The Life of the Party

Christopher Ames

The Life of the Party

FESTIVE VISION
IN MODERN FICTION

The University of Georgia Press

Athens & London

© 1991 by the University of Georgia Press
Athens, Georgia 30602
All rights reserved
Designed by Louise M. Jones
Set in 10/14 Palatino
The paper in this book meets the guidelines for
permanence and durability of the Committee on
Production Guidelines for Book Longevity of the
Council on Library Resources.

Printed in the United States of America

95 94 93 92 91   5 4 3 2 1

Library of Congress Cataloging in Publication Data
Ames, Christopher, 1956-
The life of the party : festive vision in
modern fiction / Christopher Ames.
p. cm.
Includes bibliographical references and index.
ISBN 0-8203-1290-8 (cloth : alk. paper)
1. English fiction—20th century—History and
criticism.   2. Festivals in literature.   3. American
fiction—20th century—History and criticism.
4. Manners and customs in literature.
5. Literature and anthropology.   I. Title.
PR888.F47A44   1991
823'.9109—dc20   90-11144   CIP

British Library Cataloging in Publication Data available

To the memory of my father,
the best of all my teachers

CONTENTS

ACKNOWLEDGMENTS

Acknowledgments, no doubt, make dull reading for the unacknowledged. But in a work that stresses the importance of community in the life of the individual, it is fitting for me to acknowledge the support of my own community. My first thanks are owed to those who had the patience to read this study in its earliest forms, and the goodwill to encourage me to continue working. Lucio Ruotolo read many early drafts with care and good humor. Albert Guerard reminded me (often) of the need to keep critical prose alive by engaging the energy of the imaginative writing that was my subject. Robert Polhemus offered the invaluable example of *Comic Faith* and much-needed encouragement besides. To Arturo Islas I am grateful for insightful advice on Fitzgerald. Without the criticism and guidance of these people, I doubt this book would have come to fruition.

I had the mixed blessing of a topic that made for good party conversation. As a result, valuable suggestions and ideas have come from sources too numerous to name. I must, however, record those whose particular suggestions led to lasting changes or additions: Ken Pottle, Patti Joplin, Ted Andrews, and Rick Bliss. I owe special thanks to Eric Mallin, whose continual wit and precision of thought was ever an encouragement and example, and whose detailed comments on the introductory chapters helped me over a difficult impasse.

I have benefited from the support of my colleagues at Agnes Scott College, especially the early and unflagging support of Pat Pinka. Peggy Thompson has consistently offered needed perspective, humor, and graceful advice, for which I will remain indebted. I should also acknowledge a faculty development grant that provided useful support for the writing of chapter 6.

Two portions of the book have appeared, in somewhat different form, in journals. Chapter 6 was developed from "Coover's Comedy of Conflicting Fictional Codes," which appeared in *Critique* 31, no. 2 (1990), reprinted with permission of the Helen Dwight Reid Educational Foundation. Published by Heldref Publications, 4000 Albemarle St., N.W., Washington, D.C. 20016. Copyright, 1989. Part of Chapter 5 was developed from "War and Festivity in *Gravity's Rainbow*," which appeared in *War, Literature and the Arts* 1, no. 1 (1989). I am grateful for the permission of both journals to include that material.

My final thanks are closer to home. Special thanks go to Mike Ames for advice on publishing matters and general encouragement, and to Roberta Ames for reading the manuscript with patience and support over the years of its composition. My words of thanks are not finally adequate, however, to express my debt to my wife, Kimberly Ames, who has had to live the life of the party in more ways than she might have expected. At the least though I will acknowledge her consistently astute editorial help; the rest exceeds the range of my expression.

The Life of the Party

Festive Vision

> When we compare the present life of man with that
> time of which we have no knowledge, it seems to
> me like the swift flight of a lone sparrow through the
> banqueting-hall where you sit in the winter months
> to dine with your thanes and counsellors. Inside
> there is a comforting fire to warm the room; outside
> the wintry storms of snow and rain are raging. This
> sparrow flies swiftly in through one door of the hall,
> and out through another. While he is inside, he is
> safe from the winter storms; but after a few moments
> of comfort he vanishes from sight into the darkness
> whence he came. Similarly, man appears on earth
> for a little while, but we know nothing of what went
> before this life, and what follows.
>
> —Bede, *A History of the English Church and People*

ede's simile remains evocative after thirteen centuries,
striking a chord that resonates from the Old English epics into
modern literature. These stirring lines speak the essence of festive vision; Bede's words identify the warmth and fellowship of
communal feasting with the brightness of life itself, as they depict an existence harrowed by the frightening prospect of death.
The structural dynamics of this scene recur throughout Western
literature in scenes of festivals and parties: the light and warmth
of the human community transforms the outer darkness into an
image of loneliness and death, and the feast becomes a symbol of
life celebrated in the presence of death. Of course, Bede's parable

is meant to direct us from this life to the one beyond by contrasting the brevity of life's joys with the eternity of the wintry blasts. Yet its lasting power arises from the opposite effect; for in choosing a feast as the occasion against which the bleakness of fate stands out most harshly, the passage calls attention to the pre-Christian rites that performed a sacred function analogous to the Christian consolation that the speaker later offers. The literary image of Bede's swallow derives its power, no doubt, from its ability to convey both the richness of earthly joys and the contrasting iciness of mortal brevity. Religious consolation offers a means of facing this tension, but so too does the celebration of the feast itself.

As Christianity spread through Europe, it carved out an uneasy co-existence with pagan festival, from which emerged the extraordinary character of medieval Christian festivals: a voice affirming life through communal celebration and expressing sacred meanings in a variety of popular forms. As Peter Burke has summarized: "In traditional European popular culture, the most important kind of setting was that of the festival."[1] With great success, the medieval church assimilated popular festivals into the Christian calendar. Even the lengthy and often riotous "carnival" became a pre-Lenten festivity. But the festive spirit predated Christianity, and that spirit reemerges later in more secular forms as Western society, during and after the eighteenth century, becomes less centered on the church. In the modern world parties have inherited the central sacred function of festival: they celebrate life by creating communities united against the darkness of the night. The gripping image of Bede's swallow continues to hold force. Outside, in the regions of darkness, the cold symbolizes the harshness of fate into which we each perish alone; inside, around the warmth of the fire and the abundance of the feast, the evanescent community of souls gathers and celebrates. Bede's image reaches to the heart of the festive vision. It articulates festivity as a basic human need, responding to the forces of nature and culture, the processes of growth and decay, and the vagaries of the human spirit encountering these forces. In literature, as in life, festivity has a crucial role, and the festive vision in modern literature continues to affirm the power and relevance of Bede's metaphorical swallow.

By "festive vision" I mean life conceived in terms of celebration. The impulse to celebrate helps define and create community, and the celebration itself allows individuals to come to grips with mortality. Peter Burke and Mikhail Bakhtin argue that such a vision was once the norm, that festivity once played an indisputably central role in human life. Now that our culture is more fragmented, self-conscious, and self-critical, the centrality of celebration is less evident. As a result it is the literature of festivity, in the modern period, that has stressed the ritualistic value of contemporary celebrations. As we examine novelistic versions of the prevalent party scene—from Clarissa Dalloway's formal party to the bloody bash at Chez Raoul in *Gravity's Rainbow*—we learn how crucial festivity is to the modern writer and to the manner in which modern literature represents experience. In many novels the reader encounters a compelling festive vision, an angle of fictional approach defined by celebration. The literature of festivity forms a significant subgenre of fiction, and understanding its conventions, patterns, and inspirations will illuminate individual works as well as larger genres, particularly the novel.

When we begin to think of novelists who feature prominent scenes of parties in their work, we encounter a list almost dauntingly large. In addition to the writers considered in detail in this study, one could examine from the twentieth-century British and American canons alone Henry James, Edith Wharton, Carl Van Vechten, Nathaniel West, E. M. Forster, D. H. Lawrence, Graham Greene, Nancy Mitford, Malcolm Lowry, P. G. Wodehouse, Jack Kerouac, Ken Kesey, William S. Burroughs, and Donald Barthelme. So pervasive is the party scene that one could generate many similar but distinct lists. I hope that as my study focuses on the festive vision of seven novelists, it will inspire the reader to consider the ramifications and resonances in a variety of other works. I have chosen to avoid a catalog approach and to concentrate on seven writers in whose work parties play a powerful, significant role: James Joyce, Virginia Woolf, F. Scott Fitzgerald, Evelyn Waugh, Henry Green, Thomas Pynchon, and Robert Coover. This selection comprises the different periods of twentieth-century literature: the classic modernist period of authors whose earliest works preceded the First World War; the fascinating period between the wars in both Britain and America; and the post–World War II era tentatively and provocatively termed postmodernism. These different eras or generations present different and developing visions of festivity, and these seven writers all express a profound interest in the thematics of festivity through their extended and

strategic party scenes. Close attention to these scenes and their relationship to each author's oeuvre helps elucidate the role of festivity in
modern literature, a role with significant stylistic consequences. But such
conclusions depend on certain assumptions about how parties function
in cultures; contemporary celebration must be viewed, at the outset,
in the context of a developing festive tradition. The role of parties in
the modern novel grows out of the more clearly established connection
between carnival festivities and earlier literary forms.

Modern parties have their basis in ancient traditions of feasts, banquets, and communal drinking. Plato's *Symposium*, for example, illustrates the banquet tradition of antiquity and captures the intimate connection between the social gathering and the discourses of drama,
rhetoric, and philosophy. Love—the topic at this particular party—is
characterized by Aristophanes as the guiding spirit of festival itself: "It is
Love who empties us of the spirit of estrangement and fills us with the
spirit of kinship; who makes possible such mutual intercourse as this;
who presides over festivals, dances, sacrifices."[2] Dialogue and revelry
mingle at the boundary between art and philosophy. And from Aristophanes' hiccups to Alcibiades' drunken entrance, the intermingling of
seriousness and festivity remains evident. An equally vivid, though contrasting, banquet in Roman literature is Trimalchio's dinner, the most
extended scene surviving from Petronius's *Satyricon*. Again, the work testifies to contemporary banquet traditions as well as to their literary and
satiric possibilities. The comic excesses of the feast, the various poems,
songs and other entertainments woven into the text, and the mock-death
conclusion in which Trimalchio commands his slaves to "Imagine that
you're present at my funeral feast," all point to ritualistic and recurrent
characteristics of festivity.[3]

Parties also have a significant functional link with religious festivals,
Christian and otherwise. The feast as an enjoyment of God's bounty
has always borne a problematic relationship with Christian austerity,
but the communion of shared eating and drinking had such powerful
pagan roots that it was never wholly extirpated from Christian celebration. Christian and Neoplatonic literature opposes the sensual feast
to the heavenly, but as often as not the two are allied in popular customs. Frank Kermode has demonstrated the prevalence of this "banquet
of sense" theme in Renaissance poetry.[4] The sensual feast is compared

disparagingly to spiritual communion, and sensual experience and indulgence are characterized as bestial obstacles to Platonic love and Christian spirituality. Kermode establishes convincingly the significance of
this allegorical topos in Andrew Marvell, Ben Jonson, George Chapman,
and Shakespeare. But it is worth noting, in Shakespeare particularly, a
countertheme that suggests the ambivalent spiritual status of festivity in
Renaissance thought. Embodied in the festive figures of Falstaff, Toby
Belch, and *Measure for Measure*'s Lucio and Pompey is a celebration of
the vitality of the sensual banquet. This vitality is inevitably defended in
each play on the basis of its richness and universality: "If sack and sugar
be a fault, God help the wicked!" (*1 Henry IV*, 2.4); "Dost thou think,
because thou art virtuous, there shall be no more cakes and ale?" (*Twelfth
Night*, 2.3); "Vice is of a great kindred, it is well allied; but it is impossible
to extirp it quite, friar, till eating and drinking be put down" (*Measure
for Measure*, 3.2). These memorable lines show how the joyous feast of
the many can be opposed to the narrow path of the few. Both voices are
present in Shakespeare and no clear resolution emerges. Other Renaissance writers, notably Jonson, present this same ambivalence toward
festivity—celebrating and vilifying the banquet of sense.[5] The same tension arose sociopolitically in the struggle between Puritan antifestive
forces (or reformers) and church and folk supporters of festivity. The
antifestive forces were eventually victorious, and, for several reasons,
the mixed pagan and Christian festive life waned after the seventeenth
century.[6]

In terms of direct evolution, our modern parties probably derive most
directly from the social entertainments that became popular as folk festivals disappeared in the eighteenth century. The *Oxford English Dictionary*
dates the use of the word *party* as "a gathering or assemblage for social
pleasure or amusement . . . especially of invited guests at a private home"
from 1716.

By way of example, the dictionary uses *party* approvingly in the phrase
"parties of pleasure." As secular activity came to occupy greater amounts
of leisure time and as the growth of towns and cities contributed to the
decline of community-wide popular festivals, there was an increase in
the importance of drawing room gatherings, salons, dances, masquerades, and balls. In *The Politics and Poetics of Transgression* Peter Stallybrass
and Allon White describe this phenomenon as "re-territorialization": "A

sort of refined mimicry sets into the salons and ballrooms of Europe in which the imagery, masks and costumes of the popular carnival are being (literally) put on by the aristocracy and the bourgeoisie."[7] The literature of the Restoration and eighteenth century reflects the fascination with these new kinds of social gatherings—the women's banquet at Horner's lodging house in William Wycherley's *The Country Wife,* the passions of Belinda's drawing room in Alexander Pope's *The Rape of the Lock,* Colonel Ambrose's ball in Samuel Richardson's *Clarissa,* the masquerades in Henry Fielding's *Tom Jones* and *Amelia.* These scenes testify to a growing excitement from private social gatherings and to an increased literary appetite for scenes of contemporary life and comedy of manners.[8] As George Etherege tells his audience in the prologue to *The Man of Mode,* "Your own follies may supply the stage." Many Restoration comedies opened with similarly self-conscious explanations of the new focus on everyday social life. Terry Castle describes the phenomenon: "In the guise of presenting a faithful record of modern manners, English novelists had fortuitously revivified the ancient literary image of the carnivalesque."[9] A new locus of social activity was emerging, and with it a new literary focus. Poor and rural peoples remained closer to traditional festival and carnival forms, but the change from earlier religious and communal rites to more secularized and exclusive social occasions appeared eventually in all classes of modern industrial society in the nineteenth and twentieth centuries. In short, the rise of "parties of pleasure" follows the growth of the middle class and the urbanization of the West. As privacy became increasingly formalized, communal festivity became impractical and undesirable, but the need for festive release remained. Emerging as a phenomenon of bourgeois society, private parties belonged to a secular and individualized weltanschauung that has persisted into the twentieth century.

Yet secularization and increasing individualization involved a complementary transformation of secular rites into functionally sacred forms and a development of new definitions of community. Cultural needs, once served by a community organized around a strong church, remained important but were served by evolving cultural structures. Parties formed a crucial part of this cultural shift, embodying, in secular form, many religious functions and creating celebrative communities that reflect and respond to the increased alienation and separateness of modern society. Literature also participated in this shift; as Lionel Trilling (and Matthew Arnold before him) argued, "[Modern literature] is expected to provide the spiritual substance of life," in part because organized religion no longer does so.[10] In particular, festive literature, with its possibilities for comic communion and catharsis, takes on religious force.

The modern party reflects a displacement of earlier festive forms as the conditions that fostered those festivals changed. Studies of festivity in traditional and ancient societies provide anthropological models that reveal the centrality of festive excess, and we can see this festive excess reenacted, albeit in a repressed and attenuated form, in the private parties in modern society. In light of these similarities the literary use of festivity assumes a cultural significance. Structural and functional connections between modern celebrations and ancient and primitive festivals help us understand the sense in which Clarissa Dalloway's party is truly an "offering," Tim Finnegan's wake a resurrection, Dick Diver's party "magical," and Pirate Prentice's Banana Breakfast a "charm" against aerial bombardment. Theories of festivity also reveal connections between festivity and literature. Festive and literary acts enable communal celebration and understanding; they articulate human responses to life and death.

Parties and Festivals

The sacred character of festivity arises from its communal nature and its difference from ordinary life, a difference of which participants are aware and which they demonstrate through their altered emotions and behavior. In the most important theoretical treatment of festivity, Emile Durkheim connects the birth of the distinction between the sacred and the profane (and thus the birth of religion itself) with the festival—the "effervescent" social occasion. It is through participation in heightened communal events that preliterate peoples develop a perception of a bifurcated life: an everyday existence characterized by work, familiarity, and limited contacts with others, set off against a festive existence characterized by transgressive behavior, integration with the community, and ritual. The transformation involved in the festive world introduces individuals to forces greater than themselves, which, in Durkheim's analysis, introduce religion. The distinction between communal festivity and daily routine becomes the distinction between the sacred and the profane: "So it is in the midst of these effervescent social environments and out of this effervescence itself that the religious idea seems to be born." [12] Thus Durkheim argues that celebration has indistinguishable social and religious functions. Primitive festivals are sacred affairs but also "means by which the social group reaffirms itself periodically." [13]

Festive difference depends on "excess," an idea developed by Roger Caillois in *Man and the Sacred,* which describes festival as sacred transgression. Generalizing from a broader body of primary research, but following Durkheim's basic theories, Caillois emphasizes the importance of exaggerated, extreme behavior, "for destruction and waste, as forms of excess, are at the heart of the festival." [14] Similarly, Nietzsche in *The Birth of Tragedy* discusses the importance of the Dionysian element in culture and asserts that during festival "*excess* reveal[s] itself as truth." [15] The sacred character of the festival paradoxically involves sacrilege—deliberate inversions of roles and violations of rules. As transgression, Caillois argues, the festival re-creates the world of primordial chaos, the world before social rules and distinctions, and thus, when it returns to normality, reenacts the creation of order. Festivals rejuvenate society: "The world must be created anew." [16] Bakhtin, in discussing festival and literary genre, calls this "the very core of the carnival sense of the world— the pathos of shifts and changes, of death and renewal. Carnival is the festival of all-annihilating and all-renewing time." [17]

Festival thus shares the ambivalence of the sacred, and its very ambivalence allows for an affirmation of life. Festivals celebrate violation of rules and decorum as well as the return of the everyday world. This contradiction makes possible a celebration of life that does not ignore suffering or transience. Seasonal festivals celebrate the natural rhythm of decay and rebirth (taking such forms as ritual crowning and discrowning, the burning of an effigy of winter, the consumption of harvested goods, etc.); rites of passage affirm the changes of individual life; and periodic festivals commemorate the continuity of the community as opposed to the mortality of its individual members. Beyond these specific incarnations, festivity celebrates life in the broadest sense, by heightening emotion, integrating individuals into a community, and reenacting the birth of order from chaos. Festivity involves "the universal assent to the world as a whole," or as Nietzsche writes: "To have joy in anything, one must approve everything." [18]

The celebration of life through festivity involves a more complex encounter with death, however. We can see this in the anthropological treatment of sacrifice and mortuary ritual. Caillois qualifies his discussion of "festival" by asserting that "it would have to be correlated with a theory of sacrifice."[19] And René Girard in his study of the origins of religion cites this claim of Caillois's at the outset of his treatment of festival. Girard emphasizes the loss of distinctions that accompanies the merging of individual and group in festivity. Echoing Caillois's assertion that festivals re-create the primordial chaos, Girard develops a theory in which all ritual reenacts a sacrificial crisis, a crisis stemming from the violence he argues is the natural result of loss of social distinctions. Sacrifice— literal, or ritualized into symbolic form—becomes part of the festival as a means of discharging violence. It channels the violence of individuals no longer protected by hierarchy and law (and thus no longer assured of their "place" in society) into a safe outlet—a sacrificial victim chosen and killed by the community as a whole. Girard makes two assertions essential for this study: the festive transgression involves potential violence stemming from the frightening ramifications of loss of identity; and the process by which order returns to a society includes some sort of cathartic encounter with death, usually in the form of a ritual descended from actual sacrifice.[20]

Girard's view of the regenerating power of ritual sacrifice has affinities with Bakhtin's emphasis on carnivalistic ambivalence. Bakhtin argues that death, viewed from an individual perspective, manifests itself fearfully as utter annihilation, but when viewed from a communal perspective, it becomes part of a cycle of regeneration in which the community continues to live. This latter sense, he argues, forms the heart of seasonal festivals and celebrations of change: "Birth is fraught with death, and death with new birth."[21] Girard and Bakhtin differ radically in their valuation of disorder, yet they both suggest a common cultural significance for ritual death: festivity enacts a symbolic triumph over death to purge the community of its fear of violence and destruction.[22]

Here we can see, more specifically, how festivals incorporate the basic functions of religion: they involve the individual in a community of participant believers and in so doing make that individual better able to live with the tribulations of life and with his or her own mortality.[23] Festivity's ritual treatment of death approaches religious status by affirming life in a public setting through systematic, ritualized performance.[24]

The ritual presence of mortality in festivals is paralleled by the festive treatment of actual death in certain cultures.[25] Durkheim observes: "A common misfortune has the same effects as the approach of a happy event: collective sentiments are renewed which then lead men to seek one another and to assemble together."[26] Mourning the dead, we honor the value of their lives. Death's significance arises in part from the worth of the life it terminates, and in honoring the value of specific lives, people celebrate the value of life itself. Death represents the greatest challenge to celebration—the confrontation of known and unknown. Death also becomes the necessitating force for celebration: it is that which must be celebrated against. Sharing the ambiguity of the sacred, death epitomizes "all those forces whose dominance over man increases or seems to increase in proportion to man's effort to master them."[27] As the most exclusively private event, death requires public acknowledgment, and as the final rite of passage, it demands celebrative recognition. Death rituals in traditional cultures and the more familiar wakes of modern European society provide a model for all celebrative gatherings because they demonstrate how celebration exists in the face of death and depends for its authenticity on achieving a symbolically successful encounter with mortality. Funeral and wake rituals confirm the individual's social identity and reassert the community's vitality in the face of the omnipresent threat. Other celebrations make the same affirmation, though no corpse is literally present; they require, I will argue, some sort of symbolic or ritualistic equivalent of the corpse or, in Girard's terms, the sacrificial victim. The death encounter, most apparent in wakes and funeral rituals, animates celebrations of all kinds.

This brief survey allows us to formulate a tentative description of the general characteristics of festival.[28] A festival is a communal controlled transgression in that ordinary rules of behavior are set aside for a delimited time. The festival is thus characterized by its radical difference from everyday life. The festival's excessive and sacrilegious behavior affirms life but necessarily involves some kind of ritual encounter with death, culminating in a cathartic, rejuvenating return to the normal social order. In the process individuals sacrifice their identities to participate as a communal entity, inviting potential violence and loss of control, threats that become defused by the return to ordinary life. Our key concepts in defining the controlled transgression are thus: difference, excess, affirmation of life, and ritual encounter with death.

This general description of festival, drawing upon anthropological formulations, applies remarkably well to parties in modern society. Parties form a clear contrast to ordinary existence, usually through excessive behavior: partygoers dress more extravagantly, eat and drink more, talk more volubly, and stay awake later into the night than usual. Entering a party one submits to the demands of its antidecorum: the party asks the guest to leave behind any particular mood and cares from the outside world and, figuratively, to don a celebrative mask. When parties celebrate no particular occasion, their heightened festive energy springs from an uncomplicated affirmation of life itself. Parties celebrating more specific occasions normally parallel the seasonal rites (as in Christmas parties, Thanksgiving dinners, spring garden parties) or rites of passage (parties honoring birthdays, graduations, advances in employment, weddings) that festivals traditionally honor. Similarly, as a form of intensified leisure activity, parties function cathartically as controlled transgressions, allowing different and excessive behavior within a limited time and place.

Finally, the modern party contains the phenomenon I call the ritual encounter with death. The simplest, most familiar manifestation is the carpe diem assertion, "Eat, drink, and be merry, for tomorrow we die." The fleetingness of life's pleasures, so poignantly captured in Bede's swallow image, requires commemorative celebration. Parties express a desire to grasp and delight in earthly pleasure through a joyfulness that is inseparable from the awareness of the temporality of such pleasure.[29] A larger sense in which the life of the community is affirmed against the individual mortality of its members also appears at parties. The life affirmation of traditional death rituals continues today not only in wakes but also in other kinds of modern parties where symbolic encounters with death contribute to the sense of celebration. The burning of manmade light through the nighttime darkness symbolically affirms life against the inevitability of death. And the greeting of dawn after an all-night party suggests ritual resurrection, as in the concluding scene of Virginia Woolf's *The Years*.

Specific symbolic encounters with death may be veiled, but in literature death appears symbolically in parties with remarkable thematic consistency. Reading the text of our culture, writers illuminate rituals to which habit and manners may have blinded us. Consider the many images of dead people in Joyce's "The Dead"; the role of Septimus Warren Smith in *Mrs. Dalloway*; the central death in Katherine Mansfield's

"The Garden Party"; the mysteriously absent host in *The Great Gatsby;* the mistaken and real deaths in *Parties,* Carl Van Vechten's chronicle of prohibition decadence; the dead pigeon in Henry Green's *Party Going;* the three party-related deaths in Waugh's *Vile Bodies;* the horrifying conclusion of Graham Greene's "The End of the Party"; the honored guest turned sacrificial victim in the scatological banquet in *Gravity's Rainbow;* the unexplained murders in Coover's *Gerald's Party.* In each case the author introduces death into the party in order to comment on the celebrative affirmation. The presence of death may attest to the party's triumph, or it may evidence its failure to encounter mortality; in other cases, the symbolic incarnation of death warns against the fatal dangers of excessive behavior. In any case, the encounter with death becomes inseparable from the festive occasion, a legacy from primitive and medieval festivals.

There are, however, several important differences between early festivals and modern parties. Though we can connect the cultural functions of parties to the religious impulse, modern parties are rarely explicitly dedicated to religious events, and they generally do not require or involve belief in the supernatural. More important, modern parties engage only a select segment of the community, and the process of selection may well be based on class and social hierarchy, thus reinforcing the social distinctions community-wide festivals sought to efface. But these significant differences are not primarily differences of kind; they simply reflect diachronic changes in society. Secularization and increased individualization mark, inescapably, the development of modern society, and celebration reflects these changes. We have seen how parties evidence the decline of explicitly sacred aspects of life yet illustrate the investing of secular ritual with sacred importance. Similarly, we should recognize that our communities are far too large to participate in genuine community-wide celebrations (except in the broadest sense of mass culture). Our increasingly isolated existence, however, renders parties all the more essential in providing some concrete sense of a society capable of being experienced with immediacy. And though the exclusive nature of invitations may reinforce class distinctions, parties can still dissolve barriers within the newly created community.

Stallybrass and White argue that the historical triumph of bourgeois norms of behavior pushed carnival practices to the margin of society so that the carnival spirit came to be acknowledged only negatively as something demonic that must be repressed. They also acknowledge that such sublimation led to a social displacement in which aspects of the popular carnival emerged in other forms and locations. They point to the carnival elements of "bourgeois bohemias, like surrealism and expressionism,"[30] but I would add that the bourgeois house party retains at least a festive potential in its modern version of licensed excess. Thus the tension that results between the social marginalization of celebration and the continued centrality of the need for festive affirmation structures the controlled transgression of the modern party. The historical pattern generally interpreted as a decline or disappearance of popular, community-wide festivals is more appropriately viewed as a repeated displacement of carnival into different, increasingly private forms.

The language used to describe festivals provides a vocabulary for examining parties as well. Within twentieth-century British and American culture, parties vary widely, of course, with respect to the differing subcultures of the partygoers. The following study reflects many of those different subcultural practices without attempting to survey or categorize twentieth-century leisure activity. By drawing an analogy to festivals, I wish to demonstrate how modern parties reflect the culture as it is structured by universal human needs expressed under changing social conditions.

Though fiction writers have explicitly and implicitly employed this analogy, ethnographers writing on festivals have largely dismissed parties in discussing modern inheritors of festival. It is difficult, however, *not* to apply their general interpretations of festival and culture to modern parties. Indeed, parties more directly display the festive spirit than the mass gatherings, civic festivals, or state holidays anthropologists usually cite. Caillois provides an intriguing example in an appendix to *Man and the Sacred*. He argues that war is the modern equivalent of festival and enumerates the parallels suggested by the excess of war, the rejection of traditional moral behavior, and the omnipresence of death.[31] Suggestive as these parallels are, they seem desperate when Caillois dismisses the importance of modern celebrations: "Today . . . festivals have lost almost all reality." In contemporary society, as Caillois perceives it, "attenuated and infrequent festivals grow out of the gray background symbolizing the monotony of contemporary existence and seem scattered, crumbling, and almost submerged, [possessing only] some miserable vestiges of the collective euphoria that characterized the ancient celebrations." [32]

In part, Caillois's vituperative devaluation of the modern in favor of the ancient stems from a failure of the imagination: he compares primitive rites to modern festivals only in the most literal sense of holiday celebrations and mass public gatherings. The celebrative rituals of parties—private, informal subgroupings of a local society—do not attract Caillois's consideration in spite of their potential intensity and vital exuberance. [33] More important, his devaluation of modern experience fails to allow for the critical capacity with which modern man approaches culture. Modernity is characterized by the ability of the individual to question the basis and the specific characteristics of his or her culture. Surely a mixed blessing, this critical capacity creates the possibility, even the necessity, of alienation, just as it opens society to new forces for change. At the same time, the critical capacity that alienates us from our own society colors our perspective on ancient and primitive cultures, allowing us to posit an artificial and simplistic unity of individual and culture. We tend to assume that the manifestations of traditional culture were commensurate with that culture's needs, but we would never assume that about contemporary culture. The same antibourgeois idealization of ancient and preliterate culture dominates the recent theories of play. [34] We must correct for this parallax of historical judgment by not devaluing the affirmative celebrations of our culture and by not idealizing those of the past.

Some writers on festival, notably those included in Victor Turner's 1983 anthology, *Celebration: Studies in Festival and Literature,* approach contemporary festivity more favorably; they acknowledge that "people in all cultures recognize the need to set aside times and spaces for celebratory use." But even those writers who are willing to consider parties as rituals exhibit a persistent hostility towards modern festivity and a skepticism about the celebrative validity of parties. [35] A recent collection of essays on contemporary manifestations of festivity, for example, ignores the topic of the private party in favor of the "town celebration," which the book's editor describes as "North America's most widespread and familiar type of festival." [36]

In short, though contemporary anthropology seems increasingly willing to consider the relations between parties and festivals, it still soft-pedals the significance of modern informal celebrations. This impulse stems from certain persistent habits of thought: a focus on the literal descendants of festival, in particular nostalgic folk festivals and civic holidays; a reluctance to see what were once explicitly sacred cultural functions now served by secular activities; and the distorting power of cultural alienation, which repeatedly makes unfavorable the comparisons of our society to those more ancient. The critical forces that make alienation a given in this age will not disappear or be expiated through revivified celebrations. Yet the ability to sense the failure of our celebrations at times should allow us to see the seriousness of their potential as well as appreciate their occasional success. Our functional models of golden-age ancient cultures have made us uncomfortable with the notion of "failed" rituals. Nevertheless, failed ritual has become a crucial metaphor in modern literature, and in developing this trope, many fiction writers have come to assert as well the power and importance of our attempts to celebrate life communally.

Failed ritual becomes significant only when the ritual itself is granted cultural importance. Understanding the significance of festivity thus requires a terminology for discussing the role of festivity with regard to its success or failure in satisfying cultural needs. Once we establish a distinction between the festive and the nonfestive (and include most of the functioning of society under the nonfestive), does the festive world threaten or strengthen the cultural structures of the nonfestive? Is festivity inherently subversive in its expression of repressed desires and its challenge to traditional hierarchies, or is it inherently conservative, preserving the social order by channeling antisocial impulses into a harmless, ritual outlet?[37] Whether parties are described as affirmations of life invigorating the community or catalysts of change celebrating the communal process while advancing it, either possibility is a paradigm for an ideal party. Parties can, and often do, fail in the eyes of participants, hosts, or observers, and the tensions implicit in controlled transgression suggest the extremes of such failure: excess of control or excess of release.

If the fear of chaos, intoxication, or misbehavior is extreme, the party will be sterile: social distinctions will be reinforced rather than suspended and the play of the party will so resemble the mundane character of everyday life as to become pointless—as in the querulous boredom at the Mad Tea Party, which, like Humpty-Dumpty's unbirthdays, lacks extraordinariness and so succumbs to ennui. Yet the fear of chaos is justified, for a party always has the potential to lose control. Dangers lie in the suspension of the rules of everyday behavior and the surrender of the self to the group. The wildest of parties can turn into an orgy of violence and destruction, as in Dostoyevsky's *The Possessed* or in the novels of William Burroughs or Thomas Pynchon.

Between these extremes lies the feverish decadence we have come to associate with the party behavior of the alienated, particularly in the form of the excessive party-going of an aimless leisure class. Fear of chaos can render a party stultifying, but fear of boredom has an equally numbing result in which transgression itself is pursued with a worklike tenacity that undermines the potentially liberating spirit. The heart of decadence is desperation—an overeager pursuit of gaiety, leisure, and spontaneity.

Thus the potential affirmation of life is imperiled by both the stultifying effects of social control at one extreme, and the disorder and destruction possible in the suspension of control at the other. Accordingly, the failed party in literature has become a powerful symbol for the gap between cultural expectations and individual experience. This framework I have called controlled transgression should remind us of the dangers involved in oversimplifying the modern applications of the study of festival or play.

Durkheim focuses on festivity as a force that re-creates and renews the community regardless of the violence of its taboo-breaking. Girard argues more pointedly that the very violence of the ritual reaffirms the social order by allowing the social order to return triumphantly. Most anthropologists have followed this view of festivity as a release of subversive impulses that inevitably strengthens the community. When Victor Turner, on the other hand, developed his theory of liminality, he emphasized the potential for cultural change in periods when rules are suspended. We cannot view cultures as static, he argues, and we must see in festive rites of passage the imaginative medium that allows for cultural passage and transformation as well.[38]

In the context of modern cultures, many writers have gone further than Turner by suggesting the revolutionary or subversive character of play and festival as well as "carnivalized" literature and art. In an article on the politics of transgression Allon White examines the controversy over whether transgression (literary or social) is intrinsically radical. He contrasts the anthropological position "that transgression is merely a licensed infraction of the rules which in fact consolidates and conserves the rules by periodically allowing them to be broken" with that of writers such as Julia Kristeva, who follows Bakhtin "in assuming an a priori identity between formal transgressions at the level of language and revolutionary change at the level of social institutions." White convincingly criticizes both views as "a false essentializing of transgression" and argues that "the question of the political dimensions of sexual and aesthetic transgression can only be answered historically."[39]

Nevertheless, the tension between control and transgression, between licensed release and subversive violence, forms a structural dynamic for festivities, valid in the abstract formulation as well as the specific manifestation. That anthropologists emphasize the cathartic function probably results from their global perspective in which encounters with radical change are much rarer than observances of the maintenance of the status quo. The contrary emphasis on revolutionary possibilities may reflect the political climate in which those theorists wrote: Turner's development of the notion of liminality during the antiwar protests in America in the late sixties; Kristeva's attack on authoritarian linguistic constructs in Paris after the uprisings of 1968.

Given the warning not to essentialize transgression, we can perhaps gain some valuable insights into modern festivity from this debate. Historical investigation, such as Le Roy Ladurie's investigation of a Mardi Gras carnival that turned into a political rebellion, shows that festivity can be subversive under particular circumstances but often fails to disturb the status quo: "Popular festivities and social change do not always go hand in hand."[40] Ladurie documents the convergence of the social, political, and religious forces that created a situation in which the carnival did indeed turn into rebellion, the masks into massacres.[41] Assertions about the political content of festive forms per se have no value outside such a specific historical matrix. In general terms, the most we can say is that reaffirmation and subversion are both latent in celebration. Celebration seems to require such a conflict between order and chaos, stability and change, to move toward a resolution—whether that resolution is revivification of the traditional hierarchy, progressive modification of it, or violent reaction against it. Similarly, the degree to which celebrations stress affirmation or revolution reflects the participants' relation to the society and to one another. The character of celebrations thus becomes a barometer of social conditions and alienation. This relationship becomes crucial in the modern literary use of parties to dramatize the individual's relation to society. By contrasting, for example, the effects of festive license in one of Virginia Woolf's party scenes with the effects in an Evelyn Waugh scene, one can gauge the different relationships the characters have with their societies.

Like festivals, parties relate multivalently to the societies in which they take place; we cannot assume they serve a unitary function or that they represent a perfect ideal. Parties succeed and fail in differing degrees, and they vary in cultural function. Yet, beneath the many manifestations of the festive spirit, there exists a recurrent and inescapable need to create new worlds in which we can celebrate and affirm our life in this world.

The Party and Literary Form

The cultural significance of parties forms a necessary background to this study, but my primary focus is on the party's considerable significance in modern literature. A definitive study of the modern party as cultural event remains to be undertaken. Because this study is predicated on the assertions that modern parties partake of qualities essential to older festivals and that the relationship of the modern party to the novel form parallels the traditional relationship between festivity and literature, a discussion of ethnographic studies and the pioneering literary genre studies of Northrop Frye, C. L. Barber, and Mikhail Bakhtin occupies this introduction. But as we move into the close examination of individual literary texts, sociological and ethnographic material will emerge only as it illuminates the literary issues that form the core of this study. The study of festive vision not only follows the development of a significant modern trope but also argues that an engagement with festivity has shaped the formal development of the novel genre.

Festivity has a unique and profound relationship with literary art, and in modern literature this relationship reveals itself through the important roles that parties play in the novel. The literary spirit has always been intimately tied to the festival spirit, and an interrelationship, which transcends one merely serving as content for the other, continues between them. Much of the study that follows will examine how parties function symbolically, structurally, and thematically within individual works to make up a writer's distinctive festive vision. In most cases, though, the party functions structurally to shape the narrative: the party epitomizes the multivocal openness of the novel genre.

The clearest origins of our literary tradition lie in the festivals out of which Greek comedy, tragedy, and possibly epic poetry developed. Historical evidence suggests that drama originated in religious and Dionysiac festivals, and the literature of the fifth century B.C. that has shaped our notions of comedy and tragedy testifies to this link.[42] Early Anglo-Saxon poetry, too, was performed at festive occasions—at feasts or at mead halls. But the argument that comic and tragic forms originated in festival has more profound implications than the mere fact that communal festivities provided an occasion for performance. The precursors of literary art were rituals themselves, and through its symbolic nature art has retained some of this ritual character.

In their discussions of Shakespeare's dramatic genres, Northrop Frye and C. L. Barber both advance important arguments for the continuing literary relevance of festivity in the Renaissance. Frye argues that the festive origins of drama are inseparable from its structural patterns: though dramatic performances become independent of actual festive occasions, the patterning of their plots and imagery retains the stamp of the festive community. Comedy, Frye argues, moves toward the creation of such a festive community: "The moment that this social unit crystallizes is the moment of the comic resolution. In the last scene, when the dramatist usually tries to get all his characters on the stage at once, the audience witnesses the birth of a renewed sense of social integration. In comedy as in life the regular expression of this is a festival, whether a marriage, a dance, or a feast."[43] Frye draws a crucial parallel here as he notes the shift of the festival pattern from audience to stage ("In comedy as in life"). By Shakespeare's time dramatic performances were not exclusively part of folk festivals, but the connection between festive and literary spirit remained: they present similar visions of the world.

In Shakespeare, this vision grows out of the festive capacity to create another world. Frye argues that Shakespeare's comedies develop the medieval folk tradition of the "green world" originating from "the dramatic activity that punctuated the Christian calendar with the rituals of an immemorial paganism."[44] From the pattern of medieval festivals (such as the Feast of Fools or the Feast of the Ass) comes the pattern of Shakespeare's comedies. Comedy follows festival both in this ability to enter temporarily into a world beyond the limitations of normal existence, and in the faith that the resolution of individual problems should occur in a context that embraces the whole society. In modern literature, Frye observes, the connection between successful festivity and a comic, affirmative ending remains crucial, and interrupted or failed festivity remains linked to a tragic, or at least alienated, sensibility.[45]

Barber's detailed study of the relation between Shakespeare's comedies and the festive holidays of Elizabethan England explores the broader relation between festive patterns in life and in art. He warns that the study of influence cannot be separated from a study of the basic functional unity between festivity and drama: "the holiday occasion and the comedy are parallel manifestations of the same pattern of culture, of a way that men can cope with their life."[46] Barber's conclusions on Shakespeare are relevant to other literary forms. Barber's "parallel manifestations" emerge in a form he labels "the saturnalian pattern," a dynamic process consistent with what we have termed controlled transgression. He sees comedy moving "between poles of restraint and release in everybody's experience."[47] On one level, Barber notes, the comic conflict occurs over the very issue of celebration: we see a "communion of merrymakers" opposing, at least temporarily, those antagonistic to earthly pleasure and celebration. But the conflict between festive release and repressive social norms moves toward a resolution that Barber calls "clarification." The forces of celebration, pleasure, and love do not so much triumph over their opposition as establish a coexistence with it. Festivity challenges absolutes, not only the absolute authority of the puritanical antifestive spirit but also the idealism of young festive lovers who must learn the inevitability of the return to the mortal world and its limitations. As Frye also notes, the comic pattern culminates in return and social unity; the green world does not unequivocally triumph. Barber sees the return as an endorsement of a new perspective that combines vitality and mortality: "It is indeed the present mirth and laughter of the festive plays—the immediate experience they give of nature's beneficence—which reconciles feeling, without recourse to sentimentality or cynicism, to the clarification conveyed about nature's limitations."[48]

Thus the triumph over death and solitude—what Frye describes as "the ritual pattern of the victory of summer over winter" and the merging of "individual release [and] social reconciliation"—requires a recognition of death's power and inevitability.[49] Such is the "clarification" necessary to authenticate the festive affirmation. The temporary green world of festivity allows, in literature and life, in festivals and in parties, an affirmation of *this* world.

In his several studies of the influence of carnival on literature (and particularly on the novel), Mikhail Bakhtin emphasizes a similarly complex interplay between the "official" world and the world of carnival release. "Ambivalence" and "joyful relativity" are the terms he uses to communicate what Barber calls the "vitality in mortality." Carnival or festive license does not simply consist of an inversion of everyday norms, a strict opposition to official culture; rather carnival expresses "the inevitability, and at the same time the creative power of the shift-and-renewal, the *joyful relativity* of all structure and order."[50] The ambivalence of carnival practices stems from their all-inclusive nature; inherently antihierarchical, they cannot wholly reject even the attitudes they ridicule. In its ideal form, carnival, like comedy, attempts to embrace everything; it generates a view of the world that accepts contradictions and opposites and indeed recognizes in contradiction the mystery of existence. At the core of carnivalistic ambivalence lies the natural pattern of death and rebirth. Bakhtin develops this point with many examples from ancient and medieval festivals including the recurrent image of "pregnant death," the "primary carnival performance [of] mock crowning and subsequent discrowning of the king of carnival," the practice of burning an effigy of winter, and the remarkable *sia ammazzato* candle ceremony, which Goethe describes in "The Roman Carnival."[51]

In defining the nature of carnival, Bakhtin strikes many chords familiar from anthropological investigations. He emphasizes the "other-worldness" of festivity, its difference: "The men of the Middle Ages participated in two lives: the official and the carnival life. Two aspects of the world, the serious and the laughing aspect, coexisted in their consciousness."[52] He also describes what I have termed "excess," emphasizing particularly blasphemy and the celebration of the body in food, drink, and sexuality. But Bakhtin's description of festivity differs in his repeated emphasis upon the all-inclusive, popular nature of festive life and his assertion of its radical opposition to official culture. For Bakhtin, festival does not resolve as neatly as in Frye's notion of comic reconciliation. Rather, the festive otherness or antiauthoritarianism persists in an ongoing popular culture given voice by periodic festivals. The essence of carnival remains community, "a pageant without footlights and without a division into performers and spectators." The force that brings together individuals ordinarily separated unites all categories of human perception: "Carnival brings together, unifies, weds, and combines the sacred with the profane, the lofty with the low, the great with the insignificant, the wise with the stupid." [53] Bakhtin celebrates this view of the world, both as it appears in carnival and as it appears in the literature shaped by carnival. [54]

In his essay "From the Prehistory of Novelistic Discourse," Bakhtin examines an eclectic sample of ancient and medieval literary genres—from macaronic biblical parodies to Greek romances to liturgies for drunks and parodies of grammatical treatises—in an attempt to outline various historical characteristics of the developing genre of the novel: the mixing of languages (polyglossia), the focus on the present, the parodying and adaptation of other literary forms, and the importance of laughter. [55] In his studies of Rabelais and Dostoyevsky, he relates these formal characteristics directly to festivity—to ancient feasts and saturnalia and to medieval holiday carnivals. He accomplishes this relation in several ways. First, he demonstrates the literal influence of carnival on literature—the inclusion within Rabelais, for example, of elements of medieval carnivals, such as blasphemies. He also describes the use of carnivals, feasts, and banquets as settings in works such as the *Satyricon, Cyprian's Supper*, and, of course, Rabelais. Further he identifies similar themes in festivity and literature—the glorification of the body in comedy, for instance, or the celebration of intoxication.

His most far-reaching claims, however, unite the characteristics of carnival and the novel analogically. Bakhtin argues that the novel, like the carnival world, is seriocomic, parodic, and tending toward the all-inclusive. The seriocomic nature of the novel reflects carnivalistic ambivalence, which is the inability to judge or reduce the totality of experience into an unequivocally tragic or comic vision. Parody, which Bakhtin demonstrates is inseparable from the novel, presents a version of the primary carnivalistic gesture—the ritual crowning and discrowning of the carnival king.[56] Parody also shares in carnivalistic ambivalence: we can never wholly separate the heroism from the mocking of it—"ambivalent carnival laughter burns away all that is stilted and stiff, but in no way destroys the heroic core of the image."[57] Thus the indeterminacy of ironic distance, endemic to the novel, mirrors the ambiguous relationship between the carnival upside-down life and the official life.

Most important, Bakhtin argues that inclusivity defines both the festival and the novel. The novel has always been a mixed bag, characterized by its continual willingness to adapt extraliterary discourse and other genres into its form. The novel grows from a carnivalistic attitude toward the world, which forms in Bakhtin's words, "the clamping principle that [binds] all these heterogeneous elements into the organic whole of a genre." Bakhtin advances the radical argument that carnivalization transformed the novel genre and literature as a whole: "In the subsequent development of European literature . . . carnivalization constantly assisted in the destruction of all barriers between genres, between self-enclosed systems of thought, between various styles, etc.; it destroyed any attempt on the part of genres and styles to isolate themselves or ignore one another; it brought closer what was distant and united what had been sundered. This has been the great function of carnivalization in the history of literature."[58] Passages such as this one have opened Bakhtin to the charge of idealizing folk tradition and exaggerating its subversive potential.[59] Though Bakhtin's language is at times hyperbolic, his overall consideration of carnival astutely recognizes the limits of official license; he celebrates the dialogic spirit that is potential in festive expressions, even when they are constrained. Bakhtin's theories of carnivalization, like all of his theories of language and literature, have been extraordinarily influential and controversial. "Every reader seems to make his own Bakhtin," one critic notes.[60] Yet this confusion testifies to the range and suggestiveness of Bakhtin's thought. My concern is not so much to explicate or be faithful to Bakhtin as to make worthwhile use of certain aspects of his work that seem particularly illuminating for modern literature.

Bakhtin anticipates one of my primary claims for the party in modern literature: that it allows abstract issues, particularly the social character of the individual and his or her own response to mortality, to be given dramatic life. "Carnivalistic thought . . . lives in the realm of ultimate questions, but it gives them no abstractly philosophical or religiously dogmatic resolution; it plays them out in the concretely sensuous form of carnivalistic acts and images. Thus carnivalization made possible the transfer of ultimate questions from the abstractly philosophical sphere, through a carnival sense of the world, to the concretely sensuous plane of images and events—which are, in keeping with the spirit of carnival, dynamic, diverse and vivid."[61] Parties enact, in the modern context, the symbolic drama of death and rebirth central to carnival. And the enactment depends on the problematics of individual and group.

But Bakhtin stops short of such applying his theory of carnivalization to modern festivity. Bakhtin's historical argument locates the apex of carnival in life and literature in the Renaissance: "Beginning with the seventeenth century, folk-carnival life is on the wane: it almost loses touch with communal performance . . . its forms are impoverished, made petty and less complex." Into the Renaissance, carnival directly influences literature, but as folk-carnivals lose their force, "carnival almost completely ceases to be a direct source of carnivalization, ceding its place to the influence of already carnivalized literature; in this way carnivalization becomes a purely literary tradition."[62] The novel remains a carnivalized genre but loses its actual contact with the festive spirit in life. Again we see familiar sources cited for the decline of festivity: urbanization that makes community-wide celebrations impossible; and the replacement of the church by the state as central authority in people's lives. This point of view determines Bakhtin's evaluation of later literature, including his characterization of nineteenth-century literature as "humdrum [and] solemn" and his dislike for modern satire in which, he believes, the laughter becomes nihilistic, not unifying like carnival laughter.[63]

Bakhtin does assert, however, that the festive spirit did not wholly disappear from culture: "Even within bourgeois culture the festive element did not die. It was merely narrowed down. The feast is a primary, indestructible ingredient of human civilization; it may become sterile and even degenerate, but it cannot vanish. The private, 'chamber' feast of the bourgeois period still preserves a distorted aspect of the ancient spirit; on feast days the doors of the home are open to guests, as they were originally open to 'all the world.' " [64] Bakhtin continues in this passage, almost in spite of himself, to enumerate the characteristics of "chamber feasts," that is, parties: their abundance and excess in food, drink, and dress; the importance of greetings, toasts, dances, and games; and their non-utilitarian nature. But he fails to see the continuing relevance of parties, what he calls the "bourgeois truncated forms of these celebrations," to the novel.

Bakhtin observes that the liberation from social hierarchy in medieval festival was extremely important precisely because of the rigidity of that hierarchy. Though festive celebrations can no longer embrace the whole community, open their doors to "all the world," the absence of such a community is perceived as a problem in modern society that festivity can then address, just as festivity once addressed the rigidity of class hierarchy. Thus the party becomes increasingly important as a way to assuage the alienation of the individual from society. With the secularization and urbanization of Western life and the decline and repression of traditional festivity, the need for community and the problems of facing mortality and defining one's own worth and purpose do not disappear; rather they intensify, and the party becomes a medium through which these needs are expressed and, in some ways, fulfilled.

But the party is not the only palliative; as a carnivalized genre, the novel responds to changes in society and its festivities. The development of the modern novel is concurrent with the growth of the private party as the primary means for celebration. As different as the two phenomena are, they address similar needs. Literature attempts to forge a union between the public and the private, though, as Allon White points out, the development of bourgeois society is, to a large extent, the converse: the growth of ideologies that assert the independence of the individual from social forces. Frye reminds us that comedy is intrinsically social: "The essential comic resolution . . . is an individual release which is also a social reconciliation. . . . But all real comedy is based on the principle that these two forms of release are ultimately the same." [65] Thus the comic impulse in literature remains at odds with the growing individualism of modern society.

In *Masquerade and Civilization* Terry Castle studies the popular eighteenth-century entertainment of the masquerade and its representation in the contemporary literature. By focusing on the century in which,

Bakhtin contends, the carnivalesque gave way to rationalist individualism, Castle offers fascinating insight into the repression and relocation
of festivity. Castle allows that eighteenth-century English masquerades
were, unlike earlier popular festivals, "physically set off from the surrounding urban macrocosm," and that licentious behavior was "somewhat more restricted at private masked parties held in the townhouses
of the aristocracy."[66] But she convincingly demonstrates how masquerades, aided by the license and metamorphosis of costume, continued
indeed to articulate the festive impulse. Though she follows the spirit of
carnival a century further than Bakhtin would countenance, and wittily
characterizes Bakhtin's approach as an "intensely elegiac . . . myth of a
modern fall away from the golden world of carnival (with bourgeois individualism cast as the satanic principle)," Castle concludes by accepting
Bakhtin's analysis when describing the disappearance of masquerades
at the close of the eighteenth century: "The masquerade was the last
brilliant, even brittle eruption of an impulse inexorably on its way to
extinction."[67] Nevertheless, Castle's analysis of masquerade's role in the
Age of Reason is powerful testimony to the continuance of the festive impulse even as it is rendered socially marginal by "the new seriousness"
of nineteenth-century decorum. As particular forms of festival succumb
to historical change and the apparent decline of folk culture, celebrative
impulses manifest themselves in new or varied forms—primary among
them, the private party, an entertainment which develops concurrently
with the bourgeois novel. The tendency of the novel genre to include
multiple voices and to focus on everyday life, the present, and local communities remains festive in character. The party is particularly amenable
to novelistic re-creation because it highlights these issues and provides
a thematic parallel to narrative openness.

Ian Watt's *The Rise of the Novel* chronicles the development of the English novel from this very point where Bakhtin marks the end of direct
interaction between carnival and literature. Like Bakhtin, Watt associates
the bourgeois novel with the development of individualism and locates
the beginning of the process at the end of the seventeenth century. But,
unlike Bakhtin, Watt does not see individualism simply as a force that
pushes authentic community into a literary, as opposed to a folk, tradition. Rather he posits individualism as a problem and as a condition that

makes the modern novel possible because the novel reflects this struggle for social identity. Watt argues that the French and English novel develops as it attempts to reconcile the apparent tension between self and society and the accompanying stylistic focus on one or the other. Later novelists may vary their emphases on individual or society, but the novel form becomes capable of comprehending experience from both perspectives. Indeed "the basic terms of [novelistic] inquiry have been dictated by . . . the problematic nature of the relation between the individual and his environment." [68] Bakhtin might stress the dialogic nature of the novel, which renders it congenial to such a tension or multiple voicing, and he would certainly avoid the terms that suggest a static opposition of self and other.

Nevertheless, it is instructive to follow Watt's reading of a novelistic tradition that Bakhtin tends to ignore. [69] Significantly Watt sees Jane Austen as preeminent in the "successful resolution" of the problems his initial contrast of Fielding and Richardson raised. Austen presents "a sense of the social order which is not achieved at the expense of the individuality and autonomy of the characters." [70] Looking forward, Watt cites James, Balzac, Stendhal, and Proust as inheritors of Austen's resolution and focus. We cannot avoid noticing that these are all consummate novelists of the social occasion and that parties repeatedly figure as the dramatic locus for the interaction of individual and society in these writers' works. Austen's novels epitomize the importance of the social occasion to modern fiction, and their prodigious influence arises partly from the deftness and power of Austen's use of parties. The ball or dance in an Austen novel is, first, a medium for courtship, as the narrator announces in *Pride and Prejudice:* "To be fond of dancing was a certain step towards falling in love." But Austen's parties are also metaphors for the release from antisocial isolation into the comic give-and-take of the world. In *Emma,* Emma Woodhouse's adult liberation is blocked by a father who comments, "The sooner every party breaks up, the better," and a potential lover who naively quibbles that "Fine dancing . . . like virtue, must be its own reward." [71] The "union" with which the novel literally ends becomes larger than the marriage of Knightley and Emma. It is an integration into society of the sort that Frye identified as the comic resolution. The centrality of party scenes in the work of nineteenth-century novelists follows the more ambivalent use in the eighteenth century of the openly transgressive masquerade, which Castle explicates in novels of Richardson, Fielding, Burney, and Inchbald.

Parties figure prominently throughout Victorian fiction in spite of the antifestive spirit critics like Huizinga and Bakhtin seem to associate with that period. Perhaps the importance of festivity is clearest in a somewhat idiosyncratic writer such as Thomas Love Peacock, whose comic novels of conversation clearly continue the spirit Bakhtin identifies with Greek *symposia:* a multiplicity of viewpoints combined with parody and the license of intoxication to reach a communal truth higher than the official, monologic voice of reason or moralism. Peacock's novels revolve around the country houses that provide their titles, but more profoundly the works center on the weekend parties that create festive communities within those houses. The formal carnivalistic inheritance so apparent in Peacock appears, with a different focus, in Thackeray's *Vanity Fair,* where social reality is depicted through the framing conceit of a carnival performance, and the image of society converging in the marketplace forms a backdrop for the performance of the author's puppets.

A similar sense of a teeming marketplace of social interactions infuses Dickens's novels, though in a less clearly carnivalized fashion. And the festive settings of Peacock and Thackeray have their modernized, bourgeois equivalents in the parties of Trollope and Meredith. In Trollope, as in Austen, parties provide the occasion for social business as well as play; they emerge as new communities in themselves. Robert Polhemus calls Trollope "the novelist laureate of parties" and notes how Trollope's social realism reflects a "tribal sense of life."[72] Though Meredith uses parties less frequently than Trollope, parties still appeal to Meredith as perfect occasions for the revelation of human folly. Virginia Woolf even uses the description of a tea party as a paradigm for discussing Meredith's epical style.[73] No survey of Victorian fiction can ignore its eminently social and secular character and fail to see how those characteristics find expression in party scenes and in the larger carnivalistic spirit that weaves art from a multiplicity of voices.[74]

Since party scenes are naturally suited to dramatic presentation they are important to the modernist concept of dramatic fiction, what Henry James calls "scenic" presentation. A party, like any event, may still be told rather than shown, but parties by nature offer fertile scenic possibili-

ties. Party scenes demand the manipulation of a great many characters in
a montage of faces, names, and voices; they multiply the artistic oppor-
tunities for showing character through dialogue. As Henry James said of
his most scenic novel, *The Awkward Age:* "I revelled in this notion of the
Occasion as a thing by itself, really and completely a scenic thing."[75] The
modernist predilection for dramatic presentation in fiction reflects not
only a distrust for the implications of narrative omniscience but also a rejection of the view that character can be known in the abstract. In its use
of multiple viewpoints, the modern novel participates in the genre's proclivity toward the dialogic and carnivalesque. The dramatic possibilities
of party scenes allow for the vivid portrayal of the social self.

Carnival gave literature a solution to the problems posed by the official
culture of the ancient and medieval worlds, much as parties shape the
approach of more recent novelists to the fragmentation of modern secular society. From the eighteenth century to the present, the party—as a
festive mingling of different voices, elements, and characters—becomes
a symbol for the novelistic enterprise itself. In a narrow sense, parties
simply belong to the middle-class cultural milieu that has become the
novel's subject. And for stylistic reasons, parties function, as Bakhtin
has noted of carnival, to provide concrete dramatic presentation of abstract issues. But in a larger sense the parallel Bakhtin poses between the
all-inclusiveness of carnival and the breadth of language and genre embraced by the novel applies potently to the relationship between parties
and the modern novel.

For this study the most relevant concept of Bakhtin's dialogics is his assertion that festive content is intimately tied to a carnivalized world view,
with explicit consequences for the novel genre. Bakhtin thus suggests a
powerful and provocative intersection of thematics and stylistics. In examining modern fiction in light of the idea that the party has succeeded
the festival in cultural function, I have looked at the relation between
party scenes and narrative style. What I have discovered is a variety of
manifestations of the festive influence on narrative technique, manifestations that are largely consistent with the relationship Bakhtin explores
between carnival and novel. Not surprisingly, the sense of carnivalized
genre is clearest in classic modernists and contemporary writers, more
problematic and less clear in the writers between the wars. In Joyce's
fiction we see the development of an affirmative presentation of fes-

tivity accompanied by increasingly multivocal narratives as we move from *Dubliners* to *Finnegans Wake*. In Woolf's novels we see the thematics of "party consciousness" leading to a complicated concept of self for both character and narrator, finally leading to a plural vision of narrative voice in *Between the Acts*. In Pynchon's fiction, festivity is explicitly antiauthoritarian, and that antiauthoritarianism leads to a fracturing of narrative authority as well, including the dissolution of the main character, Slothrop, in *Gravity's Rainbow*. In Coover's novel *Gerald's Party*, the party becomes a fertile mixing ground for different styles and creates a festive comedy of genres. Fitzgerald, Waugh, and Green remain problematic, in part because they are ambivalent toward the aesthetic imperatives of modernism. Fitzgerald's social realism is resistant to double-voicing, and his interest in parties and festivity creates a tension evident in his struggles and experiments with narrative voice. Waugh's satirical bent is potentially even more hostile to multiple voicing of narrative, but in *Vile Bodies* the force of the central parties explodes the satire into a comical apocalyptic vision—a "happy ending" unusually suggestive in its black comedy. In Henry Green, the between-the-wars writer with the closest ties to modernist experimentation, the novel-long party scene in *Party Going* ironically generates increased narrative authority, which Green then undermines through multivalent (even mystical) symbolism. All three between-the-wars writers examined here inherit the creative tension between two novelistic traditions—the realistic and the carnivalistic. This tension makes their work distinctive, and, as with all the writers considered here, their treatment of parties clarifies how they define the novel genre and how they have created a style within it.

The three-part structure of this book emphasizes the connection, embodied in the paradigm of controlled transgression, between festive vision and novel form. In Part 1, "Death at the Party," I discuss how the classic modernism of Woolf and Joyce uses reminders of mortality to reassert the ritual significance of celebration against the threat of the overly controlled party, the formal noncelebration. This vision of formality as threat to festive affirmation inspires the stylistic experiments: the desire for a truly carnivalistic spirit generates narrative openness and multivocality. At first the experimentation is tentative, as the voice of Septimus Warren Smith is brought into Clarissa's party, or the echoes

of Michael Furey resound in Gabriel's consciousness. Eventually the carnivalized narrative voice becomes truly multiple—in "Oxen of the Sun"
and the riotous wake of Finnegan, and in the narrative "we" and fertile
interruptions of *Between the Acts.*

In Part 2, "The Party Between the Wars," we see the literary consequences of the clash between the carnivalesque and those narrative
stances that are less amenable to double-voicing. Fitzgerald's work can
be read both as a continual exploration of the dangers and redemptive
possibilities of parties and as a series of (not always successful) experiments with narrative perspective, from the dramatic form of "The Broken
Lute" in *The Beautiful and Damned* to the narrator "within and without" in
Gatsby, to the shifting narrators (and chronologies) of *Tender is the Night.*
Waugh's entire career presents a conflict between the appeal of the festive spirit of his subject matter and the satiric distance and moral stance
of the narrator. *Vile Bodies* makes this tension most apparent as the party-
going (at once vital and decadent) undermines and complicates the satiric
posture of the narrative voice. Similarly, Henry Green's commitment to
an unintrusive narrator collapses under the force of the many voices at
play in the stagnant party of *Party Going.*

It is no accident that this particular narrative tension surfaces in fiction
given over to parties of the decadent model. The decadent striving for
vitality against the fear of boredom creates a social double bind that in
turn inspires a narrative paradox. These novels simultaneously aspire to
festive multiplicity and reject decadent cacophony.

Finally, in Part 3, "Beyond Decadence," we encounter the extreme of
controlled transgression imperiled by loss of control. But having abandoned the search for narrative certainty that characterized the between-
the-wars generation of writers, novelists such as Pynchon and Coover
are free to revel in the carnivalesque possibilities of the festive occasion
and the festive novel. The ritualistic character of festivity, which modernism located beneath the shallow celebrations and which later writers
lamented as lost altogether, reemerges in postmodern works. But the
festive rituals of the postdecadent world also present the potential for
violence and loss of our humanity, as *Gravity's Rainbow* and *Gerald's Party*
reveal.

The life of the party in twentieth-century fiction is very much a life of the modern novel. The transformation of the threat of failed festivity—from excess of control, to decadent posturing, to excess of transgression—parallels the changing modernist experiments with narrative multiplicity. Surely modern literature presents other fertile intersections of thematics and stylistics, but the story of festive form offers a particularly illuminating anatomy of modern fiction.

PART 1
Death at
the Party

When Clarissa Dalloway thinks in surprise, "Oh . . . in the middle of my party, here's death," Woolf locates in the encounter with mortality the central authenticating experience of secular literature and festivity. We have identified how the rise of the party accompanies a secularization of modern culture and how that secularization creates for literature an increasingly sacred function. To satisfy these ritualistic expectations, literature and celebration must demonstrate an encounter with the reality of death. We see this encounter insistently framed in festive settings in the works of Woolf and Joyce: only when Clarissa Dalloway is forced to confront the death of Septimus Smith does her party as "offering" gain plausibility; only through similar encounters in Joyce—the young boy with the dead priest in "The Sisters," Gabriel Conroy with Michael Furey in "The Dead," Stephen with his mother in *Ulysses*—can Dedalus's exclamation "Long Live Life!" ring true.

The failed party in modernist literature is thus typically the one that fails to transcend the everyday and offer a vitalizing engagement with death's omnipresence. When the controlled transgression of the party is stifled by too much control, we see an essential modern topos. The force of the narrative is then likely to work against excessive control through satire, subversion of narrative authority, or the depiction of alienation (usually on the part of a sympathetic central character). In turn, the very spirit of modernist narrative experimentation celebrates the vitality of excess, both thematically and formally.

This vision of liberating festivity is especially congenial to the writers experimenting with narrative form. The festive visions of Joyce and Woolf display increasing awareness of the carnivalistic consequences of festive themes. Indeed, their most extreme experimental and carnivalized texts appear almost contemporaneously and at the ends of their careers: *Finnegans Wake* and *Between the Acts*.[1] Joyce's text pushes the limits of multiple languages, discourses, myth, and farce—all superimposed upon a central scene of resurrection at a wake. Woolf experiments with plural narrative and an aesthetics of interruption as she mingles historical pageant and house party against the backdrop of impending war. The collocation of experimentation with multiple narrative voices and scenes of festivity encountering death is crucial to the literary consciousness of the age.

Bringing ritualistic expectations to scenes of social festivity is characteristic of British modernism. Repeatedly we see the superficial social occasion failing to engage vital human concerns: in the awkward teas of *Howards End* and the unsuccessful "bridge party" of *A Passage to India;* in the teas and ices of "Prufrock" that postpone the "overwhelming question"; and in the images of failed ritual in *The Waste Land*. One of the most powerful scenes in modern British fiction occurs in *Women in Love* when Lawrence sets the drowning of Gerald Crich's sister in the heart of the Crich annual fete. This placement dramatizes the submerged mortality that saps the lifeblood from the party guests, who have been characterized as decadent *fleur du mal*. In all of these works, the failed festivity is linked to a rejected superficiality associated with the Victorian past.

In the most provocative modernist works, a stylistic departure from past conventions is also clear. Indeed, it is in this regard that the festive visions of Joyce and Woolf are most fully carnivalized—perhaps because they perceive the potential of the party as well as its all-too-often failings. Much of what makes Joyce and Woolf so important to the continued development of the novel can be found in their use of parties. Bakhtin argues that the continued development of the novel genre depends upon "maximal contact with the present (with contemporary reality)" and a "stylistic three-dimensionality, which is linked with the multi-languaged consciousness."[2] The modernist engagement with these characteristics is manifested in experiments with narrative voice, often in the presentation of contemporary social scenes (most notably in the insistent setting of *Between the Acts* in "the present"). The inclusiveness of the Bakhtinian carnivalesque emerges most obviously in the novelistic propensity for "incorporated genres"—a quality again most apparent in the historical pageant of *Between the Acts* but also found in the festive moments of *Ulysses* ("Oxen of the Sun" [symposium] and "Circe" [drama]), and in the overarching dream/drama of *Finnegans Wake*. Of course, scenes of festivity are not the sole locations of such narrative experimentation, but, as the works of Joyce and Woolf demonstrate, they are especially amenable sites for the development of the novel genre's most radical and vital characteristics.

Perhaps some sense of the appeal of the party scene as a locus for challenges to the unitary narrative voice can be gained from reflection on the word *party* and its contemporary meanings. The word has, of course, a variety of familiar meanings, from social gatherings to political organizations to a single individual who is "party to a dispute." In the general classifications of definitions offered in the *Oxford English Dictionary* a remarkable antithesis between two groups of meanings appears: party can mean "a company or body of persons" or "a single person considered in some relation." The difference between these meanings evokes the tension at social gatherings between individual and group and the corresponding tension between monologic and dialogic conceptions of novelistic discourse. To the writers considered in this section, the ambiguous relation of individual to group and part to whole outlines the central problem of contemporary experience and art. Modernist art springs from a fascination with individual consciousness, but it is a consciousness that has been radically assaulted by the Darwinian, Marxist, and Freudian challenges to the autonomous self. In the twentieth century the quest of the hero becomes a pilgrimage toward reintegration, a desire of the alienated self to return to or rediscover a nourishing community. The alienated protagonist standing apart from the communal banquet of life emerges as a powerfully suggestive figure for modern humanity, and scenes of parties enact dramas of cultural alienation and identification.

Part and *whole* also suggest *fragmentation*, a word crucial to the modernist perception of experience and conception of artistic form. Contemporary social interactions as well as the inherited past appear fragmentary to the modernist writer. The stylistic conclusion toward which these perceptions tend challenges narrative authority and suggests that voice in literature must be plural and multiple. Literary interpretation as well as psychological self-definition proceeds on the faith that by experiencing the part we can come to know the whole, but such a faith necessitates negotiations among multiple points of view. When the individual or "party" is brought into the social context, the communal possibilities for life and literature intensify. Modernist literary experimentation thus maps an intersection of narrative multiplicity and social community, often envisioned in explicitly festive terms, including an encounter with death at the party.

1. "The Dead" and the Wake

PARTIES IN JOYCE

hrough Joyce's work we can trace a recurrent essential scene: a social gathering haunted by the symbolic or literal presence of death. This image of death at the heart of festivity, or, conversely, celebration in the face of mortality, is central in Joyce's fiction. If we read Joyce attuned to his vision of festivity and mortality, we will discover not only a significant thematic trope running through his work but also a consistent stylistic development toward an increasingly carnivalized narrative. As Joyce rewrites the scene of death at the party in various contexts, the vision of festivity and community grows more positive and the narrative becomes increasingly open to the genre-shaping forces Bakhtin has linked to carnival: mixing of modes, mixing of discourses (heteroglossia), free play with narrative voice, and the inclusion of folk carnival elements. David Hayman suggests that Joyce's "creative life is in some senses a record of his gradual mastery of the comic range, his conquest of joy in the name of serious literature, and the reduction of his characters to clowns gesticulating against the moving screen of history."[1] Studying the transformations of the recurrent basic scene will highlight Joyce's technical innovations and illuminate his distinctive festive vision. That festive vision offers us two powerful, polarized

39

visions of festivity engaging mortality—"The Dead" (1914) and *Finnegans Wake* (1939). These framing works remain classic paradigms for the failed party and the regenerating power of festivity, respectively. In *Ulysses* (1922) the "Oxen of the Sun" and "Circe" chapters use festivity as the context for stylistic experimentation to a virtually unprecedented degree, and they remain models for the parodic and phantasmagoric possibilities of literary festivity. Ultimately, Joyce celebrates human fellowship and the communities built around food and drink and talk. Joyce celebrates these communities through the mingling of literary and folk discourses, which finds its fullest expression in the many voices of *Ulysses* and *Finnegans Wake*. Joyce's concern with festivity, however, emerges clearly in his early writing as well.

The Wake in *Dubliners*

Late in "The Dead," after Gretta has cried herself to sleep, Gabriel remains awake meditating on the events of the evening. Gabriel's reverie moves from a recollection of the party to a vision of the Morkans' house transformed into a wake for Aunt Julia: "Poor Aunt Julia! She, too, would soon be a shade with the shade of Patrick Morkan and his horse. He had caught that haggard look upon her face for a moment when she was singing *Arrayed for the Bridal*. Soon, perhaps, he would be sitting in that same drawing-room, dressed in black, his silk hat on his knees. The blinds would be drawn down and Aunt Kate would be sitting beside him, crying and blowing her nose and telling him how Julia had died. He would cast about in his mind for some words that might console her, and would find only lame and useless ones. Yes, yes: that would happen very soon" (*D* 222–23).[2] The image not only culminates the incessant signs of morbidity that fill the otherwise hollow celebration of "The Dead," but it recalls the final tableau of "The Sisters," the first story of *Dubliners*. This tableau, glimpsed in "The Dead" and crucial to "The Sisters," develops into a Joycean topos. The Irish wake—a communal gathering and celebration on the occasion of an individual's death—exemplifies Joyce's concerns with mortality and human attempts to cope without the consolations offered by a now-rejected religious tradition.

The first full treatment of the wake as symbol occurs in "The Sisters," which is essentially a story of failed ritual. Ritual is evoked in the opening paragraph by the young boy's vigilant checking of Father Flynn's window "night after night" and his realization that the priest's death would be signalled by "the reflection of candles on the darkened blind for I knew that two candles must be set at the head of a corpse" (D 9).[3] The boy's memories of the priest are also dominated by rituals, both sacred and secular. The boy had visited the priest regularly, typically taking a packet of "High Toast" snuff as a present or offering. "High Toast" suggests both high mass and a secular toast; the ritual of the boy handing the snuff to the priest, who covers himself in little clouds of smoke, ironically suggests an altar boy handing incense to the priest at Mass.[4] The priest's lessons to the boy had stressed the power and mystery of priestly office, in particular the ritual powers of hearing confession and offering communion: "[He] showed me how complex and mysterious were certain institutions of the Church which I had always regarded as the simplest acts. The duties of the priest towards the Eucharist and towards the secrecy of the confessional seemed so grave to me that I wondered how anybody ever found in himself the courage to undertake them" (D 13). The story shows the priest failing in both these sacred duties—breaking a chalice and, later, in a state of nervous collapse, laughing to himself in the confessional. "Grave" and "undertake" reveal the morbid turn taken by the supposedly life-affirming rituals of the Church. The final images of the story confirm the emptying of ritual significance: the body of the priest holds an idle chalice on its breast while Eliza distantly recalls the priest's vague disgrace, "wide-awake and laughing-like to himself" (D 18).

Against the rituals reserved for priests, Joyce poses the human rituals of mourning—the wake. Florence Walzl has documented how the wake in "The Sisters" is characterized by "scrupulous adherence to Irish funeral practices," a scrupulousness intensified by Joyce in the story's revisions.[5] A wake can be seen as uniting a community at a time of sorrow, honoring a past life through vigorous celebration, and reaffirming that communal life continues in the face of individual death. Certainly the wake in "The Sisters" accomplishes none of these cultural goals. The room is dark and run-down; the empty fireplace is described twice. The three women exchange hollow clichés broken by awkward and solemn silences. The boy pretends to pray but cannot, encounters with horror the ugliness of what Eliza had termed a "beautiful corpse," and participates in the sherry and crackers "communion" partially and reluctantly. Joyce shifts from the sacred to the secular communion and shows the failure, here, of both.

If anything positive resides in "The Sisters," it is the boy's liberating disillusionment: "a sensation of freedom as if I had been freed from something by his death" (*D* 12). Walzl sees the boy's final taking of a glass of sherry as emblematic of his partial enlightenment, his seeing through the empty clichés and rituals.[6] Another critic suggests that the act presages the artistic epiphany and that the story suggests "Ireland might . . . begin confessing itself to and through the priest of art."[7] Certainly, later versions of the wake scene in Joyce do suggest possibilities for both individual awareness and social communion. The basic elements of the wake scenes—a social gathering around an unmistakable symbol of death—remain open to various treatments. In "The Sisters" the pallid surviving figures of authority, from the elderly sisters to the imbecilic Old Cotter, offer little hope of liberation. But in "The Dead" the encounter with death becomes, at least, *potentially* illuminating, and in *Finnegans Wake* the festive wake grows into a comic emblem of the transcendence of mortality. The essential terms and dynamics of Joyce's festive vision, however, are evident in the failed festivity that opens his first published work.

The image of death in the midst of festivity appears most directly in "Clay," the story of a family gathering on Halloween. Joyce originally attempted a story set on Christmas Eve but abandoned it in favor of a tale set on the night associated with unquiet spirits and ghosts. The story, in almost childlike language, pictures the tiny ("very, very small") Maria surrounded by large and intimidating objects, from the "big copper boilers" to the "big bell" to the "huge mugs" of tea filled from "huge tin cans." Diminutive Maria's eagerly anticipated evening out is presented as a series of minor miscues and mistakes. She is flustered at the bakery, uncomfortable on both crowded trams, and finally leaves her expensive plumcake behind. At the party inordinate anxiety attends searches for a missing nutcracker and then a missing corkscrew. Even the highlight of the evening, Maria's rendition of "I Dreamt That I Dwelt," is marred by her omission of the poignant second verse, a "mistake" of which, Joyce implies, all the listeners are aware.

But the core of this story is the "clay," a word mentioned only in the story's title. In spite of the deliberately oblique language with which Joyce describes the story's climax, what happens is clear enough. In a traditional game of fortune-telling, in which the other participants have picked prayerbook, ring, and water (emblematic of religious vocation, impending marriage, or impending travel, respectively), Maria is led by the mischievous children to pick the clay, emblematic of death: "She felt a soft wet substance with her fingers and was surprised that nobody spoke or took off her bandage. There was a pause for a few seconds; and then a great deal of scuffling and whispering. Somebody said something about the garden, and at last Mrs Donnelly said something very cross to one of the next-door girls and told her to throw it out at once: that was no play. Maria understood that it was wrong that time and so she had to do it over again: and this time she got the prayer-book" (*D* 105).

Certainly the alternatives—death or the religious life—suggest the limited possibilities for the Irish in general as well as provide an uncomfortable reminder of Maria's unmarried state. But the circumspect treatment of the "soft, wet substance" and what it represents is more suggestive in the context of the holiday and its particular festive traditions. Of all the pagan festivals assimilated by the Christian church, Halloween is the one that most clearly maintains its pagan character, specifically in the comical, theatrical (and non-Christian) representations of death and the spirit world. Halloween remains essentially a folk-carnival encounter with mortality. This significance is heightened by the traditional Celtic calendar, in which October 31 is Samhain Eve, "the prologue to the death of the Celtic year and the beginning of winter."[8] The seasonal "Feast of the Dead" of Irish folk tradition participates in the global traditions of associating seasonal change with individual mortality and communal regeneration. The festive encounter with death becomes life-giving: a ritualized way of incorporating mortality into the pattern of seasonal change, thus making it less frightening.

These festive traditions exist only dimly in the background of Joyce's story. The clearest example is the clay, the reminder of our end, here dug up from "the garden." The dimness of this festive background is exactly the point, however. In this hollow Hallow's Eve celebration the hints of the bold festive encounter with death are sublimated, drowned in politeness and defused ritual. The title of the story points directly to the death at the heart of the celebration, but the story itself hides that reality. Unnamed, encountered by Maria only when she is confused and blindfolded, and thrown out at once, the clay is expunged from the Hallow's Eve party. The emptiness of the celebration lies in its denial of mortality; this denial is the source of the miscues, awkwardness, and overall sterility. The Dubliners of this story, like Joe in Maria's opinion, are "good fellows," but their festivities mirror their lives: crucial spiritual truths lie buried beneath empty, worn-out rituals, pseudogenteel politeness, and middle-class pretension. No wonder Joe muses longingly for the past, exclaiming, "There was no time like the long ago" (*D* 106). The party in "Clay" is but a feeble ghost of the spirit of Hallow's Eve.

"Ivy Day in the Committee Room" offers a third important manifestation of death at the social gathering: the absent guest or absent guest of honor. Stout-quaffing by election canvassers takes place on Ivy Day, the anniversary of the death of Parnell, whose spirit is evoked both implicitly and explicitly by the bedraggled drinkers. Joyce adapted this device from Anatole France's use of Jesus as the "absent protagonist" in "The Procurator of Judaea."[9] The comparison of Parnell to Jesus— as betrayed king—is also explicit in "Ivy Day," as elsewhere in Joyce.[10] Joyce creates then not only a figural parallel but a complementary sense of absence—an empty chair in the committee room, the shade of Parnell. The absent protagonist technique and the Christ parallel both work ironically. The petty bickerings, distrustfulness, and selfishness of the canvassers for conservative but nationalist Tierney pale ironically before the political dedication of the "Chief." And the possibility of resurrection, or of the hero's death becoming a worthwhile sacrifice, diminishes as the Christian context changes into the context of secular politics under King Edward. As in "The Sisters" the story depicts incomplete communion, here a sort of Last Supper reenactment, but with the traitors still present and the Lord permanently departed. As in "Clay," vitality seems to reside in the past: "Musha, God be with them times! . . . There was some life in it then" (*D* 122). "Ivy Day" presents a truncated festivity that is neither party nor wake but partakes of both. The present is repressed by history not buoyed by it, and the pseudowake offers no hope of rejuvenation. "Ivy Day" also anticipates the Christmas dinner scene in *A Portrait of the Artist as a Young Man,* where the spirit of departed Parnell excites a vigor that is otherwise absent from the tense celebration (and is quickly repressed when it emerges).

"The Dead" brings together many of the themes and images evoked in earlier *Dubliners* stories. As it depicts a New Year's party dominated by the ambiguous "dead," the story powerfully combines the earlier images of death at the party: as in "Ivy Day" there exists a recurrent sense of past greatness by which the present pales in comparison (and a related sense of absent protagonists); as in "Clay" various minor miscues reveal a deeper morbidity and death-in-life; and as in "The Sisters" two elderly women appear as feeble vessels to carry the celebrative possibilities for the future. But "The Dead" also presents a stylistic departure: much longer than the other stories, it develops the full and ambiguous character of the protagonist in much greater depth and with greater sympathy than in the preceding stories. Gabriel's anxieties about self-presentation and alienation from his community presage the struggles of young Stephen Dedalus in *Portrait* and the more mature ambivalences of Leopold Bloom in *Ulysses*. Much more is invested in our qualified sympathies for Gabriel Conroy than in our distant relations to the other Dubliners. The critical controversy over how to interpret Joyce's presentation of Gabriel (with what mixture of sympathy and irony) mirrors the controversy over narrative distance in *Portrait*. Joyce moves away from the stable ironic detachment of *Dubliners* to a style that creates dialogic open-endedness about human character and renders judgment problematic.[11] This stylistic change accompanies a different view of festivity. Though still a vision of failed potential, "The Dead" invokes festive possibilities more seriously and hopefully than the earlier stories in *Dubliners*.

> "All the Living and the Dead":
> Festive Potential in "The Dead"

Roger Caillois describes the myths attendant upon New Year's festivals: "The dead leave their abode and invade the world of the living. All barriers are broken and nothing any longer prevents the trespassers from visiting their descendants during this suspension of universal order that the change from old to new year connotes."[12] This ethnographic description seems particularly appropriate to Joyce's emphasis on the presence of the dead at the holiday party given early in the new year. The title invites our first inquiry, "Who are 'the dead'?" But the story's death symbolism is so ubiquitous that our initial question has too many answers. We can only answer it after we understand the nature of the party and its relation to the final scene between Gretta and Gabriel in the Gresham Hotel. Meanwhile we can observe how a party is created, both artistically and in reality, through the establishment of borders that will come to symbolize the forces of life and death. "The Dead" illustrates how parties set up symbolic frames in order to comprehend abstract spiritual concerns through the realm of everyday life.

A party delineates by definition; it is not a casual or spontaneous affair. Human enterprise must work to bring together a group of people to dance away the night. The participants come in response to invitations; they arrive at a special place at a designated time. The invitation transforms the host's home and the night hours of the party. This consecration is a large part of a party's magic, investing with significance the physical edifice around the party. Doors and windows become portals between kingdoms. The excluded waif can peer into the party, a window affording the view, the door (and perhaps a doorman) blocking entry; Bede's swallow may flitter in and out showing the contrast between realms; the loner, or the hero, can look out the window, place himself on the Stygian border between realms, and inevitably choose one or the other. Parties sharpen our sense of the boundaries of human community and of the paradoxes of individual identity in the social group.

Lily is the agent of transition in "The Dead" and her point of view opens the story, as she is "literally run off her feet" shuttling arriving guests from the cold outside to the dressing rooms—ladies upstairs, gentlemen below—where they shed their coats and tidy themselves before the hostesses escort them to the upstairs party. We have here a vivid sense of changing worlds. The traditional contrasts that hark back to Bede's swallow are present: the harsh coldness and severe snow outside; the warmth of fires, food and drink, and human fellowship inside. But this symbolism is present only by force of implication, the result of the accumulated tradition of a party which has "never fallen flat" in thirty years.[13] The fragrant cool air "escaping" from the "crevices and folds" of Gabriel's coat is one of the few positive images of the three introductory pages it takes to get Gabriel and Gretta indoors. Indeed, the descriptive details of the story's opening subtly depict a scene more grim than festive. In this brief passage we learn that Lily is overworked, the doorbell "wheezy," the hallway and stairs "dark," the aunts "old," "quite grey," and "feeble." Gabriel's first comment—that it takes his wife "three mortal hours to dress herself"—sets in motion the death imagery soon to become prevalent. Gabriel's first social encounter, with Lily, the pale caretaker's daughter, is unnerving, as his reference to marriage unexpectedly incites her bitterness.

Joyce reverses the traditional warm/cold and life/death imagery characteristic of parties and exemplified in Bede's swallow image. During the party Gabriel goes to the window to look out at the cold, but his thoughts do not reflect a sense of comfort at the communal hearth: "Gabriel's warm trembling fingers tapped the cold pane of the window. How cool it must be outside! How pleasant it would be to walk out alone, first along by the river and then through the park! The snow would be lying on the branches of the trees and forming a bright cap on the top of the Wellington Monument. How much more pleasant it would be there than at the supper-table" (D 192). The window becomes the border between community and solitude, a warm manmade environment and a cold natural one; but Gabriel sees the natural solitude as nourishing and refreshing, the manmade warmth as stifling. Joyce carefully builds this sense of stifling warmth, from Lily's paleness accentuated by the gas flame, to Mr. Browne's hot face and the "heated" exchange between Miss Ivors and Gabriel, to the detailed description of the "hot work" of carving. This reversal of the hot/cold imagery parallels a reversal of the life/death symbolism. The reader begins to identify the party with death, the cool air outside with life. Joyce's careful symbolic descriptions suggest a morbid reversal of traditional imagery. Something has gone wrong with this celebration.

Let us first consider the nature of this party. An annual Christmastime event of thirty years standing, the party is traditionally well attended. Lily informs us that "everybody who knew [the Misses Morkan] came to it"—friends, family, music pupils, and members of Julia's choir. Joyce introduces thirteen guests by name, as well as Lily and the three hostesses, but the organized dances, the references to unnamed young men, and the fact that the guests eat in two shifts suggest a gathering considerably larger. There are quadrilles and lancers, singing and piano performances, and an elaborate dinner featuring a well-cooked goose, a ham, and special Christmas pudding. Gabriel, the senior male family member of the group, traditionally carves the goose and delivers the after-dinner oration. In all, it appears to be a festive affair, fittingly graced by music and centering on a traditional feast and a traditional dinner speech.

If we consider the successful party as a controlled ritual transgression of everyday social restrictions in which dance, feasting, intoxication, and social mingling create an atmosphere wild, celebrative, and gay, and if we see the failed party as characterized by either an excess of control or an excess of transgression, it is easy to see how this party fails. The aging aunts reflect the weariness of the party, the excitement of which has given way to a concern with maintaining decorum and the mere motions of celebration. Conversation is frequently interrupted, not by the excitement of so many people interacting, as we would expect at a party, but rather because the topics have become dangerously controversial or, in Joyce's words, "grown lugubrious." Browne's energetic comments on liquor to three young ladies are overfamiliar, and they instinctively ignore him; Mary Jane steers the conversation away from racial topics when Freddy Malins introduces them and away from religious questions when the pope's banning of women in choirs and the behavior of monks are discussed. As in "Clay" the sense is of overcautiousness in response to a perceived fear of disorder. Argument is prevented by changing the subject of discussion; the talk of monks sleeping in their coffins, morbid enough in itself, is cut off and "buried in silence." The recurrent safe topic becomes the greatness of the past and this, in turn, is the theme of Gabriel's well-received speech.

Mary Jane's dull academy piece on the piano parodies the participatory joy music can instill at a party. Its sterile technical rendition is followed by overly zealous fake applause from the young men who have ducked into the back room to replenish their stout. The rest of the party strains in polite applause. Later, Julia's more heartfelt song culminates in the slightly drunken clapping and compliments of Freddy Malins. This is, first of all, perceptive realism: Joyce subtly captures social mannerisms characterized by a mixture of insincerity and general goodwill. But these particular manifestations symbolize a more pervasive malaise, an infection that spreads beyond the party to the entire society.

Freddy Malins is our misplaced Bacchus, representing intoxication as threat. Throughout party literature social attitudes toward intoxication reveal the degree to which everyday decorum can be suspended. Here, at an overly formal, ordered affair, intoxication is not communal but rather an individual aberration that must be suppressed. Freddy's alco-holism is indeed sad, but here it primarily demonstrates how out of place the festive is at this party. His laughter and conversation are embarrass-ingly loud, his applause overhearty, his comments inappropriate. The party cannot embrace him because it fears his bacchanalian potential. To welcome Freddy Malins wholeheartedly means to yield the defenses against group intoxication and, subsequently, loss of control. Fear of disorder rules.

The climax of the unsatisfying social rituals is Gabriel's speech. Gabriel intends to emphasize both the traditional and redemptive characteristics of the occasion—"the tradition of genuine warm-hearted courteous Irish hospitality" (D 203)—but instead delivers a speech overwhelmed by ref-erences to the passing of generations and to old age. Gabriel speaks of the new generation lacking "those qualities of humanity, of hospitality, of kindly humor which belonged to an older day" (D 203). Ironically, he concludes his reflections by saying, "I will not linger on the past" (D 204). New Year's is an appropriate time for looking to the past, but it is also a moment that reaches toward the regenerative potential of the future. That potential is missing from Gabriel's speech.

Gabriel's insecurity emerges contextually to the reader of the story rather than to the auditors of his speech. To the reader Gabriel's speech brings to a climax the developing morbidity of the story and directs the partygoer's energies outward toward "the dead." His tribute to the past becomes a funereal incantation that ironically cites, as the prime source of vitality, the two elderly aunts he has characterized to himself as "ignorant old women" (D 192).

The sterility of the party as a whole is paralleled in the hero's distance from whatever conviviality survives at the gathering. Gabriel's sense of his superiority to the party guests centers on his education and literary background. The very qualities that make him the best candidate for giving the dinner speech also make him feel his speech will not be under-stood. His attitude prevents him from any kind of communion with the other guests. Not only is he defensive towards Lily and Miss Ivors, but he is barely polite toward Mrs. Malins and "moody and cold" toward his wife. Gabriel even becomes "slightly angered" in the humorous discus-sion of galoshes with Gretta and his aunts. At the party we see Gabriel only in two unpleasant conversations, delivering his speech, and reflecting in solitude. Gabriel at the window, looking out and longing to be away from the throng: this is his essence, the alienated soul at the party. And yet we feel as he places his trembling fingers upon the tablecloth in preparation for his speech, that he desires the acceptance of the group; he longs to be part of them and to be admired. But he remains separate, at the dinner taking "no part in the conversation" (*D* 198), and symbolically distinguishing himself from "all the gentlemen" by having celery instead of pudding.

Thus the party in "The Dead" fails in several ways. From Gabriel's point of view it fails to be a vehicle to social integration: he guards his sense of self so jealously that his social encounters turn sour and he longs to be alone, and, as we will see, alone with Gretta. But Gabriel's reflective consciousness acts as a screen on which we see the larger failures of the party. The party atmosphere is poisoned by a fear of excess (in drink, dance, and conversation) and by a morbid fixation on the superior qualities of the dead. Instead of the vibrant life of the party defining mortality as the threat against which we celebrate living, the dead are perceived as the source of vitality. The spirit of the past mingles with the aged sterility of the guardians of the present to create an unhealthy rivalry between the living and the dead. The terms have become reversed, as Gabriel's speech demonstrates: the dead are those at the party. In imitating the rituals of the vibrantly remembered dead, the party guests achieve not their vitality but their deathlike quality. The life-in-death of the previous generation is mirrored by a death-in-life at the party. Death is neither placated nor ritually triumphed over at this party; it ubiquitously infiltrates the living. In discussing the chaotic party in *Violence and the Sacred*, Girard argues that "The holiday-gone-wrong serves nicely to symbolize decadence."[14] Here we see the other extreme, in which the once vital ritual of the party, now stiff and lifeless, becomes a metaphor for a declining society.

If "The Dead" were more like the earlier *Dubliners* stories, it would end in the party's melancholy dissolution, perhaps with the confusion over cab directions pointing to the uncertainties of the new year. But the story continues and follows Gabriel and Gretta from the party to their remarkable encounter at the Gresham Hotel. The general sense at the party of the greater vitality of bygone generations is personified in Gretta's vivid recollection of Michael Furey.

Gabriel's final, mystical vision is related to the festive rituals of parties in which one can sense the connection between one's individual experience and the accumulated transcendent unity of the culture. The story moves from the failed community of the party, to the failed union of husband and wife, to the utter loneliness of the self facing its own inevitable extinction. But in the final vision it turns to the spiritual union that was potential but unachieved in the earlier events of the night. This vision necessitates innovations in both symbolism and narrative voice. The final unitary vision depends upon a suggestion of, and ultimately a challenge to, dualistic interpretation. The conclusion creates a narrative voice both individual and multiple, and the latter section of the work develops a symbolic construct that undermines the dualistic symbolic values introduced earlier in the story. The two worlds suggested by Gabriel peering out the window are finally insufficient; Joyce introduces a more complex symbol for the relationship between life and death. The vehicle is the stairway, the passage between the realms of upstairs and downstairs. Scenes at the party, the hotel room, Gretta's remembered experience in Galway, and even a painting at the Morkans' house involve a carefully noted separation between upstairs and downstairs. Nine separate scenes in "The Dead" involve stairways, and considered as a group they reveal the process by which the story creates and then undermines its own structural dualism.

The opening paragraph makes it clear that the party is taking place in a two-story house and that the men leave their coats downstairs with Lily while the women leave theirs with Kate and Julia upstairs. The separation of the sexes and the placement of women above men are significant details, as the later scenes will reveal. Here it is merely interesting to note that these details are given such attention in the opening paragraph and that the separation of the upstairs party from the ground floor entry causes the hostesses to keep "walking after each other to the head of the stairs, peering down over the banisters and calling down to Lily to ask her who had come" (*D* 175). Joyce continues to devote a great deal of attention to the hostesses looking anxiously down the stairs (*D* 181, 196). Gabriel finds himself staring "blank[ly] down the staircase" when Miss Ivors leaves, and he fears he has offended her. Similarly, Gabriel ventures down the "dark stairs" when he is dispatched to check on Freddy Malins's sobriety.

Taken by themselves, these staircase scenes appear to be little more than naturalistic details. But Joyce's naturalism in *Dubliners* is highly symbolic and his details significant. The two-story architecture of the party and the staircase between levels take on deeper significance when they are considered in light of the more obviously important scenes that follow. In these scenes we see not only two levels—the upper identified with women and the party, the lower identified with men and the excluded outside world—but we also see a dark passageway that connects them.

The turning point of the story is the magnificent tableau scene at the end of the party:

> Gabriel had not gone to the door with the others. He was in a dark part of the hall gazing up the staircase. A woman was standing near the top of the first flight, in the shadow also. He could not see her face but he could see the terracotta and salmonpink panels of her skirt which the shadow made appear black and white. It was his wife. She was leaning on the banisters listening to something. Gabriel was surprised at her stillness and strained his ear to listen also. But he could hear little save the noise of laughter and dispute on the front steps, a few chords struck on the piano and a few notes of a man's voice singing.
>
> He stood still in the gloom of the hall, trying to catch the air that the voice was singing and gazing up at his wife. There was grace and mystery in her attitude as if she were a symbol of something. He asked himself what is a woman standing on the stairs in the shadow, listening to distant music, a symbol of. If he were a painter he would paint her in that attitude. Her blue felt hat would show off the bronze of her hair against the darkness and the dark panels of her skirt would show off the light ones. *Distant Music* he would call the picture if he were a painter. (D 209–10)

We learn later that she is listening to "The Lass of Aughrim," the song that her childhood lover, Michael Furey, used to sing to her. The memory of him leaving his sickbed to bid her good-bye, an act of folly that cost him his life, is reawakened.

It is tempting to read the misunderstanding that begins here between Gabriel and Gretta as simply a manifestation of Gabriel's egotistical blindness, but Gabriel is indeed responding to his wife's sensitive mood. The music has moved her and evoked her deepest feelings; unconsciously he responds to that, never suspecting that she could be moved by someone else. Gretta's interest in Michael Furey breaks the accustomed familiarity that has deadened her relationship with her husband, and Gabriel responds to it: "There was grace and mystery in her attitude."

The spatial details of this scene articulate Gabriel's alienation. Gabriel is downstairs in the dark, as in the opening scene. Though looking up the staircase, he cannot see the upper floor; instead he sees the shadowy outline of a woman he identifies as his wife. She too is looking upward and listening, but Gabriel cannot hear the music she does. The passage carefully emphasizes the limitations of Gabriel's vision and understanding: he sees only the lower half of his wife's figure, not her face; he sees her in black-and-white, not color; and he is in the dark and out of hearing. He is excluded from his wife's world; failing to perceive the auditory source of her enchantment, he switches his attention solely to the visual.[15] He conceives of the scene as a painting; imaginatively he puts a frame around it that excludes the source of the music by centering on Gretta, the listener. In Gabriel's "painting" Gretta becomes the subject. No longer a part of the mediating passageway, she is enthroned on a level of her own.

The painting Gabriel imagines has a clear parallel in the painting of the balcony scene of *Romeo and Juliet* he examined earlier at the party (D 186). There, too, the hidden man observes the woman from below. She is, he discovers, thinking of him, and the scene has the poignant power of romance: the gap between the lovers will be bridged by a heroism propelled by love. In this fashion Gabriel misreads the tableau scene. Gretta is not thinking of him, and the tragedy of *Romeo and Juliet* gives us a clue to the direction of Gabriel's romantic impulse: a confusion of the living and the dead. In the beautifully rendered tableau scene, Gretta stands poised between her living and dead lovers, but it is the dead lover that is alive to her at this moment. Gabriel, however, sees the same scene in only two terms—himself and the woman he desires. Gabriel simplifies to comprehend and also to subjugate. He desires to be alone with Gretta, and his excitement is kindled by his memories of "their secret life together."

Gabriel's desire to escape a public setting for the supposed freedom of solitude is a response typical of a self-conscious individual at a lifeless party. When Gabriel's disgust for the pettiness of his aunts and the lively sociability of their party reaches its height, he daydreams, as we have seen, of a cooling, refreshing solitude that would liberate him from the suffocation of the party's warmth: "How pleasant it would be to walk out alone, first along by the river and then through the park!" (D 192). Perceiving his own shortcomings through the reflecting medium of the dull community of the party, Gabriel's desires focus on being alone with Gretta. The trip from the Morkans' house to the Gresham Hotel is dominated by this desire, the antithesis of the party spirit. Gabriel thinks fondly of the private aspects of their love, the "moments of their life together, that no one knew of or would ever know of" (D 213). He imagines a tender scene ensuing at the hotel: "He longed to be alone with her. When the others had gone away, when he and she were in their room in the hotel, then they would be alone together" (D 214). When they actually arrive at the hotel, Gabriel feels that "they had escaped from their lives and duties, escaped from home and friends" (D 215). Gabriel's obsessive desire for solitude, envisioned as escape, demonstrates how directly his passion for Gretta grows out of his failure at the party and the failure of the party to provide a sense of community. Alienated from the community festivity, Gabriel seeks fulfillment in a union with Gretta free from the alienated and threatening Other of society. But at the hotel he discovers the Other in the specific form of a rival lover whose memory fills his wife's thoughts. Gabriel's attempt to frame the picture, to limit the world solely to himself and the object of his desire, fails; the Other he sought to avoid is discovered, ultimately, within himself.

The move toward self-examination begins in the dark ascent to the hotel room. Careful description details the three-person procession up the stairs. A sleepy porter leads the way with a flickering candle; Gretta follows, again between two men, her head bowed; Gabriel comes last, "his arms . . . trembling with desire to seize her" (D 215). His lustful passion takes the form of jealous desire though he still knows nothing of Gretta's thoughts of Michael. The animating force of the unknown rival is remarkably clear in the language of his desire: "he longed to defend her against something and then to be alone with her" (D 213); as he begins to notice her preoccupation, "he longed to be master of her strange mood" (D 217); and "he longed . . . to crush her body against his, to overmaster her" (D 217). Rather than physically overpowering her, though, Gabriel inquires about her distant look and discovers she has been thinking of Michael Furey. He continues to deny the importance of the rival: "He did not wish her to think that he was interested in this delicate boy" (D 219). Oddly, it is when Gretta reveals that her old lover is long dead that Gabriel's jealousy emerges explicitly and the denial of Michael Furey's importance a moment before gives way to an encounter with him, a comparison that reveals to Gabriel his own weakness: "While he had been full of memories of their secret life together, full of tenderness and joy and desire, she had been comparing him in her mind with another. A shameful consciousness of his own person assailed him" (D 219–20). This is followed by his self-appraisal as a "pitiable, fatuous fellow." As Gretta responds to his questions with more details about her brief relationship with Michael Furey, Gabriel is gripped by "a vague terror," and Michael Furey is transformed into "some impalpable and vindictive being . . . coming against him, gathering forces against him in its vague world" (D 220). Michael Furey is becoming the Other, the figure of Death and of death's power to seduce the living.

Gretta narrates her final encounter with Michael when he came to bid her good-bye in Galway: "Then the night before I left I was in my grandmother's house in Nuns' Island, packing up, and I heard gravel thrown up against the window. The window was so wet I couldn't see so I ran downstairs as I was and slipped out the back into the garden and there was the poor fellow at the end of the garden, shivering" (D 221). Again we have the familiar scene: the woman above and the man below, the stairs in between. Gretta traverses the stairs to reach him, but it does no good; the real separation between them is not the staircase, which is after all a vehicle of transcendence, a means of connecting the separate levels. Rather, the separation inheres in their mortality. But death also unites them, and the separation is not merely one of the living and the dead, of the girl who will survive and the boy who will perish. The stairs represent the possible contact between the two worlds, which is given voice in the story—the memory of the boy that will survive in the woman to be rekindled on the staircase at the Morkans' and at the Gresham Hotel.

Gabriel holds Gretta's hand as she cries herself to sleep. When he drops it and walks to the window, we see Gretta literally fade from his consciousness. Finally he fixes on Michael Furey, the image of the passionate, eternal youth he wishes he were. Gabriel wishes to become the kind of man capable of exciting Gretta's passion and worthy of her love. His encounter with the Other is an encounter with the self he would like to be, just as at the party he is struck by the disjunction between his knowledge of himself and the social image he hopes to project. Through Michael Furey Gabriel encounters his own mortality and his limitations.

But this weakened sense of self that the contrast with Michael Furey forces him to confront also fades. Gabriel enters the passageway that connects the antithetical worlds—the dark link between the sexes, between the community and the self, between the party and the outside world, between the living and the dead: "His own identity was fading out into a grey impalpable world: the solid world itself which these dead had at one time reared and lived in was dissolving and dwindling" (D 223). Such loss of distinctions represents a kind of death-in-life, a journey perhaps to actual death. In any case, the loss abandons the distinctions by which we live and the distinctions that have functioned in the dispassionate narrative style of the earlier stories. The mysterious force of the last two paragraphs of "The Dead" arises in part, as John Paul Riquelme argues, from the ambiguous "merger of the character's interior speech with the narrator's storytelling." [16] Gabriel's vision fades into a vision that looks "all over Ireland" and a voice that speaks of the community of "all the living and the dead" (D 224). Gabriel's visionary self-criticism differs from the terse endings of the previous stories because it holds a potential for rebirth; it posits a connection between seemingly exclusive worlds and thus allows for transcendence. The gap between the self and others, whether between the individual and the community at the party, between the society and its past, or between a man and a woman, is the interstice that must be traversed. Thus, Gabriel Conroy sets out on his journey westward, which is both a journey to death in the traditional sense and a journey to a renewed vitality represented by the westerners—Miss Ivors, Gretta, and Michael Furey. These are not, however, contradictory readings. For where else but to death does growth take us? The experience of Gabriel Conroy shows the potential for spiritual growth along the journey to death.

It remains only potential because Joyce chooses to end the story with the loss of identity, the fading into sleep or death that also ends *Ulysses* and *Finnegans Wake*. He does not describe the next morning. The story emphasizes growth and self-encounter in ambiguous process, not as completed. Joyce chooses not to reestablish the formal distinctions by which we live, and the story ends in a union of opposites.[17] Joyce's broadening festive vision leads to the creation of a deliberately more ambiguous character and story. This fertile ambiguity involves a suspension, or at least a recasting, of narrative authority. This new vision is naturally more conducive to the novel form, and it is within that genre that the rest of Joyce's fictional achievement lies.

"The Dead" presents a failed party as a symbol for a lifeless society. Through the figure of Gabriel Conroy, Joyce dramatizes the dynamics of the party's failure on an individual scale. The struggle between the locked labyrinth of the self and the generosity required to give oneself to other people is cast in terms of a struggle between vitality and morbidity. To participate in the community of the party, or to participate in the dynamics of a marriage, requires a certain surrender of autonomy. The celebration of life requires an awareness of life's transience, its ultimate fragility. Love requires a realization of the self's fragility in contact with the immediate other. Both experiences suggest that static oppositions must give way. And Gabriel's final vision is, appropriately, one of community—"all the living and the dead." The force of the prose rhythms and the implied depth of Gabriel's emotional experience show how the encounter with death intensifies life experience. Riquelme expresses the connection between Gabriel's self-revelation and the festive community: "Conroy discovers his necessary connection to people he has taken for granted and even disdained. By the end of the story, he understands his inextricable relationship to a community, a relationship that is implied as well by the teller's stance in the fusion of voices."[18] Gabriel's alienation from the party and his distance from Gretta are of a piece. Both conditions arise from anxieties particularly characteristic of modern self-consciousness, and Joyce's fictional treatment involves a rejection of the stable self and its narrative counterpart.

"Dance of Death": Celebration in *Ulysses*

Ulysses has no formal party scene as in "The Dead," and yet the importance of festivity to the novel, particularly in the context of the encounter with mortality, should not be underestimated. The significance of festivity as a carnivalizing narrative force also becomes abundantly clear in *Ulysses*. Joyce's method, which Eliot aptly characterized in his "*Ulysses*, Order, and Myth" as "manipulating a continuous parallel between contemporaneity and antiquity," leads to the repeated comparison of modern secular behavior to sacred and mythic rituals. The multiple historical perspectives that shadow the Dublin present of the novel make us conscious of how the activities of the present day participate in archetypal and historical traditions. The multiple perspectives often deflate contemporary life through ironic or mock heroic contrast, but as often the ritual parallels suggest a vibrant depth to everyday experience. The background of a history of ritual celebrations and festivities is nowhere clearer than in the "Oxen of the Sun" and "Circe" chapters.[19] These chapters form a sort of climax to the novel as Stephen and Bloom are brought together and the evening revelry reaches its height. Significantly, these chapters also bring to fullest development the theme of coping with mortality. The link between bereavement and maturity emerges in the book's opening scene as Mulligan and Stephen quarrel over how Stephen mourns his mother's death; the theme is further explored through Paddy Dignam's funeral and Bloom's musings about his father's and infant son's deaths in "Hades." Both dressed in black, Stephen and Bloom stand apart as human memento mori. In "Oxen of the Sun" both Stephen and Bloom are assailed by painful memories of their losses; in "Circe" they both experience cathartic visions of those whom they have lost. That these memories and visions are framed by the drunken symposium of medical students and an inebriated outing at a brothel is consistent with Joyce's festive vision. That these two chapters present the most daring and successful examples of the mingling of narrative voices is consistent with the connection between festivity and the carnivalized novel.

At the core of "Oxen" is a knotty nexus of Joycean transformations. The clearest perhaps is the analogy between procreation and artistic creation. This parallel is combined with the familiar Joycean concept of the priest of art in which the sacred embodiment of the word becomes the secular epiphany of art. These two parallels—relating art to the physical and to the sacred—inform the multiple levels of discourse: the drinking revels of the medical students and Stephen and Bloom are expressed through an evolutionary history of styles of English prose and a rough pattern of embryological development set against a background of sacred fertility rituals. Lindsey Tucker suggests that the chapter not only describes "the development of English, the evolution of fauna, the growth of the human foetus, but the development of ritual."[20] The symposium-like gathering of drinkers allows Joyce to create a version of that simultaneous existence of "the whole of the literature of Europe from Homer," which Eliot identified in "Tradition and the Individual Talent" as the proper possession of the modern writer. Joyce's stylistic parodies display a startling virtuosity and create a comic opacity of language, but the multiple styles also evoke a rich palimpsest in which the modern social gathering is written over a history of celebrations from Platonic symposia to Anglo-Saxon feasts, gatherings of Arthurian knights, the Last Supper, eighteenth-century entertainments, and Dickens's sentimental colloquies.

The gathering of "right witty scholars" debating all manner of conceptions, births, and misbirths with comic rigor suggests the initial dialogic paradigm of the symposium and "the convivial atmosphere of Socratic discussion" (*U* 341). The references to Landor's *Imaginary Conversations* and to *Aristotle's Masterpiece* (a pseudonymous seventeenth-century work of sex education)[21] suggest the proliferation of learned and pseudo-learned symposia through the ages. The chapter itself becomes such a symposium, the festive table of the novel where the discourses of generations are brought together. Like the chapter and like *Ulysses* as a whole, "the debate which ensued was in its scope and progress an epitome of the course of life" (*U* 340). Many have noted the Joycean self-reference involved in the description of "a language so encyclopaedic" and the "chaffering allincluding most farraginous chronicle" (*U* 341, 345). Indeed the all-inclusiveness of "Oxen" and *Ulysses* as a whole reflects the festive and dialogic spirit of the symposium. No work (save perhaps Rabelais or *Finnegans Wake*) better illustrates Bakhtin's formula of the carnivalistic mixing of styles combined with the liberating undermining of parody than does "Oxen of the Sun."

The note of ritual so crucial to art, procreation, and festivity is struck in the chants of the opening paragraph of this chapter. The arrival of Bloom at the hospital and his invitation to join the party are couched in the language of Anglo-Saxon customs for offering hospitality to strangers. The imagery also echoes the customs of Greek culture that afforded hospitality to the wanderer Odysseus. Bloom becomes "the watcher in ward wary," "the seeker," "the traveller Leopold," "childe Leopold," and "sir

Leopold that was the goodliest guest" (*U* 316–18). Later his reluctance to
join in the sacrilegious mockery sets him apart further and he is dubbed
"the stranger." Still, Bloom, though different, is accorded the hospitality
traditionally offered the wayfaring stranger.

The chronological march of styles provides a historical reprise of the
languages of hospitality, reminding us how central the sharing of food
and drink is to human community. "And full fair cheer and rich was on
the board that no wight could devise a fuller ne richer" (*U* 317). Beer
and wine are praised as examples of primitive magic: "And also it was
a marvel to see in that castle how by magic they make a compost out of
fecund wheat kidneys. . . . And they teach the serpents there to entwine
themselves up on long sticks out of the ground and of the scales of these
serpents they brew out a brewage like to mead" (*U* 317). When Stephen
parodies the Last Supper, the language—"quaff ye this mead" (*U* 320)—
invokes other festive traditions as well. The languages of drinking customs range from the identification of thunder as "Old Nobodaddy was
in his cups" to the passing of "a flagon of cordial waters . . . (a whole
century of polite breeding had not achieved so nice a gesture)" (*U* 330).
The confused drunken language at Burke's includes a variety of toasts
compressed into a startling paragraph of liquor language: "expensive
inaugurated libation"; "Have you good wine, staboo?"; "*Nos omnes biberi-
mus viridum toxicum*"; "Rome boose"; "other licensed spirits"; "Health
all! *A la vôtre!*" (*U* 348). Here, in the confusion of tongues, the language
afforded strong drink in different centuries and cultures merges in the
intoxicated phantasmagoria.

Multiple tongues suggest the feast of the Pentecost as well as Babel,
and several critics have noted the importance of Pentecostal images to
"Oxen."[22] Tucker argues that the gathering in "Oxen" echoes the Pentecostal feast as well as the earlier Hebrew Shabuoth and the later Lord's
Supper in the common "close identification of food with spiritual forms
of sustenance," as in the Pentecost where "the flames are like tongues,
the spirit is 'poured' into the apostles and they are fed a new kind
of food."[23] Certainly Stephen, saturated in the religion in which he no
longer believes, uses the Lord's Supper as a metaphor connecting artistic creation to the table of the feast: "Now drink we, quod he, of this
mazer and quaff ye this mead which is not indeed parcel of my body
but my soul's bodiment" (*U* 320). But these parallels grow increasingly

ironic in force, and we are reminded that, as for Stephen, little more than "a capful of light odes can call [his] genius father" (*U* 339). And from Bloom's perspective we see the jolly medical apostles as "those who create themselves wits at the cost of feminine delicacy" (*U* 333). The festivity in "Oxen" functions within the tradition of ritual celebrations, but the Homeric parallel also suggests a violation of ritual, a crime against fertility. In this context (remembering that it is here that Bloom and Stephen meet) the alienation Bloom and Stephen both feel from the revelry becomes significant.

For at this lively and bawdy party during which a "bouncing boy" is born to Mina Purefoy and a fertile thundershower quenches the Dublin drought, the specter of mortality nevertheless haunts both Stephen and Bloom—the two figures dressed in black, one presiding over the celebration, the other an outsider invited to join. That Bloom is reminded of Rudy, his son lost in infancy, is natural given the occasion and the topics of discussion: "No son of thy loins is by thee. There is none now to be for Leopold, what Leopold was for Rudolph" (*U* 338). The narrator's bold proclamation initiates Bloom's complex reverie in which he thinks of his lost son, of the wasteland vision of sterility he had earlier in the day, and of himself as a young boy. Throughout the day Bloom has struggled with the guilt attending both his father's and his son's deaths as well as his wife's adultery. The equanimity with which he meets these challenges is offered as a tacit model for the younger generation and particularly for Stephen, whose guilt over his mother's death seems an obstacle to his own adulthood and creativity.

Joyce emphasizes this connection—Bloom as a model for the maturity Stephen lacks—by interpolating Stephen's death reverie into the middle of Bloom's vision. Stephen is reminded of his mother's death in the midst of his assertion of his artistic powers as "lord and giver of life . . . encircled . . . with a coronal of vineleaves" (*U* 339). Joyce continues to pair the issue of Stephen's creativity with his mourning for his mother: "All could see how hard it was for him to be reminded of his promise and of his recent loss. He would have withdrawn from the feast had not the noise of voices allayed the smart" (*U* 339). Once again Joyce places reminders of mortality in a festive context in such a way as to stress that the festivity fails to expiate the anxieties but rather attempts to ignore them. "Oxen of the Sun" continues the model in which the presence of death demonstrates the failure of the purgative encounter with mortality, not its success.

Nevertheless, "the noise of the voices allayed the smart," and the festive symposium of "Oxen" continues to swell to a climactic uttering of "the word." The word is here, comically, *Burke's*—the name of a bar, but it does lead Stephen and Bloom on to the final successful cathartic encounter with death in "Circe." It is also interesting that the conclusion of the development of prose styles is not a single modern style but rather an unbridled mingling of styles. The final pages of "Oxen" depict the modern tongue as heteroglossia, a vivid cacophony of the carnival square. Languages fuse and transform, alcohol abounds, "the white death and the ruddy birth" are celebrated, fights break out, some of the party (Mulligan and Bannon) disappear, and goodnights mingle with sounds of fire brigades and vomiting. The chapter ends with a carnivalistic blasphemy oddly placed in the mouth of an American evangelist: " 'Come on you winefizzling, ginsizzling, booseguzzling existences! . . . Shout salvation in King Jesus. You'll need to rise precious early, you sinner there, if you want to diddle the Almighty God' " (*U* 349). We are ready for the full-blown festivity of fiction in Circe:

CROFTON: This is indeed a festivity.

BLOOM: (*solemnly*) You call it a festivity. I call it a sacrament.

(*U* 399)

Hugh Kenner cleverly suggests that "Circe" is a hell for the reader who has sinned in "Oxen" by trying to read through the prose styles to a sense of what "really" transpired. Kenner points out that "nothing, in 'Circe,' distinguishes 'real' from 'hallucinatory.' "[24] Nevertheless, he effectively demonstrates that most of the grotesque actions, apparitions, and bizarre events must occur outside the characters' consciousnesses, because the characters exhibit no signs of being altered by them. The obvious exception is the apparition of Stephen's mother's ghost, which Stephen clearly sees and the others do not. The parallel apparition of Rudy to Bloom perhaps shares the same ontological status within the drama of the chapter. Otherwise, the reader experiences a vast phantasmagoria of images, appearances, and magical transformations overlaid upon the action of a brothel visit in Nighttown. One of the most fruitful approaches to the chapter has been psychoanalytic, viewing the "hallucinations" as a drama of the characters' unconscious minds enacted by the narrator for the reader.[25] It is also illuminating, however, to see how much of the hallucinated or surreal material belongs clearly to the carnival tradition, both in content and style.[26] Hayman suggests Joyce uses folk tradition as a structuring device: "In order to keep from losing all sense of form [Joyce] drew heavily on the traditional means of presenting chaos: pantomime, feast of fools, mock tribunal, saturnalia . . . etc."[27] Of course these folk traditions are all overlaid on the context of a contemporary social outing or "travelling party."

The sense of a drama "without a division into performers and spectators" pervades the chapter.[28] Through costumes, individuals metamorphose into a variety of scandalous incarnations, and all during the episode we experience the *monde invers* of carnival blasphemies and celebration of the lower body. The participants of the carnival are, essentially, the citizens of the novel; it is as if "Circe" were the carnival square for all the characters and tropes and props of *Ulysses*. This novelistic carnival presents two actors in clearly leading roles: Bloom as carnival king (both crowned and discrowned) and Stephen as artist/priest (engaged in parodying the mass). The most explicitly carnivalized of Joyce's celebrations, the evening at Bella Cohen's fittingly culminates in a dance of death and a liberating cathartic encounter with mortality.

Bakhtin describes the "life of the carnival square" as "full of ambivalent laughter, blasphemy, the profanation of everything sacred, full of debasing and obscenities, familiar contact with everyone and everything."[29] Throughout "Circe" we observe such blasphemies and obscene transformations. Myles Crawford hawks the *Freeman's Urinal* and *Weekly Arsewipe* (*U* 374). Boylan invites Bloom to "apply your eye to the keyhole and play with yourself while I just go through her a few times" (*U* 462). Bello's humiliation of Bloom concentrates on the excremental as well as the sadomasochistic. Stephen, as his drunkenness reaches a height, recites catalogs of perversions, from the mythic, "Queens lay with prize bulls," to those of the peep show barker, "Caoutchouc statue woman reversible or lifesize tompeeptom of virgins nudities very lesbic the kiss five ten times. Enter, gentlemen, to see in mirror every positions trapezes all that machine there besides also if desire act awfully bestial butcher's boy pollutes in warm veal liver or omelet on the belly *pièce de Shakespeare"* (*U* 464, 465).

Laughter runs throughout the chapter, specified over thirty times in stage directions or onomatopoeic renderings: the ambivalent laughter of Virag's "diabolic rictus" (*U* 424); Bello's "guffaws" and "loud phlegmy laugh" (*U* 437, 443); Ben Dollard's "abundant laughter" (*U* 426); Stephen's loud laughter at his own riddle (*U* 456); Bloom's feeble attempt to laugh with Corny Kelleher (*U* 495); and several instances of "general laughter" (*U* 376, 377, 463, 466). The mixture of vicious psychic attacks and sadism with lighthearted joking and minor blasphemies leads to a comic (though often painful) debunking of the novel's own values, from Stephen's seriousness to Bloom's charity and Molly's femininity.

The carnival sense is furthered by the stage directions that describe comically lavish costumes. Bloom's mother appears "in pantomime dame's stringed mobcap, widow Twankey's crinoline and bustle, blouse with muttonleg sleeves buttoned behind" (*U* 358); Molly appears as an eastern Queen of Sheba (*U* 359); Mulligan emerges in motorcycle garb (*U* 402); Kevin Egan passes through in a "black Spanish tasselled shirt" (*U* 483); and King Edward "levitates over heaps of slain, in the garb and with the halo of Joking Jesus, a white jujube in his phosphorescent face" (*U* 482). The stage directions of closet drama far exceed what can actually be staged, and Joyce exploits that linguistic power, particularly in the multiple comic transformations of Bloom from a dapper dancer in "a purple Napoleon hat with an amber halfmoon" to triumphant ruler in "a crimson velvet mantle trimmed with ermine" and stage Irishman "in caubeen with clay pipe stuck in the band [and] dusty brogues" (*U* 364, 392, 407).

Against this background of masquerade, carnival blasphemy, and laughter, more specific rituals are enacted. The most extended and clearest is the crowning and discrowning of the carnival king, the most fundamental of carnival rituals.[30] The carnival king is typically a representative of the ordinary folk who is singled out for temporary festive treatment. The carnival ritual endows him with a sacred character, which implies both exaltation and debasement. Just as the carnival period is temporary, so is the reign of the king; the ceremony of his discrowning parallels the end of festivities (Lent succeeding carnival, winter succeeding autumn). In Bloom's trial in "Circe" where he is charged with protean sexual indecencies, he asserts, "I am being made a scapegoat of" (U 373). John Vickery asserts that "an important part of [Bloom's] nature and role in the novel squares most nearly with an adaptation of . . . primitive sacrifice."[31] Indeed, the carnival king is a successor of earlier ritual sacrifices and follows the sacrificial pattern.

Bloom is promoted to lord mayor of Dublin and eventually "emperor-president and king-chairman" in the ceremony of Bloomusalem (U 393; 390–407). In this lengthy digression Bloom leads triumphal processions and ceremonies, renders judgment on legal controversies, and initiates utopian reforms (including "weekly carnival with masked licence" and "free money, free rent, free love, and a free lay church in a free lay state" [U 399]). Bloom also performs various entertainments including juggling and magic, dancing a Highland fling, and taking part "in a stomach race with elderly male and female cripples" (U 397). The Veiled Sybil declares herself a "Bloomite" and asserts that Bloom is "the funniest man on earth" (U 401). Finally she dubs him "My hero god" and sacrifices herself.

At this point, the height of the identification of Bloom with carnival king and thus with primitive heroic gods, the festivities turn to discrowning and the voices of the mob attack Bloom. "This is midsummer madness," Bloom protests in desperation (U 402), but it is too late: the exalted must be brought low. In classic carnival fashion, Bloom in asses' ears is pilloried, and "All the people cast soft pantomime stones at Bloom. Many bona fide travellers and ownerless dogs come near him and defile him" (U 405). The "pantomime stones" perfectly epitomize ritual sacrifice (or stoning), as do the carnival taunts of "You hig, you hog, you dirty dog!" (U 405). Certainly, it is fair to read Bloom's role of carnival king as subconscious wish fulfillment and his discrowning and subsequent humiliation with Bello as a dramatization of suppressed anxiety. But it is also salutary to view this process in carnival terms, in which folk customs of ridicule serve to "debase the hero and bring him down to earth, they make him familiar, bring him close, humanize him . . . [burn] away all that is stifled and stiff, but in no way [destroy] the heroic core of the image."[32] The extremes of "Circe" allow Joyce to develop

the psychological fullness of the carnival process of exaggerated exaltation and debasement. These extremes enrich and humanize our view of
Bloom as both comic hero and Everyman figure.

Stephen Dedalus does not function as prominently as Bloom in the narrative carnival of "Circe." But in his drunken dialogue, his piano playing
and dancing, and his final encounter with the guilt-hallucinated ghost,
Stephen plays a significant festive role. In the context of "Circe," we realize how the Joycean concept of the artist as priest of the imagination
fits into the upside-down world of carnival. As incipient artist, Stephen
has no real status in Dublin society; he is reminded of this by Mulligan, Deasy, George Russell, Lynch, and even Private Carr during the
course of the day. Thus the masquerade as mock priest, which Stephen
begins in "Oxen" and develops in "Circe," is a carnival-like imitation
of the higher order permitted in the time of festive license. Of course,
both Joyce and Stephen wish to assert the artist's claim to valid spiritual authority, not simply carnival impersonation. But Stephen's role as
mock priest in "Circe" demonstrates how great the artist's stake is in the
festive world.[33]

Mistaken as a priest by Privates Carr and Compton at the beginning of "Circe," Stephen "chants with joy the *introit* for paschal time"
(*U* 352). Paschal time (Easter to Pentecost) offers an unusually joyous
mass, and the time is associated, as Bakhtin explores in depth, with
the *risus paschalis*, during which "laughter and jokes were permitted
even in church. . . . The jokes and stories concerned especially material
bodily life, and were of a carnival type."[34] Lynch characterizes Stephen's
drunken liturgy and theological speculations as "Pornosophical philo-
theology. Metaphysics in Mecklenburgh Street!" (*U* 353). When Cardinal
Simon Stephen appears in response to Florry's assertion that Stephen
is "a spoiled priest," he wears "a rosary of corks ending . . . in a corkscrew cross" (*U* 427). Stephen continues to play the roles of professor,
priest, and artist in the spirit of carnival mockery, though he longs to lay
a serious claim to the title of artist. As we have seen, Stephen lacks maturity and experience, and his adolescence is defined by his restricting tie
to an image of a devouring mother. Just as his self-characterization in
"Oxen" as "lord and giver of life" reminded him of his mother's loss
and distanced him from the celebration, so too does his carnival play
as artist-priest culminate in a horrifying vision. This vision initiates the

series of events that leads to the debunking and humanizing of Stephen. In a short period of time Stephen goes from being lord of the dance of death and proclaimer of "Long live life!" to being laid low (crowned?) by a British private.

Zoe and Stephen initiate the dance, and in the chapter's hallucinatory medium it broadens into a dance of hours, reminding us that time is the true carnival hero. The stage directions struggle to keep pace with the whirling waltz: "All wheel whirl waltz twirl Bloombella Kittylynch Florryzoe jujuby women. Stephen with hat ashplant frogsplits in middle highkicks with skykicking mouth shut hand clasp part under thigh" (*U* 472). At the conclusion of the dance, amidst calls of "Encore," Stephen characterizes the dance as a "dance of death," and it is then that the other couples fall aside and Stephen confronts his mother's ghost.[35] Stephen begs his mother for knowledge from beyond the grave: "Tell me the word, mother, if you know now. The word known to all men" (*U* 474). But the ghost of May Goulding offers no supernatural knowledge, only familiar guilt: she challenges Stephen to pray and repent and "Beware God's hand." Stephen senses in his horror that the ghost represents his guilt and the religious and social conventions that foster it: "No! No! No! Break my spirit, all of you, if you can!" (*U* 475). He rebels against all the ghost represents; his satanic *non serviam* is framed by the carnival blasphemy "Shite!" and the cry of "Nothung!" Stephen, with his "augur's rod," shatters the light and brings the festivity to an end. In his drunken argument with the British soldiers in the street outside, Stephen provides a fitting coda to his struggle with oppressive Irish guilt and mortality: "Damn death. Long live life!" (*U* 482). In a cathartic moment, Stephen has culminated a ritual battle with death, and though he is knocked down and almost out by the privates, he remains alive. Bloom's crowning and discrowning and Stephen's ritual battle with death both amount to festive affirmations of life. The shifts of change, death, and renewal, to invoke Bakhtin's phrasing, are celebrated in a ritual context that allows a nonfatal encounter with those forces. The chapter ends with Bloom's vision of Rudy overlaid upon the prone youngster, Stephen. The vision is clearly his counterpart to Stephen's encounter with his mother's ghost. The ritual patterns in "Circe" offer us an interpretive clue: in spite of its potent horrors the chapter should be read as cleansing and affirmative.

"Circe" is a long way from "The Sisters." Yet both the similarities and differences are instructive. In Stephen's "Long live life!" we can detect an echo of the young boy of "The Sisters" feeling freed from something by the priest's death; in the apparition of Stephen's mother we can detect the oppressive clichés that dominate *Dubliners*. But where "The Sisters" hinted at the real festive encounter with death by demonstrating its absence, "Circe" expands the elements of *Ulysses* into a full-blown carnival with a *danse macabre* climax. And the presence of Bloom, a character of a complexity unanticipated in *Dubliners*, allows for the expression of a whole range of carnival elements excluded from the world of *Dubliners*. The festive visions are complementary, not antithetical: *Dubliners* faithfully sketches a world drained of meaningful ritual and celebration; "Circe" expresses (through the narrative as much as the characters) the liberating possibilities of festive excess. The role of fiction in creating an alternative world of festive and comic possibility is obviously much greater in *Ulysses*. The principles of the carnival world are vividly at play in the multiple discourses and parodies in *Ulysses*, and the festive style emerges most naturally in the chapters describing festive content, "Oxen" and "Circe."

Frothearnity and Funferal:
Festivity in *Finnegans Wake*

Joyce's final version of the recurrent scene of death and festivity is the Ur-story of Tim Finnegan, which resonates throughout the multiple levels of *Finnegans Wake*. Joyce used the title of his final work to underscore the regenerative power of celebration: just as the title of *Ulysses* called attention to the book's Homeric parallels, the title of *Finnegans Wake* highlights the traditional story of Tim Finnegan, whose wake is the subject of a popular stage ballad. The story is simple: Tim Finnegan, a hod-carrier fond of liquor, tumbles to his death from his ladder on a day he has had too much to drink. At his wake his friends gather and place beer at his head and whiskey at his feet. In the riotous party that follows, an argument rages, a bottle is thrown, and the spilled liquor revives the corpse. This tale no doubt seems as far removed from the grim wake in "The Sisters" as the style of *Finnegans Wake* from that of *Dubliners*, but both the naturalistic tale and the folk-like ballad essentially present failed and successful versions of the same cultural rite. Joyce's lifework shows a consistent development that takes us from one side of the wake vision to the other; his stylistic metamorphosis is intimately tied to the transformation of the subject matter. The revivifying festivity absent from the early *Dubliners* stories, hinted at in "The Dead" and begun in the revelry of "Oxen of the Sun" and "Circe," reaches fruition in Joyce's final work—perhaps the most clearly carnivalized work in the English language.

In "Bakhtin and *Finnegans Wake*" Denis Donoghue suggests that Bakhtin's concepts of heteroglossia and dialogism provide a helpful means of approaching *Finnegans Wake* and relating it to Joyce's earlier innovations with narrative voice. Donoghue asserts that the radical difficulty of the *Wake* comes from the mixing of discourses within a single word or phrase: "one word or phrase contains both the root and its travestied development." [36] He concludes that Bakhtin's notion of polyphony helps us understand Joyce's stylistic achievement. Certainly this is the case: *Finnegans Wake* epitomizes the narrative use of multiple discourses and heightens the potentially subversive effects of dialogism with regard to meaning and interpretation. I would like to advance Donoghue's argument a step further and propose that the style of the *Wake* is consistent with certain themes that Bakhtin would aptly designate as "carnivalistic." Donoghue notes correctly in his summary of Bakhtin that "Bakhtin is not interested in carnival and grotesquerie as mere themes." [37] But a crucial premise of Bakhtin's analysis of the novel genre is that certain thematic elements are indissolubly linked with the novel's dialogic nature: "*The source of carnivalization was carnival itself.* In addition, carnivalization had genre-shaping significance; that is, it determined not only the content but also the very generic foundations of a work." [38]

Finnegans Wake illustrates this interrelatedness in a complex way. Any paragraph that sets out to define the subjects or themes of *Wake*—to say what the book is "about"—is foolhardy. Still, I would like to suggest a related web of themes in *Finnegans Wake* that cohere in the realm of carnival: Tim Finnegan's fall and resurrection; the night world of sleep and dreams and "death's second self"; a cyclic pattern of history characterized by archetypal repetitions and regenerations; the story of an Irish tavernmaster and his family as a prototype of all family struggles. Renewal through the continuance of history ("the seim anew") implies a festive sense of regeneration, the heart of celebrations ancient and modern and certainly the heart of the wake, in which the living community survives the individual death. The magical transformations of *Wake*-language reflect these various thematic levels: as in *Ulysses* historical palimpsest creates a blurring of multiple meanings (when HCE is a contemporary Irishman, Tim Finnegan, Finn MacCool, as well as Adam, referential language is apt to show some strain); the logic of dreams allows for linguistic metempsychosis through the subconscious and the free play of the imagination; intoxication, a quality tied to Tim Finnegan and his mourners as well as to HCE and his customers, fosters (as in the last pages of "Oxen of the Sun") a narrative intoxication. Dreams, intoxication, festivity, and the vast metamorphoses of history all play with metamorphosis and change and contribute to the festive world of carnival and parties and the transformations of the novel. In reading *Finnegans Wake* as comic work of the night world, then, we should be alert to the importance of festivity—those rites of the night that seek a comic, social affirmation in the heart of circadian darkness.

The dense text of the novel contains many brief allusions to elements of the Tim Finnegan story: there are frequent plays on the title "Finnegan's Wake" and the name Finnegan as well as variations on the choric line "lots of fun at Finnegan's wake." In this allusive context the name Finnegan echoes in Joyce's play with Finn MacCool, and the first name Tim blends into the motifs of "Time, please!" and "Tip." But there are at least four fuller versions of the story that present, in one guise or another, the basic elements of the narrative: the building of a wall by a drunken masterbuilder or hod-carrier; his fall from the ladder (often associated with the thunderclap); the party at the wake with its liberal eating and drinking; and the revival or waking of the corpse signalled by a version of "Thanan o'dhoul, do ye think I'm dead?"[39]

The importance of the "Tim Finnegan" theme is accentuated by its appearance at the very beginning, in the book's overture (*FW* 3–7), and then again in the opening chapter (*FW* 23–28). Two other full versions occur, both associated with descriptions of HCE and his protean crime. The first is in Question One of the twelve questions apparently posed by Shem to Shaun in book 1, chapter 4 (*FW* 126–139), and the second is in response to the command "Recount" in the "Yawn" chapter, (3.3). Appropriately the ballad themes also reappear in Section 4 where they prepare for the cryptic "Finn, again!" in the penultimate sentence of the book.

These fuller versions make it clear that Tim Finnegan is a prominent metamorphosis of the changeable HCE. Tim Finnegan unites, para-
nomastically and thematically, Humphrey Chimpden Earwicker, Dublin
tavern host, and Finn MacCool, great Irish mythic hero. Shem's question (*FW* 126–39) unites characteristics of Finnegan and HCE and derives
from Shaun the answer, "Finn MacCool." To the reader familiar with
Bloom-Odysseus, Tim Finnegan is a logical choice for a Joycean hero. On
page 4 we learn that "Bygmester Finnegan, of the Stuttering Hand . . .
lived in the broadest way immarginable." This tells us not only of Tim
Finnegan's free style of living, but also that he is a marginal character
of broad significance, a masterbuilder with a shaky hand. Tim Finnegan and HCE are comic heroes like Bloom, though they are blurred in
the broader dream farce of *Finnegans Wake;* they face life with broad and
imaginative schemes but repeatedly fail—falling down again and beginning anew on the never-finished wall. "Tim Finnegan" contains "time,"
"fin" (the end), and "again" (the new beginning). Like all humankind he
is a sinner, not quite repentant, whose sins engender life. In the realm
of HCE's "hydrocomic establishment," Finnegan will "sin again . . . to
make grim grandma grunt and grin again" (*FW* 580).

The wall and the fall become emblematic of the two aspects of human
existence, work and play. The wall is construction and thus civilization.
Made possible by the first fall and the original sin, its greatest manifestation is the Tower of Babel, which in turn is a model of *Finnegans Wake*
itself—a massive project the hubristic ambition of which creates a fertile but confusing babble of tongues. The wall and the tower are forever
uncompleted, not only because they seek a perfection beyond human
grasp, but because humankind continues to fall off the ladder. Work is
but one aspect of human existence balanced by that driven repetition of
the fortunate fall, the desire to play: "to rise in undress maisonry upstanded (joygrantit!), a waalworth of a skyerscape of most eyeful hoyth
entowerly, erigenating from next to nothing and celescalating the himals
and all, hierarchitectitiptitoploftical, with a burining bush abob off its
baubletop and with larrons o'toolers clittering up and tombles a'buckets
clottering down" (*FW* 4–5). Here we actually hear the ladder tipping
at the height of the architectonics, as the maisonry upstanded becomes
upended and the builder finds "escape" contained in the skyscraper.

Drink is the agent of Finnegan's fall, but it is not until the wake that the
party really begins. Jubilation and merriment are the stuff of parties and,

Joyce tells us, of wakes as well. With the corpse at the center, his friends celebrate life: it's a "prepronominal *funferal*" (*FW* 120), a "grand funferall" (*FW* 111) with "Jests, jokes, jigs and jorums for the Wake lent [by] the late cemented Mr. T. M. Finnegan R.I.C." (*FW* 221). All in all, there's "lovesoftfun at Finnegan's Wake" (*FW* 607). Laughter and intoxication are the constants at the wild party of Finnegan's wake: "Hohohoho, Mister Finn, you're going to be Mister Finnagain! Comeday morm and, O, you're vine! Sendday's eve and, ah, you're vinegar! Hahahaha, Mister Funn, you're going to fined again!" (*FW* 5). Laughter and drink (the vine) make the mourning a comedy in which the corpse is made whole (Finnagain), but made whole to return to the "funnaminal world" (*FW* 244) in which aging (vine to vinegar) and future falls (fined again) await.

Drinking, then, causes the fall, fuels the celebration at the wake, and serves as resurrecting agent for the awakening; it is a ubiquitous presence in the world of *Finnegans Wake.* John Bishop asserts that "one would be hard pressed to find a page in *Finnegans Wake* that did not name a variety of kinds and brands of alcohol."[40] Unlike at the party in "The Dead," the view of intoxication in *Finnegans Wake* is, I think, primarily affirmative; it is a world which does not exclude Freddy Malins. Joyce asserts the communal power of drink—"Drouth is stronger than faction" (*FW* 336)—and its life-giving power—"Ireland sober is Ireland stiff" (*FW* 214). The party endorses "lebriety, frothearnity and quality" (*FW* 133), and there is indeed "Hops of Fun at Miliken's Make" (*FW* 176). Intoxication, along with the dream state, provides a sort of objective correlative for the transformations of language in the *Wake.*

The "frothearnity" comes also from the primitive sense of communion that drinking can establish. Group intoxication is a kind of communal journey, the drink piloting a united swing in mood. Thus, Joyce's Everyman hero is here a tavernmaster, HCE, "host of a bottlefilled" and "lord of the barrels" (*FW* 310, 311). The quaffing of drink is pictured as a heroic "mouth burial": "Slake your thirdst thoughts awake with it . . . We rescue thee, O Baass, from the damp earth and honour thee. O Connibell, with mouth burial! So was done, neat and trig. Up draught and whet them" (*FW* 311; Bass and O'Connell's are popular ales). The spirit here is of Falstaff, tavern king. Prospero's promise in *The Tempest* that "Every third thought shall be my grave" is also echoed with the suggestion that the heroic mouth burial can overcome morbidity. But at the wake the communal significance of drink is also eucharistic, religious: "Stay us wherefore in our search for tighteousness, O Sustainer" (*FW* 5). The communion involves not only drinking *to* the dead but drinking *of* the dead. The custom of bringing food and drink to a wake is given a special turn in Joyce's version of "Finnegan's Wake" in which the corpse, laid out between barrels of beer and whiskey, is depicted as centerpiece of an elaborate feast:

> Grampupus is fallen down but grinny sprids the boord. Whase on the joint of a desh? Finfoefum the Fush. Whase be his baken head? A loaf of Singpantry's Kennedy bread. And whase hitched to the hop in his tayle? A glass of Danu U'Dunnell's foamous olde Dobbelin ayle. But, lo, as you would quaffoff his fraudstuff and sink teeth through that pyth of a flowerwhite bodey behold of him as behemoth for he is noewhemoe. Finiche! Only a fadograph of a yestern scene. Almost rubicund Salmosalar, ancient fromout the ages of the Agapemonides, he is smolten in our mist, woebecanned and packt away. So that meal's dead off for summan, schlook, schlice, and goodridhirring. (*FW* 7)

Here Finnegan becomes the mystical salmon that Finn MacCool eats to attain wisdom, but the loaf of bread is his head as well, and the ale seems to flow from the corpse. "Agapemonides" suggests agape and the "love-feast" or "love-supper" in the early Christian tradition of honoring the Last Supper through shared meals.

We need to explore the meaning of a love feast commemorating Tim Finnegan rather than Christ. Clearly it is a secular communion in the same sense that Finnegan's resurrection will be a "secular phoenish" (*FW* 4), combining a secular phoenix with a spectacular finish. Appreciating the communion without divine transubstantiation takes us to the heart of Joyce's vision of the sacred character of secular rites. Spawning the night-revelry of the wake, Finnegan does, in one sense, die so that others may live. Religion provides a way of coping, of living, with our mortality—Christ dies so that we shall not die. In Joyce's world, outside Christianity, the same human religious function exists: we celebrate the things of this world—food, drink, community—in the presence of death so that we may ritually triumph over it and thus live with it. A wake epitomizes this revelry in the face of death, the sweetness of life heightened by the cold reminder of its transience. At the wake the communion of the living with one another is a partaking of the corpse—the host, in both senses of the word.

The party at Finnegan's wake surges forward, a communion propelled by bread and ale. It clearly lacks the chaos-fearing restraints of the party in "The Dead" as seen in the chaos that ensues as well as in the linguistic metamorphoses. When the whiskey bottle smashes, the precious fluid revives the corpse. In the first rendering of the story this climactic moment is signalled by *"Usqueadbaugham!"* (FW 24), which includes the Gaelic word for whiskey *usquebaugh*. Like the climactic moment in *Ulysses* when Stephen screams "Nothung!" and smashes the chandelier, the height of chaos—"shattered glass and toppling masonry"—promises a new life from the wreckage of the old. "Usqueadbaugham" mingles life and death: *usquebaugh* means "water of life" etymologically, while the *ad* and *am* suggest *usque ad mortem*, "even unto death." Later versions of the wake in *Finnegans Wake* follow this pattern with the exclamations "Whiskway and mortem" (FW 510), and *"Uisgye ad Inferos!... Usque ad Ebbraios!"* (FW 497) suggesting *usque ad inferos* ("even unto the dead") and *usque ad ebrios* ("even unto the drunk").

Thirsty not dead, Tim Finnegan revives. His exclamation, "Thanam o'n dhoul, do ye think I'm dead?" is given overtones of drink in Joyce's versions: "Anam muck an dhoul! Did ye drink me doornail" (FW 24) and "saouls to the dhaoul, do ye. Finnk. Fime. Fudd?" (FW 499). On a symbolic level this whiskey-induced resurrection represents the regenerative power of parties and the life-celebrating force of the wake, an occasion not simply for mourning the soul passed but for looking to the future of those present—life unto death. The inebriation is the wild spirit of excess, the bacchic aspect of humanity given reign in the world of comedy and festivity. Joyce's inclusive novel embraces the Dionysian spirit of indulgence and intoxication and reflects that spirit with a language under the influence, a Dionysian style.

The "spirit" world at the wake has a double meaning: the spirit's life hereafter and the distilled spirits here. "We purposely say nothing of the stiff, both parties having an interest in the spirits" (FW 82). But all stiffs are not corpses, as "The Dead" demonstrates. The all-inclusive *Wake* contains the antithesis of the Dionysian spirits of "Finnegan's Wake." Shaun, one polar extreme of the twin descendants of Earwicker-Everyman, often

represents authority and holier-than-thou censure and thus raises a puritanical voice against parties. He is frequently pictured as the nay-sayer,
harsh and falsely knowing, as epitomized in his pompous lecture to
Issy (3.2), in which he resembles Polonius, weaving a philosophy derived from aphorisms and received opinion into a sycophantic paean to
the powers that be. At these times Shaun represents the world of order
and rules that blinds itself to the positive power of humanity's excesses
and passions. Not surprisingly, his first commandment is "Thou shalt
not smile" (*FW* 433). His objections to parties are harsh and numerous.
He views them as weakening rather than purgative: "Especially beware
please of being at a party to any demoralizing home life. That saps a
chap" (*FW* 433–34). Parties are seen not as communal but common, and
as bad habits bound to lead to worse ones: "Don't on any account acquire a paunchon for that alltoocommon fagbutt habit of frequenting and
chumming together with the braces of couples in Mr. Tunnelly's hallways (smash it) wriggling with lowcusses and cockchafers and vamps
and rodants, with the end to commit acts of interstipital indecency as
between twineties and tapegarters, fingerpats on fondlepets, under the
couvrefeu act. It's the thin end; wedge your steps!" (*FW* 435–36). Finally,
Shaun expresses the familiar fear of excess, pictured here in terms of
loss of respect, hangovers, and dangers of driving home: "When parties
get tight for each other they lose all respect together. By the stench of
her fizzle and the glib of her gab know the drunken draggletail Dublin drab. You'll pay for each bally sorraday night every billing sumday
morning. . . . And beware how you dare of wet cocktails in Kildare or the
same may see your wedding driving home from your wake" (*FW* 436).

The wake, as a model for all parties, brings out the real source of
Shaun's objections. His lengthy sermon to his sister, Issy, includes in-
structions for proper behavior at his wake: "So now, I'll ask of you, let ye
create no scenes in my poor primmafore's wake" (*FW* 453). We begin to
see what Shaun fears, when he cites specifics from Tim Finnegan's wake:
"I don't want yous to be billowfighting your biddy moriarty duels, gobble
gabble, over me till you spit stout" (*FW* 453; Biddy incites the argument
that leads to the liquor being spilled ["spits stout"]). Shaun doesn't want
a Finnegan-like resurrection because, convinced of his blessedness, he is
happily off to the next world: "Lo, improving ages wait ye! In the orchard
of the bones. . . . we shall all be hooked and happy, communionisti-

cally, among the fieldnights eliceam, *élite* of the elect, in the land of lost of time. Johannisburg's a revelation! Deck the diamants that never die!" (*FW* 453). Like all moralists who preach against the stuff of life in view of heavenly reward, Shaun here sees the true communion and happiness in the heavenly feast. His puritanical disapproval of the festival spirit is part of a greater view of eternal self-indulgence. His view is the religious extreme that rejects all of this world in the act of positing another; it is the same spirit that sought to stamp out the pagan festivals incorporated into early Christianity.

Shaun's "revelation" has its counterpart in the description of Tim Finnegan "with a bockalips of finisky fore his feet. And a barrowload of guenesis hoer his head" (*FW* 6). Joyce envisions other worlds but refuses to see them as antithetical to our own: "The tasks above are as the flasks below" (*FW* 263). In the liquor-bedecked corpse of Finnegan is our beginning and our end—genesis and Guinness ("guenesis"), the *fin* of "finsky," and the apocalypse of "bockalips."[41] For the triumph of life celebration is not ignorance of death or apocalypse but a courageous toast in the face of it.

Joyce explicitly asserts the universality of the Tim Finnegan story. The sense in which Tim Finnegan's rise, fall, wake, and resurrection are archetypal illuminates the ritual significance of the party. "Life . . . is a wake," writes Joyce (*FW* 55), and he posits the experience of Finnegan's wake as part of a collective unconsciousness: "If there is a future in every past that is present *Quis est qui non novit quinnigan* and *Qui quae quot at Quinnigan's Quake!*" (*FW* 496–97). The premise is that all living beings—carrying the accumulated products of centuries of civilization, what we now call "culture" and what Joyce here calls "every past that is present"—have a future, and that future is the common fate of the grave. If this is the case, and surely it is, then Finnegan's questions are appropriate: "Who is there who does not know Quinnigan" and "Who, which, how many [are] at Finnegan's Wake?" The answers are, respectively, no one and everyone. His producers are his consumers: this is both the paradox of culture, which we create while we are created by it, and of the communion in which we consume the body that, dying, gives us life.

Joyce's abstractions, however, always take bodily form, just as the revivification of the spirit that parties represent is rendered palpable in the waking of Tim Finnegan. One hundred pages from the abstract *Qui, quae, quot* we again meet Finn incarnate: "Behold, he returns; renascenent; fincarnate" (*FW* 596). The following passage rewards particularly close examination because it reinforces the Joycean connection between sleep and death and also a parallel connection between dreams and parties:

> You mean to see we have been hadding a sound night's sleep? You
> may so. It is just, it is just about to, it is just about to rolywholy-
> over . . . The untireties of livesliving being the one substance of a
> streamsbecoming. Totalled in toldteld and teldtold in tittletell tattle.
> Why? Because, graced be Gad and all giddy gadgets, in whose words
> were the beginnings, there are two signs to turn to, the yest and the
> ist, the wright side and the wronged side, feeling aslip and wauking
> up, so an, so farth. Why? . . . Why? Every talk has his stay, vidnis
> Shavarsanjivana, and all-a-dreams perhapsing under lucksloop at least
> are through. Why? It is a sot of a swigswag, systomy, dystomy, which
> everabody you ever anywhere at all doze. Why? Such me. (*FW* 597)

Indeed we have been had, the proper exclamation when we realize a story is but a dream, as we do in the *Alice* books, *Finnegans Wake*, and in our nightly dream activity: for all the while we have been sound asleep. About to "rolywholyover" we are not only about to roll over in bed, wake up, and start over but also about to wake from our glimpse of the holy wholeness of "livesliving" experience—an entire unity, "untireties"—which is of one substance existing in the substrata or collective unconscious of the subtrance. The *Wake* starts at night and ends in the morning, just as sleep and most parties do. This reversal of the traditional "night follows the day" forms a pattern of regeneration suggested in the "two signs . . . the yest and the ist": the west (sunset) and the east (sunrise); and in the "yes" (Molly's final word of acceptance) and the "is" (the continual being represented in Issy's life flowing from Anna Livia's at the re-cycle of the book's end: "Is is" [*FW* 620]). Joyce's phrase "So an, so farth" presents the passing of generations as an ongoing process through its blending of "so on and so forth" with Anna the mother, and HCE, the father. "Feeling aslip and wauking up" parallels the sleep cycle

with Finnegan's slip and his subsequent wake (with overtones of the regenerative powers of the auk's egg from Bloom's descent into sleep, see
U 607).

The repeated "Why?" of this passage asks "Why do we all die—tot/
all?" It asks why we wake one day to find that all of life has passed like
a dream. And the answers, yoking opposites, are found in the everyday
process of sleeping and waking. Bishop's *Joyce's Book of the Dark* is the
best discussion of this crucial parallel of sleep and death. Bishop sees
the *Wake* as realistic documentation of what fiction has turned away from
representing: the world of sleep and the process of dying. He shows how
Joyce is true to what little physiological and psychological knowledge we
have of sleep and death.

The parallel of sleep and death, which "The Dead" introduces, is suggestive in that dreams and parties, both subjects of *Finnegans Wake*, are
symbolic triumphs against the night. In a dream the individual in som-
nolent rehearsal of death asserts his continued existence. This dream
activity involves the operation of a sort of collective unconscious, the culturally accumulated imagery of dreams. At parties communities gather
and stay awake through the night in a ritual triumph over death. Toward
this tend the ceremonies of eating, drinking, carousing, and greeting
the dawn. As in dreams, the individual surrenders some autonomy to a
collective experience. The symbolic imagery of dreams and the ritual triumph of parties are combined in the dream of Tim Finnegan's wake; the
corpse is literally given new life, revived by the power of the community
revelling. The dream discourse of the *Wake* thrives within the context of
the carnivalized novel: the transformations of the unconscious, the accre-
tion of associations onto words and images, require a nonauthoritarian
narrative multivoicing.

"Every talk has his stay . . . and all-a-dreams perhapsing under lucks-
loop at least are through" (*FW* 597). Dreams, parties, novels, and life
must end. The pattern of sleep and waking suggests a resurrection, as
does the potentially cyclic ending of *Finnegans Wake*. But such regeneration has to be seen, finally, in communal terms, in terms that see
continued life not in the individual but in the sense of contributing to a
process, a dying so that others may live. In the final section of *Finnegans
Wake*, which culminates with the death of Anna Livia Plurabelle, we see

the role of the Tim Finnegan story and the ritual of his wake in asserting this vision of our end.

The phrase "lovesoftfun at Finnegan's Wake" (FW 607) connects the celebratory fun of the wake and the love that animates a party (and its potential sexual unions as well) with Anna Livia's final monologue, which begins "Soft morning, city!" and plaintively echoes the word "soft" until the final kiss of "Bussofthlee, mememormee" (FW 628). We get a preview of the final monologue and life's final moment in the grand rehearsal of the wake: "We'll have a brand rehearsal. Fing! One must simply laugh. Fing him aging! Good licks! Well, this ought to weke him to make up. . . . Don't forget! The grand fooneral will now shortly occur. Remember" (FW 617). "Fing!" (in German) commands "begin," the again in Finnegan. To begin is to enter into the world in which we age. To celebrate life is to travel toward death, toward the grand funeral. Parties, whether they be wakes or not, are rehearsals for the final wake (as Gabriel realizes when he sees all the elements of his aunt's wake at the party). The ritual is both a triumph over death and a preparation or rehearsal for it. At the party, as at the funeral in "Hades," we sense our own end and live the harder for it. The farcical play of the Wake leads to Joyce's comic credo: in the face of a potentially tragic vision we "must simply laugh." Through our own vitality we remember the vitality of those now dead who have given us life. Anna Livia's dying plea "mememormee!" is a serious memento mori: she pleads, as did Hamlet's ghost, "Remember me!" and in that memory sees also "more me." Having lived and given of herself, to husband, children, and others, Anna Livia can see her ending as somehow plural and reach out to the participants of Finnegan's wake: "End here. Us then. Finn, again!"

This brief discussion touches on only a few of the festive levels of Finnegans Wake, but the suggestions of the Tim Finnegan story resonate through the work and its central concern with regeneration and multiplicity in a context of farce, parody, and laughter. A fuller study of the festive elements of Finnegans Wake would include examinations of the trial of Festy King, the riddle of the Prankquean, ballad-maker Hosty as host and artist figure, The Mime of Mick, Nick and the Maggies, closing time at HCE's pub, the performance of Butt and Taff, and the rites of dawn in book 4. Here, I just wish to suggest that Joyce's treatment of the story of Tim Finnegan is the last and most affirmative in a series of death festivities in his fiction. Similarly, the many languages of *Finnegans Wake* represent the culmination of a consistent pattern of carnivalization. To ignore the festive elements in Joyce's fiction is to deprive it of much of its emotional force and to miss the structural significance of Joycean celebration: "that pride that bogs the party begs the glory of a wake while the scheme is like your rumba round me garden" (*FW* 309).

2. The True Self

PARTIES IN WOOLF

"My present reflection," Woolf noted in 1925, "is that people have any number of states of consciousness and I should like to investigate the party consciousness" (*DVW* 3:12). This now famous quotation is a good starting point for appreciating the thematic and stylistic importance of parties to Woolf's fiction. The diary entry is related, of course, to the genesis of *Mrs. Dalloway* (1925), but the importance of party consciousness extends through Woolf's subsequent writing. In *Mrs. Dalloway* we first encounter the thematic centrality of the party scene: Clarissa's party is the culminating event and the locus for the revelation of the eponymous hero's consciousness. In *To the Lighthouse* (1927) Mrs. Ramsay's dinner party becomes a unifying center to which the dispersing characters hearken back. In *The Years* (1937) characters of many generations gather at a concluding party that draws together the novel's dominant motifs. Even *The Waves* (1931), Woolf's novel furthest removed from the milieu of society, concludes with a social gathering that, like Clarissa Dalloway's party, takes on aspects of a ritual sacrifice.[1] Finally, in *Between the Acts* (1941) a rural pageant and a society gathering are intertwined to produce Woolf's most clearly carnivalized novel.

Woolf's investigation of the party consciousness in 1925 led to her most dramatically experimental novel up to that date, *Mrs. Dalloway*—a major shift towards formal innovation. The convergence is no accident. In exploring the party consciousness, Woolf discovered the novel's polyphonic capacity, its ability to subvert its own unitary narrative authority through the use of multiple voices and discourses. Woolf's desire to present the individual as the interaction of many selves evolves into a questioning and reshaping of the narrative self. A vision of both self and narrative voice as multiple becomes the basis of Woolf's stylistic experimentation, an experimentation that begins most clearly in *Mrs. Dalloway* and culminates in her provocative and clearly multivoiced last novel, *Between the Acts*.

Mrs. Dalloway and *Between the Acts* are two closely related novels of festive vision, novels in which the thematic center and genre-shaping force is a contemporary celebration. A high society party including the prime minister differs greatly from a village pageant hosted by the gentry; and the stream of consciousness of *Mrs. Dalloway* is a long way from the highly allusive, often-interrupted prose of *Between the Acts*. But together they reveal Woolf's particular festive vision: a belief in the redemptive potential of the secular festive communion and in the work of art as crucible for that problematic communion.

Mrs. Dalloway: "For there she was"

"It is to express character," Virginia Woolf asserts, "that the form of the novels, so clumsy, verbose, and undramatic, so rich, elastic, and alive, has been evolved" (CE 1:324). Though Forster objected that Woolf's formal experiments were incompatible with the successful creation of character, this was clearly the end toward which they were directed.[2] Woolf's preoccupation with the inadequacy of traditional fiction's methods of creating character is clear in all her novels and particularly evident in the celebrated essays "Modern Fiction" and "Mr. Bennett and Mrs. Brown." The inadequacy of earlier methods, she felt, came from a static and materialistic definition of the self. Thus, the justification for formal experiments was not aesthetic but realistic: the novel must bend to accommodate a more dynamic sense of self as product of memory, desire, self-awareness, and the unconscious, as well as of society. This concern with dynamic presentation of character informs Woolf's frequent use of party scenes in her fiction: what better way to show the interaction of self and other? The same issues that attend defining the autonomous self complicate the issue of narrative authority, and Woolf's "party consciousness" develops into a strategy for subverting or limiting narrative authority and liberating the festive multiplicity of discourses.

Mrs. Dalloway more than any other of her works focuses on the revelation of the true self: set as a problem in various ways throughout the book, it is epitomized in the simplicity and inevitability of the concluding sentence: "For there she was." Early in the book Clarissa rejects easy summations of character or self: "She would not say of herself, I am this, I am that" (*MD* 15). But moments after this liberating vision of the complexity of her existence, she feels the acute sense of definition that comes from knowing how much of one's life is past and how much of one's future is determined: "There being no more marrying, no more having of children now, but only this astonishing and rather solemn progress with the rest of them, up Bond Street, this being Mrs. Dalloway; not even Clarissa any more; this being Mrs. Richard Dalloway" (*MD* 14). Clarissa alternates between expansive and narrow visions of herself; the problem is not susceptible to an easy answer: who, or what, is Clarissa Dalloway?

When Peter Walsh considers theories of the self Clarissa had once voiced to him, he perceives, with the author, the tremendous difficulty of knowing a person: "It was unsatisfactory, [Clarissa and Peter] agreed, how little one knew people" (*MD* 231). Clarissa's proposal for a solution suggests Woolf's technical objective: "to know her, or any one, one must seek out the people who completed them; even the places" (*MD* 231). So *Mrs. Dalloway* becomes an intensely social novel, though it is named for one character and features Woolf's most sustained use of stream of consciousness, an inner-directed narrative technique. The same novel that treats the nature of the self and its relation to others is also the novel in which a party scene, important throughout Woolf's fiction, most clearly forms the dramatic center. The connection between party and self remains crucial, for in Woolf one's authentic being can only be discovered in a social context; authenticity emerges only when the accumulated experiences of solitude are engaged by the vibrant life of the community. As Mabel Waring muses in "A New Dress," the finest story of Woolf's sequence surrounding *Mrs. Dalloway:* "For a party makes things either much more real, or much less real, she thought. . . . She saw the truth. *This* was true, this drawing-room, this self, the other false" (*MDP* 58).

If we follow the movement of *Mrs. Dalloway* attuned to the question

of what is the true self, we will see how important Clarissa's party becomes in framing an answer. We can see precisely what Clarissa only
knows intuitively—that her party is a kind of religious "offering." We
also see how the festive occasion becomes a stylistic model for Woolf's
novelistic "offering." The complication of the idea of "self" necessitates
a complication of narrative voice, and the multiple voicing of the party
scene becomes a crucial means for Woolf's escape from the limits of the
individual perspective.

We can also understand the social emphasis in *Mrs. Dalloway*, with
its central party and its various characters' walks through the London
metropolis, as a manifestation of Woolf's refusal to find ultimate authenticity in solitude.[3] Reflections in solitude do have an extremely important
place in Woolf's writings and are significant in *Mrs. Dalloway*, but they
need to be approached with an awareness of the romantic vision of solitude Woolf radically rejects. To feel returned to oneself from the artifice
of social life in moments of solitude is a common experience. Social
intercourse repeatedly makes us aware of how we adopt poses to create certain effects, and awareness of role-playing suggests that a truer
self chooses to play the roles.[4] But Woolf resists the temptation to reject social selves as inauthentic. Rather she uses stream of consciousness
and what she calls her "tunnelling process" to show that the private self
coexists with the public appearances. In *Mrs. Dalloway* Clarissa's private
self with its recurrent questions and familiar memories is as present at
her lively party as during her repose in the attic room. Woolf's narrative
style strives to make interior experience coextensive with everyday life.

Possessed by a sense of the difficulty of living and of the act of will
required in order to live, Woolf is aware of the seductive dangers of solitude. Throughout Woolf's novels are scenes in which the protagonist
must willfully extricate himself or herself from the trancelike symbolic
surrender to death in moments of solitude. The moment of visionary
intensity that solitude can offer requires that the hero waken from that
vision and carry it back into the bustling world of life. The most extended
dramatization of this experience is Bernard's final soliloquy in *The Waves*,
his refusal to "sit on and on, silent, alone," his walking out into the street
to confront the enemy, Death, at the break of day that ambiguously bodes
"some sort of renewal" (*W* 296). We will see a similar moment in *Mrs.
Dalloway* as Clarissa gathers the strength to return to her party. And in

Between the Acts, this narrative pattern is repeated in the several scenes of interrupted silences, the most dramatic of which is the triumphant rainshower during the pageant.[5]

In *Mrs. Dalloway* Clarissa demonstrates another way in which the quest for the true self must lead from solitude to society. The confrontation with the prospect of death is the primary authenticating experience of the reflecting self in solitude. But while the imagination of the solitary experience of death creates a bedrock of selfhood within the consciousness, the same imaginative experience suggests the dissolution of the self. Examining the precise moment when Clarissa contemplates her own end, we see the redefinition of the autonomous self (which death ends absolutely) as the social self, which shares an essence with its environment:

> Did it matter that she must inevitably cease completely; all this must go on without her; did she resent it; or did it not become consoling to believe that death ended absolutely? but that somehow in the streets of London, on the ebb and flow of things, here, there, she survived, Peter survived, lived in each other, she being part, she was positive, of the trees at home; of the house there, ugly, rambling all to bits and pieces as it was; part of people she had never met; being laid out like a mist between the people she knew best, who lifted her on their branches as she had seen the trees lift the mist, but it spread ever so far, her life, herself. (*MD* 12)

Thus the portrait of Clarissa Dalloway—the parallel quests of reader, author, and character to define the true self—must include both "the streets of London" occupied by "people she had never met" and the friends of whom she is a part, "the people she knew best." The narrator follows this path, moving freely into the minds of people who know Mrs. Dalloway, following them and Clarissa through the London streets, and culminating in Clarissa's party where Clarissa becomes both the "pointed; dartlike; definite" figure at the head of the stairs and the permeating spirit of the party, laid out like a mist among the guests.

There are several ways of presenting the individual's relation to society in the novel. In the bildungsroman, for example, society can be shown through a series of encounters between the hero and different segments of society. Thus, Julian Sorel of *The Red and the Black* encounters the village bourgeoisie, the church, the military, and the urban bourgeoisie. We see the same representative series of life encounters in Joyce's *Portrait* and in Samuel Butler's *The Way of All Flesh;* their generalizing power is quite apparent. But the focused world of a single day, as in *Mrs. Dalloway,* invites two particularly appropriate and complementary techniques: the walk through the city and the party—the hero travelling through the community and the bringing of the community into the hero's home.

The street scenes that occupy the first two-thirds of *Mrs. Dalloway* have multiple functions. They allow for the introduction of various characters before their appearance at the party; for the development of psychological background through the "tunnelling process" of presenting characters' memories; for the anticipation of the party through the characters' expectations; and for the examination of the problem of creating a community of separate selves. Only the last point depends necessarily on the public setting; the others demand only some showcase of significant characters before the party begins. In sketching so much of the character depth through the scenes of London perambulation, Woolf creates a sense of social environment and develops the narrative technique (which will be essential at the party) of juxtaposing interior monologue with external action and description.

This characteristic Woolfian narrative technique is discussed by most of the better studies of Woolf's narration. The technique is a product, first, of the narrator's omniscience, which controls the rendering of the character's unvoiced thoughts. J. Hillis Miller points out that in "any given page of *Mrs. Dalloway* [the reader is most often] plunged within an individual mind which is being understood from within by an ubiquitous, all-knowing mind."[6] James Naremore stresses the narrator's distinctive voice that modulates, controls, and unifies the different perceptions of various characters.[7] In addition, this omniscience and unity of voice allow Woolf to bring the thoughts of the individual character into the same plane as speech, action, and description of setting. The following sentence is typical: "She had a perpetual sense, as she watched the taxi cabs, of being out, out, far out to sea and alone" (*MD* 11). It is while she is watching the cabs that Clarissa reflects on a recurrent, indeed perpetual, feeling of loneliness.[8] The narrative simultaneity of private thought and public vision is the technical counterpart for Woolf's intuition that the deepest aspects of the self are still engaged and alive in social situations.

The street scenes in *Mrs. Dalloway* display Woolf's sensitivity to how much of the private life—one's self-evaluations and thoughts of family, friends, love, death, and religion—takes place in random, frequently interrupted moments in the midst of everyday routine. Clarissa muses about life and death, her illness, and her family while shopping for flowers; Peter Walsh fantasizes about a romantic encounter or recalls his past while strolling through London. This technique highlights the fragmentary, unsystematic character of the individual philosophy but also demonstrates the depth of ordinary experience: one need not be a philosopher to participate in the great human questions.[9] Above all, Woolf's narrative fusion refuses to separate the private self from the social context; the social self exists simultaneously with the private self, and thus a true self can exclude neither aspect of consciousness. The narrative movement blurs the distinct boundaries of character and environment by subsuming the revelation of both into a unifying but multivalent voice.

Woolf's essay on the pleasures of exploring the London byways, "Street Haunting—A London Adventure," describes departing from one's house as the shedding of a narrow self formed in solitude. Though she notes an anonymity to urban existence, her language here reveals the social experience to be liberating: "The shell-like covering which our souls have excreted to house themselves, to make for themselves a shape distinct from others, is broken" (*CE* 4:156). The pleasure and liberation come from an engagement with others that the experiences of solitude, essential and valuable as they are, cannot provide. The particular revelation that the city holds is of the variety of human existence, and this variety challenges any illusions about a simple unitary essence that the solitary soul may have fabricated: "Is the true self this which stands on the pavement in January, or that which bends over the balcony in June? Am I here, or am I there? Or is the true self neither this nor that, neither here nor there, but something so varied and wandering that it is only when we give the rein to its wishes and let it take its way unimpeded that we are indeed ourselves?" (*CE* 4:161). These questions are raised by the vibrancy of the city and what Woolf deems, in this dialogic essay, "the insecurity of life." This same questioning of identity takes place in the minds of Clarissa and Peter as they move through sun-warmed London.

Woolf's "Street Haunting" essay is presented, like most of the London perambulations in *Mrs. Dalloway*, from the point of view of the wanderer. But the narrator in *Mrs. Dalloway* deliberately breaks that focus in two important scenes—the royal car and the skywriting airplane (*MD* 19–29; 29–42). These two consecutive scenes occur quite early in the book and allow the narrator to suggest the presence of a great many people: it is through these scenes, primarily, that Woolf communicates the sense of a bustling metropolis. They also serve a political purpose, introducing the themes of state and empire on the one hand, and commercial enterprise on the other—both linked by the memories of the recent war that add poignancy to the symbols of state and fear to the sound of an airplane. But these two scenes are linked more profoundly in that they are both scenes of interpretation. The skywriting is most blatantly a paradigm for our interpretation of signs, involving, as it does, vague letters promising a message and interpreted by one fellow as "a symbol for the human soul." The royal car is equally a problem in interpretation, for a "square of dove grey" in the window is developed variously into the image of the Queen, the Prince of Wales, and the Prime Minister.

These dramatic scenes of a community of interpreters themselves invite two different interpretations. Readers respond to these episodes as emblematic of either the unity of society or the disparateness of the supposed interpretive community. Miller suggests the former: "Such transitions [the mysterious royal motorcar and the skywriting airplane] seem to suggest that the solid existing things of the external world unify the minds of separate persons because, though each person is trapped in his own mind and has his own private responses to external objects, nevertheless these disparate minds are unified by the fact that you and I, he and she, can all have responses, however different they may be, to the same event, for example, an airplane skywriting. To this extent at least we all dwell in one world."[10] Jeremy Hawthorn, by contrast, acknowledges that these scenes are taken to represent "moments when the group in a Virginia Woolf novel becomes like a single person," but he goes on to argue that "surely at this point we are reminded more of the atomism of the crowd—each member of it solipsistically interpreting the message in different ways."[11]

Woolf carefully balances these two perspectives, which animate the interpretive scenes. Certain key sentences unmistakably focus on a unity of some kind: "Every one looked at the motor car" (*MD* 21); "For thirty seconds all the heads were inclined the same way" (*MD* 25); "Every one looked up" (*MD* 29); "As they looked the whole world became perfectly silent" (*MD* 30). These sentences locate the unity in the act of interpretation, as Miller suggests, rather than in the substance of the interpretation. But Woolf balances these congruities of group experience with the idiosyncrasies and uncertainties of interpretation. When she states that "there was nothing to be seen except a square of dove grey" (*MD* 19), she immediately follows with an evocation of the power of rumor and mystery, the qualifying nature of which is signalled by the initial "yet." This effusion is immediately countered with the qualification: "But nobody knew whose face had been seen. Was it the Prince of Wales's, the Queen's, the Prime Minister's? Whose face was it? Nobody knew" (*MD* 20). She describes the paucity of details that have generated the excitement: "The face itself had been seen only once by three people for a few seconds. Even the sex was now in dispute" (*MD* 23). Then Woolf immediately counters with a qualifier: "But there could be no doubt that greatness was seated within" (*MD* 23).

The narrative counterpoint between communal unity and diversity of interpretation is even more dramatic in the skywriting episode. Here the pattern is reversed: unified action is established first and diversity introduced by the word "but": "But what letters?" (*MD* 29); "But what word was it writing?" (*MD* 31). Most pointedly, the varying interpretations appear as the characters voice the words they read:

> "Glaxo," said Mrs. Coates. . . .
> "Kreemo," murmured Mrs. Bletchley. . . .
> "It's toffee," mumbled Mr. Bowley. (*MD* 29, 30)

The skywriting letters, like an author's nightmare vision of her own work's insubstantiality, are by nature fleeting: "Only for a moment did they lie still; then they moved and melted and were rubbed out up in the sky" (*MD* 29). These scenes disperse the narrative voice and authority into a multiplicity of voices making up the community. Woolf's treatment of the party continues this essentially dialogic approach to truth established early in the novel.

Diversity—what Hawthorn labels atomism—is a necessary condition of life seen up close. Only death, or the utter absorption of madness into the self, allows one to stand so far from the stuff of life as to see no contradictions, no disparateness, no detail. Woolf celebrates the world of detail, the inescapable diversity of life. Yet the separateness of the individuals in a society, which, finally, these scenes do reveal, remains problematic. The stopping of the motorcar may be a momentary "gradual drawing together of everything to one centre" (*MD* 21), but this momentary illusion gives way to the varied interpretations, the dangers of the communal worship of royalty (which Woolf aptly mocks), and the powerful feeling of "the impossibility of reaching the centre" (*MD* 280–81). To be true to life is to recognize the final separateness of individuals—the relativity of their perceptions, the loneliness of their lives, and the limitations of human contact. These street scenes celebrate life, but they also hint at a pervasive loneliness.

Acknowledging the separateness at the heart of life, Clarissa proposes her parties as a solution: "What did it mean to her, this thing she called life? Oh, it was very queer. Here was So-and-so in South Kensington; some one up in Bayswater; and somebody else, say, in Mayfair. And she felt quite continuously a sense of their existence; and she felt what a waste; and she felt what a pity; and she felt if only they could be brought together; so she did it. And it was an offering; to combine, to create, but to whom?" (*MD* 184–85). To Clarissa, at least, her parties are an attempt to bridge the separateness of selves, to create a community. She explicitly thinks forward to her party at the moment in which the magical and unifying power of the royal car's presence is most intense: "She had seen something white, magical, circular, in the footman's hand, a disc inscribed with a name,—the Queen's, the Prince of Wales's, the Prime Minister's?—which, by force of its own lustre, burnt its way through. . . . And Clarissa, too, gave a party. She stiffened a little; so she would stand at the top of her stairs" (*MD* 24–25). This passage echoes the almost primitive fire-bearing imagery associated with Clarissa's party. The party, she thinks, will be magical and unifying. Like the moment in which royalty appeared, it will hold together a group of separate selves.

The party itself strives to fulfill these ambitions sketched so powerfully in the novel's early scenes. The party also provides a narrative means for Woolf to escape the tyranny of the single voice and of the authoritarian concept of the unitary self. Woolf presents the details of the party almost entirely through the multiple experiences of host and guests. Woolf uses no set description of the house, the party preparations, or the guests. The descriptive elements remain tied to characters' thoughts and perceptions. As Miller points out: "In *Mrs. Dalloway* nothing exists for the narrator which does not first exist in the mind of one of the characters."[12]

Nevertheless, we learn certain particulars of Clarissa's elegant party. We know that the preparations are elaborate: Clarissa buys flowers, mends her dress, and adjusts the crystal dolphin to her liking, but her leisurely efforts cap a concerted effort by her staff, which includes her maid, Lucy; a cook, Mrs. Walker; her assistant; and three additional servants "hired for parties" (see *MD* 42, 56–57, 253–54).

The party begins with a small dinner downstairs and follows with a much larger party upstairs (*MD* 253–54). The formality of the affair is indicated by the traditional separation of the sexes after dinner: the women adjourn and the men sip Imperial Tokay. Then, as the first party guests not invited to dinner arrive, the men finish their liqueur and join the women upstairs. The new guests also perform a ritual gender separation before being introduced: the women go to a separate cloakroom while the men wait in the hall. Then at the top of the stairs, the reunited couples and other guests are formally announced by Mr. Wilkins, one of the servants specially engaged for parties (and, it seems, specially groomed for ostentatious formality).

As these formal trappings suggest, attendance is by written invitation. But Clarissa does invite Peter and, reluctantly, Ellie Henderson at the last minute. Sally Seton, now Lady Rosseter, attends without an invitation and thereby pleasantly surprises Clarissa. Not only more formal than the party in "The Dead," this affair is much larger. The rapidity with which guests arrive emphasizes this, as does Clarissa's observation later that rooms of her house were far too crowded to allow dancing (*MD* 259, 271).

Peter Walsh characterizes those attending as "infinite numbers of dull people," but admits that at Clarissa's parties, "odd unexpected people turned up; an artist sometimes, sometimes a writer" (*MD* 116). The dull people, we learn indirectly, are primarily politicians or other figures connected with the government. These range from obsequious figures like Hugh Whitbread (who is savagely lampooned through Peter Walsh's point of view) to Richard Dalloway's friends from Parliament, to a large number of lords and the Prime Minister himself. The social status of the guests is very high, as Sir Harry's joke about "these circles" being above him, and his thoughts about Clarissa's "damnable, difficult upper-class refinement," indicate (*MD* 267). Present, though clearly in the minority, are university people (*MD* 263, 267), and young people (*MD* 269).

Conversation is the communal focal point, yet the most striking characteristic of Woolf's narrative is the paucity of directly rendered dialogue. James Naremore comments on this technique: "Except for occasional snatches of speech, all we get are summaries of conversation. Usually the interplay between characters is twice removed from direct presentation: every scene is refracted through the minds of the characters, and their thoughts in turn are refracted through Mrs. Woolf's elegant voice. The result is a curious qualitative unity."[13] This technique, while it unifies the voice of the fiction, allows for a very complex presentation of the interaction between speech and internal emotions. It allows Woolf to satirize the superficiality and inanity of the conversations and yet spare the characters, or at least preserve them for a different, more qualified, judgment. The conversations that the narrator intermittently reveals are almost all superficial and uninteresting (Sally and Peter's discussion of Clarissa is a possible exception); they are social rituals, valuable for the communication they may symbolize rather than the information they communicate.

Woolf's technique allows us to see that Ellie Henderson's comments on the weather represent a shyness and an unwillingness to risk herself in human interaction, an unwillingness Clarissa sees as selfish, and Richard as pitiably sad. Sir and Lady Bradshaw's small talk, on the other hand, reveals a callousness to human suffering and a worship of authority that Clarissa (as well as Richard and, it seems, the narrator) finds reprehensible. At the same time, Clarissa's hostess greetings, which seem to Peter "effusive and insincere," are defended by the narrator through Clarissa's thoughts on the importance of her party. The refrain, "How delightful to see you," is given different meanings in different contexts: early in the evening it reflects Clarissa's anxiety about her party's failure, but later it demonstrates her excitement with the party's apparent success.

Woolf derives three technical advantages from her preference for indirect discourse: she presents individuals as deeper and more complex than their conversations alone might suggest; she unveils the different personalities concealed beneath the party chatter; and she presents the conversations and personalities of individuals from different points of view. Contrast this with Hemingway's extensive use of direct dialogue in *The Sun Also Rises* or Anthony Powell's direct discourse in his party-centered novel, *Afternoon Men*. In both novels the authors' objectives are to reveal the shallowness of the characters and their limitations from the narrator's consistent and unflinching point of view.

Still, Woolf avails herself of some of the satirical potential of a high society party. In her diary, she wrote about the work which was to become
Mrs. Dalloway: "I want to criticise the social system, and to show it at
work, at its most intense" (*DVW* 2:248). Many readers have felt that this
particular objective was either abandoned (because social criticism seems
more prominent in the earlier "Mrs. Dalloway in Bond Street") or unsuccessful because the author grew too enamored of her hero to criticize her
social aspirations effectively. These readers are inevitably disappointed
because Clarissa comes off too well to be the vehicle of an extended
social critique. Certainly the most pointed and witty social criticism of
the book is directed at other characters. A good portion of the party scene
is devoted to mocking the presumption and stateliness of Clarissa's most
prominent guests: the pompous Hugh Whitbread, Sir Harry (the painter
of "cattle standing absorbing moisture in sunset pools"), Millicent Bruton
(raising a Union Jack in heaven) and Aunt Helena Parry (the "indomi-
table Englishwoman"). To Clarissa's credit, she is a partner in much of
this perceptive critique of pomposity.

Wit, humor, and a social criticism that is restrained yet pointed characterize Woolf's depiction of the upper-class party guests in *Mrs. Dalloway*,
but Woolf is admittedly far more interested in showing the social system
at work than in leveling a critique. And work it does, in a positive, liberating sense. For finally, the pompous figures' aimless talk of the weather,
bare-shouldered girls catching cold, or Darwin's interest in Asian orchids
is unimportant if some kind of magical communion can take place at the
party, momentarily triumphing over the agonizing separateness of selves
and the feebleness of so much social intercourse. Such a communion,
if it does occur, does not take place in the realm of conversation or of
realistic description of physical phenomena. That is why there is com-
paratively little descriptive or conversational detail in Woolf's rendering
of the party.

The party spirit has the power to overcome the separateness of selves
and in so doing suspend the traditional boundaries of self, place, and
time that form the realistic set of coordinates which, during most of the
novel, orient memories and reveries. Throughout *Mrs. Dalloway* the characters' minds travel freely while the movements of their bodies in space
and time are carefully mapped and chronicled by the author. Following
the temporal specificity of Big Ben and the spatial guidelines of London
place names, Avrom Fleishman has divided *Mrs. Dalloway* into twenty-

one sections labeled by situation and time. In addition, he has mapped
the characters' routes through London. The chart he provides, however,
reveals a striking gap in the chronological specificity of the novel.[14] There
is no reference to time between Peter's preparations for the party (not
long after six P.M.) and the tolling of Big Ben at three A.M. near the
end of the party and the book. Time disappears in the excitement of the
party, and Woolf's narrative style, here freed from moving her characters through the streets and their daily appointments, is perfectly suited
for suspending narrative chronology. Neither providing external description nor staying within a single character's consciousness long enough to
portray the dwindling of the evening, Woolf presents a variety of social
interactions and portraits that, while not devoid of all temporality, are
freed from the ominous tolling of Big Ben, which has symbolized time's
remorseless reduction of the future. All the references to aging as a narrowing of horizons tied to the leaden circles of Big Ben (first a warning,
then the sound—irrevocable) momentarily give way.

The liberating moment is clearly marked: it is when Ralph Lyons
pushes back the curtain to continue talking. Before this moment Clarissa
had suffered a typical host's anxiety—she worried that her party would
fail. Her sense of success and failure is quite clear: a failed party maintains the separateness of individuals—"people wandering aimlessly,
standing in a bunch at a corner" (*MD* 255). Clarissa's sense of the party's
failure at this moment is exacerbated by Peter Walsh's presence and the
particularly masculine criticism of her parties he represents. In response
to Peter's implicit criticism of her party, Clarissa defends her sincerity
(to herself) by arguing for the seriousness of the enterprise to which
her effusiveness is dedicated. In terms she recognizes as hyperbolic, she
imagines herself "drenched in fire," burned to cinders by the intensity
of her refusal to drift silently apart from others. More calmly, she affirms
that "she did think it mattered, her party, and it made her feel quite sick
to know it was all going wrong, all falling flat" (*MD* 255). These terms will
be important later when, learning of Septimus's death, Clarissa searches
her heart for what truly matters in life. Here this meditation focuses her
anxious hope that from the separate individuals milling about her lighted
rooms, some worthwhile whole will be created.

Clarissa recognizes that synergetic creation in the moment that Ralph
Lyon beats back the curtain to continue talking: "And Clarissa saw—she

saw Ralph Lyon beat it back, and go on talking. So it wasn't a failure after all! it was going to be all right now—her party. It had begun. It had started" (*MD* 258–59). On the most literal level she senses the party is successful because Ralph's engagement in conversation makes him oblivious to his environment: the talk must be important if the outside interference cannot distract him. But his gesture is richly symbolic. Its inadvertence represents a loss of self-consciousness; Ralph acts without thinking, breaking the hold of deliberate action upon the stiff, lifeless party (consider the contrasting deliberateness of Richard's attempt to engage Ellie in conversation). Further, the gesture represents the inside triumphing over the outside. The human community in the indoor, artificially lighted world attains precedence over the elements outside. Again the window acts as a border between worlds, and the party's beginning is an unconsciously rebellious "beating back" of the wind and the alien forces of death and darkness. The unconsciousness here is important too, for that quality demonstrates the absorption of the individual into the party. The surrounding details and the physical environment are no longer important; people and community are. Significantly, Ellie Henderson is the one who so carefully notes details ("It was quite a treat just to see the lovely clothes," [*MD* 257]) because she does not participate in the party; she is not absorbed in it. One senses that when she tells Edith all about the party, it will be the kind of detailed naturalistic description that Woolf so carefully avoids. Ellie Henderson appreciates the trappings of the party but is blind to its spirit, and this materialism emerges in the contrast between her implied narrative mode and Woolf's.

At the moment Clarissa detects that the party has truly begun, she feels a loss of identity. Standing at the top of the stairs "was too much like being—just anybody, standing there" (*MD* 259). The creation of a communal spirit involves a certain loss of identity. Clarissa's position, rooted to the top of the stairs, suggests the artist refining herself out of existence, or at least stepping back from her creation. As Lucio Ruotolo points out in his discussion of this scene: "The good hostess, like the good writer, while technically in charge, remains unseen. . . . Having created the festivity, her task is now to allow the party to develop a life of its own."[15] In this new state, at once relieved of her anxiety and distanced from her deliberate, individual, torch-brandishing participation, she thinks that "oddly enough she had quite forgotten what she looked like" (*MD* 259). This is clearly the antithesis of her feeling moments before that Peter "made her see herself" (*MD* 255). The loss of identity brings with it a loss of self-consciousness that is, in part, a move toward a more authentic being: "Every time she gave a party she had this feeling of being something not herself, and that every one was unreal in one way; much more real in another" (*MD* 259).[16] Following this reverie Clarissa considers the qualities that make a party extraordinary— the breaking of routine, the fancy dress, the feeling that new things are possible in speech. She realizes we can perhaps become more real by shedding our everyday pose and seeing what we can create of ourselves in a new role.

The key to the paradox of the party bringing out both the real self and the self's public mask is the simultaneous existence of the two selves, or judgments of the self. Woolf's complexities of style and thought are directed against a simplistic unitary concept of being. She can accept neither the view that the authentic self is the self in solitude nor the view that the public self shaped in social interaction is the sole true self. The excitement and communal involvement of the party—what Clarissa identifies as losing herself in the process of living (*MD* 282)—is a triumph over the self-doubt that alienates one person from others, and over the seductive spell of solitude that promises one will "fear no more the heat of the sun" (*MD* 283). For this triumph does Clarissa "kindle and illuminate," for this moment when the irrevocable passage of time is negated. But this triumph is also incomplete.

The timeless spell of the party is broken when Lady Bradshaw relates Septimus's suicide to Clarissa. "Oh! thought Clarissa, in the middle of my party, here's death, she thought" (*MD* 279). Lady Bradshaw's recounting of the incident is viewed by Clarissa as an intrusion, a violation of the sanctity of her party. It is the introduction of precisely what the party spirit triumphantly, if temporarily, excluded—death.

Clarissa withdraws into a nearby room and acutely feels the carefully wrought celebrative edifice of her party crumbling: "The party's splendour fell to the floor, so strange it was to come in alone in her finery" (*MD* 279–80). We should recognize this as a classic gesture of party scenes, established in literature, made more familiar by theater and film: the individual stepping apart from the whirl and gaiety of the party, usually to a window, a balcony, or an outdoor garden, some border from which he or she can look out into the darkness with the distanced noise of the celebration as background. This withdrawal stands for a poignant solitude, for one is perhaps never as alone as when one stands apart but close to a celebrating crowd. Gabriel Conroy tapping the window pane, Clarissa Dalloway approaching the window through the empty room: both participate in what has become a symbolic gesture of loneliness and reflection.

This scene is the most powerful in the book. Surely intended as the climax, it draws together all the novel's thematic strands. Woolf clearly intended that the party scene should "knit together everything," and the most difficult strand to include was obviously Septimus, whose character, though doubling Clarissa's, is unknown to her (*DVW* 2:312). As well as bringing Septimus's "insane truths" into the sane compass of Clarissa's reflective consciousness, this withdrawal scene brings death into the party. By death, I mean here the way in which the awareness of mortality shapes our perceptions as we live. The sense of time that the novel has linked to Big Ben is mortality's most obvious manifestation: not merely duration, or sequentiality of events, the tolling of Big Ben symbolizes the encroachment of age, the distancing of the past, and the sense of dissolution into air, which, as we have seen, Clarissa identifies with death. Clarissa's parties are magical because they allow the participants to lose themselves in a communal fete and transcend the limitations that awareness of mortality and separateness impose. But this party becomes, for Clarissa, extraordinary ("But what an extraordinary night!" she thinks at the close of this scene [*MD* 283]) because she is able to combine the liberating loss of self of the party with the essential revelations of solitude. Returning to the party she carries the solitude experience into the community so that she can truly feel that, uniting the two realms of experience, "[Septimus] made her feel the beauty; made her feel the fun" (*MD* 284).

To understand the dynamics of this scene and how Clarissa combines the self in society with the self in solitude, we must see how Woolf synthesizes the antithetical elements of the novel within this scene. Symbolic values infuse with meaning the presences that fill the scene—Septimus Warren Smith, the old woman who lives next door, and Clarissa. The concept of the literary double is frequently invoked to characterize the relationship of Septimus and Clarissa.[17] As the major writers on "the double" point out, though, the concept includes a wide variety of psychological and literary constructs.[18] A few of these constructs are particularly relevant to *Mrs. Dalloway* and to the literature of parties as a whole. Since party scenes so often raise questions about the interrelationship of public and private selves, the vision of the double as one facet of the divided self recurs significantly. With this version of the double is associated a particularly apt and characteristically literary pair of symbols: the mirror and the window. These symbols are so prevalent in literature that they have a life and tradition of their own; yet in Woolf, as in Joyce, their use is powerful and fresh. Woolf's symbolic use of the window in the scene of Clarissa's withdrawal is worth comparing with the earlier depiction of Clarissa in front of the mirror.

Mirrors are a potent, recurrent literary symbol, not only because of the appeal of the Narcissus myth (given renewed vitality by Freud) but because the mirror is such a pregnant symbol for the literary enterprise itself, and as such an appropriate vehicle for self-reference. The root image of art as a mirror held up to nature is complicated by the paradigm of art as the image of the author, product of both self-reflection and self-presentation—terms that already suggest the multivalence of mirror imagery especially applicable to party scenes. For in looking into a mirror we reflect upon ourselves as individuals (people only truly known to ourselves), and at the same time witness how that self appears to others. Mirror-gazing is generally a private experience, an occasion for self-examination. But in looking into a mirror one also travels imaginatively outside oneself, visualizing how one appears to others. This is frequently a rehearsal gesture, a preparation (even, perhaps, a literal "making up") for engagement with others. Like the party itself, the mirror dramatically juxtaposes private experience and public image. Two-dimensional and reversed, mirror images unavoidably symbolize the divided self.

Thus mirrors have a realistic place as a party accoutrement, a symbolic link with the themes parties in literature evoke, and a special affinity with the literary enterprise as a whole. But the very applicability of the mirror image endangers it: it may easily become hackneyed. Aware of this, Virginia Woolf introduces her own explicit mirror scene parenthetically and then expands it, through Clarissa's own consciousness of her social roles, into a meditation on the complexity of self-definition:

> As if to catch the falling drop [of life's passage], Clarissa (crossing to
> the dressing-table) plunged into the very heart of the moment, trans-
> fixed it, there—the moment of this June morning on which was the
> pressure of all the other mornings, seeing the glass, the dressing-table,
> and all the bottles afresh, collecting the whole of her at one point (as
> she looked into the glass), seeing the delicate pink face of the woman
> who was that very night to give a party; of Clarissa Dalloway; of
> herself.
>
> How many million times she had seen her face, and always with the
> same imperceptible contraction! She pursed her lips when she looked
> in the glass. It was to give her face point. That was her self—pointed;
> dartlike; definite. That was her self when some effort, some call on her
> to be her self, drew the parts together, she alone knew how different,
> how incompatible and composed so for the world only into one centre,
> one diamond, one woman who sat in her drawing-room and made a
> meeting-point, a radiancy no doubt in some dull lives, a refuge for the
> lonely to come to, perhaps; she had helped young people, who were
> grateful to her; had tried to be the same always, never showing a sign
> of all the other sides of her. (*MD* 54–55)

Twice Woolf has Clarissa call her mirror image her "self." But then she
qualifies it: the image is her self drawn together into one center by
conscious effort. This self-composition locates the self in the engagement with other people. The reader should also recognize the familiar Woolfian act of will required to venture from solitude to community. Here community is both limiting and life-giving: limiting in that it
leaves behind the complexities and depths of the character that somehow others can never know, and life-giving in that it demonstrates the
character's generosity in existing for others, engaging in life. The scene
moves from multiplicity (of inner selves) to the diamondlike unity of the
mirror image and to multiplicity again (this time of self as perceived by
different people). Woolf's technique presents the simultaneous existence
of public and private to give existential depth to the glittering moment.

Clarissa's drawing herself together into a socially presentable whole
in this scene has its obvious counterpart in her return to the party in
the book's climactic scene. In both, she pulls herself together to meet

the gaze of others. The latter scene, however, reverses the pattern of the mirror scene by focusing on "people feeling the impossibility of reaching the centre which, mystically, evaded them" (*MD* 280–81), rather than on the drawing together of the self into such a center. To stress the thematic shift, Woolf has Clarissa looking through a window rather than a mirror. In fact, what Clarissa sees through the window is shockingly like a mirror image; but it is a mirror image of a different self.

Septimus Warren Smith functions as a double in that he seems to embody repressed aspects within Clarissa. As doubles Clarissa and Septimus are twin heroes: Clarissa representing the comic hero successfully integrated into society, and Septimus the tragic hero exiled by the very nature of his being.[19] In the integrative process of the climactic scene in which Clarissa imaginatively experiences Septimus's suicide, he becomes the *pharmakos* or sacrificial victim.[20] Quite explicitly, his death contributes to her heightened sense of vitality.

Septimus and Clarissa never meet; thus the thematic parallels that link them operate on a narrative level wholly outside the characters' awareness.[21] Despite the sympathies the story of Smith's suicide engenders in Clarissa, their visions and experiences are, finally, separate. The link between "sane and insane truth" is complex: these truths are neither identical nor exactly parallel. The actual "contact" between them is limited to the scene of Mrs. Dalloway's withdrawal, and Clarissa learns little more about him than the literal circumstances of his suicide and that he is a victim of delayed shell shock. But on the basis of her limited knowledge, Clarissa is deeply moved: Septimus's apparent agony at what Clarissa feels is the inexorable separateness of beings and the impossibility of communicating authentically with others is juxtaposed with the levity and light magic of her party. Lady Bradshaw's story disrupts Clarissa's engagement with the party precisely because it shows a more tragic, more rash way of dealing with the very problem toward which Clarissa directs her parties. Within herself Clarissa recognizes the depths of despair that lead one to suicide, and she wonders if her parties, conceived as an offering to life, are meaningless by comparison. This is the question she wrestles with in the empty sitting room.

There she experiences Septimus's fatal fall in a paragraph framed by her outrage at the Bradshaws' talking of death at her party. The structure strangely mimics the actual suicide, which is framed by Holmes's intrusion into Smith's home and his sedation of Rezia. The Bradshaws similarly force the account of the suicide into Clarissa's home, and she feels the violent "forcing of the soul" Sir Bradshaw represents as in the name of deified "Proportion and Conversion." The radical lack of proportion in the flinging away of one's life moves her. To Mrs. Dalloway, Septimus's suicide is an act of courage and defiance because it refuses the consolations of life, it insists on facing squarely the final tragedy of existence—that we each perish alone. Our mortality and our inevitable separateness from each other are the truths that we cannot bear to face constantly; these truths we must forget momentarily in our intoxication with life. Powerful poetic diction renders the heart of this revelation: "A thing there was that mattered; a thing, wreathed about with chatter, defaced, obscured in her own life, let drop every day in corruption, lies, chatter. This he had preserved. Death was defiance. Death was an attempt to communicate; people feeling the impossibility of reaching the centre which, mystically, evaded them; closeness drew apart; rapture faded, one was alone. There was an embrace in death" (*MD* 280–81). "Wreathed about with chatter" is the key phrase here, for it describes the centrality of the tragic realization within the vibrant circle of society. The chatter can obscure the thing that matters or it can include it. Here Clarissa focuses on how it obscures: the social world is blind to a basic truth of existence. Death is the authenticating experience; only it can free one from the insincerity of life.

The embrace of death is a freedom from the constant pain and frustration that are the conditions of existence. "Embrace of death" echoes the novel's refrain from *Cymbeline*, "Fear no more the heat o' the sun / Nor the furious winter's rages," which invites one to leave the world's tempests for eternal calm. The embrace of death frees one, Clarissa thinks, from the "awful fear" at the "depths of [the] heart": that one is incapable of living "this life, to be lived to the end, to be walked with serenely" (*MD* 281). This thought indicates how the balance has begun to shift in Clarissa's perceptions. She began by contrasting the courage of suicide with the truth-denying weakness of maintaining everyday calm. Now, life is seen as an immensely difficult task, one that requires skill and continual effort. Defined as such, choosing to live becomes both courageous and imbued with the suffering of others. Dramatically, Woolf presents the image of death at the party: "It was her punishment to see sink and disappear here a man, there a woman, in this profound darkness, and she forced to stand here in her evening dress" (*MD* 282). Sharing in the suffering of others, including now Septimus, Clarissa realizes the depth of her achievement, the everyday human triumph of living. Thus she can say in the next paragraph that "she had never been so happy" (*MD* 282). The quality of this happiness is carefully defined as the interpenetration of two distinct experiences—the unself-conscious engagement in life, and the extraordinary self awareness of moments such as these: "No pleasure could equal, she thought, straightening the chairs, pushing in one book on the shelf, this having done with the triumphs of youth, lost herself in the process of living, to find it, with a shock of delight, as the sun rose, as the day sank" (*MD* 282). To emphasize again, the joy is not simply in losing herself in the process of living, but in the combination of that feeling with the shocks that put the process of living in perspective. Thus, Clarissa begins here to acknowledge that death belongs at her party, that as an offering to life, the party cannot wholly exclude the darkness against which it is constructed. An offering requires a sacrifice, some gesture to the greater powers. Clarissa walks to the window to look at the sky; she reverses the gesture against the "outer" that Ralph Lyon's beating back of the curtain represented. She wants to look out into that wilderness upon which she has constructed her offering.

"She parted the curtains; she looked. Oh, but how surprising!—in the room opposite the old lady stared straight at her!" (*MD* 283). Here the window functions as a mirror, and Clarissa sees herself as she will eventually be—an old woman going to bed. Mrs. Dalloway's withdrawal from the party balances two separate and equally significant visions.[22] The profound resonance she feels in response to Septimus's suicide has its complement in the image of the old woman. For the old woman is equally Clarissa's double.

The old woman is commonly taken to symbolize the separateness of selves and the "privacy of the soul"—the very conditions that Clarissa's party seeks to overcome.[23] But that reading relies primarily on the earlier scene in which Clarissa watched the old woman and concluded "here was one room; there another" (see *MD* 191–93). Though there is still a contrast between the quiet and darkness of the neighbor's house and the light and noise of the Dalloways' party, this later scene differs significantly in emphasis. In spite of the apparent regularity of the neighbor woman's movements (which the earlier scene stresses), the later scene is extraordinary because, to Clarissa's obvious surprise, "the old lady stared straight at her." Unlike the earlier scene in which the woman was "quite unconscious that she was being watched," the woman now mirrors Clarissa's posture and causes Clarissa to wonder if she "could see her."

To see the old woman solely as a symbol of lonely isolation is to miss the powerful bond between her and Clarissa. The "supreme mystery" (*MD* 193) is not only that a room so near can contain a life unknown to Clarissa and completely different from hers, but also that the old woman's life is somehow fundamentally the same in the daily courage of living and in the accomplishment of routine as life diminishes. To muse "here was one room; there another" notes not only separateness but similarity: a woman in a room, a woman at a window. The old woman personifies approaching age and growing loneliness, which have both been associated with Clarissa through her response to the tolling of Big Ben and her vision of narrowing beds. Here the woman is going to bed and is explicitly connected to Big Ben ("Gigantic as it was, it had something to do with her" [*MD* 192]). The old woman represents the alternative to suicide. She represents the courage to continue living in the heat of the sun and the furious winter's rages. This is the courageous alternative Clarissa accepts at the moment the clock begins to toll and she realizes that she does not pity Septimus and that she must return to the party:

> The clock began striking. The young man had killed himself; but she did not pity him; with the clock striking the hour, one, two, three, she did not pity him, with all this going on; There! the old lady had put out her light! the whole house was dark now with all this going on, she repeated, and the words came to her, Fear no more the heat of the sun. She must go back to them. But what an extraordinary night! She felt somehow very like him—the young man who had killed himself. She felt glad that he had done it; thrown it away. The clock was striking. The leaden circles dissolved in the air. He made her feel the beauty; made her feel the fun. But she must go back. She must assemble. She must find Sally and Peter. And she came in from the little room. (*MD* 283–84)

At the beginning of this scene a report of death destroys the sanctity of Mrs. Dalloway's party; at the end, the death has enriched it. At the beginning her sympathy for Septimus leads her to experience his suicide and to see it as perhaps the proper alternative for her;[24] at the end, equally sympathetic, she sees Septimus's death as enriching life. Septimus's death becomes a ritual sacrifice incorporated into the heart of the party, invigorating the community he had threatened. Death becomes the center of the party.

Faced with an unavoidable link between alienation and social existence, some modern psychologists and philosophers have seen in madness an authenticity that transcends the inauthenticity endemic to society.[25] This line of thought has led some readers to see in Septimus and his suicide the final authentic alternative to a society dominated by conversion and proportion. But Woolf knew madness too well to romanticize it. Woolf knew the tragic isolation of insanity, an isolation that radically invalidated the authenticating claims made for madness. In spite of the truths one can sense in Septimus's view of the brutality of social conformity, his rejection of life is ultimately tragic. Septimus does not represent a higher truth than Clarissa's synthesis.[26]

Even if one does not celebrate Septimus's madness, it is tempting to see the embrace of death his action implies as the only final alternative the book offers to the corruption of the flesh and spirit. Miller concludes that the impossibility of reaching the center is "the ultimate lesson of *Mrs. Dalloway*," and that "in spite of [Clarissa's] love of life she will reach peace and escape from suffering, only in death." The narrator, Miller concludes, is identified with the "region of death," and the only alternative to the impermanence of the unity found in social life is "in the enduring language of literature."[27] Within Clarissa's world, he argues, Septimus's suicide represents the only possible communion. Miller ultimately deems Clarissa's party a failure and locates the affirmation of the book outside her world in the permanence of literary art. But such a reading distances us far too much from Clarissa: it suggests her emotional experiences and revelations do not culminate in an affirmation the reader can imaginatively share. Finally, I think it ignores the spirit of the book and Clarissa Dalloway's engagement with the enduring questions that transcend her local existence. *Mrs. Dalloway* is Woolf's most affirmative book, and it deliberately locates that affirmation in nonliterary experience (in contrast with the role of artist Lily Briscoe in *To the Lighthouse*, for example). And Clarissa's party is one of the most clearly successful, as we shall see, in the literature of parties. As Sasha Latham muses in the last short story of the *Mrs. Dalloway's Party* sequence, "A Summing Up": "This, she thought, is the greatest of marvels; the supreme achievement of the human race. Where there were osier beds and coracles paddling through a swamp there is this; and she thought of the dry, thick, well-built house, stored with valuables, humming with people coming close to each other, going away from each other, exchanging their views, stimulating each other. And Clarissa Dalloway had made it open in the wastes of the night" (*MDP* 67–68). Rare is the paean to a party so eloquent.

But such praise is not unqualified, and Sasha Latham's judgment of Clarissa's party is balanced by estimations less generous, which complicate the endorsement of the festive world by suggesting its limitations. Woolf, however, anticipates the reader's criticisms of Clarissa and her parties by incorporating them in characters to whom Clarissa can respond. Richard sees his wife's parties as silly excitement; Peter sees them as representing Clarissa's stiff and formal side; Sally Seton fears Clarissa is a snob. All three of these characters come together in the scene that occurs simultaneously with Clarissa's withdrawal into the empty room. There, in a remarkably moving passage, Sally, watching Richard's kindhearted generosity toward a party guest, realizes the transcendent value of community and friendship, of Clarissa and her parties:

> How generous to her friends Clarissa was! and what a rare quality one found it, and how sometimes at night or on Christmas Day, when she counted up her blessings, she put that friendship first. They were young; that was it. Clarissa was pure-hearted; that was it. Peter would think her sentimental. So she was. For she had come to feel that it was the only thing worth saying—what one felt. . . .
> "Richard has improved. You are right," said Sally. "I shall go and talk to him. I shall say goodnight. What does the brain matter," said Lady Rosseter, getting up, "compared with the heart?" (*MD* 291–92, 296)[28]

Parties are not simply good vehicles for Woolfian themes; they are models for the artistic process itself. As J. J. Wilson notes: "The party has the potential for joining outer and inner experience, the individual with humanity, the instant with the constant, all goals of Virginia Woolf's art."[29] Party-giving becomes an analogy for artistic creation, reflecting within the fictional realm the struggles and desires of the author. Party-giving creates a certain order out of chaos, structuring, by invitation, a community from disparate individuals. Like the work of art, the party is a temporary pocket of anti-entropy; within boundaries of time and space, random experience is ordered into a larger entity with coherence and shape. This is the entity Clarissa identifies when, noting approvingly that Ralph Lyons has beat back the curtain to keep on talking, she thinks that the newly arrived guests enter "into something now, not nothing" (MD 259). The sharp borders of the party (doors, windows, garden walls, etc.), which set it apart from the outside world, function like the covers of a book or the frame of a painting, designating that a distinctive world exists within, distinctive because more controlled and ordered than the vagaries of day-to-day existence.

When we say that parties are "artificial," we stress their connection with artwork; we are aware of the painted theatricality of social life. The concept then of discovering one's true self at a party is analogous to the idea of reaching truth through fiction: both the party and the artwork use artifice to get closer to life and assert, by their very existence, a belief in imagination and the social occasion. When Oscar Wilde spoke of the truth of masks and counseled young men to be as artificial as possible, he had in mind the masked ball as well as Shakespeare's stage, the social occasion as well as the work of art. The partygiver and the artist create an imaginary world that exists both within the everyday world and apart from it.

Such imaginary worlds thus have their own complexities and interactions. Once the party becomes that "something," it has a life of its own; brought into being by the host, it attains an independent existence. Lucio Ruotolo observes that "the problem of making a successful party, like the problem of making a good book, is to create conditions that will inspire mutuality."[30] We perceive a forced quality when fictional characters bear no life beyond being vehicles for authorial manipulations; so, too, can an overzealous partygiver take the life and spontaneity out of a party. Clarissa knows when to withdraw, and she prides herself on allowing people to remain themselves, even freeing them to be more themselves at her parties. So too does Woolf temper the authority of the narrator by letting the characters shape the content of the narrative voice. For transgression to occur in the context of ritual, there must be freedom as well as control, individual idiosyncrasy as well as communal pattern. Maria DiBattista acknowledges the interplay of these forces through the metaphorical connection of the party and the artwork: "[Woolf] feels, like Clarissa, that this dispersed spectacle of life can and should be collected and assembled and created into new, more human forms. . . . This power of making a world of her own is the power exercised by the narrator. . . . She is nameless, never inflicts her individuality, yet succeeds in combining and creating out of the diffuse matter of life a work of art." [31]

The organizing "power" of host and narrator suggest the problematics of narrative authority that would increasingly concern Woolf. The party inevitably reflects the projected personality of the host, and Clarissa's party risks becoming merely an offering to herself.[32] Similarly, narrative per se invites an authoritative voice that can transmute the literary text into the linguistic manifestation of the author's ego. But, as Bakhtin has chronicled, the novel genre includes a great variety of maneuvers that can undermine this monologic force of narrative through parody and multiple voicing. In *Mrs. Dalloway* Woolf tempers narrative control by rendering the consciousness of many characters. The effect, a sort of Joycean parallax, does not so much undermine narrative authority as it undermines Clarissa Dalloway's conscious authorship of her own self. The "true self" of the novel's protagonist emerges, then, only in the interaction of various consciousnesses and includes Clarissa's symbolic connectedness to Septimus and her rejection of the authoritarianism of Bradshaw and Kilman. The final "For there she was" is rendered from outside Clarissa. While the party bears the impress of its creating host, it also exhibits an independent life which, in turn, shapes the host's authorial self (most radically through the "intrusion" of Septimus). Similarly, Woolf's use of multiple perspectives surrenders a certain amount of authorial control to the richness of ambiguity. Clarissa's self extends beyond her conscious awareness to be completed by others; so too must the literary enterprise inevitably await completion in the diverse community of readers and interpreters.

The importance of the connection between festivity and artwork and between host and artist emerges more explicitly—that is, less metaphorically—in *Between the Acts*, the novel that contains Woolf's most radical undermining of narrative authority. In depicting the village pageant written and directed by Miss La Trobe, Woolf merges festivity and artwork and subjects the figure of the controlling artist to complex scrutiny. Miss La Trobe, the social outcast, and Clarissa Dalloway, the successful social matron, are poles apart, but as organizers of social functions they bear significant similarities. These similarities appear most prominently when Miss La Trobe thinks of the pageant (and her playwriting) as her "gift": "She could say to the world, You have taken my gift! Glory possessed her—for one moment. . . . It was in the giving that the triumph was" (*BTA* 209). And her creative gift, as a director as well as playwright, is seen, as is Clarissa's party-giving gift, as bringing out the gifts of others: "People are gifted—very. The question is—how to bring it out? That's where she's so clever—Miss La Trobe" (*BTA* 59). The moments in which Miss La Trobe agonizes in the background over whether her play is failing echo Clarissa Dalloway's anxieties for her party. So too we find an echo of the approving hostess at the moment in which La Trobe feels the "play had begun," taken on a life of its own. The figure of Miss La Trobe hidden in the background and disappearing at the pageant's close has narrative implications similar to Clarissa's withdrawal from the party. Both Miss La Trobe and Clarissa are most successful when they relinquish control of their creations and allow (and revel in) the interactions of chance, environment, and the various guests or actors.

But in *Between the Acts* the figure at the heart of the festivity is clearly an artist, and Woolf's criticism of narrative control becomes far more overt: Miss La Trobe's character bears marks of Doris Kilman as well as of Clarissa Dalloway and Lily Briscoe. Her struggle to maintain artistic control is dramatized to show both its futility and to show the liberating festive quality that can emerge when the artwork is liberated from that authoritarian control.

Both *Mrs. Dalloway* and *Between the Acts* reflect Woolf's concern with the individual and collective determinants of the self. But *Between the Acts* is more radically focused on the collective entity—the "we"—whereas *Mrs. Dalloway* remains oriented to the individual (though Woolf has greatly complicated that concept). An exploration of *Between the Acts* will illuminate the extent to which the party consciousness Woolf explored in *Mrs. Dalloway* continued to shape her narrative experimentation throughout her career. Woolf's party consciousness reaches beyond the thematic realm, culminating in *Between the Acts,* a carnivalistic novel in the most profound sense.

Between the Acts: "Joy, sweet joy, in company"

Like *Mrs. Dalloway, Between the Acts* unfolds on a single day, a day significant because of the festivity planned for it. But the titles of the two works illustrate crucial differences in focus and structure. *Between the Acts* is liminal or marginal by design; it follows a variety of characters, who are granted more or less equal narrative attention, through social activities that take place before, after, and between the acts of the village pageant performed at Pointz Hall. The focus on a single character that the title *Mrs. Dalloway* announces is replaced in *Between the Acts* by a multiple, communal perspective: " 'I' rejected: 'We' substituted . . . we all life, all art, all waifs & strays" (*DVW* 5:135).

Between the Acts presents two festivities: a contemporary social gathering and a nostalgic village pageant (with a historical theme). The interplay of the two sheds considerable light on festive transformations as we observe what Bakhtin would term a "bourgeois chamber feast" juxtaposed with a survival of an older, more inclusive village festivity. Though the village festivity is formal enough to separate spectators from participants, it is still more inclusive than the classbound society at Pointz Hall. The pageant is authentically communal, and yet it is enough of a "survival" to seem traditional and even quaint. The family at Pointz Hall is transformed into a party by the arrival of William Dodge and Mrs. Manresa the morning of the pageant—a point Woolf makes several times. The two guests are "uninvited, unexpected, droppers-in, lured off the high road by the very same instinct that caused the sheep and the cows to desire propinquity" (*BTA* 37). They bring their own food and drink, even glasses, asking nothing but "society apparently, to be with [their] kind" (*BTA* 38). Throughout the novel Woolf draws various parallels between these two societies—the small, upper-class gathering at the country home and the broader pageant of the villagers. In both social realms, we observe a heightened consciousness of role-playing. In the pageant and the party we see a social or artistic whole created out of a myriad of fragmentary quotations. And in both pageant and party, the polyphonic play of quotations is set off against silence and absence.

These parallels allow Woolf to explore the interaction of art and festivity, of creation and community.

In building a novel around a village festivity hosted by the country manor, Woolf can draw on not only the traditions of village pageants (and Forster's contemporary venture into the genre) but on a separate novelistic tradition representing such festivities—a tradition that includes such memorable scenes as the Ullathorne party in *Barchester Towers*, the village fete in Huxley's *Crome Yellow*, and the Criches' annual party in *Women in Love*. What made for powerful scenes in those works becomes here the framework for an entire novel.

The parallel social occasions allow Woolf to exploit the dramatic metaphor of role-playing and the self-consciousness it engenders. In the pageant the audience relishes the rich double focus created by recognizing both the villagers and the roles they play, whether Mrs. Otter of End House plays an aged crone or the village idiot plays the hindquarters of an ass. These vivid examples of role-playing attune the reader to subtler social masks worn by the Pointz Hall crowd. Mrs. Manresa casts herself as "Nature's child" and imagines Giles as her "surly hero." Dodge's unpronounceable homosexuality becomes a label or type affecting how all relate to him, inspiring Giles's disgust and Lucy Swithin's sympathy. Giles and Isa enact less obvious roles, but from Giles's donning of a cricket outfit to Isa's audible muttering of verse, their poses prepare husband and wife for their ultimate archetypal roles as sparring lovers, roles which resume after the book's final, and explicitly theatrical, lines: "Then the curtain rose. They spoke" (*BTA* 219). This vision of society as drama—that "we act different parts; but are the same" (*BTA* 192)—is familiar, even proverbial. But, though familiar, the concept of role-playing complicates the notion of authentic selfhood, as Woolf had explored in *Mrs. Dalloway*. The concept of the performing self becomes particularly rich in fiction that contains embedded or framed performances—the play-within-the-play or the-play-within-the-novel. The self-consciousness of such literary devices complicates the illusion of mimesis by underscoring the ubiquity of role-playing and by undermining the notion of a unitary, knowable self.[33] Accordingly, we see the mirror scene of *Mrs. Dalloway* transformed as Isa stands before a "three-folded mirror" looking at "three separate versions of [herself]" (*BTA* 13). This image of multiple reflections foreshadows the final scene of the pageant in which the players hold up moving glasses which catch, fragment, and animate the reflections of the audience (see *BTA* 183–85).

The presentation of character in *Between the Acts* goes beyond the patterns of the luminous halo suggested by "Modern Fiction" or the notion of the self completed by others epitomized in *Mrs. Dalloway.* Character becomes a vision of scraps, fragments, and multiple reflections. This is not to say that the visions of character—or life in general—lack any coherence or unity; indeed there is a great deal of emphasis in the novel on harmony, wholeness, and historical pattern. But whatever pattern exists is constructed out of fragmentary, incomplete pieces, and Woolf's novelistic enterprise reflects the multiplicity of voices, roles, and echoes that characterize a social group. The old-fashioned pageant with the villagers donning costumes and playing multiple roles symbolizes the complexity of social role-playing through a dramatic metaphor. Woolf implies that our contemporary social gatherings present the same sort of multiple focus taken for granted in the village pageant.

Both the pageant and the Pointz Hall party are filled with interruptions and lacunae. Woolf uses ellipses and dashes liberally to reflect sentences and thoughts left unfinished. She uses parentheses to intersperse audience comments and natural sounds into the speeches of the pageant. Actors in the play frequently forget their lines or have their words obscured by the wind. Through all these devices Woolf creates an insistent aesthetics of interruption whereby the fertile conversational dynamics of the festive setting (always open to interruption) are transmuted into the work of art as a whole.

Hillis Miller suggests that the interrupted rhythms of *Between the Acts* reflect Woolf's attempt to break the inheritances of male tradition implicit in familiar rhythms, continuity, and harmony.[34] Lucio Ruotolo in *The Interrupted Moment* argues that openness to interruption is crucial to Woolf's creativity. Like Miller he stresses that interruption and discord subvert the tempting artistic tradition of "wholesome proportion." But Ruotolo suggests further that "to be open to life in Woolf's fictional world is to remain open to an aesthetic of disjunction situated at the heart of human interplay."[35] The fragmented narrative in *Between the Acts,* manifested in short paragraphs, frequent shifts in perspective, liberal use of ellipses and dashes, and the thematic focus on entrances and exits, mirrors the qualities of effervescent social activity. Part of the justification of interrupted prose thus stems from a realistic impulse. Joyce similarly used sentence fragments in the stream-of-consciousness passages of *Ulysses* to give the illusion of the shorthand of thought; Woolf interweaves terse external description with narration of thought in *Mrs. Dalloway* to reflect how mental operations occur in the fragmented context of daily life. *Between the Acts* carries fragmentary narrative further by demonstrating how much of talk and thought, especially in a social setting, is incomplete and unfinished. The narrator resists translating the oft-interrupted flow of dialogue and thought into a more eloquent and ordered fictional form.

But the realistic basis of stream of consciousness offers only an incomplete explanation of Woolf's incessant narrative interruptions in *Between the Acts*. Indeed, interruption itself becomes, ironically, a theme in the novel, inviting the reader to connect the frequent instances of and explicit references to interruption. Interruption and fragmentation form one of the most consistent motifs of the novel. The sense of incompletion begins in the text's opening scene when Mr. Haines leaves both a sentence and a thought unfinished as Isa enters the room. The theme is deepened when Isa muses that " 'Abortive' was the word that expressed her," and complicated when Miss La Trobe grimaces at "the torture of these interruptions" and views the interval as "her downfall" (*BTA* 15, 79, 94). The frequent instances of unfinished sentences and interrupted thoughts resonate with the prominent thematic emphasis given the refrain of "scraps, orts and fragments" and with the sense of betweenness suggested by the title and the novel's expectant ending. Interruption constitutes both technique and theme in *Between the Acts* and is rooted in the intersection of style and substance implicit in the notion of carnivalized literature. The festive setting is by nature multivocal, not conducive to the prolonged utterance of a single voice. The experience of a partygoer building an afternoon or evening out of various brief and fragmentary interactions, or of the spectator at an outdoor pageant hearing the play's text mingled with the sounds of nature and the comments of an audience, is akin to the experience of the reader of Woolf's novel who is invited to filter, complete, connect, or simply enjoy a variety of voices and themes. The novelist, to be sure, has the option of filtering experience herself and presenting an artistic whole more unified than a social experience. Every artist does this to some extent, but Woolf chooses here to exaggerate interruption perhaps to counterbalance more effectively the narrator's univocal tendencies.

Party consciousness becomes, as Woolf explores it, a creative awareness that has significant narrative consequences. The heightened individual experience in the festive setting requires openness to interruption and participation in collective being, as Durkheim realized in locating the birth of the social and the sacred in the "effervescent" gathering. The problem for the fiction writer is how to keep that collective effervescence alive in the linear and ordering medium of written language. The playful and subversive development of the novel genre forms a history of such attempts to invigorate the social and plural elements in a medium as much ingrained in solitude as the book. Accordingly, Woolf's last novel reproduces, exaggerates, and exemplifies the jerkiness (to echo a word used often in *Between the Acts*) of human exchange.

Woolf's fragmentary, multivoiced narrative also devotes explicit attention to how various art forms transform and represent the incomplete truth of experience. These explorations also link the novel's two festivities. Both festivities involve quotation, misquotation, pastiche, and parody, and both grant a precedence to music and theater over literature. That the fragmentary whole of *Between the Acts* is composed of many quotations and allusions is one of its most striking characteristics. The quality is reminiscent of *The Waste Land*—though in a far different frame—and the resemblance is heightened by Woolf's explicit use of Swinburne's swallow and of the nightingale, both important allusions in Eliot's poem.[36] Woolf's musing over the meaning of fragments also echoes Eliot's concern with "these fragments I have shored against my ruin." It is of course natural that the historical pageant should be richly allusive: "There's the whole of English literature to choose from" (*BTA* 59). The pageant's sequence of historical pastiches, culminating in a chaotic representation of the present, provides a dramatic parallel to Joyce's "Oxen of the Sun" chapter in which the various styles of English prose follow one another toward a baffling confusion of dialects. But in *Between the Acts*, the Pointz Hall conversations, as well as the pageant, are woven of quotations, largely through Isa's mingling of her own improvisational verse and remembered bits of English poetry. Again, the narrative serves to expose rather than disguise how the present plays with the past. The recognition that literature lives in the minds of readers in the form of fragmentary quotations, treasured touchstones, and hazy memories is very much in the foreground of this novel and seems a part of Woolf's conscious qualifying and diminution of narrative authority. She foregrounds the artist's fearful recognition that the audience retains only bits and pieces of the artistic whole.

The awareness of the limits of narrative authority perhaps accounts for the negative view of books presented in *Between the Acts*. Woolf's novels and particularly her essays have offered a powerful testimony to the continued vitality of literature actively read, savored, and criticized. But in *Between the Acts* books are largely seen as inanimate props in a country gentleman's library. Lucy Swithin reads guiltily in the *Outline of History* but keeps drifting back to prehistoric moments. (That particular book seems to epitomize the masculine penchant for order Woolf satirized in her version of Whitaker's Table of Precedency in "A Mark on the Wall.") Against this masculine, encyclopedic outline is opposed the historical vision of the pageant at the heart of which are three dramas of romantic intrigue (Elizabethan, Restoration, and Victorian) and the personification of England as a woman.

The aphorism that "books are the mirrors of the soul" is asserted, but deflated. It was the remark of "a foolish flattering lady" touring Pointz Hall; in this case, the narrator suggests, they mirror "a tarnished, a spotted soul. . . . [a] shuffle of shilling shockers" (*BTA* 16). "Book shy" Isa views the collections of poetry, "lives," and antiquarian studies with distaste, preferring the immediacy of the newspaper.[37] Bartholomew views the same books later in the day with ambivalence: "A great harvest the mind had reaped; but for all this, compared with his son, he did not care one damn" (*BTA* 116).

Against the posited sterility of books Woolf places not only the humble parodic play but also music and, more surprisingly, conversation, which the novel associates insistently with music. The musical metaphor has always been a potent creative source for literature, from Sir John Davies' "Orchestra" to Joyce's "Sirens" and Eliot's *Four Quartets*.[38] The aspiration of other arts to the "condition of music" as Pater so eloquently phrased it is usually attributed to music's power to move the audience without the troubling mediation of a referential function. But the appeal in *Between the Acts* arises largely from music's polyphonic capabilities, its capacity to combine many voices without fragmentation and interruption, the possibility of building a harmony through artistic structuring of discrete and apparently discordant elements. "Music makes us see the hidden, join the broken," the narrator ventures and then defines the hidden as explicitly multivocal: "the many-tongued much syllabling" voices of nature. Music is described as both "intoxicating" and "expressive of some inner harmony" (*BTA* 94, 119). It seems to image not so much the desire to order or outline in hierarchical fashion but the dream of blending many voices into a whole where they complement one another rather than strive for precedence.

Music—so prominent in the novel through the pageant's gramophone, the audience's foot-tapping and humming, and the analogous oft-cited bird song—is of course traditionally associated with festivity, though it is noticeably absent from Clarissa Dalloway's party. Woolf, however, ventures a bolder analogy when she compares conversation to musical harmony, a comparison that occurs at least five times in the novel. The first instance of this remarkable comparison offers an explicit simile:

> The words were like the first peal of a chime of bells. As the first peals, you hear the second; as the second peals, you hear the third. So when Isa heard Mrs. Swithin say: "I've been nailing the placard on the Barn," she knew she would say next:
> "For the pageant."
> And he would say:
> "Today? By Jupiter! I'd forgotten!"
> "If it's fine," Mrs. Swithin continued, "they'll act on the terrace . . ."
> "And if it's wet," Bartholomew continued, "in the Barn."
> "And which will it be?" Mrs. Swithin continued. "Wet or fine?"
> (*BTA* 21–22)

Here the sense of voices complementing and completing one another is colored by the familiarity of the conversation—they say this every year. But as this metaphor recurs, it broadens to encompass a repeated pattern whereby human voices begin out of silence and accumulate to create the musical harmony of conversation.

The metaphor is developed gradually. When Isa and William overhear someone practicing scales on a piano, the music begins as individual notes, the notes become associated with letters and these form a word. When a tune begins it sparks the accompanying lyrics and then hints of a richer polyphony:

> A.B.C., A.B.C., A.B.C.—someone was practising scales. C.A.T. C.A.T. C.A.T. . . . Then the separate letters made one word "Cat." Other words followed. It was a simple tune, like a nursery rhyme—

> The King is in his counting house
> Counting out his money,
> The Queen is in her parlour
> Eating bread and honey.

> They listened. Another voice, a third voice, was saying something simple. (*BTA* 114–15)

This simple scene suggests a reenactment of the birth of language in an explicitly polyphonic context.

This pattern of gradually building voices is replicated in the scenes that show talk growing out of silence. Silence is the essential counterpoint shared by music and talk; it punctuates, precedes, and follows the sounds: "Silence made its contribution to talk" (*BTA* 49). *Between the Acts*, like all of Woolf's novels, depicts silence and solitude with compelling force. But the silence is always broken, just as the silence between Isa and Giles will, it is implied, be broken after the curtain rise of the book's final line. The empty dining room graced by two portraits (the silent medium of painting) forms the scene for what was in manuscript Woolf's most extended meditation on silence.[39] In published form the passage is much reduced but still eloquent: "Empty, empty, empty; silent, silent, silent. The room was a shell, singing of what was before time was; a vase stood in the heart of the house, alabaster, smooth, cold, holding the still, distilled essence of emptiness, silence" (*BTA* 36–37). This profound emptiness is the void of solitude upon which all life is built. Here, beyond solitude, the narrator is stripped of any attachment to character and becomes a disembodied voice singing of what was before time was. As much as Woolf experimented with effacing the self from narrative, that ultimate narrative voice remained unavoidable—from the scene following Rachel Vinrace's death in *The Voyage Out* to the "Time Passes" section of *To the Lighthouse* and the empty dining room in *Between the Acts*.

The silence of the dining room, like the pause when a conductor raises the baton before the orchestra plays, opens into the music of human interaction: "Across the hall a door opened. One voice, another voice, a third voice came wimpling and warbling: gruff—Bart's voice; quavering—Lucy's voice; middle-toned—Isa's voice. Their voices impetuously, impatiently, protestingly came across the hall. . . . Coming out from the library the voices stopped in the hall. They encountered an obstacle evidently; a rock. Utterly impossible was it, even in the heart of the country, to be alone? That was the shock. After that, the rock was raced round, embraced. If it was painful, it was essential. There must be society" (*BTA* 37).

The musical modulation from silence to society recurs frequently in the single day of *Between the Acts,* in which the festive social element is necessary to complete the self of solitude and to resist the deathlike seduction of silence. *Between the Acts* is a novel filled with lapses into silence or inactivity followed by the vital reawakening of the social impulses. The jerky rhythm of the book can be thought of as numerous shakings into wakefulness. The comments about the view or the invitation to see the greenhouse may be trite, or the conversation may be hostile or antagonistic (as Isa and Giles's promises to be), but only out of such initiations can human contact and life flourish.

The most dramatic of the novel's many silences is the ten-minute silence designed to represent the present time in Miss La Trobe's pageant. Taking to the logical extreme Colonel May's assertion that "they don't need to dress up if it's the present time" (*BTA* 175) La Trobe anticipates John Cage by presenting the now as emptiness and silence. The absence of stage entertainment foregrounds the audience—they become the play—but having been transformed from their roles as passive observers, the audience is unable to return simply to their natural selves. They are caught in a liminal state between spectacle and spectator: "They were neither one thing nor the other; neither Victorians nor themselves" (*BTA* 178).

Woolf does not go as far as La Trobe; she does not offer us a blank page. Instead she fills the dramatic void with Miss La Trobe's sense that this part of the play has failed: "This is death, death, death, she noted in the margin of her mind; when illusion fails" (*BTA* 180). Woolf moves the thought from the margin of La Trobe's mind to the center of narrative attention: the failure of illusion—of sound, conversation, fiction, the drama of human life—is death, but into this void the rain falls, like a natural tear abhorring a vacuum. The filling of the empty air with the rain—"all people's tears"—represents the social and artistic creation of life upon the void. It is followed by music: "Music began—A.B.C.— A.B.C. The tune was as simple as could be. But now that the shower had fallen, it was the other voice speaking, the voice that was no one's voice. And the voice that wept for human pain unending" (*BTA* 181). The rain, the music, and the mingled sounds of audience and actors point to a collective voice or urge to create that is communal, like the fabled Anon of Woolf's planned next work or like the unidentified voice on the gramophone as the audience leaves. The pageant becomes, like the novel, a bittersweet tribute to the social desires of humankind, and the vision of art, in the mingled measure of conversation and folk song, is festive in essence.

At the heart of the book is another scene of silence and emptiness filled by festivity. Woolf presents the teatime interval in the Barn by opening the scene before any people enter. Like the dining room the Barn presents a profound emptiness graced, at first, by only the bodiless (or characterless) narrative voice. The Barn has sacred and historical associations and it receives a potent peroration: "The Barn, the Noble Barn, the barn that had been built over seven hundred years ago and reminded some people of a Greek temple, others of the middle ages, most people of an age before their own, scarcely anybody of the present moment, was empty" (*BTA* 99). But the emptiness exists only in human terms. Closer narrative examination shows that the "empty" barn is filled with animal life: mice, swallows, "countless beetles and insects," a dog and puppies, a bluebottle, and a butterfly. Still the barn seems empty to Mrs. Sands, who leads the servants in. Once again, society follows nature and fills the silence with a musical swelling: "And the company entered. . . . The Barn filled. Fumes rose. China clattered; voices chattered" (*BTA* 101, 103). In the midst of the social duties of the tea, Lucy Swithin stands out looking at the swallows. She marvels at the swooping swallows that return every year and at the migration of the birds itself, predating the barn, predating civilization: " 'Swallows,' said Lucy, holding her cup, looking at the birds. Excited by the company they were flitting from rafter to rafter. Across Africa, across France they came to nest here. Year after year they came. Before there was a channel, when the earth, upon which the Windsor chair was planted, was a riot of rhododendrons, and humming birds quivered at the mouths of scarlet trumpets." (*BTA* 108).

Swallows fly throughout the day's narrative, twice dancing in droves through the pageant (*BTA* 182, 192), and Lucy is clearly associated with them. Her first words of the day are, "How those birds sing!" (*BTA* 9), and her brother's repetition of "Swallow, my sister, O sister swallow" reinforces the association. The most apparent referent of the allusion is the myth of Procne and Philomela as treated by Swinburne and Eliot. Philomela, raped and deprived of her voice by Tereus but telling the story of her violation through her weaving, is a powerful symbol for the female artist in particular, and for any artist transmuting suffering into song in general. Procne, the betrayed wife who kills her son Itylus and is transformed into a swallow, is an ambivalent figure. In the Swinburne poem that Bartholomew quotes, the nightingale chides the swallow for forgetting her pain, singing during the day, and flying south again. Bartholomew may intend a similar criticism of what he takes to be his sister's superstitious "whole-making" and ignoring of facts.[40] Certainly the spirit of the barn passage suggests that Lucy (rather romantically) sees the swallows as emblems that transcend the petty and passing human suffering below.

But the context here—the swallows flying in the empty barn and growing excited as it fills with villagers—suggests another antecedent: Bede's image of the swallow and its double-edged reflections on mortality and festivity. The swallow flitting through the mead hall epitomizes the brevity of life and the transience of earthly feasts against the vastness of the void. Woolf echoes Bede but shifts the focus. The swallows return, and their generations outlive civilization, just as Keats's nightingale "wast not born for death." Nature implies silence and death (as Woolf often stresses), but here through the swallows it also suggests recurrence and the filling of the void with life, an example that humankind follows in celebrating against mortality. In Bede's metaphor life is tiny and fleeting, poised between infinite reaches of darkness, but in Woolf's narrative of betweenness that liminal moment is at the center. Life is lived between the acts of the greater void; the realm of the swallow in the sacred hall is the realm of festivity and fiction.

The awareness of festivity as a celebration enacted in the presence of death manifests itself repeatedly, and in various forms, in *Between the Acts*. Miss La Trobe's melodramatic association of "death, death, death" with the failure of illusion hints at a more complex association between artistic and mortal limits. Woolf's courageous experimentation with narrative fragmentation in her last novel reflects her awareness that many of her earlier notions of wholeness may have been illusory. The connection of the artistic illusion of completeness (and control over the audience) with the illusion of immortality forms a striking corollary to Miss La Trobe's hyperbole. Miss La Trobe, however, proceeds to muse over plans for another play over drinks in the pub; her extremes of anxiety and elation resolve to a viable and practical middle ground, yet suggestively hint at how festivity, artwork, and life are temporary (and perhaps ultimately illusory) reversals of the world's entropy.

Isa Oliver embodies, at times, the more familiar Woolfian sentiment, the desire to fear no more the heat of the sun. Isa, in the moments in which she is most absorbed in her pseudopoetic world, desires "To fly away, from night and day, and issue where—no partings are" (*BTA* 83). Distant from the social chatter at the interval, she begs to be allowed to "'turn away . . . from the array . . . till I come to the wishing well . . . But what wish should I drop into the well? . . . That the waters should cover me'" (*BTA* 103). Isa's rapturous identification with the aged beldame of the Elizabethan section of the pageant—"She to whom all's one now, summer or winter"—most strikingly echoes Clarissa's refrain from *Cymbeline*. As in all Woolf's fiction, the longing to surrender to rest is a temptation to be resisted. In *Between the Acts* this vision reverses the emphasis implicit in Miss La Trobe's morbid exclamation. Miss La Trobe equates chaos with death: art and life exist in the struggle to order. Death represents to her not rest but a surrender to the entropic disorder, to the randomness of the universe behind the antientropic patterns of art and nature. Isa sees death as a release from the harshness and chaos of life. The two visions are alike, however, in that they recognize that living is a struggle against a foe that demands energy and creativity.

Death is the foe against which artist, party host, and each individual struggle. This formulation points to the most pervasive morbid presence in *Between the Acts*, the specter of the coming war. Present in the frequent comments of the audience, the obsessive malaise of Giles, the newspaper reports, and the buzzing of the airplanes overhead, the prospect of war provides the unmistakable background to the pageant and the Pointz Hall sociabilities. The prospect that the war might mean not only a multitude of people senselessly slaughtered but also the extinction of a civilization and a way of life intensifies the interplay between history and the present moment. This interplay is most evident in the pageant, but it also appears in the Pointz Hall conversations. *Between the Acts* invites us to examine the relationship between festivity and war, a theme that becomes crucial in post–World War II fiction, as epitomized in *Under the Volcano, Catch-22*, and, most powerfully, in *Gravity's Rainbow*.

One aspect of the relationship between war and festival emerges from the pageant itself. The pageant presents English history as a peaceful succession of modes and styles, devoid of bloody conflict. Mortality is embodied in the pageant as part of a natural progression of aging, death, and the birth of a new generation that succeeds the old. Though there are hints of personal violence in the Elizabethan sketch, of alienation and loneliness in the Restoration bit, and of imperialism and moral coercion in the Victorian drama, the pageant is notable for its omission of the military. Colonel Mayhew is irked by this festive history: "Why leave out the British Army? What's history without the Army, eh?" (*BTA* 157). The answer seems to be a pastoral and comic vision of history as a series of stylistically different reenactments of the same human plots, whether marital or martial. The interpretive difficulty lies in the pageant's ambiguous resolution with the present day and its clear threat of barbarism and brutality. If history is seen as culminating in the present, and the present is seen as uninterpretable and ambiguous, the historical narrative adopts the ambiguity of the present, as Eliot phrases it in *Four Quartets:* "History is now and England." The approaching war will revise history and generate a different pageant from the perspective of a different present.

That is, it will do so if it creates a pageant at all. The spirit of the pageant with its stress on historical continuity in the face of individual difference is antithetical, or at least opposed, to war: "If one spirit animates the whole, what about the aeroplanes?" (*BTA* 197). The nostalgia of the pageant is intensified by the present sense of historical severance. The individual celebrating in the festive occasion is cognizant that this life's riches are not unending. That individual sense usually finds a balance in the sense that the community will endure: the festivals outlive the individual celebrant. But, here, the community faces a threat of extinction that both darkens and intensifies the celebration. The prospect of another world war clearly influenced both Forster's and Woolf's writing of pageants in 1939.[41] *Between the Acts* suggests both the poignant fragility and the necessity of festivity's life affirmation. Through such social and artistic creations we seek to counter, subdue, or control deadly violence.

The prospect of war burns most vividly in the mind of Giles Oliver, the character linked most dramatically to an image of violence and death. In a scene that Alex Zwerdling calls "the book's most shocking passage," Giles encounters an olive green snake: "choked with a toad in its mouth. The snake was unable to swallow; the toad was unable to die. A spasm made the ribs contract; blood oozed. It was birth the wrong way round— a monstrous inversion" (*BTA* 99). Zwerdling notes how well the image of "a perverse assault in which both antagonists are inevitably destroyed" symbolizes the threat of another world war.[42] This scene inverts the life-affirming associations of the cycle, of the ouroboros (the multivalent symbol of the snake devouring its tail). Feeding has become deadly, generation reversed. The image grotesquely inverts what Bakhtin identifies as the crucial dualistic carnival trope—the image of pregnant death.[43] The choking snake embodies the antifestive force or spirit that forms a backdrop to the festive novel. The celebrative response to mortality— "Eat, drink and be merry"—contrasts starkly with this morbid statement and with Giles's violent response to it. As Giles smashes the snake and toad with his foot, his clean tennis shoes become "bloodstained and sticky" and he feels relieved by the action (*BTA* 99). Throughout the rest of the day the narrator will note the blood on his shoes, the mark that sets him apart from the festivity. Just before this moment, as the audience dispersed for tea, Giles had stood out "like a stake in the tide of the flowing company" (*BTA* 96). Giles embodies, in some measure, the fascistic mindset—or at least, in the context of the novel, a need to respond to obstacles with violence. His antifestive character emerges also in his resistance to social inclusivity—his disgust with William Dodge and his recoiling from Mrs. Parker's use of "we" (*BTA* 111).

The celebrations of *Between the Acts* are staged on a fragile ground: "The doom of sudden death hanging over us," as William melodramatically puts it to Isa (*BTA* 114). Festivity always possesses a self-reflexive element, celebrating the capacity to celebrate. Though *Between the Acts*

examines the fragmentation and fragility of the social world, it nevertheless applauds, through the example of the novel itself, the festive urge.
The antifestive background of holocaust, however, threatens both individual and society, and as such the festive impulse to eat, drink, and be
merry takes on an apocalyptic cast.

The various shades of mortality come together, appropriately and
powerfully, in the pageant's period of silence showcasing the present.
This is the point at which Miss La Trobe, seized by panic, with "blood
seem[ing] to pour from her shoes" notes that "this is death, death, death"
(*BTA* 180). But, as we have seen, the rain and music fill the void with
affirmative tears. In this otherwise joyful moment Isa murmurs, "O that
my life could here have ending" (*BTA* 181). Then she imagines herself as
a sacrifice upon "the altar of the rain-soaked earth" (*BTA* 181), offered to
end tears of human pain. Once again Woolf explicitly connects festivity
with ritual sacrifice. The offerings of Clarissa, Miss La Trobe, and Isa are
speculative and poetic, not literal blood sacrifices, but they participate
in a genealogy of ritual forms whereby festivity is seen as a ritual for
bringing life out of death, a sacred substitution.

Between the Acts is a novel carnivalistic in the genre-shaping sense that
Bakhtin asserts is rare or absent in post-Renaissance fiction.[44] Not only do
pageant and celebration form the thematic focus of the novel, but the carnivalistic spirit shapes, as we have seen, the work's style and structure.
Most strikingly, the carnivalized style emerges in the mixture of genres
accommodated within the novel frame. Woolf's text, woven of artistic
fragments of the pageant and conversational fragments from its audience, epitomizes the "destruction of all barriers between genres" and the
destruction of attempts "on the part of genres and styles to isolate themselves or ignore one another."[45] By interweaving the pageant-drama with
more familiar novelistic elements, *Between the Acts* provides an interesting illustration of my crucial argument that the novel exhibits a relation
with contemporary festivity akin to the organic connection of drama and
carnival in earlier times. By writing not a pageant (as Forster did) but a
pageant framed within a festive novel, Woolf makes use of the richness
of the novel form and its particular modernity. A pageant like Forster's,
or even Miss La Trobe's, would remain nostalgic in its exclusive reliance
on a once-vigorous folk mode. Woolf's novel, including the pageant but
also the novelistic play between the acts, achieves a form expressive of

the exigencies of late modernism, and not in the least nostalgic. Woolf demonstrates what John Barth has described as "how an artist may paradoxically turn the felt ultimacies of our time into material and means for his work."[46]

This contemporaneity reveals itself also in the obsessive urge to present the present. Bakhtin asserts that seriocomical genres have their starting point in "the living *present*, often even the very day."[47] Woolf sets her novel in the present and includes within the pageant the self-reflecting silent dramatization of the present moment. As Bakhtin notes, this sort of engagement radicalizes the relationship to history through its inherent open-endedness. Pageant and novel end up in the air with ambiguous potential and a disturbing lack of finality: "The church bells always stopped, leaving you to ask: Won't there be another note?" (*BTA* 207); " 'And if we're left asking questions, isn't it a failure, as a play?' " (*BTA* 200).

Inconclusiveness transmutes historical narrative into parody and pastiche, both in the pageant and in the characters' amalgam of quotations and memories. When Bakhtin notes the centrality of parody to carnivalistic expression, he offers a simile especially appropriate to *Between the Acts:* "[Carnival parody] was like an entire system of crooked mirrors, elongating, diminishing, distorting in various directions and to various degrees."[48]

The parodic history presented by the pageant, though multivoiced in itself, is just one voice in the complex polyphony of *Between the Acts*. The interruptions, quotations, and the musically interweaving conversations contribute to the novel's undermining of traditional authority and evidence its carnival inclusivity. Monologic voices such as Giles Oliver's condescension or the Reverend Streatfield's genial interpretation are subsumed into a multivocal and festive whole. *Between the Acts*, in its refusal to conclude, forms an ironically appropriate conclusion to Woolf's lifetime of stylistic experimentation and exploration of the party consciousness.

PART 2
The Party
Between the Wars

"The commonest, one might call it
the natural, rhythm of human life
is routine punctuated by orgies."
—Aldous Huxley

"Between the wars" may be an awkward way to describe a literary generation, but the phrase accurately captures several qualities common to the writers of the thirties. First, the phrase reflects the self-conscious sense of belonging to an era, or, specifically, one decade (*Vile Bodies, Tender Is the Night,* and *Party Going* are all novels of the thirties). That sense is demonstrated in Fitzgerald's short story "The Lost Decade" (in which a man wakes, as with a hangover, having missed the thirties) and in Auden's famous summary of the "low dishonest decade." But beyond the sense of belonging to one decade, a distinct perception of "betweenness" appears in the novels of the thirties—of being ill-suited to the time, caught between an earlier, greater (and, in terms of the war, more heroic) generation and a horrifying future. Valentine Cunningham in *British Writers of the Thirties* describes the pervasiveness of "that '30s sense of being *enclosed* in and by the destructive element" as manifested in myriad scenes of prisons, hospitals, locked rooms, caves, cages, and zoos—even the insides of whales.[1] The tropes of imprisonment and immobility are crucial to the party scenes of this time—from the fogbound party trapped in the railway station in *Party Going* to the parties in the moored dirigible in *Vile Bodies* and the moored yacht in *Tender Is the Night*. Images such as the stuck car spinning its wheels in Gatsby's driveway or the zooming engine of the stationary racing car in *Vile Bodies* capture the sense of futility perceived beneath Europe's temporary peace.

The pervasive fear of imprisonment and immobility affects the festive paradigm. The typical party of this era—at least in its literary manifestation—is characterized by a frenetic and decadent avoidance of control that generates a sort of mock transgression. This decadent party expresses neither the spirit of stifled festivity nor the extreme of the party gone wild. Rather, it is characterized by an artificial straining for spontaneity and excess that ultimately leaves the partygoers unsatisfied. Typically, decadence resists the vital difference of festivity: seeing no value in the everyday world (into which festive release ordinarily resolves), the decadent strives to make the party last forever. The party without end, stripped of its invigorating carnival inversion, threatens to become the unhappy norm of ennui.[2]

The changing meaning of the word *party* was decried in the leading item of the June 27, 1922, *New York Times* "Topics of the Times" column. The *Times* argued that if current usage took hold, "a once quite respectable word will become—well, something else." Clucking its editorial tongue at the behavior of the young, the paper describes the new, unfortunate meaning of the word: " 'Party,' in its latest employment, has come to mean a gathering of persons who can have a 'good time' only when highly stimulated by strong waters, always, in these days, illicitly acquired. These assemblages consist of both men and women who evidently are incapable of conversation in a normal condition. They acquire—for each other—a semblance of wit and wisdom after two or three hours of devotion to the cup that does inebriate, but when that state has been achieved, animosities develop, quarrels arise, and not infrequently the end of the 'party' is some sorry form of the tragical." Clearly a sign of the times, this commentary is but one of hundreds discussing the behavior of young people in the period following the First World War. The *Times* article suggests that "perhaps most light on 'parties' is cast by F. Scott Fitzgerald's *The Beautiful and Damned*" by virtue of its accurate portrayal of decadent parties. The belief that the era's uniqueness could be defined by the character of its social entertainment is shared by the young writers as well as the disapproving elders. Indeed, Fitzgerald in America and Waugh in England both contributed magazine articles on the "younger generation,"[3] and both wrote novels that used frequent party scenes to capture the social dynamics of the new age. The parties in the fiction of Fitzgerald, Waugh, and Henry Green reveal the distinctive character of the American and British generations that came of age in the twenties and dominated the literature of the thirties.

Not many years separate Fitzgerald, Waugh, and Green from Joyce and Woolf. The writers in Part 2, however, all began publishing after the war, and their fiction is shaped by that new world and a particular fascination with changes in social mores—a fascination that the *Times* piece also ironically communicates. *The Beautiful and Damned* appeared in 1922, that annus mirabilis of modernism that saw the death of Proust and the publication of *Ulysses, The Waste Land,* and Virginia Woolf's first experimental novel, *Jacob's Room.* This year also heralded the publication of Emily Post's *Etiquette,* billed as "a social document . . . without precedent in American literature."[4] Codifications of manners, such as British directories of landed families, are generally rearguard actions: they appear when the standards they espouse have begun to erode visibly and are in need of reinforcement. One need only read Post and Fitzgerald side by side to see the disjunction between Post's teas and Fitzgerald's cocktail parties. Within this generation gap parties acquired a new significance, even became a sort of cause célèbre reflecting possibilities for social change as well as despair with the postwar world.

But the relation of the between-the-wars novelists to the writers of "high modernism" is a complex one. While it is fair to say that Fitzgerald, Waugh, and Green were influenced by modernist works in their early years, we see very little evidence of that influence, particularly with regard to modernist experiments with narrative multiplicity, in their writing style. In part, the resistance to modernist credos was colored by the political influence of social realism and Marxism, which generated a climate of distrust for the perceived aestheticism of high modernism (to such an extent that such distrust was shared by clearly right-wing, antisocialist writers such as Waugh).[5] The literary attitude toward the masses was at best ambivalent, as Fitzgerald's careful pairing of Socialist party and socialite party in "May Day" illustrates. This ambivalence also finds expression in the problematic attitude Waugh and Green exhibit toward the affluent segments of society whose parties they chronicle—an unsettling mixture of disgust and sympathy. We also see in between-the-wars novelists a mixed fascination and repugnance with regard to distinctively modern innovations—mass transit, mass media, automobiles and airplanes, skyscrapers, popular music and other entertainments, and the increasingly cynical rituals of social etiquette.

These attitudes generated literary styles that were particularly resistant to modernist dialogism or multiple voicing. And yet the fascination that festivity continues to hold for these writers keeps the possibilities for carnivalized narrative present, if always somehow deferred. Fitzgerald and Waugh each developed styles that tended, for different reasons, to reinforce narrative authority and limit the carnivalized multiplicity of voices. Fitzgerald's characteristic style blends social realism and a neo-Keatsian romanticism; Waugh's early style approaches satire but resists the moral center typically associated with satirical narrative distance. Bakhtin argues that satirical laughter has a harshness or one-sidedness that makes it antithetical to the double-edged spirit of carnival and parody.[6] Similarly, his hostility to novelistic realism arises from its tendency toward moral seriousness and a unitary or "objective" viewpoint, both of which are antithetical to the comic spirit of the carnivalesque. Though Bakhtin tends to overstate the dynamics of his history of genre, we do see in writers such as Fitzgerald and Waugh a turning away from modernist narrative experimentation, combined, however, with the festive life as subject matter. As a result, the very struggle between the competing influences toward narrative authority and dialogism defines the style of these writers. Similarly, Henry Green, whose explicit resistance to narrative intrusion has clear modernist roots, ironically compromises that stylistic precept in order to manage the many voices of *Party Going*.

This very tension is consistent with the decadent model of controlled transgression. Since the striving for festive excess becomes a desperate pose, it becomes difficult for the writer, as observer of the decadent facade, to open the narrative to the forces of carnivalization. Fitzgerald, Waugh, and Green exhibit the second of our three paradigms of festive vision. No longer is propriety (social or literary) the existing, stale tradition that the novel can oppose; the decadent party has become the social given and the conventions of nineteenth-century fiction have already been shattered by a previous generation. Against decadent ennui it is difficult either to celebrate transgression or to advocate the return to decorum. Thus the fiction of the time maps an important region between modernist narrative experimentation and postmodern linguistic play.

3. Charioted by Bacchus

PARTIES IN FITZGERALD

Ay, in the very temple of Delight
Veil'd Melancholy has her sovran shrine,
Though seen of none save him whose
    strenuous tongue
Can burst Joy's grape against his palate fine;
His soul shall taste the sadness of her might,
And be among her cloudy trophies hung.
—John Keats, "Ode on Melancholy"

When Fitzgerald characterizes the twenties in his 1931 essay "Echoes of the Jazz Age," the party emerges as a metaphor for the age. The era started with a "general decision to be amused that began with the cocktail parties of 1921" but had its true origins in the memento mori lesson of the First World War, which led a generation to conclude "eat, drink, and be merry, for to-morrow we die" (*CU* 15–16). Fitzgerald invokes the festive metaphor in describing the spread of the jazz age ethos: "The sequel was like a children's party taken over by the elders, leaving the children puzzled and rather neglected and rather taken aback.[1] By 1923 their elders, tired of watching the carnival with ill-concealed envy, had discovered that young liquor will take the place of young blood, and with a whoop the orgy began. The younger generation was starred no longer. A whole race going hedonistic, deciding on pleasure" (*CU* 15). The language of festivity—"party," "carnival," "orgy"—reflects Fitzgerald's serious belief that a culture could be interpreted through its celebrative core. In his fiction the party accordingly becomes much

131

more than a tour de force for the novelist of manners. The party scene becomes a crucial means for relating individual disillusionment to societal decline; the party is the liminal territory in which individual and group collide. A sense of collision, or tension between opposing forces, is consistent with Fitzgerald's status as a novelist between traditions. Though aware of and attracted by the modernist innovations of Joyce and Proust, Fitzgerald was as strongly influenced by the earlier manner of Compton MacKenzie. Similarly, Fitzgerald's work remains caught up in a tension between the social focus of the novel of manners and a romantic individualism of a decidedly Keatsian strain. His scenes of parties frame the struggle between these conflicting influences and the concomitant struggle with novelistic form that characterized his career.

Party scenes chronicle Fitzgerald's development and experimentation, in both narrative and thematic terms. As Fitzgerald sketches a decadent caricature through dramatic form in *The Beautiful and Damned* (1922), a party scene serves as the occasion for his first experiment with point of view. The Nick Carraway participant-narrator of his next novel is a justly celebrated technical device that accounts for much of that work's laudable unity. But the unity of *The Great Gatsby* (1925) denies part of Fitzgerald's vision, a vision that is hinted at in the contrast between the structural importance of parties to the novel and their thematic unimportance to Gatsby's romantic quest. Only in *Tender Is the Night* (1934) does Fitzgerald succeed in bringing his conflicting emphases—on the dynamics of society and the capacities of the heroic individual—into fruitful contact. This novel most clearly presents Fitzgerald's Keatsian vision within a story of individual dissolution; here, the party embodies the transcendent possibilities of community toward which the characters aspire. The party at the Villa Diana becomes the narrative center, and events (including subsequent parties) can be located by their distance from its informing spirit. Overall these works reflect not so much a development throughout Fitzgerald's career as a repeated struggle characterized by recourse to different narrative strategies, at the center of which remains Fitzgerald's appreciation of the richness and complexity of contemporary celebration.

Fitzgerald saw in parties a metaphor for the corruption and dissolution of an age, and a canvas for painting society as "crowd" as well as for depicting individual alienation from the group. Through most of his fiction Fitzgerald explores the failed party as metaphor for individual tragedy and social decline. This theme figures in *The Beautiful and Damned* and *The Great Gatsby* as well as in some of his best stories—"May Day," "The Baby Party," "The Rich Boy," "The Bridal Party," "Babylon Revisited," and "Crazy Sunday." Only in *Tender Is the Night* does Fitzgerald show the party at the height of its potential, and even there it prefigures the collapse that lies ahead and the decadent, empty parties that will characterize that collapse.

Fitzgerald's parties explore the possibilities and limits of pleasure in the modern world: from Anthony and Gloria's drunken binges to the transcendent illuminations of the Divers' party. Such scenes map the range of Fitzgerald's festive vision. His novels also explore different means of commingling the voices of narrative, though Fitzgerald never allows himself the full multivocal potential of the carnivalized novel. Fitzgerald instead prefers the compromise of the narrator "without and within" (in Nick Carraway's terms), a perspective mingling ironic detachment and romantic subjectivity. These contradictions of Fitzgerald's place in early modernism are reflected in the changing but continually significant role of celebration in his fiction.

The Beautiful and Damned:
The Party in the Decadent Age

Life's meaninglessness, Edmund Wilson argues with disapproval, is the theme of Fitzgerald's *The Beautiful and Damned*.[2] But in true decadent, self-conscious fashion, the perception of life's meaninglessness becomes a pose itself, a pretense excusing dissolute behavior.[3] These poses covering poses emerge most clearly in the parties that fill the book, and particularly in the party rendered as drama, which serves as Fitzgerald's first significant experiment with narrative form. Through this scene, and the novel as a whole, Fitzgerald develops a sophisticated conception of the meaning of decadence in social behavior.

Parties become the center of Anthony and Gloria's existence early in their married life. Since the spirit of decadence represents a rejection of the socially accepted, the parties appropriately begin as a response to Anthony's decision to accept a job in "the bond business," a short-lived concession to his grandfather's sense of propriety. Before Anthony's first day at work, Gloria leads Anthony and a few friends on as "gay and joyous a bacchanal as they had ever known" (*BD* 224). Thus begins the sequence of increasingly frenetic parties: "It was with this party, more especially with Gloria's part in it, that a decided change began to come over their way of living. The magnificent attitude of not giving a damn altered overnight; from being a mere tenet of Gloria's it became the entire solace and justification for what they chose to do and what consequence it brought. Not to be sorry, not to loose one cry of regret, to live according to a clear code of honor toward each other, and to seek the moment's happiness as fervently and persistently as possible" (*BD* 226). At the heart of this plan lies the temporal contradiction between the moment and the continuous, between the spontaneous character of "the moment's happiness" and the premeditated quality of "to seek."

Fitzgerald uses two main techniques for creating the decadent party atmosphere: he uses plural generalizations to convey the sense of similar, almost continuous, parties; and he creates a single decadent party with grotesque exaggeration to culminate the accelerating, chaotic decline of decadent behavior. In *The Beautiful and Damned* sentences such as "These 'parties' gradually became their chief source of entertainment" (*BD* 227) suggest an ongoing series of parties occurring offstage. Frequently, typical chacteristics are sketched in a paragraph that refers to no particular party: "They filled the house with guests every week-end, and often on through the week. The week-end parties were much the same. When the three or four men invited had arrived, drinking was more or less in order, followed by a hilarious dinner and a ride to the Cradle Beach Country Club" (*BD* 235). And there are more specific summaries: "There had been many parties—people broke things; people became sick in Gloria's bathroom; people spilled wine; people made unbelievable messes of the kitchenette" (*BD* 296). The continuous character of the parties weakens the sense of transgression and difference; they become a norm in themselves.

This process of "becoming" is not static but rather accelerates toward a crisis. That crisis comes in the most clearly decadent party in Fitzgerald's fiction, the set piece within *The Beautiful and Damned* entitled "The Broken Lute." The use of dramatic form with elaborate, italicized stage directions often cast in inflated diction makes this scene stand out from the rest of the book. This stylistic device is used for a literal dramatic effect, to heighten the scene's coherence as a "set piece," and to accentuate the grotesque nature of the comic behavior. Joyce uses the same device, for similar reasons, in the "Circe" episode of *Ulysses* (published the same year), linking, as Fitzgerald does, wild, drunken behavior to dramatic presentation. But critics have tended to fault Fitzgerald for breaking the narrative continuity: Arthur Mizener asserts that Fitzgerald "still seemed to think there was some special virtue in passages written in play form"; Richard Lehan sees this segment of the plot development as a whole (Adam Patch disinheriting Anthony) as "the crudest kind of narrative device."[4] The attempt to mix grotesque humor with the movement of a realistic novel toward its ironic climax admittedly creates tonal problems. It is difficult to know, for instance, how to read the following description of Muriel Kane: "Her bosom is still a pavement that she offers to the hoofs of many passing stallions, hoping that their iron shoes may strike even a spark of romance in the darkness" (*BD* 270). But these excesses are consistent with the strained extremity for which Fitzgerald is here striving, and the dramatic effectiveness of the scene is too often over-looked. In a mere fifteen pages Fitzgerald manipulates nine characters into a whirling climax that captures the typical qualities of decadence: he frames the scene with two revealing, symbolically significant exchanges concerning intoxication and abstinence; he mingles good party cheer with a growing animosity between Maury Noble and Fred Paramore and between Anthony and Gloria; and he believably catapults the characters into a frenzied chaos that prepares for the deflating entrance of Adam Patch. In the process Fitzgerald creates one of his funniest episodes.

The dramatic effect is heightened by the gradual introduction of characters. First, the empty house sets the scene; then the flute music announces the Japanese servant, Tana. Fitzgerald next introduces a foil character to intensify the irony of the upcoming scene. Fred Paramore, a teetotaler and an aggressively Protestant social worker, arrives to renew acquaintances with his Harvard friend, Anthony. His quick observation of the signs of a party in the empty house (empty glasses and filled ash-trays) and his ethnological question of the Japanese servant reveal his pretension and show how out of place he is in Anthony and Gloria's world. Maury Noble then enters before the rest of the group, which allows for an amusing contrast between his learned, alcohol-fueled cyni-cism and Paramore's naive social idealism. Paramore is an example of Virginia Woolf's "man who loved his kind," and his sudden immersion into the sophisticated decadence of Anthony and Gloria's circle creates a comic chiaroscuro. After Maury arrives as harbinger of the Patch party, Anthony and Gloria enter with their traveling entourage—novelist Dick Caramel, Muriel Kane, and Rachel and Rodman Barnes. The party is under way.

Drink and decadence become topics of conversation as Maury and Fred spar over the issue of social responsibility and Gloria chastises Anthony for getting so drunk that he pays for everything and rudely flirts with all available women. These two conversations form an effective counterpoint on the issue of intoxication, which is central to this scene. Maury and Fred are disputing on the societal level. Having progressed from "'Proof' down to 'Distillery'" on the whiskey bottle (*BD* 267), Maury drunkenly scoffs at Fred's charitable social work and his pretense of broad-mindedness. Maury reacts to Fred's superiority, which he feels undermines any real empathy for the people he is trying to save. Maury exaggerates his celebration of decadence in order to bait Fred's moralistic, pejorative view of it. The narrator even comically invokes the word: "Whether PARAMORE is lingering in the gray house out of politeness or curiosity, or in order at some future time to make a sociological report on the decadence of American life, is problematical" (*BD* 270).

While Fitzgerald shows clear scorn for Fred's moralistic position, the conversation between Anthony and Gloria reveals how far Fitzgerald is (even in 1922) from being unaware of the devastating influences of drink. The deterioration of the relationship between Anthony and Gloria emerges in these group scenes as well as in their arguments alone between binges. Anthony and Gloria's argument, and Gloria's charge that drinking makes Anthony simple, create a tension that affects the rest of the party.

Fitzgerald divides the guests and the progression of the party into two parts by interposing the stage direction: "By nine o'clock these can be divided into two classes—those who have been drinking consistently and those who have taken little or nothing" (*BD* 269). As much as intoxication can unite a group by providing a communal change in mood, it can also divide it. But Maury seeks devilishly to entice the nondrinkers into the spree, addressing Fred: "'Well, such a broad-minded man should consider the raised plane of sensation and the stimulated optimism contained in this cocktail'" (*BD* 271). Paramore accepts with the condition, " 'If a fellow can drink like a gentleman—' "(*BD* 271). Surely a popular phrase of the time, this saying is also mocked by Faulkner in his jazz age novel *Sanctuary,* where it becomes the refrain of the irresponsible drunkard, Gowan. Here it highlights the attempt to ignore the tension between festive intoxication and everyday rules of behavior. One does not drink in order to continue behaving like a gentleman; intoxication invites a temporary freedom from the normal hierarchy that the ambiguous term "gentleman" evokes. Nevertheless the party quickly intensifies as the teetotaler becomes drunk and the partygoers dance to Tana's bizarre Japanese flute train song. At the height of the chaos Maury appropriately offers a profane toast (what Bakhtin would identify as a "carnivalistic blasphemy"): " 'Here's to the defeat of democracy and the fall of Christianity' " (*BD* 273).

The reference to a "fall" suggests the relationship between decadent behavior and a declining system of values and alerts us to the images of the late stages of decadence that fill the entire scene. The stage-direction introduction, for example, evokes the decadent qualities of overripeness and artificiality: "There are dying flower scents upon the air, so thin, so fragile, as to hint already of a summer laid away in time. . . . On the table is a dish of fruit, which is real but appears artificial" (*BD* 261). In their drunken behavior the guests, and Fred Paramore in particular, evince decadent pose and imitation, a sense of the real appearing artificial. Paramore is not simply drunk; he is intoxicated with the very idea of being drunk: "So enraptured with the notion that he increases the effect by simulating funny-paper staggers and even venturing an occasional hiccough" (*BD* 273). The decadent emphasis on "lowness" combines with narrative mimesis as the fiction warns us that life will imitate bad art: "But the grotesque, the unbelievable, the histrionic incident is about to occur, one of those incidents in which life seems set upon the passionate imitation of the lowest forms of literature" (*BD* 274). The event is the entrance of Anthony's millionaire, prohibitionist grandfather, around whom the gaiety grinds to a halt. Witnessing this debauched scene confirms his gravest suspicions and completes his alienation from Anthony. Grandfather Adam Patch leaves without a word, and Anthony and Adam never meet again. At Adam Patch's death, Anthony finds he has been disinherited.

The entrance of Adam Patch violates the sanctity of the festive, "green world" suspension of the everyday. As millionaire temperance supporter and vengeful moralist, Adam Patch represents the status quo in exaggerated form. A classic blocking character, he hovers outside the major scenes of the book, providing a plot structure and asserting his presence by antithesis. Though Adam Patch's world is antithetical to Anthony's festive world, his money has provided the means by which Anthony's festive world survives, and this perhaps damns Anthony from the start. Such dependence is certainly the ironic point of the ending: Anthony's rebellion against his grandfather's values drains him of all life by the time he finally inherits (through lengthy lawsuits) his grandfather's position and wealth.

Decadence perverts the comic pattern. Adam Patch should be inefficacious in the festive world that excludes him; instead, his power emerges clearly as his entrance paralyzes the party. The transition from the green world of festivity and youth to an adult world of renewed vigor and unity very obviously fails. The poison of Adam Patch's world is so extreme that it renders the decadent antidote deadly as well. The decadent behavior is so clearly a reaction to the moralistic world that it unwittingly demonstrates that world's continued power.

Ultimately, this party is death-centered in a way that offers no possibility for renewal. The opening description of the scene even suggests a death's-head presence: "[On the table] are grouped an ominous assortment of decanters, glasses, and heaped ash-trays, the latter still raising wavy smoke-ladders into the stale air—the effect on the whole needing but a skull to resemble that venerable chromo, once a fixture in every 'den,' which presents the appendages to the life of pleasure with delightful and awe-inspiring sentiment" (*BD* 261). Adam Patch's entrance provides the skull for this mock altar. Gossip will have it afterwards that "that party in Marietta *killed* Anthony's grandfather" (*BD* 299), but in effect it kills Anthony, draining him of spirit and hope and beginning the decline that culminates in his breakdown. The breakdown appropriately takes the form of a plunge into second childhood, as Anthony mindlessly retreats into his stamp collection. The young inherit the world, but in *The Beautiful and Damned* it is only after the struggle has thoroughly debilitated them.

Fitzgerald's use of the climactic and exaggerated party evinces a mature understanding of the internalized decay endemic to decadent behavior.

But, as the various party scenes illustrate, Fitzgerald has defined his narrative point of view as a sort of sympathetic satire—a limited perspective that is particularly uncongenial to Fitzgerald's sense of individual passion as the motivating force for literature. Fitzgerald sought a narrative mode and social perspective that was neither as subjectively direct as the bildungsroman form in *This Side of Paradise* nor as ironically distant as the third-person narration of *The Beautiful and Damned*. In *The Great Gatsby* Fitzgerald discovered a narrative solution of sorts, a perspective that mitigated the ironic flavor of satire and allowed for a presentation of human passion and "greatness."

The Great Gatsby: "Delivered From the Womb of Purposeless Splendor"

There is a certain irony in the fact that *The Great Gatsby* comes so readily to mind when one thinks of parties in literature, and this irony is consistent with the method of the novel. Parties, though structurally and stylistically important in *The Great Gatsby*, are, finally, thematically insignificant. Structurally, social occasions shape and organize the novel; stylistically, parties are natural vehicles for Fitzgerald's social realism as a novelist of manners in what he himself dubbed the jazz age. But Fitzgerald never seems wholly comfortable in the novel of manners mode because it conflicts with the passionate, romantic individualism that characterizes the most elevated moments in his writing. Therefore, in *The Great Gatsby* the significance of parties as social canvas emerges ultimately through their contrasting unimportance to Jay Gatsby. *The Great Gatsby* presents absence and emptiness as themes, and such images fill the novel: the absent host at the early parties, the empty house and ill-attended funeral at the end, the vacant stare of Dr. T. J. Eckleburg, and the empty wasteland into which he gazes. The emptiness and insignificance of Gatsby's parties contrast with the stylistic force and structural importance the parties clearly possess. In *The Great Gatsby* the lack of authentic festive spirit or a desire for it stands out, but against *Gatsby's* irrelevant festivity will emerge the centrality of the festive spirit in *Tender Is the Night*.

When Edith Wharton wrote to Fitzgerald praising *Gatsby*, she singled out for special admiration "that seedy orgy in the Buchanan flat, with the dazed puppy looking on."[5] It should cause little surprise that Wharton cites a party scene, particularly the party scene most directly concerned with class difference and social mobility. Both Wharton and Fitzgerald assert the importance of close observation of social behavior. Parties are essential to their fiction because they illuminate the interplay of class, boundary, and mores within the actions of the individual. For both novelists social occasions are not merely rich subjects for realistic novels; they are crucial arenas for the fulfillment of individual destiny.

Fitzgerald demonstrates his inheritance from Wharton most brilliantly in *The Great Gatsby*, and the cocktail party hosted by Tom Buchanan and his mistress offers a particularly good example. The scene studies how finely tuned the American awareness of class can be, as it follows Myrtle Wilson's afternoon transformation from vital spirit imprisoned in the valley of ashes of American poverty to petty socialite fluttering about in her newly created illusionary world. Fitzgerald's careful notation of social and physical borders structures the scene. Tom Buchanan exercises his leisure-class privilege by selecting a woman beneath him for his pleasure (just as one of his previous scandals involved a chambermaid). But for Myrtle, Tom represents a way out, a shining knight to rescue her from damnation on earth. When her affair with Tom first begins, she repeats to herself as a tonic the phrase, " 'You can't live forever; you can't live forever' " (*GG* 36). Myrtle's affair with Tom is not merely a matter of sexual passion (on the afternoon of the party those needs are satisfied in a brief absence from the living room). No, Myrtle Wilson's love affair is an escape into a world in which she can feign privilege and position. Therefore, she must entertain: she creates her own set of social boundaries and a world in which she can exorcise her low class status. With her lover as companion, and Nick, her sister, and the neighboring McKees to play host to, her "intense vitality . . . so remarkable in the garage was converted into impressive hauteur" (*GG* 30–31).

But Myrtle's ascendancy is temporary and limited, as she discovers when, in Tom's eyes, she oversteps her bounds. At the end of the party she attempts to assert her equality with Daisy by loudly repeating Daisy's name, and Tom brings her reign to an end by "[breaking] her nose with his open hand" (*GG* 37). The crisis reaches its bloody conclusion in the bathroom, as so many of Fitzgerald's crises do, because it is the only private room in the house that has been opened up for a party. One of the final visions in the New York apartment is of "bloody towels upon the bathroom floor," an image that will reappear centrally in *Tender Is the Night*.

Fitzgerald carefully manipulates the description of the party to give a sense of progress through time. He interrupts dialogue with indications of time passing: the increased haziness of the intoxicated narrator; the guests' increasing abandon in conversation and movement; the gradual dimming of the sunlight; and the emergence of artificial light in the darkness. Standing in the little world constituted by Myrtle's party, Nick Carraway moves, like Gabriel Conroy and Clarissa Dalloway, to the window and speculates on the relationship between the microcosmic community within the apartment and the myriad communities without: "Yet high over the city our line of yellow windows must have contributed their share of human secrecy to the casual watcher in the darkening streets, and I was him too, looking up and wondering. I was within and without, simultaneously enchanted and repelled by the inexhaustible variety of life" (*GG* 36). Fitzgerald gives us the best critical description of his narrative relation to his fiction—"within and without," "enchanted and repelled." From the border he has so meticulously described, the observer narrates "riotous excursions with privileged glimpses into the human heart" (*GG* 2). To possess special insight into parties, characters must be able to withdraw from the midst of the celebration and perceive the boundaries that define it against the dark outside world.

The shift from this smoky, stifling indoor party at the Buchanan apartment to the glittering festivities in Gatsby's garden is the novel's most startling juxtaposition, and it suggests how parties structure the book. Swept on the tide of music, which is notably absent from Myrtle Wilson's afternoon debauch, the descriptions of Gatsby's parties shimmer with intoxication, jazz, and the magic of nighttime: "There was music from my neighbor's house through the summer nights. In his blue gardens men and girls came and went like moths among the whisperings and the champagne and the stars" (*GG* 39). Fitzgerald precedes Nick's first narration of a Gatsby party with a three-page description of the parties in general, using the technique from *The Beautiful and Damned* of suggesting a series of similar affairs for which a single description suffices. Fitzgerald comically evokes the weekly pattern of party and aftermath: "On week-ends his Rolls-Royce became an omnibus, bearing parties to and from the city. . . . And on Mondays eight servants, including an extra gardener, toiled all day with mops and scrubbing brushes and hammers and garden shears, repairing the ravages of the night before" (*GG* 39). This rhythm not only captures the relation between weekend festivities and the return of the workweek but also between the upper-class host and his guests and the workers and servants needed to make their entertainment possible. So when Fitzgerald describes the "five crates of oranges and lemons" arriving every Friday to leave as a "pyramid of pulpless halves" on Monday, he is careful to explain that they are juiced by an electronic machine operated by a butler's thumb. Within just a couple of pages Fitzgerald evokes a season of parties and a rhythm of festive excitement and restoration, all based upon a specific economic underpinning.

The Great Gatsby, however, is primarily a scenic novel, in Henry James's sense of the term.[6] Explanations of personal histories or the general progress of events through time are kept at a minimum, while fully realized dramatic scenes are used to narrate the story. Fitzgerald relies so completely on direct presentation of dramatic scenes that he has Nick apologize for it, explaining after the first of Gatsby's parties: "Reading over what I have written so far, I see I have given the impression that the events of three nights several weeks apart were all that absorbed me" (*GG* 56). Like the ambivalence of "within and without," Fitzgerald's shifts between dramatic scene and narrative reflection demonstrate some dissatisfaction with the limitations of Nick's point of view. Yet it is Nick's double nature as participant and narrator that allows for the essentially scenic novel to acquire moral depth.

All but one of the nine chapters of the book are oriented around social occasions or parties. The first three chapters map the extremes of the novel's microcosmic world with parties in East Egg, New York City, and West Egg. Chapter 4 begins with the famous guest list Nick has composed after observing a season of Gatsby's parties, and again we see Fitzgerald's skill in suggesting an accelerating succession of parties. Nick's lunch with Gatsby and Meyer Wolfsheim forms the dramatic heart of Chapter 4, as Fitzgerald uses a social occasion to portray the relativistic moralities of Gatsby's business world. Chapter 5, at the center of the book, is the showcase for Nick's tea in which Gatsby and Daisy awkwardly reunite, and Nick's presence on the tour of Gatsby's mansion reminds us how important it is that the occasion be social rather than intimate. Chapter 6 shows us another of Gatsby's parties, this one different because the goddess to whom they have been offered is in attendance. Though chapter 7 opens by describing the end of the parties, it too has its dramatic center in a social occasion—the sweltering cocktail party in rented rooms at the Plaza. Only chapter 8, in which Gatsby embraces the nothingness into which his dream has dissolved, is devoid of a unifying, central social occasion. Ending with Gatsby's death, it prepares us for the final public gathering—Gatsby's ill-attended funeral, an ironic complement to his crowded and lively parties.

The Great Gatsby is built of parties that serve as backdrops for the developing tragedy of Gatsby's failed love and the senseless deaths of Myrtle Wilson, her husband, and Gatsby himself. Yet important as the parties are to Fitzgerald's narrative technique, their failure lacks the significance of failed parties in *The Beautiful and Damned* and *Tender Is the Night*. Elaborate facades, Gatsby's parties, like the sealed books in his library, remain devoid of meaning. Nick's opening description of Gatsby's parties prepares us for a festive transformation that we can only understand when it fails to occur. The diction and prose rhythm suggest a swelling crescendo, a movement of the party as a whole towards consummate ecstasy: "The bar is in full swing, and floating rounds of cocktails permeate the garden outside, until the air is alive with chatter and laughter, and casual innuendo and introductions forgotten on the spot, and enthusiastic meetings between women who never knew each other's names" (*GG* 40). This passage continues the gauzy imagery of insubstantiality begun in the Buchanans' breezy drawing room. Fitzgerald then ties the growing intensity of the party to the coming of night, an image that will be central in his next novel: "The lights grow brighter as the earth lurches away from the sun, and now the orchestra is playing yellow cocktail music, and the opera of voices pitches a key higher. Laughter is easier minute by minute, spilled with prodigality, tipped out at a cheerful word" (*GG* 40).

Nick describes the parties from the perspective of the gap between host and guests. Nick's formal invitation, delivered by Gatsby's chauffeur, distinguishes him from other guests and reinforces his place of narrative privilege as observer and participant. The invitation initiates his eventual closeness to Gatsby but points to the overarching irony of Gatsby's parties—the total lack of communion between host and guests. Nick views both with disapproval, though he is closer to Gatsby in his sympathies and perceptions. He will finally make this choice explicit when he shouts to Gatsby, " 'They're a rotten crowd. . . . You're worth the whole damn bunch put together' " (*GG* 154). Nick describes the openness of the party at the outset and notes that few of the guests actually know Gatsby; instead they merely "conducted themselves according to the rules of behavior associated with amusement parks" (*GG* 41). The amusement park suggests an impersonal public arena rather than a home, and mechanical amusement rather than human interaction.

Nick disapproves of this anonymity; to him it suggests a world without center. The party without a present, living host is like a world without God in which anything is permitted—liberating and empty. The mysterious Gatsby of the party has affinities with the billboard of Dr. T. J. Eckleburg—both survey with unseeing eyes, both preside over realms of emptiness. Uncomfortable in such an impersonal, uncentered environment, Nick immediately sets off in search of the host in order to orient himself. Through most of the party Nick will be occupied by this search until he finally meets up with Gatsby in understated anticlimax.

Nick moves through "swirls and eddies of people [he] didn't know," himself a boat against the current (*GG* 41). When he asks for Gatsby, strangers gawk at him in amazement, so he settles at the bar, which, Fitzgerald aptly notes, is the one place "where a single man could linger without looking purposeless and alone" (*GG* 42). Fortunately he meets Jordan Baker who will accompany him throughout the evening. She almost speaks the host's name but is interrupted before she can utter it: "I remembered you lived next door to—' " (*GG* 42). The interruption is caused, fittingly, by two girls who introduce themselves by saying, " 'You don't know who we are,' " and move out of earshot by the time Jordan responds (*GG* 43). Forgotten names and hosts never met suggest the party's anonymity and cloak the scene in mystery.

When Jordan and Nick settle into a conversation, they are with five people with indistinguishable, mumbled names. The conversation turns to Gatsby and his overly generous replacement of a gown torn at an earlier festivity. Gatsby's name is introduced through questioning and ambiguous ellipsis:

> "He doesn't want any trouble with *any*body."
> "Who doesn't?" I inquired.
> "Gatsby. Somebody told me—" (*GG* 43)

This opening leads to the first round of malicious gossip about Gatsby, at the end of which the small group "all turned and looked around for Gatsby" (*GG* 44). Nick's quest continues to fail: Gatsby is not at the crowded bar or on the steps or the veranda. Neither at the heart of the party nor surveying it, he is simply and mysteriously absent. Nick and Jordan's search takes them into the library where they encounter the drunken man with owl-eyed spectacles. This inebriated visionary, like most of the guests, has been ambiguously "brought." In this famous scene the owl-eyed man testifies with drunken wit to the artifice of the library. Like the party, the library is realistic but not real. The books, though real, remain unread. Their uncut pages testify to the fragility of the illusion: "if one brick was removed the whole library was liable to collapse" (*GG* 46). Later Nick will penetrate to the secret of Gatsby's parties, just as the owl-eyed man has discovered the secret of the library. For now, Nick seeks only to find the host, but the controlling presence of a central enigma has been established. Gatsby is as mysterious as his parties: understand why he gives them and you will understand the man himself.[7]

Against a Dantesque background of couples dancing in "eternal grace-less circles" varied only by sundry stunts and entertainments, Nick and Jordan rest in their search for Gatsby to quaff "two finger-bowls of champagne." At this point a man engages Nick in conversation because he recognizes him from the army. Warming to conversation Nick confesses bewilderment at having not met the host, only to discover that the man he's speaking to is, indeed, Gatsby. The ironic interplay of recognition and bewilderment, search and discovery, is complete. Gatsby then reveals his magnificence in the way Nick will memorialize him—with a gesture. He smiles a Cheshire cat smile, which vanishes into its very openness: "It was one of those rare smiles with a quality of eternal reassurance in it, that you may come across four or five times in life. It faced—or seemed to face—the whole external world for an instant, and then concentrated on *you* with an irresistible prejudice in your favor. It understood you just as far as you wanted to be understood, believed in you as you would like to believe in yourself, and assured you that it had precisely the impression of you that, at your best, you hoped to convey. Precisely at that point it vanished" (*GG* 48). A fine understanding of party dynamics infuses this description. Gatsby's smile accepts you as you want to portray yourself; the gesture is so caught up in images of images that it has lost all contact with reality. Though Fitzgerald clearly valued social skills and, in particular, a winning smile, he presents this gesture as magically elusive, the smile of the nonexistent host who derives his existence from people's impressions of him. Its emptiness represents the artificiality of the party mask reduced to the absurd, and it makes Nick as curious as the rest of the guests about Gatsby.

In contrasting the smile directed to "the whole external world" and the smile directed to one individual, Fitzgerald foreshadows the incompatibility he will explore between the intimacy of romantic love and the public, communal interaction of a successful party. Fitzgerald recognizes that the party requires people to smile at the whole external world, whereas a love affair often calls for a pushing aside of the external world. Lovers, wholly wrapped up in themselves, are out of place at a party. They fit in only if they suspend their intense involvement with one another. Jordan sums up the tension between private and public when she naively asserts: "I like large parties. They're so intimate. At small parties there isn't any privacy" (*GG* 50).[8] Of course, Jordan's paradoxical comment has a familiar meaning. Once a party reaches a certain size it breaks into a variety of ever-changing groups and thus relieves everyone from the communal spotlight. But here this comment stresses the anonymity and lack of community at Gatsby's parties: it is almost like being alone. The anonymity even grants license, but it is not the festive license of the feast of fools or controlled transgression. The license comes from feeling completely unobserved. "God sees everything," an enraged George Wilson proclaims later in the book (*GG* 160), but Wilson's eyes look out on Dr. Eckleburg's uncomprehending stare. Gatsby's parties are "intimate" because they create no true community.

The details of the ending of the party further underscore Gatsby's distance from his guests: he remains sober, even becoming increasingly so, "as the fraternal hilarity increased" (*GG* 50). He surveys the guests from afar during the playing of the *Jazz History of the World* and offers a ritual gesture of farewell as the oblivious guests squabble over the exiting traffic jam. Nick's final impression of the evening captures Gatsby's distance from the community of his parties: "A sudden emptiness seemed to flow now from the windows and the great doors, endowing with complete isolation the figure of the host, who stood on the porch, his hand up in a formal gesture of farewell" (*GG* 56). The emptiness that separates Gatsby from the jazz world of his parties becomes, at this point, merely another part of his mystery. But the nature of the mystery is hinted at in Gatsby's public and private smile, and in Jordan's comment on the intimacy of large parties. For, as Nick learns from Jordan, Gatsby's parties are far from being ends in themselves. Rather they are, like his enormous house, his hydroplane, and his silk shirts, part of his monument to Daisy Fay, the woman he loves. Having lost her because he lacked wealth (Fitzgerald's persistent theme), Gatsby strives to win her back through displays of wealth, the greatest of which is his ostentatious house, which the narrator ironically calls "his ancestral home." Touring the vast edifice later with Nick and Daisy, Gatsby offers his own explanation for his parties:

> "That huge place *there*?" she cried pointing.
> "Do you like it?"
> "I love it, but I don't see how you live there all alone."
> "I keep it always full of interesting people, night and day. People who do interesting things. Celebrated people." (*GG* 91)

But it takes little reflection to realize that Gatsby's explanation of his parties is inadequate. He hardly finds his guests diverting or interesting; they do nothing to assuage his loneliness. Jordan reaches the true answer to the mystery when she asserts that Gatsby bought the house across the bay from the Buchanans and entertained lavishly on the hope that his parties would draw Daisy to him (*GG* 80). The parties are simply a means toward reaching Daisy, a way to find her and impress her. To Gatsby the lavish parties are incidental, merely one part of a five-year effort to win back the golden girl who rejected him for a millionaire. Nick connects the explanation with his first image of Gatsby, alone and trembling to embrace something in the darkness across the bay: "Then it had not been merely the stars to which he had aspired on that June night. He came alive to me, delivered suddenly from the womb of his purposeless splendor" (*GG* 79). The mystery dissolves and, with it, the parties; the true man takes shape when the purpose of his splendor is revealed. This end, the winning of Daisy, obviates the purposelessness that characterizes the true festive spirit. What purpose parties do serve in the larger cultural context—celebration, catharsis, building a community, triumphing over mortality—are all beyond the level of individual human aspiration. Gatsby's motives are utilitarian and underscore his alienation from his guests. The community of the party becomes inconsequential to the novel as the host's spiritual absence is explained. The explanation of the mystery of Gatsby's parties explains the enigma of Jay Gatsby himself.

The "purposeless splendor" of Nick's first Gatsby party is contrasted with the "peculiar quality of oppressiveness" of the party Tom and Daisy attend with Nick (*GG* 105). Just as when Gatsby shows Daisy his house and "revalue[s] everything . . . according to the measure of response it drew from her well-loved eyes" (*GG* 92), he values the party solely in terms of Daisy's response. And she doesn't like it. As Gatsby concludes, " 'She didn't have a good time' " (*GG* 110).

Gatsby's most lavish tribute to Daisy fails to win her heart. The reader may wonder why his party fails where his silk shirts succeeded. Perhaps an explanation lies in the disjunction between public and private values. Daisy's love for Gatsby has always been private, even secret, for in that private world his charm could be separated from his youthful poverty, and now, from his criminally gained wealth. The party is a public affair, which she attends with her husband. And her husband notably scoffs at the West Egg celebrities: "I was just thinking I don't know a soul here" (*GG* 106). Thus it is no surprise that Nick concludes that "except for the half-hour [Daisy had] been alone with Gatsby she wasn't having a good time" (*GG* 107).

Daisy's disappointment infects Nick as well as Gatsby and shows him another side to the party. He finds this affair different from Gatsby's others: "It stands out in my memory from Gatsby's other parties that summer. There were the same people, or at least the same sort of people, the same profusion of champagne, the same many-colored, many-keyed commotion, but I felt an unpleasantness in the air, a pervading harshness that hadn't been there before" (*GG* 105). Nick's "within and without" narrative versatility allows him to see the party with new eyes: "I was looking at it again, through Daisy's eyes. It is invariably saddening to look through new eyes at things upon which you have expended your own powers of adjustment" (*GG* 105). Nick begins to share Daisy's distaste for the party, and this allows Fitzgerald to compress the vulgarity and futility of the jazz age excitement into a single astounding passage: "[Daisy was] appalled by [West Egg's] raw vigor that chafed under the old euphemisms and by the too obtrusive fate that herded its inhabitants along a short-cut from nothing to nothing. She saw something awful in the very simplicity she failed to understand" (*GG* 108). This excerpt evokes Bede's swallow passage, which characterizes the festive brightness of life as an instant framed between two infinite reaches of darkness. Daisy penetrates to the emptiness of the party, or at least to the figure of death—that "too obtrusive fate"—that lurks behind the eating, drinking, and merriment. She wants her love for Gatsby free of the constraints of the earthly, the public, and the temporal. In contrast to Myrtle Wilson, who revels in the public excitement of her affair because "[she] can't live forever," Daisy wants to refuse mortality and embrace Gatsby in some world free not only of death but of Tom and her commitment to respectability. The parties disappoint her because they show how far from Gatsby's world she has grown and how dangerous a leap she must make if she wants to leave Tom for Gatsby.

The enormity of this evening's failure emerges in Gatsby's talk with Nick in the late hours of the night after the last of Gatsby's anonymous guests has departed: " 'I feel far away from her. . . . It's hard to make her understand.' " Nick assumes he means "understand the party" and asks: " 'You mean about the dance?' 'The dance?' He dismissed all the dances he had given with a snap of his fingers. 'Old sport, the dance is unimportant' " (*GG* 111). More than anyone else, Gatsby understands the insignificance of his parties. To him they are nothing at all, and his disdain emerges symbolically in the rubble of the party's aftermath as he paces "up and down a desolate path of fruit rinds and discarded favors and crushed flowers" (*GG* 111).

The parties are over. The next Saturday night "the lights in his house failed to go on," and, the narrator comments, "his career as Trimalchio was over" (*GG* 113).[9] As Nick summarizes: "the whole caravansary had fallen in like a card house at the disapproval in her eyes" (*GG* 114). From that final party onward, the movement of the book is decisively down-hill, an accelerating rush toward that "all too obtrusive fate," the death that awaits Gatsby and his illusions of capturing a mythic, romantic past.

Just as the central image of the first half of the book is Gatsby's enlivened mansion, so is the deserted house stripped of its superfi-cial vitality the central image of the second half. Against Gatsby's bril-liantly described parties is posed the overwhelming mood of the party being over. Although so many guests had been unable to find Gatsby, George Wilson (with Tom Buchanan's assistance) has little trouble find-ing Gatsby, and kills him. Wilson acts under the mistaken impression that he is shooting his wife's lover, not his wife's lover's rival. The mul-tiple ironies converge in this tragic "holocaust" (GG 163). The image of the antiparty continues as Nick calls the guests Gatsby never knew, trying to rouse a respectable crowd for Gatsby's funeral. Nick invites many of those who had been uninvited guests at the parties, and it is hardly surprising that they all refuse to come. The parties they attended bore no stamp of Gatsby's spirit; the guests never knew him and so the death of the absent host creates no vacancy in their lives.

Gatsby's father attends, bearing a photo of Gatsby's mansion "more real to him now than the house itself" (GG 173). In the pouring rain, the owl-eyed man joins Nick, Gatsby's father, and the loyal servants at Gatsby's final party. When Nick relates that no other of Gatsby's guests paid their respects, Owl-eyes responds: " 'Why, my God! they used to go there by the hundreds. . . . The poor son-of-a-bitch' " (GG 176). A fitting epitaph delivered, appropriately, by a nameless guest.

In the novel's final scene, a ghostly image of Gatsby's parties lingers on in the empty shell that was his home. The parties stand, in their crowning insignificance, for the grandeur, indeed the greatness, of Gatsby's single-minded illusion, "his incorruptible dream" that distanced him from "the whole damn bunch" (GG 155, 154). Nick offers the elegiac comment: "I spent my Saturday nights in New York because those gleaming, dazzling parties of his were with me so vividly that I could still hear the music and the laughter, faint and incessant, from his garden, and the cars going up and down his drive. One night I did hear a material car there, and saw its lights stop at his front steps. But I didn't investigate. Probably it was some final guest who had been away at the ends of the earth and didn't know that the party was over" (GG 181).

Tender Is the Night:
Plagued by the Nightingale

Like Jay Gatsby, the protagonist of *Tender Is the Night* is most prominent in his role as "host." Dick Diver's most characteristic role replicates Gatsby's most prominent, though finally unreal, public image. But unlike Gatsby, Dick Diver presides over a festive community that is often vital and always important as a setting for moments of individual crisis and revelation. "The whole damn bunch" of Gatsby's guests, who remain nameless and uncomprehending, become, in *Tender Is the Night*, a carefully sketched, memorable group of American expatriates whose interaction allows for the presentation of Dick and Nicole as socially shaped individuals. Fitzgerald depicts Dick Diver's marriage to Nicole Warren and its eventual dissolution against what he deemed a "background . . . in which the leisure class is at their truly most brilliant & glamorous." [10] This background "brilliance" is not proved inconsequential or superficial as it is in *Gatsby*. Instead, Dick Diver's "intricate destiny" remains bound up with the community he hosts and with his social role. As the reader learns more about Gatsby, the elaborate parties seem increasingly less important to Gatsby's essential character; on the other hand, Diver's role in the festive community changes with his character, always revealing significant aspects of his personal makeup. The parties in *Tender Is the Night* chronicle and explicate Dick's personal tragedy, and, in a broader sense, they reveal the power and danger contained in the festive world's promises of plenty and happiness.

In *Tender Is the Night* Fitzgerald presents a more complex analysis of the failure of personal and societal dreams. The book is more unwieldy and convoluted than the exquisitely structured *Gatsby* precisely because its hero has no "single dream," no informing mystery holding the key to his psyche. The style of *Tender Is the Night* suggests an impressionistic rendering of the irreducibility of life itself; it lacks the guiding, moralizing consciousness that provides the thematic continuity in *Gatsby*. *Tender Is the Night* is Fitzgerald's mature work, representing, in its complexities of characterization and narrative style, some degree of resolution to the conflicts that characterize his earlier fiction.

Part of the narrative power of *Tender Is the Night* arises from the impressionistic, *in medias res* opening that plunges the reader, like the naive and innocent Rosemary Hoyt, into the heart of the Divers' social milieu. The opening magic of the Divers' Riviera world and the initial portrayal of Dick's finely developed social skills enhance the poignancy of his dissolution and provide a basis for it.[11]

Tender Is the Night begins, as does *Gatsby*, with a careful delineation of social distinctions and boundaries. Beginning from Rosemary's viewpoint, we never doubt that we are reading a work in the tradition of the novel of manners. Consider the emphasis on natural and manmade borders in the first sentence: "On the pleasant shore of the French Riviera, about half way between Marseilles and the Italian border, stands a large, proud, rose-colored hotel" (*TN* 3). The action will begin on a shore— a natural border—located midway between a French town and the Italian border. The Americans in the novel will move among the cultures these manmade borders delineate. Even the hotel's rose color symbolizes the tension between extremes, the mixing of red and white, as well as suggesting the youthful bloom of Rosemary Hoyt. More explicit social boundaries appear when we view this beach through Rosemary's gaze a few paragraphs later. She observes how "each family possessed the strip of sand immediately in front of its umbrella" (*TN* 5). Beyond this observation of territorial behavior, Rosemary notes how the people on the beach are divided into two groups—the tanned ones under the beach umbrellas she has just described and fairer-skinned tourists beneath hand-parasols who "were obviously less indigenous to the place" (*TN* 5). Rosemary seats herself "between the dark people and the light," suggesting her role at the beginning, as a narrator both "within and without."

Though Fitzgerald presents the Divers' enchanted Riviera dinner party from Rosemary's point of view, he includes a few pages of introductory description that deliberately deviate from Rosemary's perspective. It is, perhaps, an awkward strategy, requiring a few paragraphs later the rather blatant introductory phrase, "To resume Rosemary's point of view."[12] But as much as Fitzgerald wants the reader to share Rosemary's innocent appraisal of Dick and Nicole's party, he finds it essential to preface the party with a scene that sketches its setting and intention. Giving the party is a creative as well as social act—what Rosemary judges "an act of creation different from any she had known" (*TN* 19)—and Fitzgerald presents the party as a structured work arising from deliberate intention.

In the brief diversion from "Rosemary's angle," (*TN* 25–28) Fitzgerald highlights the contrast between socially gregarious Dick and moody, independent Nicole. The afternoon before the party, Nicole walks through her garden, alone and self-sufficient. The tangled mass of flowers suggests decadence and overripeness, as does the abandoned wheelbarrow lying across a garden path "atrophied and faintly rotten." Walking through the rich blooms of her Mediterranean garden, Nicole wears an artificial camellia (*TN* 25). Tucked away in Nicole's garden is Dick's workhouse, a structure that will take on meaning only after the tension between the Warren money and the Diver ambition has developed. Dick emerges from his workhouse and addresses Nicole, ridiculously, through a megaphone. The absurd dramatic situation makes several points about Dick and Nicole's relationship. Dick and Nicole share strength and power but draw them from different sources: Nicole from her overripe dream garden and from the forceful serenity of her own voice emerging from solitude; Dick from the ascetic quarters of his workhouse and from the public flourish of his megaphone, one of his "many light mechanical devices" (*TN* 27).

Through his megaphone Dick announces his intentions for the party in a remarkable speech amplified by context as well as mechanical device: " 'I want to give a really *bad* party. I mean it. I want to give a party where there's a brawl and seductions and people going home with their feelings hurt and women passed out in the cabinet de toilette. You wait and see' " (*TN* 27). Indeed, the reader will discover all these promises fulfilled—though the seduction of Rosemary does not occur until years later. But beyond foreshadowing Nicole's collapse in the bathroom and McKisco's duel with Tommy Barban, this passage illuminates the violent energy inherent in parties. Nicole characterizes it as part of "[Dick's] excitement that swept everyone up into it," an "excitement about things [that] reached an intensity out of proportion to their importance, generating a really extraordinary virtuosity with people" (*TN* 27). This is a fine description of how a party arbitrarily heightens experience. In the observation that follows, the metaphor of violence recurs: "[Dick] sometimes looked back with awe at the carnivals of affection he had given, as a general might gaze upon a massacre he had ordered to satisfy an impersonal blood lust" (*TN* 27). The extremity of this simile recalls Caillois's assertion that warfare is the modern equivalent to festival, but suggests here, more specifically, that "carnivals of affection" exact a price by intensifying what is combative and potentially violent in the unleashed human spirit. Festive "excitement" is inherently ambivalent because of the variety of emotions freed in the release from the repression of everyday acceptable social behavior.

Dick expands on his motivation for wanting a "bad" party in a conversation with Rosemary at the party. He explains that the affair commemorates the end of the summer season, bringing it to a fittingly dramatic and cathartic conclusion: " 'Well, this is over—this part of the summer is over. . . . Maybe we'll have more fun this summer but this particular fun is over. I want it to die violently instead of fading out sentimentally— that's why I gave this party' " (*TN* 38). We should recognize here the celebration of death and resurrection characteristic of New Year's parties and wakes. As Bakhtin notes, festivity celebrates change and transition— process over remembrance, community over individual. Dick's desire for the season to die violently offers another version of the presence of death at the party: the artificial acceleration of threatening natural forces by the ritual process. Ritual enacts, symbolically and in a more temporally condensed form, the natural process of growth, death, and rebirth. Ideally, the ritual acceleration quickens the path from growth to death in order to minimize decay (or "fading away"). Ritual death—whether represented by the numbness of intoxication, the end of the party, or the parting of friends after the festivities—becomes release from the pain of dissolution. Keats's desire "to cease upon the midnight with no pain" suggests the festive attempt to extinguish decay. This motivation inspires the most evocative and successful social occasion in the novel and contrasts with the latter half of *Tender Is the Night*, which narrates Dick's decline and concludes with what Fitzgerald, following Conrad, termed a "dying fall." [13] The party in the Goldings' yacht later in the novel will symbolize the prolongation of decay; at the novel's outset, however, the more youthful and spiritually intact Dick Diver inspires a liberating version of ritual death in which the power of the moment of joy arises from its brevity.

Toward this moment of joyous union the party itself progresses. After a brief précis of Dick's social skills, the narrative jumps to the actual scene. Dick's abilities as host suggest a sincere attempt to synthesize individual and group; his manner toward the guests leads them to believe in their own distinction, what Fitzgerald aptly terms "the proud uniqueness of their destinies, buried under the compromises of how many years" (*TN* 28). Dick's politeness creates in others a confidence in that heightened sense of a true inner self, which Virginia Woolf also saw emerging at social gatherings. But this inner self is immediately plunged into the all-inclusiveness of Dick's "amusing world."

Upon Rosemary's entrance we resume her point of view. The first few paragraphs describe the party's radical difference from everyday life and demonstrate the process of transformation that marks the beginning of a party. Even the movie director, Earl Brady, seems to Rosemary to be metamorphosed, "as if his differentness had been put on at the gate" (*TN* 28). This positive awareness of artifice is implicit in "the intensely calculated perfection of Villa Diana" (*TN* 28), which suggests the inherently contradictory, yet invigorating, "planned spontaneity" of the social occasion. The arrival of the guests even seems to accelerate the setting of the sun and the coming of the festive kingdom of darkness: "While the first guests arrived bringing with them the excitement of the night, the domestic activity of the day receded past them gently, symbolized by the Diver children and their governess still at supper on the terrace" (*TN* 28). Fitzgerald uses the children as a dramatic (and literal) chorus ushering in the festive night; at Brady's request they sing "that song about 'Mon Ami Pierrot.'" The dramatic setting of the song suits both Dick and Nicole on one level, and the party as a whole on another. Suggesting a failed love affair in which both pen and candle are impotent, "Mon Ami Pierrot" locates its only hope in the opening of the door for both the love of God and, in a subsequent verse, the god of love. Appropriately, the song sketches a world where, as in the "Ode to a Nightingale," and as at the Villa Diana, there is no light except "*au clair de la lune*."[14] But through the festive figure of Pierrot, the moonlight takes on carnival as well as romantic significance.[15] The Divers, whatever their impotencies or lost fires, open their doors ("*ouvrez la porte*") to the community in hope of forging some connection under the spell of the moonlight. "'New friends,'" Dick remarks later, "'can often have a better time together than old friends'" (*TN* 31). "Mon Ami Pierrot" hints at a relation between failed love and failed community that combines with the imagery of moonlight to reinforce the image patterns of the novel. The singing here also heightens the sense of artifice and performance that help create a party's difference. Rosemary thinks: "On such a stage some memorable thing was sure to happen" (*TN* 29).

In this manner Fitzgerald sets the scene. What follows is a masterful blend of dialogue and description. By interrupting directly rendered dialogue with a more generalized narrative recounting that collapses time, Fitzgerald can include a great deal of actual dramatic presentation while still rendering the entire party scene in twelve pages.[16] Our sense of the party's nature comes largely from Rosemary's reflective and descriptive passages that set the dialogue in accurate temporal and scenic contexts. Often brief snatches of conversation are incorporated into these descriptive passages for illustrative purposes and to make the deliberate alternation more subtle. Fitzgerald is conscious of the multivocal potential of party scenes but resists or controls that potential. His maintaining of narrative control contrasts with the subversions of narrative authority we have seen connected with the presentation of festivity in Woolf and Joyce. Nevertheless, in the party's dominant scene, the dinner itself, Fitzgerald communicates more powerfully than anywhere else in his fiction the transcendent possibilities of celebration.

The first significant withdrawal from direct dialogue follows Nicole and Abe's conversation about sawing a waiter in half. Rosemary's reflection signals how much time has passed and how the party's mood has changed: "They had been at table half an hour and a perceptible change had set in—person by person had given up something, a preoccupation, an anxiety, a suspicion, and now they were only their best selves and the Divers' guests" (*TN* 32). In the phrase "their best selves" Fitzgerald echoes Woolf's affirmation of the authenticity inspired by a party's effervescent excitement. That parties bring out some shining best self, though an idea crucial to Woolf, is not common in Fitzgerald's treatment of parties. No other party scene in his novels suggests anything so positive about the interaction of self and community. We certainly do not see the best selves of Anthony and Gloria or Gatsby and Daisy at parties. This passage makes an important corollary point, however: these best selves are created at the expense of some individual identity; each person must give something up, put on "their best selves" to act the communal role of "guest." In giving up their cherished personal anxieties, the guests make a leap of faith—an action that requires effort and generosity: "So now they were all trying, and seeing this, Rosemary

liked everyone—except McKisco who had contrived to be the unassimi-
lated member of the party" (*TN* 32). Here the outsider is excluded, the
author implies, through his own unwillingness to believe in the powers
of the social occasion and not through a failure of the party community's
inclusiveness.

Indeed, a party, by its very nature, creates a community anew with
special temporary boundaries—such is its power to create a world. We
see the creation of a new world that affirms life in the scene's most remarkable passage, the mystical elevation of the dinner table. It provides
the key to Fitzgerald's festive vision:

> There were fireflies riding on the dark air and a dog baying on some
> low and far-away ledge of the cliff. The table seemed to have risen a
> little toward the sky like a mechanical dancing platform, giving the
> people around it a sense of being alone with each other in the dark
> universe, nourished by its only food, warmed by its only lights. And,
> as if a curious hushed laugh from Mrs. McKisco were a signal that
> such a detachment from the world had been attained, the two Divers
> began suddenly to warm and glow and expand, as if to make up to
> their guests, already so subtly assured of their importance, so flattered
> with politeness, for anything they might still miss from that country
> well left behind. Just for a moment they seemed to speak to every one
> at the table, singly and together, assuring them of their friendliness,
> their affection. And for a moment the faces turned up toward them
> were like the faces of poor children at a Christmas tree. Then abruptly
> the table broke up—the moment when the guests had been daringly
> lifted above conviviality into the rarer atmosphere of sentiment, was
> over before it could be irreverently breathed, before they had half
> realized it was there. (*TN* 34)

Fitzgerald cuts to the heart of what is celebrated at a party—"a sense of
being alone with each other in the dark universe, nourished by its only
food, warmed by its only lights." This both captures "detachment from
the world" and symbolizes the human condition. Indeed, we are alone
in the dark universe, and such inevitable solitude can be broken by our
communities when we celebrate food, light, and life together—the festive communion. The newly created world symbolizes in light and dark
the contrast between the richness of life and the omnipresence of death's

inevitability, a contrast with which we must always live, but which we experience in a powerful and unique way during transcendent moments at parties. Finally, this passage emphasizes the role of the Divers as hosts in creating this magical community. Speaking to everyone "singly and together" echoes, of course, Gatsby's private and public smile, as well as the manipulation of multivocal narrative possibilities. But here the friendliness and affection, and the party itself, are more than "successful gestures," because Dick and Nicole value the community in itself.

The transition from "conviviality into the rarer atmosphere of sentiment" again involves a loss of self, for conviviality means here pleasant feelings exchanged between individuals, while sentiment implies feelings shared. Though we are limited to Rosemary's point of view, the magic of the moment depends upon the assumption that the feeling belongs not strictly to her but to the group as a whole. Such a transcendent experience is, Fitzgerald implies, incapable of being sustained or subjected to introspection. Unlike the decadent cultivation of overripeness, it cannot be prolonged. Like the picture of life itself in Bede's swallow passage, the transcendence is fleeting; an instantaneous present, not a continual present, the moment is characterized by its freedom from consciousness of past and future. The experience enters real time when it is remembered: "But the diffused magic of the hot sweet South had withdrawn into them—the soft-pawed night and the ghostly wash of the Mediterranean far below—the magic left these things and melted into the two Divers and became part of them" (*TN* 35). The quality and value of this moment and the memory of it stand as a backdrop to the novel's picture of decline. Throughout the book the reader must return to this magical levitation to consider its value and substantiality. This transcendent experience appears similar to the "Already with thee" moment of the nightingale ode, and *Tender Is the Night* asks the same question with which the ode ends: "was it a vision, or a waking dream?"

At this moment in the party, Rosemary is "tolled back to her sole self" as Dick and Nicole disappear from the scene. The contained violence that the party also liberates begins to emerge. Violet McKisco announces she will go to the bathroom; later we learn that there she discovers something shocking, and her insistence on talking about it leads to the duel between Tommy Barban and McKisco. Only Dick's return suspends the grim mystery Tommy Barban's comment evokes: "It's inadvisable to comment on what goes on in this house" (*TN* 36). The community of the party is clearly breaking up, and the narrative focuses on Dick and Nicole's smooth handling of the guests' departures. The final tableau evokes the sadness of Dick and Nicole alone: "Down in the garden lanterns still glowed over the table where they had dined, as the Divers stood side by side in the gate, Nicole blooming away and filling the night with graciousness, and Dick bidding good-by to everyone by name. To Rosemary it seemed very poignant to drive away and leave them in their house. Again she wondered what Mrs. McKisco had seen in the bathroom" (*TN* 39). "Poignant" is crucial in this beautifully written passage. For against the shared sentiment of the party will the final emptiness between Dick and Nicole be measured so that it seems poignant, even, perhaps, tragic. What Violet McKisco sees in the bathroom is not merely evidence of Nicole's schizophrenia, but of the double nature of the Divers themselves, of their love and its shaky foundations, of Dick's sense of self and its equally fragile basis. The giving of one's self in which they have engaged exacts a high price.

The revelation of this price—the forces that will destroy the Divers' marriage and Dick's personal integrity—is suspended until much later in the book.[17] The tragic force of individual moral decline requires the successful portrayal of that individual's integrity and potential; the symbolic power of the failed party requires a successful depiction of the party's transcendent and unifying powers. A dynamism between the potential and the realized, the imagined and the inevitable, finds expression in the ambivalent personification of the night in both the novel and in Keats's ode from which the novel's evocative title is taken. The night receives profound attention not only at the party at the Villa Diana, but in the scene immediately following it, which begins, "It was a limpid black night, hung as in a basket from a single dull star" (*TN* 39). After a brief sleep Rosemary awakens at her hotel in a mystical night-shrouded mood. She is described as "suspended in the moonshine," and "cloaked by the erotic darkness" (*TN* 39). Because she is unable to sleep she ventures out into the courtyard where she learns from the weeping Luis Campion of the impending duel between McKisco and Barban. In the strange final hours of the night suspended between the excitement of the party and the chilly dawn, Abe North encounters Rosemary and remarks that she is "'plagued by the nightingale . . . probably plagued by the nightingale'" (*TN* 42).[18] This explicit reference to the nightingale (the only one in the book) fittingly recalls the title. The scene is tender: Rosemary's insomnia stems from the excitement of her first love, and her newfound feelings for Dick have blossomed under the night's power to nurture illusion. The mood of this scene and its association of beauty with the dreamlike quality of nighttime exemplify the tender incarnation of night in the novel.

William E. Doherty emphasizes this view of night imagery in his perceptive study, "*Tender Is the Night* and the 'Ode to a Nightingale.'" He argues that Fitzgerald's novel exploits a symbolic contrast between night and day: "Fitzgerald has divided his world into two parts—the night and the day. The day is reality, hard, harsh and vigorous; the night is illusion, tender, joyful, but devitalizing." Doherty supports this assertion with several scenes that suggest the night provides a welcome relief, "masking the ugliness of reality that the day exposes."[19] Doherty even associates the glare of the sun with Nicole's madness, pointing to the reason-destroying sun on the beach and the fierce afternoon sun at the Agri Fair where Nicole breaks down on the Ferris wheel. Undoubtedly, the dichotomy Doherty reveals is deliberate, but the role of nighttime in festivities and the ambivalent treatment of the tender night in Keats's ode suggest further significance. The night fosters illusion not only because it blurs the distinctions of the day but because it invites the creation of new, manmade distinctions. "Who would not be pleased at carrying lamps helpfully through the darkness?" questions Rosemary near the end of the Villa Diana party (*TN* 37). And indeed it is the spirit of illumination against darkness that brightens the Divers' party. Against the backdrop of night, the lighted up world becomes a stage, and the party a performance. Reality is curtained off, bordered in a way that the ever-receding horizon of day does not allow. By lighting a small section of the earth for a nighttime social gathering, we create a new world—smaller, more condensed and controlled than the vast community to which we belong, almost anonymously, by day.

At the same time that night shrinks the social world and the physical earth, it makes us conscious of the vastness in which our earth exists. When the stars and planets of the night sky are visible, we sense more profoundly the emptiness of space, what Joyce called "the apathy of the stars." Thus the dynamics of the primitive community gathered around the fire continue in the modern world of artificial light, for the darkness outside the circle of light—and the final annihilation it presages—remains equally frightening.

By emphasizing the evocative power of the night through the book's title and the party scene at the Villa Diana, Fitzgerald stresses the primitive, unchanging, ritualistic communion of the party—light in the darkness, life in the midst of death. And he underscores the liberating sense of difference that distances the artificially lighted performance in the night world from constant daytime toil, the endless marching towards the horizon of day. The festive world makes a worshipful and fearful offering to the night, which encloses its gatherings. But as much as festivity affirms night by taking it as the medium of human celebration, festivity also exists in opposition to the night. The ambivalent relationship to the night symbolically echoes the romantic ambivalence toward death, which is at once the enemy, sapping life of achievement or consummation, and the desired final embrace promising relief and an ultimate union closer to perfection than any imaginative state life offers. In Keats's ode, the bacchanalian revels of the sun-drenched south fade into a desire to "cease upon the midnight with no pain"; the numbing effects of intoxication foreshadow the darker loss of sensation death promises.

In their notes for a screenplay for *Tender Is the Night,* Malcolm and Margerie Bonner Lowry provide an interesting discussion of the threatening aspect of the night that Fitzgerald derived from Keats. Their argument concentrates on the lines that form the novel's epigraph (Fitzgerald omits the second and third lines):

> Already with thee! tender is the night,
> [And haply the Queen-Moon is on her throne,
> Clustered around by all her starry fays;]
> But here there is no light,
> Save what from heaven is with the breezes blown
> Through verdurous glooms and winding mossy ways.

The Lowrys suggest that Fitzgerald interprets these lines to mean the night provides no light save moonlight, which is equated with madness. "The night," the Lowrys write, "thus becomes a kind of absolute night which the moon has only made, or makes, darker."[20] Surely, the association between the moon and madness is more important to Fitzgerald than to Keats. The association of Nicole with the Villa Diana and the pointed omission of the Queen-Moon lines from the epigraph tie Nicole's breakdown in the bathroom at the party to the patterns of night imagery.

This image pattern suggested by the Lowrys also helps explain the ambivalence of Dick's role as host, for the night enchantment of the party is largely created by Dick, who radiates the light of his charm into the darkness. The association of Dick with the lamps carried helpfully through the darkness, and of Nicole with the moon, reinforces the earlier contrast between Dick's voice through the megaphone and Nicole's voice carrying naturally through the garden. The union of Dick and Nicole as hosts (epitomized in their habit of signing notes and invitations "Dicole") is a public joining of two very different natures. Nicole's light comes from a fierce inner strength finally inseparable from her madness; Dick's light comes from society, from his ability to illuminate while in the presence of others. Both are destined to vanish. And both forms of light are cast, finally, at the expense of their "sole selves." The Lowrys are correct in seeing that the novel underscores the grim conclusion that, in truth, "here there is no light." The party at the Villa Diana remains, throughout the book and in the reader's memory, a profoundly positive light in the darkness, yet it foreshadows the dark dissolution of self with which the novel will conclude.

The life of the party at the Villa Diana flows from Dick's exceptional social grace. The book emphasizes this clearly, perhaps even excessively. Dick sets guests at ease, promotes their self-confidence, charms individuals, times the stages of the party, and eases the awkwardness of departure. In the various scenes in part 1 following the party, Dick's social skills receive the dominant emphasis as he is shown to be the driving force who crystallizes one social occasion after another. Understanding Dick's social graces and why Fitzgerald foregrounds them prepares us for understanding Dick's social decline as it is portrayed through the flashback to his past and through his breakup with Nicole in the novel's present. Dick's decline grows out of his social self, not out of some dark, mysterious, private self.

We can share Rosemary's admiration of Dick's social mastery, just as we can finally appreciate the sincerity of Fitzgerald's dedication of the book: "To Gerald and Sara Murphy—Many Fêtes."[21] But while the Murphys were models for the public and positive side of Dick and Nicole, the Fitzgeralds themselves were models for the Divers' darker side. And the darker side of Dick's social ease emerges subtly from Rosemary's ebullient praises. Dick's own judgment of himself is even more revealing: "He knew, though, that the price of his intactness was incompleteness" (*TN* 117). Later when Baby Warren calls Dick's ability to " 'keep a party moving by just a little sentence or a saying here and there. . . . a wonderful talent,' " Dick calmly responds that " 'It's a trick' " (*TN* 216). Dick's self-appraisal is not mere modesty, false or otherwise; it is his somber realization that in seeking his fulfillment so thoroughly through kindling love and excitement in others, in that total abnegation of self to the hope of salvation in communal festivity, he has lost his own capacity for love and happiness. Like the narrator in the nightingale ode, Dick has become "too happy in thine happiness," his heart aching for the joy he sees around him.

Dick is almost entirely subsumed in his role as host. Standing beside his little workhouse making proclamations through the megaphone, Dick appears between his two incarnations—the public world of the megaphone and his private study. Yet even his treatise *A Psychology for Psychiatrists*, on which he expends his private labors in his tiny hut, shouts out the message the book proclaims to Dick's dying selfhood: "Physician, heal thyself!" As doctor as well as host, Dick has become excessively other-directed; and Dick's marriage to his patient symbolizes the confusion between his public and private lives. An intense craving for the love of others has rendered him incapable of personal love, for he has abandoned the sense of self from which such love must spring. Dick Diver—host, social general, psychiatrist-husband—locates his identity almost exclusively in social situations that bring his skills alive, as in *To the Lighthouse* where Mrs. Ramsay, bereft of even a first name, finds her existence most sharply defined as wife, mother, and hostess. But where she finds in her introspection a wedge-shaped core of darkness that offers strength and unity to her own conception of selfhood, Dick Diver finds only emptiness and need.

The disintegration of Dick Diver's life and marriage remains at the heart of *Tender Is the Night* in spite of the greater emphasis given his life before the collapse. Since the book's publication, the controversy over its artistic success has focused on whether or not Fitzgerald's portrayal of Dick's breakdown is convincing.[22] Dick's tragedy lacks, as I have suggested, the narrow, private and obsessive quality of Gatsby's. His is the romantic tragedy of insatiability, what Harold Bloom calls the romantic paradox in which "the taking famishes the receiver."[23] This tragedy is developed on the public level of failed festivity and suggests, as *Gatsby* does, the failure of a certain quality of dreams. This romantic paradox and its manifestation in the corruption of human aspiration emerges to a large extent through parties that explicate Dick's decline and chronicle his dissolution.

Dick's collapse reflects the romantic sources of Fitzgerald's tragic sense. In Fitzgerald's vision of life, tragedy lies not in the idealistic hero's inability to attain his goals, but rather in the inability to be satisfied by attaining them. As in the nightingale ode, the rapture of "Already with thee!" remains inescapably momentary; the intensity of the imaginative leap leads only to darkness and uncertainty. The dreamwork of the imagination is circumscribed by the inevitability of death and the limitations and compromises forced by reality. The idealist's tragic stature comes from the magnitude of his visionary goals, and thus that tragic stature is inseparable from inevitable dissatisfaction. Lionel Trilling describes this aspect of Fitzgerald's tragic heroes: "The tragic hero . . . is destroyed by the very thing that gives him spiritual status and stature. . . . From Fitzgerald's two mature novels, *The Great Gatsby* and *Tender Is the Night*, we learn about a love—perhaps it is peculiarly American— that is destructive by reason of its very tenderness."[24]

The significant experiences and achievements of Dick's life—his marriage to Nicole, his success as a psychiatrist, his romantic affair with Rosemary, his triumph as host par excellence—all fail to remain worthwhile to him once they are achieved. Referring to an earlier draft of *Tender Is the Night*, Fitzgerald wrote that, "Unlike *The Beautiful and Damned* the break-up will be caused not by flabbiness but really tragic forces such as the inner conflicts of the idealist and the compromises forced upon him by circumstance."[25] By the final version the idealism is itself shaped by circumstances; the only dreams worth having are destined never to satisfy the dreamer.

In arguing that the romantic paradox of consummation applies to Dick's ultimate inability to find happiness with either Nicole or Rosemary, it may seem we are straying far from the relation of failed festivity to Dick's decline. Yet these personal failures exemplify the overriding conflict between the festive and comic spirit of communal "replace-ability" and the individuality of heroic or tragic destiny.[26] Fitzgerald, in the carefully orchestrated scenes that dramatize Dick's emotions toward Rosemary and Nicole, significantly places striking and clear images of carnival. The complexity of two scenes in particular—Nicole's break-down after Rosemary and Dick's passion is interrupted by the dying man, and Rosemary and Dick's reunion and only sexual experience—dem-onstrate how effectively Fitzgerald interweaves the public and private aspects of Dick's destiny.

The first scene forms the conclusion to book 1. Dick is in Rosemary's hotel room, two doors down the corridor from Nicole. Their mood is a mixture of passion and the awareness that they are unable to act on it. The mixed mood is such that Rosemary in making her "most sin-cere" comment to Dick stresses their very insincerity: " 'Oh, we're such *actors*—you and I' " (*TN* 105). The refreshing honesty contributes to the tenderness of the scene. But all those emotions are shattered when Abe North stumbles in and moments later a wounded black man, Peterson, enters the room and collapses on Rosemary's bed. The strange situation becomes a perfect vehicle for showing Dick's role in relation to crises in general and to Rosemary and Nicole in particular. He immediately takes charge, carries the body into the hall, strips the bedspread, and has Nicole wash it in their bathtub. Returning to Rosemary's room, Dick, in his characteristic pose, straightens out things crooked or confused, and "smooth[s] back the grain of the plush floor rug" (*TN* 111).

Dick's smooth efforts at restoring calm, while successful in dealing with the police and the hotel, do not succeed in hiding from Nicole the true violation that has taken place. That the hotel manager is named McBeth rather blatantly calls our attention to the theme of blood that can-not be washed off. Indeed, the scene concludes by focusing on Nicole as she attempts to clean the bedspread. The paragraph in which Fitzgerald switches the focus from Rosemary to Nicole through Dick is a brilliantly crafted manipulation of point of view and imagery: "She adored him for saving her—disasters that could have attended upon the event had passed in prophecy through her mind; and she had listened in wild wor-ship to his strong, sure, polite voice making it all right. But before she reached him in a sway of soul and body his attention focussed on some-thing else: he went into the bedroom and toward the bathroom. And now Rosemary, too, could hear, louder and louder, a verbal inhumanity that penetrated the keyholes and the cracks in the doors, swept into the suite and in the shape of horror took form again" (*TN* 112). Rosemary's adoration and wild worship of Dick, the social genius who makes everything right, is building to an embrace with him when the sentence rhythm is broken by "but" and the explicit shift of Dick's attention. Dick moves toward Nicole, through bedroom and bathroom, passing through stages of increasing privacy, while Nicole's insane shrieking encounters Rosemary in reverse; Nicole's verbal inhumanity "penetrates" the narrow (and, no doubt, symbolic) keyhole and fills with horror the room in which Rosemary stands.

Nicole accosts Rosemary in her maddened state: "Nicole knelt beside the tub swaying sidewise and sidewise. 'It's you!' she cried, '—it's you come to intrude on the only privacy I have in the world—with your spread with red blood on it. I'll wear it for you—I'm not ashamed, though it was such a pity. On All Fools Day we had a party on the Zurichsee, and all the fools were there, and I wanted to come dressed in a spread but they wouldn't let me—'" (*TN* 112). This passage succeeds on several levels. First, it is clearly sexual. Nicole is right to see Rosemary intruding on her world. And undoubtedly she sees in the bloodied bedspread her own loss of virginity when her father raped her, and her current loss of Dick to Rosemary's virginal charms. The link between sex and violent aggression, which she has tried to escape through Dick, is renewed. On another level this scene reveals Nicole's ambivalent relationship to Dick's festive world. She recalls an All Fools Day party that she wanted to attend dressed in a spread. The mysterious "they" is, of course, those in charge at the asylum, and this explains the irony behind "all the fools were there." Partitioned from the world as both victim and deviant, Nicole inverts her relationship to the topsy-turvy world of festival. It is as if she is denied access to her own world.

The carnival references in this scene form a direct link to Nicole's subsequent breakdown on the Ferris wheel at the Agri Fair. Nicole claims her wild hysteria is caused by seeing Dick eye a young girl. Though this accusation is purely invention, its parallel with the earlier scene with Rosemary reminds us of the grain of truth at the core of Nicole's delusion: "'It's always a delusion when I see what you don't want me to see'" (*TN* 190). But beyond this truth lies the inescapability of Nicole's madness. She remains a victim, inheriting from her father not only the fortune of an industrial empire that conquered a nation but also the scars from the brutality and lust that subjugated her as a child.

Inescapability provokes hysteria on the Ferris wheel, a likely symbol for the destruction of individuality by the eternal cycle. The ouroboric regeneration of the wheel, with its cyclical counterpart in seasonal festivals and its carnival counterpart in Ferris wheels, can be profoundly positive, but to the individual trapped in it, and particularly to Nicole, alienated from festivity by her position as insane outcast, it can be threatening. There is a horror not only in death but in the vision of an ever-changing perpetual community, which implies a devaluation of individual importance. Just as the inversion of the Ferris wheel strips the outcast Consul in *Under the Volcano* of the few material possessions that link his identity to society (his passport, his pocket money, etc.), so too does the incident on the wheel at the Agri Fair symbolize the community's rejection of Nicole. The festive world exacts its price, especially when it becomes the only vehicle with which to conquer alienation. The love that connects Nicole and Dick has been weakened by the personal emptiness of host and doctor roles that have swallowed Dick Diver. For them both festivity threatens destruction, metamorphosing from positive celebration and purgation to a nightmarish Ferris wheel spinning eternally into darkness and madness.[27]

After the incident with the dying man, Rosemary and Dick part, not to see each other again for four years. Dick's reunion with Rosemary in Rome, as he returns from his father's funeral in America, most dramatically illustrates his decline, "the taking famishing the receiver." When Dick and Rosemary's passion first bloomed, it could not be fulfilled. Now that it can, the initial enthusiasm has waned. The scene of their reunion is cloaked in images of decadence, decline, and nostalgia. Rosemary is filming "The Grandeur that Was Rome," and the entire Roman setting emphasizes lost greatness. Fitzgerald shared Joyce's judgment that Rome was like "a man who lives by exhibiting to travellers his grandmother's corpse."[28] In this setting Dick dwindles to human proportion in the act of reaching out for emotional contact in a form not certified by the social role of host. In romantic terms that echo the fleeting union characterized in the nightingale ode, Rosemary perceives Dick fading in front of her: "A moment had come and somehow passed. For three years Dick had been the ideal by which Rosemary measured other men and inevitably his stature had increased to heroic size. She did not want him to be like other men, yet here were the same exigent demands, as if he wanted to take some of herself away, carry it off in his pocket" (*TN* 211). Fitzgerald, of course, has written this scene before, with the sexual roles reversed— it is the pattern of Gatsby and Daisy's reunion. Love, Fitzgerald suggests, must inevitably partake of disappointment, for without illusion there exists no passion, and all that the sentimental may deem tragic is revealed as melodrama.[29]

And yet the compromises of life involve the readjustment occasioned by fading dreams. Dick and Rosemary take a romantic walk and return to consummate their four-year-old, withering passion. Fitzgerald could hardly be more specific in using the language of decline: "Dick and Rosemary had luncheon at the Castelli dei Caesari, a splendid restaurant in a high-terraced villa overlooking the ruined forum of an undetermined period of the decadence. Rosemary took a cocktail and a little wine, and Dick took enough so that his feeling of dissatisfaction left him. Afterward they drove back to the hotel, all flushed and happy, in a sort of exalted quiet. She wanted to be taken and she was, and what had begun with a childish infatuation on a beach was accomplished at last" (*TN* 213). But that infatuation has become, we have seen, a mere "romantic memory": tragic dissatisfaction resides in attaining one's goals and finding them incapable of satisfying, incapable of investing life with meaning.

Rosemary and Dick meet once more, only to quarrel. Dick challenges her other relations with men and Rosemary can only reply truthfully, in refusing to compare them, that " 'you never know how you once felt' " (*TN* 219). Even the romantic memory refuses to linger. In the final words they exchange, Dick and Rosemary demonstrate the connection between their own emotional disappointment and the larger issues of their own happiness and fulfillment. Dick concludes: "I guess I'm the Black Death. . . . I don't seem to bring people happiness anymore" (*TN* 219).

Stripped of his infatuation with Rosemary, Dick walks through Rome past "the house where Keats had died." "Rome," Dick concludes, "was the end of his dream of Rosemary" (*TN* 220). As in Keats's nightingale ode, all that remains of ecstasy is confused memory, an uncertainty about whether the past experience can continue to bear value in the present.

The scene that follows in which Dick and Collis Clay get increasingly drunk and obnoxious in a Roman cabaret, and in which Dick wildly accosts a taxi driver and then strikes a policeman, symbolizes the extent of his dissolution. Drink, which had served as sacrament and as Bacchus's chariot in the book's opening scene on the beach, has degenerated to grim fortification in the tryst with Rosemary and now to obliviating narcotic in Dick's Roman debauch. Unsatisfied by the "tricks" that created his social success, Dick has lost those skills as well. The blessing of wine has become a curse, the passion of love a disappointment, and the purpose and direction of his life an uncertain haze colored by despair. Dick's Zurich "illusions of eternal strength and health" are far behind.

"I am glad you are happy," Fitzgerald wrote his daughter, "but I never believe much in happiness."[30] Dick Diver's personal decline is pictured, however, in terms of his growing inability to bring others happiness, which, in turn, given Dick's highly social nature, leads to his own unhappiness. Yet Dick's decline is also a loss of integrity, as in Frau Gregorovius's pronouncement, "Dick is no longer a serious man," (*TN* 241). Fitzgerald also offered his daughter advice on the topic of seriousness: "I think that despite a tendency to self-indulgence you and I have some essential seriousness that will manage to preserve us."[31] These qualities of happiness and seriousness are the coordinates of Fitzgerald's mapping of the self in society; they animate his vision of the human.

Understanding Fitzgerald's view of the dynamic relation between seriousness and happiness renders accessible his linking of the failure of Dick Diver, *homme épuise,* to a larger failure of cultural aspirations. Maria DiBattista discusses this tension between the festive life and seriousness —or what she calls "forbearance." She suggests that Fitzgerald equates "the decadence of post-war society with the unforbearing spirit of carnival." Thus, in reading the opening party scene, DiBattista suggests that "Rosemary Hoyt . . . is duped by the surface good cheer prevailing at the Villa Diana."[32] For DiBattista happiness defined in the festive, communal sense is at odds with individual seriousness or forbearance. While this tension is certainly at work in the conflict between Dick's public and personal lives, I think DiBattista's position neglects somewhat the affirmative aspects of festival: "The extended holiday taken by the postwar society argues a more pervasive *ubi sunt:* a goodbye to a belief in the privileged destiny of an "elect" or incorruptible self. In [*Tender Is the*

Night, The Sun Also Rises, and *USA*], carnival culminates with the destruction of once intact personality."[33] Yet we must remember Fitzgerald's warning that "the price of intactness was incompleteness." The failure of the dream of an incorruptible and intact self is inevitable. For Fitzgerald seriousness remains a precondition for happiness, even though such happiness is doomed to be but fleeting ecstasy. Both seriousness and happiness depend upon an innocence and an "epic grandeur"—a willingness to aspire to greatness combined with a willingness to give up the private, tragic self to a warm, participatory social self. The social self that Gatsby only pretended to, but that Dick Diver actually aspired to, is not without value.

Lionel Trilling helps illuminate Fitzgerald's treatment of pleasure as a goal in life, suggesting in his essay, "The Fate of Pleasure," that one of the characteristics of modernity is the loss of belief in pleasure as a moral end and its replacement by a cult of "unpleasure." Trilling cites Keats as the foremost poet of sensual pleasure and also as the prime evidence of the problematics of pleasure: "Keats, then, may be thought of as the poet who made the boldest affirmation of the principle of pleasure and also as the poet who brought the principle of pleasure into the greatest and *sincerest* doubt."[34] Though Trilling focuses on Freud and Dostoyevsky as modern exponents of the decline of pleasure as a worthy end to human endeavor, his observations are relevant to Fitzgerald and particularly Fitzgerald's use of Keats. Like Keats, Fitzgerald draws power as much from his sympathetic portrait of the sensual and earthly as from his awareness of pleasure's final inability to satisfy. Trilling argues that society has come to perceive a conflict between the ideal of pleasure and those "psychic energies [that] are a means of self-definition and self-affirmation."[35] This formulation helps explain Dick Diver's decline in terms of his very skill at extracting pleasure from social occasions; it explains how, culturally, the goal of pleasure involves a loss of authentic selfhood. But Fitzgerald does not begin with the "adversary" assumption that the pursuit of pleasure is self-denying. In fact, Fitzgerald's life and art echo Keats's poetry: not believing in happiness is the conclusion of a long process of tragic disillusionment that can take place only if life itself is pursued in good faith. The tragedy of life's failures is predicated upon the intensity of desires. The moment of frozen time—the always-desiring lovers on the Grecian urn, the prolonged midnight of "Already with thee"—eludes the timebound hero, whose life must wane past dis-illusionment into decline. But finally Fitzgerald, like Keats, is the poet of the illusion, the weaver of the dreams of pleasure, as surely as he is the chronicler of those dreams' collapse.

Though Dick's inability to love comes in part from his loss of self (in-separable from the development of his fine social skills), it also comes from the American Dream set in the context of postwar Europe. The culture-specific manifestation of Dick's tragedy is best explained by Edwin S. Fussell: "The man of imagination, fed on the emotions of romantic wonder, is tempted and seduced and (in this case, nearly) de-stroyed by that American dream which customarily takes two forms: the escape from time and the materialistic pursuit of a purely hedonistic happiness."[36] We have seen how these aspects of the American Dream form the core of Fitzgerald's festive vision. Fitzgerald also stresses the importance of dealing with death's effect on earthly pleasure and with preserving for as long as possible the capacity for seriousness and hap-piness. One way to escape time is to have things die violently—ritually or literally. But the fancy will not cheat so well, and decadent prolonga-tion results. So too does the cynical yet desperate quest for happiness outlast the capability of enjoying the ecstatic moment. The fulfillment of this corruption of festival time and the dream of happiness occurs, of course, at a party—the party at the Golding yacht that forms the ironic counterpart to the dinner at the Villa Diana.

The scene begins with Dick and Nicole at dinner, the facade of their marriage crumbling in their increasingly frank and bitter conversation. For the first time Nicole confronts the reality of Dick's emotional collapse.

> "Some of the time I think it's my fault—I've ruined you."
> "So I'm ruined, am I?" he inquired pleasantly.
> "I didn't mean that. But you used to want to create things—now you seem to want to smash them up." (*TN* 267)

Nicole's observation encapsulates Dick's social decline from the state Mary North later sums up as " 'Everybody loved you' " (*TN* 314) to what Rosemary now hears in fashionable gossip: " 'He's not received any-where anymore' " (*TN* 287). This reversal is dramatized in the novel's last party. Dick and Nicole go impulsively at Dick's vehement suggestion: " 'See that boat out there? . . . We'll go out there now and ask the people

on board what's the matter with them. We'll find out if they're happy' "
(*TN* 268). The happiness of others, which he had once tried to create, he
views now as a rebuke, a challenge, and also as a reminder of his own
abandonment of the quest.

The party on board presents the social world that has succeeded
Dick's, the new clan of the summer Riviera following the trends he and
Nicole have inaugurated. Fashionable, shallow decadence in its own
decay dominates the description. The boat itself, like the frantic, continual partying of the era between the wars, is "constantly bound upon a
romantic voyage that was not dependent upon actual motion" (*TN* 268).
Golding, the host, seems a gigantic, less refined, version of Dick; he's
implicitly (though unfavorably) compared to Dick in a reference to "his
huge bulk, which transmitted his will as through a gargantuan amplifier"
(*TN* 271 [recalling Dick's megaphone]). The second generation of American and English tourists or expatriates appears through Nicole's eyes as
made up of "fierce neurotics, pretending calm, liking the country only
in horror of the city, of the sound of their own voices which had set the
tone and pitch" (*TN* 270). The kingpin of the crowd is the Lady Caroline
Sibly-Biers whose name (a sybil upon a bier) suggests Eliot's epigraph to
The Waste Land. She appears "fragile, tubercular—it was incredible that
such narrow shoulders, such puny arms could bear aloft the pennon of
decadence, last ensign of the fading empire" (*TN* 271). Decadence has
decayed, as it inevitably will.

Dick's interaction, primarily with Lady Sibly-Biers, shows how entirely
his social skills have deserted him. Next to Lady Caroline he appears
weak yet strident: "His usually ruddy face was drained of blood; he
talked in a dogmatic voice" (*TN* 271). His perceptions are true enough
when he asserts, " 'It's all right for you English, you're doing a dance
of death,' " but his sense of tact and grace is seriously lacking (*TN* 271).
Dick appears drunk and is clearly out-of-step with the party. When the
rest of the party leave the table he "remain[s] in his seat wearing an odd
expression" and when he speaks, his voice betrays "a harsh ineptness"
(*TN* 272). The transformation from the Dick Diver of book 1 could not be
more complete.

After his failure at the party, Dick retreats to solitude on the deck,
apparently contemplating suicide. " 'It'd be a good setting to jump overboard,' " Dick remarks in a bland version of Keats's "now more than

ever." Nicole, sensing his mood, grabs his hand in what will be the last gesture tying her fate to his: "All right, she would go with him—again she felt the beauty of the night vividly in one moment of complete response and abnegation—all right, then—" (*TN* 273–74). But Dick's destiny allows no easy cessation of the pain of existence. Midnight has passed, and the pain will continue. As they drive back from the party, Dick nods off to sleep against the background of "the constant carnival at Juan les Pins where the night was musical and strident in many languages" (*TN* 275). The contradiction of "constant" and "carnival" reaches to the heart of the decadence in Dick and his society. It echoes the horror of the vision of eternity associated with the Ferris wheel, and prepares for Fitzgerald's concluding his story not with a violent denouement as in *Gatsby* but with the "dying fall."

Described as "the last hope of a decaying clan," Dick literally comes full circle, returning to the Villa Diana and the beach. Nicole senses the poignancy of the return and renders a perceptive tribute to the forever unrecoverable: "Probably it was the beach he feared, like a deposed ruler secretly visiting an old court. She had come to hate his world with its delicate jokes and politenesses, forgetting that for many years it was the only world open to her. Let him look at it—his beach, perverted now to the tastes of the tasteless; he could search it for a day and find no stone of the Chinese Wall he had once erected around it, no footprint of an old friend" (*TN* 280). His creations gone, his boundaries erased, Dick suffers a further humiliation when his attempts at youthful stunts on water skis fail. He gruffly acknowledges his own dissolution, concluding: " 'The manner remains intact for some time after the morale cracks' " (*TN* 285).

What follows is the moving description of Nicole's liberation—her refusal to continue "play[ing] planet to Dick's sun" (*TN* 289)—and the scene with Dick, Nicole, and Tommy Barban, in which Dick, half-shaved at the barber's, sits between the other two. Afterward, the marital split accomplished, Nicole watches Dick walk away in a passage that clearly echoes Marlow's final view of Jim in *Lord Jim*: "Her eyes followed his figure until it became a dot and mingled with the other dots in the summer crowd" (*TN* 311). In a marvelous last scene Dick again returns to the beach before leaving to practice medicine in America. Mary North challenges him: " 'All people want is to have a good time and if you make them unhappy you cut yourself off from nourishment.' " Dick responds by asking, " 'Have I been nourished?' " (*TN* 313). What Mary North says is true enough, but the response from the depths of Dick Diver's depleted self reveals how elusive the final fulfillment to be derived from community remains. Whatever dreams we invent, neither our friends nor our lovers can deliver us from disappointment and death. The conversation and the religious imagery of the scene suggest a multivalence to Dick's role as "host": its social meaning teeters between a religious meaning (as vehicle to communion) and a biological one (as host for parasites). Yet Dick's final gesture is to bless, though feebly, the grounds of his sacrament and the spirit of his quest: "He raised his right hand and with a papal cross he blessed the beach from the high terrace" (*TN* 314). Fitzgerald's festive vision is inseparable from his tragic sensibility, and yet it does not devalue festivity, individual dreams, or the dreamer. It does criticize a world in which the shape of human aspirations is corrupted, and it focuses on the pain in realizing that however tender the night, it offers, finally, only darkness.

The role of festivity in completing the psychological portraits of Dick and Nicole brings together the various avatars of the party in Fitzgerald's oeuvre: image of an age, model of communal dissolution and decadence, vehicle for individual transcendence. It is in the party scene, more than anyplace else, that Fitzgerald can image a reconciliation of romantic individualism and the social vision of the novelist. The successful transcendence of the Villa Diana party stands at one extreme of Fitzgerald's vision of community; the failed parties—from "The Broken Lute" to Gatsby's hollow offerings and the Goldings' yacht—constitute the inevitable corollary. The thematic extremes of festivity parallel Fitzgerald's stylistic struggles with individual and community as narrative poles. His resolution of that struggle in *Tender Is the Night*, the delicate balance of narrative voices and dramatic scenes, finally resists the openness of a carnivalized multivocal narrative. Fitzgerald's unique place in modernism emerges precisely from this festive tension that reflects the collision of novelistic traditions and modes.

4. Dark Visions of the Bright Young Things

PARTIES IN WAUGH AND GREEN

"What I always wonder, Kitty dear,
is what they actually *do* at these parties
of theirs. I mean, *do* they . . . ?"
—*Vile Bodies*

"This is a rum thing this party.
And they call it pleasure, eh?"
—Thompson in *Party Going*

merican jazz age fiction of the twenties focused more exclusively on the era as a social phenomenon. In Fitzgerald's best fiction, however, the portrayal of the younger generation is always a part of a larger tragic vision: Fitzgerald's society was his means and his milieu, mere description of it not his artistic end. But a more essentially satiric focus on jazz age society emerges in works such as Carl Van Vechten's *Parties*, the main characters of which, Dave and Rilda Westlake, are modeled on Scott and Zelda. As the title indicates, the narrative satirizes a social set whose life is driven by parties, inevitably overwhelmed by them. Van Vechten's novel illustrates a social self-consciousness typical of the literary use of parties in the period between the wars: the party-going of a particular social set becomes the specific subject and satirical target of the entire work.

Prominent as this self-consciousness was in America, it was even more characteristic of England, where the rising postwar literary generation knew each other from the close quarters of public schools, Oxford, and the narrow realm of London society. Many of the prominent writers of this postwar Oxford school—Evelyn Waugh, Henry Vincent Yorke (Henry Green), Aldous Huxley, Anthony Powell—wrote novels that focused explicitly on parties and the "bright young things" who attended them.[1] Several other luminaries of this age wrote novels depicting the antics of the younger generation: Nancy Mitford, Stella Gibbons, Cyril Connolly, Dorothy Sayers. Rather than attempt to survey themes or make broad comparisons between these writers, I would like to discuss two works that concentrate on the parties of the time and still retain literary force and emotional power: Waugh's *Vile Bodies* (1930) and Green's *Party Going* (1938). These novels represent two extremes of this generations's self-caricature: Waugh's biting, controlled satire—terse, witty, and almost unforgiving; Green's equally dark but less satirical vision of the dynamics of sociability. Both novels offer a perspective on literary style and social fashion between the wars in its particularly British incarnation. Though affinities exist with the American fiction of the time, these works present a vision of a society shaped by the First World War's transformation of Edwardian England, a transformation that mingled a sense of sophistication with an awareness of entering a new and frightening age. For both Waugh and Green the social entertainments of their generation offer a rich literary subject and inspire innovative techniques for presenting images of the modern condition.

Evelyn Waugh's *Vile Bodies*

Modernity, more than youth per se, forms the subject of Evelyn Waugh's satire of the "bright young things" of London in the twenties. *Vile Bodies* describes the frenetic parties of the English decadence between the wars, much as *The Beautiful and Damned* treats American decadence of the same period. But in Waugh the scathing, satirical indictment engulfs all he sees as modern in life, and the novel culminates in an apocalyptic and prescient vision of "the biggest battlefield in the history of the world" (*VB* 314). The remarkable progression from satirized parties to the desolate expanses of Armageddon occupies a unique place in the treatment of decadence and in the literary use of parties:

Waugh's morbid yet liberating humor offers a fresh vision of the party in twentieth-century literature.

Waugh's fiction begins with a decadent party, on the first page of his first novel, *Decline and Fall*, "dinner, three years ago [in which] a fox had been brought in a cage and stoned to death with champagne bottles."[2] *Vile Bodies* continues this treatment of eccentric celebration; its parties explicate a class, a generation, and a society. Waugh's humor dissects the youthful celebrations of the London social scene and reveals deadly stasis behind apparently constant activity, ennui behind chipper amusement, and sordid death behind lighthearted gaiety.

In his "narrative of 'decadence' in England after 1918," *Children of the Sun*, Martin Green chronicles the generation Waugh treats in his fiction, following them from Oxford in the early twenties (Waugh's subject in *Decline and Fall*) to London in the late twenties (the subject of *Vile Bodies*). Green describes a cult of youth, the Sonnenkinder, emerging in England between the wars, flowering in a period conducive to aestheticism and congenial to the types of the dandy, the rogue, and the naïf. "England as a whole, and especially London, was itself in the grip of the pleasure principle during the 1920's," Green writes, citing among other things the growing popularity of cocktail parties (either invented or imported from America by Alec Waugh), and bring-your-own or "bottle parties."[3] Green provides valuable historical details including a list of actual parties in 1928 and 1929 that served as models for the "such a lot of parties" at the heart of *Vile Bodies*. He mentions various forms of fancy dress parties and masquerade parties (including affairs centered around themes of sailors, circuses, cowboys, or "homosexual lovers through the Ages"), as well as Brian Howard's twenty-fourth birthday party, which is revealingly titled "The Great Urban Dionysia."[4] Martin Stannard, though he disputes Green's classifications of "dandy" and "aesthete," confirms the dominance of parties in the London social scene of the late twenties; he mentions specific affairs titled the "Party Without End" and a "Second Childhood Party" in which guests attended in baby clothes.[5] These wild affairs of the "bright young people" dominated the London gossip columns and provided the satirist Waugh with the raw material of his fiction. But by broadening its satirical target to include all of the society, indeed, all of civilization, *Vile Bodies* stands apart from other fiction of the time that lampooned the social scene. Waugh combines social satire with a broader wasteland vision by tying his depictions of parties to other prominent accoutrements of the modern age—telephones, automobiles, airplanes, motion pictures—and by refusing to provide any alternative vision to that offered by the frenetic parties in *Vile Bodies*.

The titles of Waugh's three great early works—*Decline and Fall*, *Vile Bodies*, and *A Handful of Dust*—adumbrate the seriousness of his dark vision of corrupted festivity. Playing on Gibbon's chronicle of the Roman Empire's demise, *Decline and Fall* suggests the crumbling of an empire that already pales by comparison with Rome. At the start of Waugh's fiction, decadence is already in decline. Similarly, Waugh's allusion to *The Waste Land* in the title of his third major work emphasizes not only the wasteland vision but also the sense that man is reduced to a handful of dust because he is alienated from meaningful tradition and stripped of the forward-looking dream of progress: "Your shadow at morning striding behind you / Or your shadow at evening rising to meet you" (*The Waste Land*, 11. 27–28). In this hollow present man becomes mere dust, reduced to a strictly physical being; he becomes a "vile body." (The phrase has a biblical source: "[Jesus Christ] shall change our vile body, that it may be fashioned into His glorious body" [Phil. 3:21]). As Yossarian realizes in *Catch-22*, the novel following the war that *Vile Bodies* foreshadows: "The spirit gone, man is garbage."[6]

The titles of these works also point to the diachronic sense of decadence defined as a rebellion against a no longer vital tradition. Behind Waugh's satire lies an ambiguous yet persistent feeling that the emptiness of modern existence results from a loss of values and once-potent sensibilities. Waugh's mocking characterization of himself in *The Ordeal of Gilbert Pinfold* as abhorring "everything . . . that had happened in his own lifetime" does not seem far from true. And the perception, cultivated in *Brideshead Revisited*, that "it was not as it had been" lurks in these early novels as well, though without much specificity about when or how society existed before the modern decline, and certainly without much hope for reversing the decline or finding any alternative to it. The failure of community is not to be mourned, Waugh implies, because the community is already beyond saving. These conclusions emerge from the specifics of Waugh's satirical treatment of parties and from the method by which he expands the parties into an epitome of the modern condition.

Like Fitzgerald, Waugh exhibits a problematic relation to literary modernism. He has been characterized as both modernist and explicitly anti-modernist.[7] Perhaps it is best to think of him as a reluctant modernist, one acutely aware of the distinguishing characteristics of contemporary society but generally negative in his valuation of those characteristics. Like Eliot, Waugh felt that the past—and particularly the European cultural tradition—held moral and aesthetic standards superior to the chaos of modern "values." But he felt that those who tried to live as if the world had not undergone a radical transformation were ridiculous anachronisms.

This attitude toward the superiority of the no longer efficacious standards of a past civilization has significant consequences for Waugh's style and tone. In many respects he is best understood as a satirist: he frequently renders characters and ideas as objects of comic ridicule and mockery in a tone that suggests narrative distance. Waugh himself argued that he was not really a satirist, since satire depends on "a stable society and presupposes homogeneous moral standards."[8] Indeed, Waugh employs a satiric method without the resolute moral center against which objects of satire can be measured. The result, particularly in Waugh's early fiction, is a negative moral and narrative center, a satire without affirmation. Similarly, Waugh practiced the modernist techniques that preferred direct presentation, dramatic scenes, and frequent use of dialogue without a moralizing narrative voice. But he never viewed narrative fragmentation or the surrender of narrative authority as causes for celebration. I fear that Waugh would have found Bakhtin's celebration of the carnivalized novel repugnant, a desperate affirmation of moral chaos. Yet his work shows that he saw the coexistence of multiple discourses as essential to presenting the modern world in prose. Perhaps we can see Waugh as one who might admit the appropriateness of the polyphonic novel to the modern age, but who would believe that to be a comment on the dire nature of modernity.

In *Vile Bodies* Waugh makes brilliant use of multiple discourses: youth slang, gossip column style, the language of evangelism, cinematic argot. In that respect his novel is a carnivalistic mingling of cultural voices. Though his satire lacks an affirmed moral center, it maintains a relatively constant distance from the novel's multiple discourses, and the plot makes Waugh's satirical intent clear. Bakhtin saw satirical laughter as inimical to the carnivalesque, and Waugh's uneasy mixture of the two demonstrates Bakhtin's thesis. This uneasy mixture of consistent narrative distance with direct representation of cultural discourses defines Waugh's unique perspective. In the works of early modernism, we are generally much closer to the communities depicted, more immediately bound up in their multiple discourses; thus the novels tend to be carnivalesque in Bakhtin's positive sense of the word. Waugh's satiric distance creates a negative carnivalization in which corrupted festivity stands for a corrupted society. Making the failed party a central object of satire, however, implicitly grants the significance of festivity. The party is central to Waugh's social vision and his narrative technique.

Vile Bodies revolves around Adam Symes and Nina Blount and their making and breaking of engagements to marry. Waugh uses Adam and Nina to poke fun at the sophisticated affectation of casualness with which the bright young people discuss their emotional lives. We learn of Adam and Nina's relationship when Adam, quite some time after disembarking from his channel-crossing, "remember[s] that he was engaged to be married" (*VB* 36). This recollection sends him to a telephone box in a tube station from which he calls his fiancée. Telephones become, in Waugh's fiction, instruments of failed communication. Here Nina alters her voice to pretend someone else is answering her phone. Unfooled, Adam identifies himself, and Nina responds with a deliberately nonplussed "Oh." Though we discover, as the book develops, a rather touching love between Nina and Adam, both of them are careful never to betray their emotions. They agree to meet later in the evening at Archie Schwert's party, and then Adam adds as an afterthought:

> "Oh, I say. Nina, there's one thing—I don't think I shall be able to marry you after all."
> "Oh, *Adam*, you are a bore. Why not?"
> "They burnt my book."
> "Beasts. Who did?"
> "I'll tell you about it tonight."
> "Yes, *do*. Good-bye darling." (*VB* 38)

Their clipped conversation carefully hides feeling behind popular slang and pseudosophistication. It is also limited by the sense of hurry that pervades the book: there is no time to talk, and even if there were, the telephone is not the proper medium for intimate or serious conversation. The alternative is Archie's party, but, of course, parties are also not conducive to lengthy, uninterrupted talk. Waugh implies that these hurried, public media shape and reflect the superficiality of the protagonists' relationship. Telephone and party conversations in *Vile Bodies* symbolize the shallowness of human interaction in the modern age.

Miscommunication permeates the novel in a variety of forms. The drunken major who owes Adam either £1 or £35,000 appears comically throughout the story, constantly foiled by various failures in communication in his attempt to make a simple transaction: at first, he does not know Adam's name ("Don't know him from Adam"); when they meet on one occasion their conversation is drowned out by the sounds of a traffic jam; when they schedule a rendezvous, another traffic jam makes Adam so late that when he finally arrives the major is too drunk to conduct business; and ironically Lottie Crump, Adam's landlady, mistakes the major for a bill collector and protects Adam by misleading the major. Indeed, Lottie Crump's primary trait is her inability to communicate, which she combines with a rather gay acceptance of unconventional youthful behavior. She constantly confuses people's names and botches introductions with a charming but frustrating innocence.

The triumph of creative mishearing is Nina's father, the senile Colonel Blount, whose constant confusion of memories and inability to remember faces or names leads to several wonderfully comic scenes in which he confuses Adam with a vacuum cleaner salesman, with a reporter for the *Daily Excess*, and finally with Ginger Littlejohn. The old man gets the upper hand when he dismisses Adam's plea for a loan by making him out a £1,000 check and signing it "Charlie Chaplin." But Adam and Nina wreak a revenge of sorts when they spend Christmas with the colonel and convince him that Adam is actually Nina's new husband, Ginger. Most of the novel's plot lines are simply comedies of miscommunication.

Colonel Blount's inability to connect faces, images, and experiences sufficiently to form a sense of continuity finds artistic expression in his love of cinema. Waugh suggests that the montage technique of motion pictures is the perfect art form for an age that lacks continuity with the past and compensates for that lack through frenzied activity and conscious imitation. Waugh took film seriously as an art form, both for its own sake and as a model for literary innovation. But in the hands of

Colonel Blount, the modern technology parodies itself: "One of [Colonel Blount's film's] peculiarities was that whenever the story reached a point of dramatic and significant action, the film seemed to get faster and faster" (*VB* 300–301). The comically ridiculous film of John Wesley is billed as painstakingly realistic—"nothing has been omitted that would contribute to the meticulous accuracy of every detail" (*VB* 202)—while, of course, it is nothing of the kind. Colonel Blount's motion picture dramatizes the corruption of art and communication in terms that Waugh develops thematically throughout the novel—the fascination with speed and the triumph of imitation.

In passing Waugh creates little tableaux that advance the theme of communication corrupted through modern technology. The auto race, itself a triumph of pointless technological vulgarity, is officiated by referees "attempting to understand each other over a field telephone" (*VB* 234), above the cacophony of brass bands and thundering engines. From this confused scene Adam sends Nina a telegram reading: "Drunk major in refreshment tent not bogus thirty-five thousand married tomorrow everything perfect Agatha lost love Adam" (*VB* 249). Adam dispatches this message while remarking that it sounds "quite clear." Nina and Adam's engagement, made by letter, postponed and renewed by telephone and telegram, eventually ends fittingly in a telephone exchange. Their face-to-face encounters are few and comically abbreviated.

In between are parties, paradigms of abbreviated and limited communication. The abortive nature of human relations in *Vile Bodies* arises not from any separation imposed by isolation or geography but from the implicit choices of the young people; indeed, their lives are heavily social. Yet when the characters do come together in social situations, their conversations are as distant, clipped, and devoid of emotion as drunkenly penned telegrams. We can see this, for example, in the promised conversation at Archie Schwert's party that Nina and Adam have when they reunite after his season in France. The mere fact that they withdraw to talk to each other is labeled "sentimental," and party activities and travel have exhausted them to the point that their discussion of their engagement is interrupted by Adam's nodding off and Nina's straying into the trivial (*VB* 67–68).

Waugh demonstrates how improved modern communication distances us further from each other. Our first view of a party—Archie Schwert's—

is filtered through the distorted images of gossip columnists throwing together a story and phoning it into the newspaper. At the end of a survey of notable guests and an anecdote about Lord Throbbing "living in a log shack in Canada which he built with his own hands, aided by one Red Indian," the narrator proclaims: "You see that was the kind of party Archie Schwert's party was" (*VB* 63–64). Yet the narrative testimony is ironic: our source is distinctly distanced and unreliable, the narrator's description of a pirated, secondhand gossip column story, delivered with spoken punctuation and spelled-out words over the telephone ("No, T for telephone, you know"). Yet, we sense that this distanced summary does do justice to Archie's parties since they are little more than a shuffling of familiar names, enlivened by occasional bits of unfamiliar gossip.

Archie's party is a "Savage Party" in which guests are to dress as "natives." This theme allows Waugh to comment subtly on the nature of festive transgression in his social milieu. The "real aristocrats" ignore the costuming and imply by their formal dress that they have come from another party. Many of the guests, however, are dressed up: Agatha Runcible as a Hawaiian, and Johnnie Hoop as an Indian maharanee (to the consternation of an actual Indian maharajah who attends). Waugh intermingles performance fictions and realities for comic effect. The civilized stiffness of pseudosophistication ironically overwhelms the savage dress, as Waugh manipulates the disjunction between the self-conscious young people and the implied extremes of primitive celebrations. Only the timid Miss Mouse actually seeks this savage intensity and considers reaching it through a removal of costumes: "How she longed to tear down her dazzling frock to her hips and dance like a Bacchante before them all. One day she would surprise them all" (*VB* 66).

Despite its primitive theme Archie's party exists within the economic complex of the English upper class; it is a mode of spending, a means of consumption: "It was too thrilling to see all that dull money her father had amassed, metamorphosed in this way into so much glitter and noise and so many bored young faces" (*VB* 64). Waugh's prose is highly suggestive: not only does he outline the economic expression the party implies and juxtapose the excitement of the party accoutrements with the boredom of the guests, but he also picks up the appropriate slang in the heightened "*too* thrilling."[9] This rating of experiences as "thrilling," "divine," or "sick-making," characterizes both the speech and ideology of the aesthete, who lives by sampling and grading sensations. The constant party-going has transformed language to the extent that when Agatha Runcible "heard someone say something about an Independent Labour Party, [she] was furious that she had not been asked" (*VB* 66). The social beat creates a new party politics; Archie's party even leads to the displacement of the new prime minister.

Waugh's criticism of the superficiality of parties sounds familiar: he argues that the structure of parties with their enforced gaiety, frequent interruptions, and inclusion of casual friends and strangers precludes true communication. But his target is not specifically the parties but the way of life dominated by such parties. This way of life wants to avoid intimate personal contact or any kind of profound conversation or thought. For the parties *are* constant, as the famous list following "Oh, Nina, what a lot of parties!" suggests. By using the parties to heighten and dramatize characteristics of modern life satirized elsewhere, Waugh also suggests a critical lack of difference at festive celebrations. *Vile Bodies* shows everyday life as fragmented and proceeding at a dizzying pace. Thus the excitement of parties hardly offers an inverted period differing from the norm. If excess has become the norm (as the newspaper entitled the *Daily Excess* suggests), parties only impotently mirror the degeneration of everyday existence. This inversion of festive inversion characterizes the decadent desire to prolong festive time because there exists no valued ordinary society to return to.

The lack of an affirmed everyday life fuels the decadent fear of the party's end, and we see this in the hysterical continuation of Archie's party by "that hard kernel of gaiety that never breaks" (*VB* 69), who head off in search of further amusement at three in the morning. This group tries Lottie Crump's hotel and Agatha Runcible's house before ending up at Miss Brown's house, the prime minister's residence. En route Waugh presents a remarkable, brief tableau of a party's aftermath: "They went up to Judge Skimp's suite, but there had been a disaster there with a chandelier that one of his young ladies had tried to swing on. They were bathing her forehead with champagne" (*VB* 69). No further comment follows in this scene. Only later, through indirect reference, do we learn that the accident was fatal, when Lottie complains that she doesn't mind the damage to the chandelier but rather "having a death in the house and all the fuss" (*VB* 78). The offstage death, like Lord Tangent's in *Decline and*

Fall, creates comedy through the incongruity between the seriousness of the event and the flippancy and misdirected priorities of the others concerned. The image of the judge bathing the dying hooker's head in champagne lingers as an emblem of the toll of excess. Flossie Ducane's death is the first of three that grow out of the parties in the book. In this scene death appears as the inevitable, yet random, conclusion of the decadent, never-ending acceleration of excessive behavior. In fact, Frederick Stopp suggests that "Death at the Party" might be an apt title for *Vile Bodies*.[10]

The traveling party, nonplussed by the injured girl in Judge Skimp's suite, proceeds to the prime minister's house where they are entertained in fine style by his daughter, Jane, who is thrilled to be finally accepted into the bright young set. In the midst of gleeful late-night snacking, gossip columnist Vanburgh telephones in a report entitled "Midnight Orgies at No. 10." Agatha Runcible stays the night and, to the horror of the prime minister and his family, appears the next morning at breakfast, somewhat worse for wear in her Hawaiian outfit. Attempting to ease matters, Agatha reads aloud from the social column, only to realize she is announcing the scandalous report of her transgression the night before in the prime minister's house. The account of the party merges with the reality. Agatha's pregnant comment is that "this really is all too bogus" (*VB* 76). She then calmly strides from the breakfast table onto the front page, making history and shedding pieces of her skimpy costume with each step: "She turned round and trailing garlands of equatorial flowers fled out of the room and out of the house to the huge delight and profit of the crowd of reporters and Press photographers who were already massed round the historic front door" (*VB* 76). "Historic" concentrates Waugh's irony by pairing the history of today's newspapers with the tradition of British rulers. With this fine convergence of satirical themes, Waugh concludes the first of the novel's many parties.

This blend of newspaper account and real life is just one manifestation of the novel's obsessive theme of the interpenetration of imitation and reality. *Vile Bodies* begins with a series of fakes connected to the popular image of the intriguing Jesuit: Father Rothschild carries a suitcase of "imitation crocodile" stamped with Gothic initials not his own, and containing, among other things, a false beard. In his appearance Father Rothschild resembles not so much a gargoyle as a "plaster reproduction" of one, as sold in tourist shops. From the beginning Waugh plays with the disguises and imitations of imitations that individuals don for their public performances. Though public life naturally requires performance as we present ourselves in a variety of situations, Waugh suggests that a pervasive adoption of poses and disguises has distanced us irretrievably from true feeling. One of the book's two epigraphs from *Through the Looking-Glass* announces this theme:

> "If I wasn't real," Alice said—half laughing through her tears, it all seemed so ridiculous—"I shouldn't be able to cry."
> "I hope you don't suppose those are real tears?" Tweedledum interrupted in a tone of great contempt.

Waugh depicts a world not simply of crocodile tears but of imitation crocodile tears; decadence imitates the already stylized. Waugh suggests that, in our confusion with public appearance, we have rendered ourselves incapable of authentic feeling. Surely the spirit evoked by the *Alice* epigraph is echoed in this poignant exchange between Adam and Nina:

> "Nina, do you ever feel that things simply can't go on much longer . . . ?"
> "No—I wish I did." (*VB* 273)

Even despair seems preferable to feeling nothing; such is the implication of the conversation's end:

> "Oh, Adam, my dearest . . ."
> "Yes?"
> "Nothing." (*VB* 273)

Waugh is fascinated by the banality of the public self, and in *Vile Bodies* he explores that most modern and extreme version of the public self—the celebrity. Daniel Boorstin offers an interesting analysis of the celebrity as "human pseudo-event" when he distinguishes between heroes and celebrities. A celebrity, he argues, is a person famous for being well known rather than for achievement or integrity. Thus celebrities, promulgated by mass media, prevail in the modern age.[11] Waugh's characters are shaped, even created, by how they are reported in the society columns. And society columns are an especially appropriate medium for creating the "human pseudo-event" because they take as their subject the world of social interaction per se. Ordinary activities become newsworthy if the people performing them are celebrities, and people become celebrities from appearing in the society pages. Much of the novel's humor comes from Waugh's deft incorporation of journalistic language to describe the social set that is partially defined by the society page mentality.

The most extreme manifestations of the artificially created celebrity in *Vile Bodies* arise when Adam takes over Mr. Chatterbox's gossip column. To ease the rigors of his job, Adam begins to invent people to write about, reasoning that "people did not really mind *whom* they read about provided that a kind of vicarious inquisitiveness into the lives of others was satisfied" (*VB* 154–55). Adam is only partially correct, for the people he invents sustain interest and he must continue to report them in his column. They take on an existence, becoming, in the minds of the social set, as real as the actual living members. The real Mrs. Hoop brags to her friends that Provna, a sculptor invented by Adam, is fashioning a bust of her son. One of Adam's fictitious anecdotes becomes canonized in an anthology of Highland legends read in elementary school. Finally, Adam creates Imogen Quest, a kind of ideal figure of the social set, "her character . . . a lovely harmony of contending virtues" (*VB* 158). Imogen becomes the greatest of celebrities: everyone claims her acquaintance; clothiers display packages apparently sold to her; other celebrities clamor to meet her: "Soon Imogen Quest became a byword for social inaccessibility—the final goal for all climbers" (*VB* 158). Waugh implies that the ultimate goal of society is a hollow fiction—the completely empty celebrity. Culminating the multiple ironies, Adam's column reports that his fictitious sculptor lauds the beauty of this fictitious celebrity, saying that she "justif[ies] the century" (*VB* 158). And, indeed, in Waugh's eyes, she epitomizes it.

The drama of successive unmaskings takes place most notably at Lady Metroland's party—a veritable collage of false images. Lady Metroland's party differs from the others in *Vile Bodies* in that it combines young and old. The mixture of guests "testif[ies] to her success," since the two generations "[differ] upon almost all questions of principle and deportment" (*VB* 131). But in *Vile Bodies* this mixture of generations does not represent the successful bridging of generational gaps or the creation of a new community. Rather it demonstrates that the differences of principle are so shallow as to be inconsequential and that the generations are harmlessly united in their common superficiality. Waugh explores this lack of contrast in more detail later, when he compares separate parties of the two generations.

Lady Metroland's party does not require savage dress, but it does provide exotic entertainment: evangelist Mrs. Melrose Ape and her choir of angels. Mrs. Ape and her angels are a traveling drama of people imitating what they are not, and they fit perfectly into Waugh's satire of parties. Some of the ironies are obvious: the angel, Chastity, is exhausted from having spent the afternoon flirting with a lesbian under the impression she was a man; later Chastity will leave the protection of Mrs. Ape to work for Lady Metroland as a prostitute in South America. Waugh suggests that Mrs. Ape's hypocritical religious fund-raising and Lady Metroland's heartless capitalism are equally forms of prostitution: indeed, one guest says of Mrs. Ape, "she looks like a *procureuse*," but adds in deference to her hostess, "perhaps I shouldn't say that *here*, should I?" (*VB* 135). In the inverted world of *Vile Bodies* both religion and the party are seen as traditions corrupted by phoniness.

Mrs. Ape's ridiculous name highlights not only her bestial nature but the larger theme of people pretending to be what they are not. Waugh brings the hypocritical religious superiority and the tradition of social snobbery into a stunning collision at Lady Metroland's. As guest of honor, Mrs. Melrose Ape begins her evangelical presentation with one of her favorite openings: "Brothers and Sisters . . . *Just look at yourselves*" (*VB* 136–37). In response to this challenge to confront their glassy essences, the guests are stirred to question their hedonistic lives: "Magically, self-doubt began to spread in the audience" (*VB* 137). Mrs. Ape's aggressive piety stirs the collective and individual guilt of the usually unreflective members of this party. In the dramatic silence that follows Mrs. Ape's command, the partygoers all manage to find some embarrassing darkness in their souls. But this overpowering mood yields to the stronger forces of society: "Suddenly on that silence vibrant with self-accusation broke the organ voice of England, the hunting cry of the *ancien regime*. Lady Circumference gave a resounding snort of disapproval: 'What a damned impudent woman,' she said" (*VB* 138). A collective release of laughter spreads, and Lady Metroland ironically glories in the failure of her honored guest. The vast pretense of British reticence and propriety has defeated the hypocritical appeal of religious guilt.

Yet this is hardly a liberating unmasking since it reveals only another mask beneath. A similar interplay of futile unmaskings animates the remarkable scene that follows. The crafty Jesuit we met amidst accumulating imagery of imitation in the book's opening paragraphs has been observing a mysterious bearded figure whose bizarre behavior has aroused Father Rothschild's suspicion: "He is bowing across the room to empty places and to people whose backs are turned to him" (*VB* 133). A powerful trio gathers to discuss the mysterious man who is wearing obscure medals and bowing to the incorporeal air: Lord Metroland, Mr. Outrage, and Father Rothschild. They represent the gentry, the state, and the Roman Church. In a farcical scene the three powerful figures hide behind curtains to observe the bearded stranger. As he begins to make a telephone call, they burst out, ordering him to remove his beard. Indeed, they are right; the beard is false, and Simon Balcairn the gossip columnist, having been unsuccessful in his desperate attempt to wheedle an invitation, slowly rips off his artificial beard. Adroitly he responds: " '*There* . . . Now I should go and make Lady Throbbing take off her wig. . . . I should have a really jolly evening while you're about it, if I were you' " (*VB* 140). The gossip writer wittily points to the reality that everyone is masked—his dissimulation is no more dishonest than theirs.

The culminating irony arises in Father Rothschild's response to Mr. Outrage's typical bafflement (he always feels left out in matters of political intrigue, whether as prime minister or party guest): " 'That,' said Father Rothschild bitterly, 'is *Mr. Chatterbox*' " (*VB* 141). The unmasking reveals the living incarnation of a pseudonym. The whole scene is too much for Outrage's already stretched credulity: " 'I don't believe there is such a person. . . . *Chatterbox*, indeed . . . you make us hide behind a curtain and then you tell us that some young man in a false beard is called Chatterbox. Really, Rothschild' " (*VB* 141). Mr. Outrage maintains his comic incredulity through Metroland's and Rothschild's patient attempts to explain to him "some of the complexities of modern journalism," that is, the twisted mazes of dissimulation, imitation, and intrigue that contribute to the controlling fictions of the society page.

The wild farce veers toward tragedy, though. The dejected Simon Balcairn, alias Mr. Chatterbox, expelled from the party, heads home to dictate his swan song. His incredible story depicts the party as a mass confessional propelled by Mrs. Ape's religious enthusiasm. One by one the celebrities rise to confess their sins, and Chatterbox's fiction strips them bare. Unmasked himself, he invents a tale of unmasking that will briefly attain the status of truth in the evanescent ink of the morning papers. Simon Balcairn then asphyxiates himself in his gas oven in a brilliantly conceived scene in which Waugh juxtaposes a variety of literary discourses: from gritty realism (noting the grime of the oven door and Simon's inadvertent attempt to cover it with a newspaper sheet containing his rival's column), to an understated description of his death, and a mock heroic eulogy in which "the last Earl of Balcairn went, as they say, to his fathers (who had fallen in many lands and for many causes, as the eccentricities of British Foreign Policy and their own wandering natures had directed them)" (*VB* 146). Mr. Chatterbox fell a good deal before his death though, scratching out a miserable living feeding unsuccessfully off the shallow social set. His discovery at the party would lead, he presumed, to the loss of his job. The death of his pseudonym provokes his own suicide. Behind the layers of imitation lurk real lives; Simon's real death reminds us, comically, even farcically, of the slow death creeping up on all those lives controlled by the multiple poses of the social world.

The commanding metaphor of *Vile Bodies* grows out of the other *Alice* epigraph:

> "Well in *our* country!" said Alice, still panting a little, "you'd generally get to somewhere else—if you ran very fast for a long time, as we've been doing."
>
> "A slow sort of country!" said the Queen. "Now, *here*, you see, it takes all the running *you* can do, to keep in the same place. If you want to get somewhere else, you must run at least twice as fast as that!"

The image of running in place, of constant exertion required merely to remain stationary, modifies the controlling metaphor of the Luna Park wheel in *Decline and Fall*. Through Silenus's speech in *Decline and Fall*, Waugh suggests a division of the world into static and dynamic characters. But in *Vile Bodies* he argues that the dynamism of Margot Metroland's set remains essentially static. In both novels Waugh seems to revel in the vitality of his most active characters; yet in *Vile Bodies* he more clearly emphasizes the pointlessness of all that expended energy. The *Alice* epigraph also suggests that the condition is not the fault of the individual but of the environment: because the Looking-Glass country is fast moving, individual effort can, at best, only keep pace. So, too, in *Vile Bodies* does Waugh depict the frenetic party-going of the bright young people as a product of the fragmentation of the age and its fascination with engines and speed.

Modern forms of transportation fill the book: the characters travel in boats, airplanes, railroads, automobiles, taxis, and racing cars. And their trips are generally bad: the book begins aboard ship with the warning, "It was clearly going to be a bad crossing" (*VB* 1). Before the novel concludes we witness several traffic jams, a fatal racing crash, and a sickening airplane ride. The power of modern technology ironically highlights the paucity of values required to put it to use. Bergsonian comedy ridicules the transformation of people into things, and in Waugh's novel people become soulless automatons, mere "vile bodies," transformed by the engines that surround them.

The grand symbol of pointless energy is the auto race. Bracketed by horrible traffic jams, the race itself puts the finest technological machines onto an ever-circling track, going nowhere at incredible speed. In describing the preparations for the race, Waugh captures the spirit of the *Alice* epigraph through the powerful image of a racing car "running in place," idling at a standstill as concerned mechanics look on: "The engine was running and the whole machine shook with fruitless exertion. Clouds of dark smoke came from it, and a shattering roar which reverberated from concrete floor and corrugated iron roof into every corner of the building so that speech and thought became insupportable and all the senses were numbed" (*VB* 226). This vision encapsulates Waugh's conception of modern life in *Vile Bodies:* fruitless exertion numbing the senses and emptying the mind through paroxysms of noise and smoke. The stationary engine represents technology without progress, machines defeating humanity.[12]

For Waugh this defeat also emerges in the fruitless exertion of parties. The party held in a "captive dirigible" symbolizes this pervasive sense of arrested or pointless motion. The grotesquely moored ship is "chic" because it has been transformed from its purpose into an object of art.[13] Comically out of place, the dirigible overpowers the natural setting: it seems "to fill the whole field" in which it is tied; the cables holding it down trip and entangle the arriving guests; and the "acres of inflated silk" unfurling above the ship "[blot] out the sky" (*VB* 168–69).

The introduction to this party recalls our introduction to the novel, as the ominous note struck by "It was clearly going to be a bad crossing" is echoed by the retrospective appraisal "It was not really a good evening" (*VB* 1, 168). The dirigible is located in a "degraded suburb" that depresses Nina and Adam and faintly suggests, through the implications of the prefixes *de-* and *sub-*, the past existence of a nobler age. In the spirit of that age a caterer has covered the bulky cables with a red carpet, but social tradition fails to disguise the vulgarity of the new, and most of the guests stumble and trip en route to the party. Inside the hallways and staircase are impossibly narrow, and awkward protrusions jab and bruise the guests. Waugh starkly juxtaposes the craving for novelty with the party's jading familiarity: "There was a band and a bar and all the same faces. It was the first time a party had been given in an airship" (*VB* 168–69). Though the dirigible is not suitable for a party, it is at least different and provides some desperately needed variation for "the same faces."

This sense of sameness and boredom seems to affect Adam and Nina as they discuss their engagement. " 'It's a bore not being married,' " Nina blandly asserts (*VB* 169), and when Adam shyly admits he would like their marriage to last " 'quite a long time,' " Nina responds, " 'Yes, it's one of the things about a marriage!' " (*VB* 169–70). The constant fast pace of social life has drained festivity of its difference and contaminated even the participants' private lives with ennui.

We see this contamination in the famous parenthetical passage from which the book's title comes:

> "Oh, Nina, *what a lot of parties.*"
> (⸬ . . Masked parties, Savage parties, Victorian parties, Greek parties, Wild West parties, Russian parties, Circus parties, parties where one had to dress as somebody else, almost naked parties in St. John's Wood, parties in flats and studios and houses and ships and hotels and night clubs, in windmills and swimming baths, tea parties at school where one ate muffins and meringues and tinned crab, parties at Oxford where one drank brown sherry and smoked Turkish cigarettes, dull dances in London and comic dances in Scotland and disgusting dances in Paris—all that succession and repetition of massed humanity. . . . Those vile bodies . . .)

> He leant his forehead, to cool it, on Nina's arm and kissed her in the
> hollow of her forearm.
>
> "*I know*, darling," she said and put her hand on his hair. (*VB* 170–71)

The tension between the public life of parties and the developing inti-
macies of young lovers that we noticed in *The Great Gatsby* emerges
here. This tender moment between Nina and Adam provides a brief
respite from the frenzied, sophisticated nonchalance of party relationships. Against the background of varying masquerades, Adam and Nina
temporarily drop theirs and seek some sort of private oasis from the un-
varying desert of parties. For behind the stunning variation of themes
around which the bright young people's celebrations have been organized lies constant mechanical repetition. "The succession and repetition
of massed humanity" argues that the world of parties has reduced individuality to a series of encounters with "all the same faces." The sense
of continual rearrangement of interchangeable parts poses a mechanistic
metaphor for humanity, and the cry of "vile bodies" augurs the triumph
of physical being over mind and soul. The passage reminds one of Hugh
Kenner's notion of "stoic comedians": the modern Stoic views existence
as a finite set of possibilities, capable of being arranged in a limited number of ways. The stoic comedian sees this mechanistic, entropic world
as the sphere of comedy and his art as a means of drawing life from
the threatening oblivion of clearly perceived finitude. The vitality that
intertwines with bitterness in Waugh's catalog of parties marks him as
a stoic comedian of sorts, in Kenner's words, "suffering our partner the
machine to mechanize all that the hand can do yet remaining obstinately,
gaily, living; courting a dead end but discovering how not to die." [14]

Waugh's comedy does operate, however, at his characters' expense,
and Adam and Nina's tender moment, born of frustration with the
parties, is not allowed to last. It is interrupted by Ginger Littlejohn, buffoon par excellence. Ginger's cheerful exuberance draws Adam and Nina
back to the world of superficial chatter of which Ginger is a master. Asked
whether he's enjoying himself, Ginger responds: " '*Rather*. I say, I've met
an awful good chap called Miles. Regular topper. You know, *pally*. That's
what I like about a really decent party—you meet such topping fellows. I
mean some chaps it takes absolutely years to know, but a chap like Miles

I feel is a pal straight away'" (*VB* 171). Ginger enjoys the party because
it offers what he values—superficial, predictable people who are easily
known. "Regular topper" suggests the comfort offered by the utterly un-
exceptionable, and Ginger's disdain for "chaps it takes absolutely years
to know" glories in the familiarity and safety of the socially shallow. The
hurried pace of life encourages snap judgments of character and a disdain for complexity and depth in personal relationships—life is too short
for that.

Lightning-fast personal judgments enliven the farcical scene that follows, as Adam, Nina, and Ginger adjourn from the dirigible party to a
"social club." There a drunk approaches Adam to announce, "'When I
see a howling cad I like to tell him so.'" When Ginger, wholly comfortable
with such a remark, comes to Adam's defense with the enlightened comment, "'Same to you, old boy, with nobs on,'" the drunk recognizes Ginger and everyone makes friends: "Any pal of Ginger's is a pal of mine"
(*VB* 173). The next logical step in this world of hastily forged acquaintances is an invitation; the party proceeds to Gilmour's (the drunk's)
room. Waugh sums up the scene in a couple of lines: "So they sat on the
bed in Gilmour's place and drank whisky while Gilmour was sick next
door. And Ginger said, 'There's nowhere like London really you know'"
(*VB* 174).

Vomiting (being sick) is a definitive part of the festive world in *Vile
Bodies*. In the opening scene Mrs. Ape's angels sing during the roughest
part of the channel crossing while some of the hardier voyagers are sick in
the lounge. Agatha Runcible draws the comparison: "'So like one's first
parties . . . being sick with other people singing'" (*VB* 19). Later Agatha
will find that it is quite like her last party, when music and cocktails surround her in her sickroom and excite her to the point of a medical crisis.
In the book's opening the image signals an important theme. Vomiting
forms part of the party world because it follows excessive drinking and
eating. As a kind of cathartic, extreme reaction to intoxication, it epitomizes excess. Images of vomiting and subsequent hangovers also stress
the body's vileness, a mixed sense of repulsion from and immersion in
the physical. Vomiting is further connected with dizzying motion and
appears in the channel crossing and Nina's airplane ride where it signals
the rebellion of the body against the unnatural pace to which life has
been accelerated.

In *Vile Bodies* vomiting ultimately expresses revulsion at humanity, as in the crucial airplane scene:

> Ginger looked out of the aeroplane: "I say, Nina," he shouted, "when you were young did you ever have to learn a thing out of a poetry book about: *'This sceptered isle, this earth of majesty, this something or other Eden'?* D'you know what I mean? *'this happy breed of men, this little world, this precious stone set in the silver sea. . . .*
>
> " *'This blessed plot, this earth, this realm, this England
> This nurse, this teeming womb of royal kings
> Feared by their breed and famous by their birth . . .'*
>
> "I forget how it goes on. Something about a stubborn Jew. But you know the thing I mean?"
>
> "It comes in a play."
>
> "No, a blue poetry book."
>
> "I acted in it."
>
> "Well, they may have put it into a play since. It was in a blue poetry book when I learned it. Anyway, you know what I mean?"
>
> "Yes, why?"
>
> "Well, I mean to say, don't you feel somehow, up in the air like this and looking down and seeing everything underneath. I mean, don't you have a sort of feeling rather like that, if you see what I mean?"
>
> Nina looked down and saw inclined at an odd angle a horizon of straggling red suburb; arterial roads dotted with little cars; factories, some of them working, others empty and decaying; a disused canal; some distant hills sown with bungalows; wireless masts and overhead power cables; men and women were indiscernible except as tiny spots; they were marrying and shopping and making money and having children. The scene lurched and tilted again as the aeroplane struck a current of air.
>
> "I think I'm going to be sick," said Nina.
>
> "Poor little girl," said Ginger. "That's what the paper bags are for."
> (*VB* 283–84)

Nina's vomiting appropriately answers Ginger's bastardization of Shakespeare; it is her equivalent to "man delights not me." Nina sees only a macrocosmic expanse of vile bodies. Dwarfed by the "things" of industrial society—cars, factories, power cables—people are indistinguishable atoms in a mass society. Their lives are reduced to an industrial version of "birth, copulation, death." The only response, Waugh darkly suggests, is revulsion. And the modern culture of comfort has even provided for that—with convenient, disposable bags.[15]

Immediately following this scene of revulsion is the description of Agatha Runcible's final hallucination. In the absurd auto race, Agatha has ended up drunk behind the wheel of a racing car by virtue of having worn a "spare driver" armband to gain access to the pits. Her terrifying experience takes her off the race course and through several collisions. Her recovery in a nursing home is marred by recurrent hallucinations of driving at full speed unable to brake or stop. Describing the final stage of her delusion, Waugh compares her vision to a motion picture, the dizzying sense of a limited horizon and the car plunging into nothingness: "There was rarely more than a quarter of a mile of the black road to be seen at one time. It unrolled like a length of cinema film. At the edges was confusion; a fog spinning past; *'Faster, faster,'* they shouted above the roar of the engine" (*VB* 284). The nightmare of acceleration into the void, the fog of confusion, culminates the increasingly darker visions of modern existence the novel offers. The voices of the nurses urging Agatha to lie down and relax augment her feeling of helplessness: " 'How could one drive properly lying down?' " (*VB* 285). As she screams " '*Faster, faster*' " a nurse sedates her, the chapter ending with the ominous reassurance of: " 'There's nothing to worry about, dear . . . *nothing at all . . . nothing*' " (*VB* 285). Echoing Adam and Nina's conclusive phone conversation, this chorus foreshadows Agatha's slip into death, her only release from the constant acceleration.

Agatha is the third and most direct casualty of the corrupted festive world in *Vile Bodies*. Her accident follows from the glib carelessness of her social set (and recalls *The Great Gatsby* and its thematic use of careless driving). Wearing the armband to be on the "inside," to crash the "party" of the mechanics in the pit, Agatha takes on her imitation identity at a fatal cost. Yet her crash is not immediately fatal, and it is the party in her sickroom that interferes with her recovery and aggravates her delusion of constant terrifying motion.

The scene opens with Adam visiting Agatha. She seems quite cogent, her usual cheerful self, and the scene is restrained. Her description of

her recurrent nightmare, however, introduces the party through a significant juxtaposition. She echoes the *Alice* epigraph in her dream: "I
thought we were all driving round and round in a motor race and none
of us could stop, and there was an enormous audience composed entirely of gossip writers and gate crashers . . . all shouting at us at once
to go faster" (*VB* 266). This *Dunciad* vision of apocalypse acts as a cue
for Miles Malpractice, who bursts in announcing that other guests are
soon to follow: "So soon there was quite a party . . . and they played the
new records and Miss Runcible moved her bandaged limbs under the
bed-clothes in negro rhythm" (*VB* 267). The party resembles the others
we have seen, replete with cocktails, inane conversation and the ubiquitous gossip columnist phoning in his story. Yet sickness lies more clearly
at the heart of this party: the image of the deluded Agatha shuffling
her bandaged limbs in bed epitomizes the slang expression "How sick-
making!" Illness and delusion form this party's center. Slipping wholly
into the world of hallucination, Agatha performs a ghastly parody of
all the parties in *Vile Bodies*. "Smiling deliriously," she is "bowing her
bandaged head to imaginary visitors," offering in benediction scattered
phrases of party slang: " 'Darling . . . How *too* divine . . . how angelic of
you all to come' " (*VB* 271). These empty phrases grow into the screams of
her recurrent nightmare, the frightening, "faster, faster!" Finally Waugh
creates a startling juxtaposition of the scene in her sickroom and the
vision in her mind: " 'All friends here,' said Miss Runcible, smiling radiantly. 'Faster. . . . Faster . . . it'll stop all right when the time comes' " (*VB*
271). The community of friends shares in her tragedy, for they too race at
an increasing pace toward oblivion. Agatha's dying vision foreshadows
the novel's apocalyptic conclusion: death at the party expands into the
death of civilization on the final battlefield.

By attacking the expressly "modern" Waugh hints at the existence of a
better world in the past, in tradition. In the later Waugh, where the promises of Christian redemption are linked with tradition, a better world is
posed explicitly. But in *Vile Bodies* he offers no such solace. Only Waugh's
insistence upon the modernity of the subjects of his satire alerts us to the
possible valorization of history and tradition. Yet the closest thing we
get to such a tradition in the actual content of the novel is the depiction
of the older generation at Lady Anchorage's party.

The Anchorage house, as its sturdy name implies, is a fitting setting for the festivities of stolid tradition. Indeed Anchorage House is one of the homes Charles Ryder is to paint in *Brideshead Revisited* as he travels about England chronicling the death of the past.[16] In *Vile Bodies* it appears as the "last survivor of the noble town houses of London . . . of dominating and august dimensions" (*VB* 174). Waugh explicitly contrasts it with creeping modernity, describing it as "lurking in a ravine between concrete skyscrapers" (*VB* 174). The sight moves Mrs. Hoop, who has a vision of Anchorage House peopled by the ghosts of the past (an odd mixture of Pitt, Burke, Beau Brummel, and Dr. Johnson, but still, tradition of a sort). Lady Circumference similarly views the current guests as the "fine phalanx of the passing order" (*VB* 175). But the party at Anchorage House is not a serious panegyric to the older generation.

Throughout the scene Waugh deflates the grandeur of the elders. A variety of remarkable similes helps accomplish this: the guests leave the cloakrooms "like City workers from the Underground" (*VB* 175); young Lady Ursula, eldest daughter of the Duchess of Stayle, wears a traditional garment "from which her pale beauty emerged as though from a clumsily tied parcel" (*VB* 177); and the hottest topic of conversation spreads through the assembled guests "like a yawn." Lady Circumference's vision of the stolid guests culminates in a simile both vast and farcical, elevating the receiving line to celestial heights: "that fine phalanx of the passing order, approaching, as one day at the Last Trump they hoped to meet their Maker, with decorous and frank cordiality to shake Lady Anchorage by the hand at the top of her staircase" (*VB* 175–76). A savagely animal metaphor characterizes the crowd as Lady Circumference views them and "sniff[s] the exhalation of her own herd" (*VB* 176).

The party contains miscommunications similar to those of the younger generation's parties. The prime minister's encounter with the oriental princess with whom he has been flirting for weeks is a good example. She attempts to thank him for his personal attention; he remains resolutely formal, leading her to stalk off in frustration shouting, " 'Oh, twenty damns to your great pig-face' " (*VB* 177). Mr. Outrage comforts himself with the cliché about West is West and East is East, as the narrator remarks that it is "a poor conclusion for a former Foreign Secretary" (*VB* 177).

Later in the evening we see Mr. Outrage's discomfort translated into cosmic terms: "Was Mr. Outrage an immortal soul, thought Mr. Outrage; had he wings, was he free and unconfined, was he born for eternity? He sipped his champagne, fingered his ribbon of the Garter, and resigned himself to the dust" (*VB* 181–82). The champagne toast and imperial order commemorate humanity as a handful of dust. Surely Waugh completely undercuts this generation as an alternative to the younger one. Perhaps this is clearest in Outrage's depressed appraisal of the value and worth of the great British tradition. Father Rothschild approaches him and comments on the young people, " 'Well, after all, what does all this stand for if there's going to be no one to carry it on?' "—to which Mr. Outrage responds, " 'All what?' " with genuine confusion (*VB* 182). If we look for an honored tradition in *Vile Bodies*, this question will be our ultimate discovery: "All what?" For a party to develop the valued awareness of communal immortality that comes with the passing of culture from one generation to the next, it must be able to affirm the worth of that culture in the first place. By this point it is too late; there appears to be nothing worth saving.

The party at Lord Anchorage's exhibits the sense of decline we saw in Joyce's "The Dead." But whereas "The Dead" suggested decline by reference to the faded greatness of the past, *Vile Bodies* pictures decline in terms of the degradation of hope for the future as embodied in the younger generation. The "younger generation" dominates the conversation at Anchorage House. Lady Circumference sweepingly characterizes them as "young toads, the whole lot of them" (*VB* 180). And the Duchess of Stayle criticizes them in terms of their parties: "And these *terrible* parties which I'm told they give!" (*VB* 180). But the novel, as we have seen, shows that those terrible parties differ only superficially from this one.

Father Rothschild's long, pompous speech concerning the younger generation's inability to devote themselves to work in an imperfect world foreshadows the ending of the book by forging a connection between lack of control over social conditions and the inevitability of a second world war. Lord Metroland challenges Rothschild's theory by failing to see a connection between the predicted war and the irresponsibility of the young:

> "Anyhow," said Lord Metroland, "I don't see how all that explains why my stepson should drink like a fish and go about everywhere with a negress."
>
> "I think they're connected, you know," said Father Rothschild. "But it's all very difficult." (*VB* 185)

Later Lord Metroland scoffs at Rothschild, thinking, "radical instability, indeed" (*VB* 187). But while he scoffs he is bearing out Rothschild's admittedly overly general theory as he complacently waits in his study for his wife's lover to leave. In Waugh's vision the pace of modern life, the superficiality of the young, the collapse of marriages, the frenetic corruption of festivity, and the coming war are all of a piece. They demonstrate the metamorphosis of humanity into vile bodies, into a grotesque mixture of the mechanical and the animal that reaches its height in modern warfare.

The parties of *Vile Bodies* become a *danse macabre* announcing the coming war, which is introduced by the novel's last chapter, "Happy Ending." This title alerts us to the novel's reversal of comic structure. Opening with the introduction of the engaged young couple, Nina and Adam, *Vile Bodies* anticipates a comic plot and a happy ending. Even the customs official who confiscates Adam's memoirs and the publisher who signs him to a ridiculously unfair contract serve as conventional blocking characters, who interfere with marriage in an arbitrary, authoritarian fashion. Nina's father's senility and obstinacy are also consistent with the traditional characterization of the old in marriage comedies. *Vile Bodies* may not adhere strictly to comic pattern, but the only plot which organizes the various scenes is provided by the young couple's attempts to marry. The penultimate chapter even suggests a potentially happy, if absurd, resolution: Nina marries the empty-headed but wealthy Ginger Littlejohn but enacts a more affirmative mock marriage to Adam, who impersonates her husband at Christmas at Doubting Hall, Colonel Blount's ancestral home. Adam and Nina waking together to a cheerful, traditional Christmas seems to promise the blissful comic resolution we wish for young lovers. Even the declaration of war appears perversely fortunate since Ginger has been away with his regiment. But "Happy Ending" reverses this expectation as Ginger returns home and Adam is sent to war. *Vile Bodies* hints at the resolution of marriage comedy only to subvert it in a morbid epilogue.

The final vision of the battlefield transmutes the critique of modernism into a ghastly version of holocaust replete with "leprosy guns" and annihilated divisions. In grim irony, Adam, the drunk major (now a general), and Chastity (now a nameless whore) meet on a desolate battlefield and drink champagne in a mud-mired Daimler. Caillois's notion of warfare as the modern equivalent of festivity is consistent with Waugh's closing vision: a decadent party at the end of time, the characters drinking to the death of civilization, much like Foppl's Siege Party in Thomas Pynchon's *V*. The two nameless characters with Adam echo the novel's insistence on lack of communication and the reduction of humans to mere bodies. The mud-mired car epitomizes the theme of pointless motion, deadly stasis in the midst of a kinetic environment, and the sounds of the battle whirling in a cyclone around the still center of the car suggest the ultimate dark issue of the frenzied party-going of *Vile Bodies*. Champagne trickles through these increasingly bleaker visions, linking the caged fox stoned to death at Oxford, the dead prostitute in Judge Skimp's suite, the despairing Mr. Outrage fingering his medals, and the medal-bedecked drunk major seducing Chastity on the world's final battlefield.

Yet a reader cannot abstract the apocalyptic ending and the satire devoid of any positive alternative from the wit, humor, and joy of Waugh's comedy. *Vile Bodies* is as consistently funny as its implications are grim, and any reading of the novel must account for its comic energy. Like all black comedy, *Vile Bodies* juxtaposes humankind's most horrible fears with an unavoidably affirmative capacity to laugh. The narrative implies a consciousness able to penetrate to the dark and comic core of our being. The potency of this sort of black humor is more liberating, I would argue, than a vision moving toward an explicit, didactic resolution, as in Waugh's later novels.

Waugh's presentation of the bright young people and their parties is animated by an unresolved tension between his thorough indictment of their superficiality and his obvious delight in their vitality. This ambivalence has a biographical basis, for Waugh was quite active in the set he satirizes and was often very concerned with garnering their attention and admiration. Yet, during the composition of *Vile Bodies*, he grew increasingly disgusted with the youthful social scene (in part because of the disastrous breakup of his marriage).[17] Of the writers considered here, Waugh presents the most thoroughly negative, consistently satirical attack on the value of parties. Yet the depth of the satire argues for the significance of the target, and the mixed feelings black humor inevitably engenders remain, finally, irreducible. I do not wish to minimize the bleakness or seriousness of Waugh's indictment of modern society in *Vile Bodies*, only to point to the necessary complexity of our response. The dance of death, we must remember, remains a dance, the inescapable rhythmic pattern of our lives.

Henry Green's *Party Going*

Henry Green baffles readers in a way that few of his contemporaries do. As Robert Ryf describes in an introduction to Green's work: "Nearly everyone who writes about Henry Green ends up calling him elusive. Nearly everyone who reads him understands why."[18] The novel on which Green labored longest, *Party Going* (1931–38), demonstrates several stylistic reasons for this elusiveness: Green's overt but broad symbolism, his avoidance of narrative commentary, and his refusal to subordinate narrative elements into a hierarchy or pattern of importance. But this oft-remarked elusiveness of Green's fiction represents a larger quality that distinguishes him from the other writers I discuss: Green's novels do not read as if they are progressing towards a revelation. Joyce may be ambiguous, but we can define the terms of the ambiguity and realize that he is carefully interpreting ambiguities inherent in life. Similarly, Woolf explores consciousness and its relation to the outside world; as we read her we experience an artistic conquest of new ground, an excitement of revealing, of capturing what is elusive or flickering in experience. In Fitzgerald we see self and society converging in an artistic pattern that culminates in tragedy. The most instructive contrast is with Green's contemporary and friend, Evelyn Waugh, who treats the same social set of *Party Going* in *Vile Bodies*. Green shares little of Waugh's satirical comedy, though his characters at times satirize themselves. Green proffers no apparent, consistent attitude towards his characters' folly, and goes further than Waugh in undermining both the voices of the characters and of the narrator who interprets and presents those voices.

Richard Gill comments that parties are "so essential to the plot and theme" of so many novels that "the title of Henry Green's *Party Going* could be fittingly used over and over again."[19] Though Green's novel is not quite so universally representative as to stand for all fiction of festive vision, Gill's comment suggests how *Party Going* may be approached in the context of literary festivity. Such an approach may provide a fresher perspective than the tendency to consider Green as either a quirky exception to or a precise representative of the Waugh and Auden literary generation.[20] The dynamics of the party in *Party Going* shed light on Green's persistent themes and his often puzzling techniques. Michael North argues that "Green's novels are based on the belief that the self is not a truth to be expressed but an expression of itself, a fiction."[21] It is in the extended and stagnated party scene of *Party Going* that these multiple fictions come into collision. The fictionality of the self ultimately extends further to the implied narrative self, and the novel reveals Green's modernist attitude toward narrative distance as well as the limitations he imposed on that narrative strategy. *Party Going* also provides the most telling illustration of Green's distinctive use of symbolism, and the paradigm of death at the party we have been exploring suggests a new way of interpreting that symbolism. *Party Going* makes an interesting companion piece to *Vile Bodies* in treating a similar subject from a less judgmental narrative stance. *Party Going* also provides a good introduction to Green's excellent and often neglected novels.

Setting is important in this novel; it contributes both situation and plot. Wealthy young Max Adey has organized a group expedition or "party" to travel from London to the south of France for a holiday. Picking up the tab for the entire party, Max has invited six guests: Robert and Claire Hignam, Evelyn Henderson, Alex Alexander, Julia Wray—all of whom have traveled with Max before on similar excursions—and Angela Crevy, who is new to the group. Max has rather pointedly not invited his girlfriend, the elegant and beautiful Amabel, who manages, however, to track him down and join the party about midway through the book. The group meets at a railway station along with several people who have come to see them off: a couple of nannies, Angela's fiance, a few servants bringing luggage, and Miss Fellowes, Claire's aunt. A dense fog has delayed all departures, however, and the station, from which commuter trains also run, begins to fill with stranded workers as well as travelers. The delay becomes so bad that Max rents a suite of rooms in the railway hotel above the station so his party can wait in comfort. Max also considerately rents another room for Miss Fellowes to rest in, for she is taken suddenly ill after she mysteriously picks up a dead pigeon, washes it, and wraps it in brown paper. Most of the book takes place in these hotel rooms with the giant, stranded crowd beneath, visible from the windows. When the fog clears enough to allow departures, the guests assemble on the railway platform to board their boat-train and the book ends.

The title *Party Going* uses the progressive tense to suggest continued expectation. Since "the party" has been defined as a traveling holiday, the evening in the hotel becomes something less than a party itself; it becomes a preface of indeterminate length, a waiting in limbo, a going-toward. The fog, the station, and the hotel rooms become active elements in the plot, creating the dilemma of the traveling party rendered immobile. The novel singles out and dramatizes Waugh's theme of arrested motion. This emerges first in the descriptions of the fog obliterating visibility, halting traffic, and trapping people in the station. The novel opens with the phrase "Fog was so dense" (*PG* 384), while an eerie passage describing Julia's walk to the station through the fog establishes the tone: "As she stepped out into this darkness of fog above . . . she lost her name and was all at once anonymous" (*PG* 388). The air becomes harsh, car headlights surrealistic and frightening, street lamps weakened or blotted out entirely: "It was like night with fog as a ceiling shutting out the sky" (*PG* 389). The fog is a powerful, invading natural force, effacing manmade distinctions of class and identity: "If it had not been for her rich coat she might have been any typist making her way home. Or she might have been a poisoner, anything" (*PG* 388–89). As a device at the opening of the novel, Green's use of the fog is reminiscent of Conrad's opening in "Heart of Darkness"—a deliberate attempt to make humanity and civilization appear insignificant.[22]

The fog's natural erasing of social distinctions incites a human resuscitation of boundaries and borders. Max's action in renting hotel rooms separates his party from the masses they have been trapped with in the station; it reinforces their membership in a privileged class. Throughout the book the separation of the guests in the hotel from the working-class crowd in the station is emphasized. The party draws divisions between inside and outside and above and below that temporarily intensify class boundaries in a world gradually effacing them.

The boundaries create distinctions at three levels. First we have the familiar border between the natural and the human—the fog that has muffled the city outside against the vast human community in both the railway station and the hotel. Indoors the masses who stand in the chilly station are separated from the wealthy who lounge in the comfort of the hotel. Within Max's world a further separation takes place as he has rented three rooms—one for the party, one next door for the very ill Miss Fellowes, and one upstairs for him to take women to (first Julia, later Amabel). One room for socializing, one for sickness, one for seduction: compartmentalization prevents contamination and rigidly separates the private worlds of sex and death from the public world of the party (for Miss Fellowes, the characters fear, may be near death).

An important passage reveals the complex interaction of these levels. Max and Julia are in the upstairs room and Julia, enacting the familiar party gesture to the outside world, walks to the window:

> She flung her window up. Max said: "Don't go and let all that in," and she heard them chanting beneath: "WE WANT TRAINS, WE WANT TRAINS." Also that raw air came in, harsh with fog and from somewhere a smell of cooking, there was a shriek from somewhere in the crowd, it was all on a vast scale and not far above her was that vault of glass which was blue now instead of green, now that she was closer to it. She had forgotten what it was to be outside, what it smelled and felt like, and she had not realized what this crowd was, just seeing it through glass. . . . She thought how strange it was when hundreds of people turned their heads all in one direction, their faces so much lighter than their dark hats, lozenges, lozenges, lozenges.
>
> The management had shut the steel doors down because when once before another fog had come as thick as this hundreds and hundreds of the crowd, unable to get home by train or bus, had pushed into this hotel and quietly clamoured for rooms, beds, meals, and more and more had pressed quietly, peaceably in until, although they had been most well behaved, by weight of numbers they had smashed every-

thing, furniture, lounges, reception offices, the two bars, doors. . . .

"It's terrifying," Julia said. "I didn't know there were so many
people in the world."

"Do shut the window, Julia." (*PG* 437)

People here are trapped on all levels—the masses physically trapped,
the upper class trapped by their own fears. Max has just finished chasing
Julia amorously around the upstairs room, while the party downstairs
shifts nervously from boredom, and the huge crowd in the station becomes walled in by steel doors and the sheer mass of assembled bodies.
The structure suggests a pyramid of claustrophobia. And yet, as Max's
protests against "letting all that in" suggest, there is comfort in the sepa-
rations imposed by the architectural boundaries.

When Robert Hignam hires a mysterious man he meets in the corridor to go below and check on Julia's luggage, the effort of leaving the
hotel is "like trying to get out of one world into another" (*PG* 481). This
nameless man appears at the party without explanation, speaking in a
strange mixture of accents, and he comments morbidly and repeatedly
on the condition of Miss Fellowes. Like Joyce's Man in the Macintosh
he embodies ambiguity and becomes the subject for creative interpretation by both characters and readers. Uniting this mysteriousness with
the man's ability to cross borders, Frank Kermode argues he is a Hermes
figure, since Hermes is god of interpretation and "god of boundaries and
messenger between worlds." [23]

Not the least of the boundaries Hermes traverses is that between life
and death, and the mysterious man's associations with morbidity participate in the book's pervasive death imagery. Here, the image of an in-
definitely long wait is explicitly connected with mortality. When, earlier,
Julia is searching for the rest of her party in the already crowded station,
she thinks that "it was like an enormous doctor's waiting room and . . .
it would be like that when they were all dead and waiting at the gates"
(*PG* 414). When she finds the party she explains to Claire, " 'My darling,
my darling, in this awful place I wondered whether we weren't all dead
really' " (*PG* 414). Surely a remarkable observation, this comment foreshadows one of Miss Fellowes's most disruptive thoughts later in the
book. Throughout the novel scenes of Miss Fellowes's feverish delusions

in bed counterpoint scenes at the party next door. In one she recalls her argument with a waitress in the crowded tea room downstairs:

> Well, she was saying, if there's no one to serve me I might just as well not be here at all. And a voice spoke soundless in answer through her lips. It said everyone must wait their turn. She replied she had waited her turn and that people who had come after had been served first.
>
> It might have been an argument with death. And so it went on, reproaches, insults, threats to report and curiously enough it was mixed up in her mind with thoughts of dying and she asked herself whom she could report death to. (*PG* 452–53)

This passage highlights the injustice of death and its omnipotence. It also suggests a broad analogy for the literal events in *Party Going*. The single evening depicted in Green's novel embodies life's uncertainty: we are all under death sentence in a waiting-room world pending our call.[24]

At the very least the situation is explicitly compared to a siege. " 'We are simply in a state of siege . . . no one's allowed in or out!' " Claire reports to a friend on the telephone (*PG* 451). And the sense of civilization outside grinding to a halt while the ominously swelling crowds gather in the station below highlights the threatening appropriateness of Claire's metaphor. In *Party Going* the indeterminate length of the situation poisons the party; the indefinite postponement of the traveling plans creates an unshakeable nervousness and annoyance that renders the party in rented rooms intolerable. No one, as we will see, is having a good time.

As tempers become short after several hours of waiting, Robert makes a remarkable suggestion for remedying the anxiety: " 'All we've got to do is to take [the tickets] with us wherever we go to have a party, because we must have one to make up for all this' " (*PG* 515). Robert wants to take the party elsewhere, assuming that if their stationary condition were planned it could be enjoyed. Were they only in hotel rooms by choice rather than by siege, they could have a fine time. But Robert's suggestion is dismissed and the party must continue under the strained conditions of arrested motion and indefinite confinement.

The party that takes place in the hotel is simply not very much fun. The characters appear to be consistently unhappy and quarrelsome, tending frequently, in their own words, "to make a fuss." Even the pretense of having a good time is only kept up briefly at the beginning, though at various times the characters try to force themselves into a party mood by having tea or cocktails. The unpleasantness, of course, is largely due to the circumstances—the uncertainty about the time of departure, worries about the luggage and servants below, and concern for Miss Fellowes. But these conditions symbolically reflect normal festive circumstances, here skewed by the unplanned; they represent, respectively, freedom from the demands of a rigid work schedule, separation from material worries, and the presence of death.

The conversations and interactions suggest, however, that some of the unpleasantness stems from the nature of the characters and how they relate, rather than from any unusual circumstances. Green's stylistic triumph in _Party Going_ is the dramatic, deadpan representation of complex social stratagems. He explores what Erving Goffmann aptly terms "impression management": he chronicles how talk and action are motivated by the conscious desire of the actor to shape a public image.[25] _Party Going_ contains dozens of examples of hypocritical behavior identified in terms of the effect it seeks to create. One of the most extended versions of this is Angela Crevy's flirtation with Alex Alexander, which she engages in to make her boyfriend, Robin Adams, jealous. As Robin turns weak with embarrassment and fear, Angela boldly proposes retiring into the bedroom with Alex. Alex plays along trying to call her bluff. Finally, they go into the bedroom and Angela directs Alex to leave by another door, then claps her hands twice to imitate the sound of a face being slapped. Her boyfriend, predictably, bursts through the door only to discover her alone and pretending innocence. She begins to chastise him and then breaks into tears; he tries to calm her muttering, "Darling, darling," and the scene concludes with the narrative comment: "By this time they neither of them knew what they were doing" (PG 450). A sadly pathetic scene, this charade illustrates Alex's earlier comment on the entire situation: " 'If it wasn't so ludicrous it would be quite comic' " (PG 416).

The novel is filled with such social stratagems—words spoken or actions taken with a consciousness of impressing an audience. When Amabel arrives uninvited while Max is upstairs with Julia, she finds she must manage a difficult situation with Max's friends. She does not know if they know whether Max is expecting her or not. As it is, the guests are understandably confused about the situation, and all eventually assent to her presence because it is less embarrassing to assume she has been invited.[26] When Alex telephones Amabel's maid to send up her things, he learns that "she had only just made up her mind to come" (*PG* 462). Alex is surprised how quickly and warmly the usually selfish Amabel thanks him for phoning, but the narrator explains that "he did not see she had done this to stop the others knowing. But he did get as far as to feel bewildered" (*PG* 462). The novel follows Alex's bewilderment in detail: first we see him deciding Amabel is uninvited and that he should warn Max she has come, then deciding that though she is uninvited he should not warn Max, until ultimately in his confusion he concludes she *was* invited. "It was easier to believe her maid had been mistaken or that she had forgotten her orders to pack the things. In this way he showed how he had been taken in by Amabel" (*PG* 466). The confusion culminating in this mistaken conclusion testifies to Amabel's mastery of impression management.

Amabel prepares for Max by taking a bath, and Green orchestrates the scene to highlight not only her beauty and her vanity but also her great skill in preparing for public performance: she dries herself "as if she were moulding something" (*PG* 480). The bathroom retreat offers solitude at the party, a motif we noted in Fitzgerald, and this hotel bathroom is appropriately supplied with mirrored walls surrounding Amabel with images of herself. She traces her name in the steamed glass and gazes at her eyes through the "A." Her carefully prepared image gazes back at her through the letters of her name—what better image for the private construction of the public self? This scene has obvious affinities with the mirror scene in *Mrs. Dalloway*. Though Woolf does not stress Clarissa's vanity or falseness, the mirror still allows the author to contrast the private self with the self composed for the public world.[27]

While Amabel takes her bath, she converses with Alex through the bathroom door. By the time she is drying herself, she is so caught up in her own beauty that she loses track of the conversation. Again, Green faithfully chronicles the elaborate minuets of social strategy: "When Alex came to an end she had not properly heard what he had been saying so she said something almost under her breath, or so low that he in his turn should not catch what she had said, but so that it would be enough to tell him she was listening" (*PG* 480). This marvelously complex sentence follows a thought process that should be familiar enough to us from social interactions, but which we rarely encounter rendered in detail in fiction. Edward Stokes has noted that *Party Going* contains a greater preponderance of long sentences than any other Green novel, and it is surely sentences like these, mirroring the complexities of impression management, that contribute to *Party Going*'s high average of words per sentence.[28] Consider the convoluted thought and syntax in the following sentence describing the interaction between Max and Amabel after they finally meet up: "He was why she changed so she would forget what she had been six minutes back, he it was who nagged at her feelings when he was not there, and when he came in again worked her up so she had soon to go out though not for long, it was his fault, but then she knew it to be hers for being like she was about him, oh, who would be this kind of a girl she thought" (PG 520).

The narrative emphasis on the disjunction between appearance and motivation, which leads to such tortured sentences, requires authorial access to the characters' thoughts, a device of which Green is quite skeptical. In his few public comments on novel theory, Green has stressed, above all, the importance of dialogue and the weakness of authorial intrusion or judgment: "Since conversation in these days is the principal means of communication between people in everyday life, I for one maintain that dialogue will be the mainstay of novels for quite a while."[29] In another article Green asks, "Do we know, in life, what other people are really like? I very much doubt it. We certainly do not know what other people are thinking and feeling. How then can the novelist be so sure?"[30]

But *Party Going*, though it contains a great deal of dialogue, has considerably less than Green's other novels, *Nothing* or *Doting*, and undoubtedly depends on a certain amount of narrative commentary, even if that commentary is filtered through the characters' thoughts. Party scenes, which appeal to authors because they offer great possibilities for presenting revealing dialogue, seem to divert Green from his usual insistence on the priority of directly rendered conversation in order to show the true dynamics behind such conversation. Indeed, the very dynamics of multiple characters in an extended party scene seem to inspire Green to explore this different narrative direction. But though he goes quite far in exploring the private composition of the public self, he also calls that narrative enterprise into question. Speculating on Amabel's power, Evelyn

Henderson concludes, remarkably, "If people vary at all then it can only be in the impressions they leave on others' minds" (*PG* 464). That is, Evelyn suggests that the surface impressions people create are, at least in the context of social relations, the only valid quality that distinguishes them from each other. The hidden assumption is that we cannot know the inner self that manages such impressions, that the private nature of inner selves renders them indistinguishable. "How impossible it is to tell what others are thinking or what, in ordinary life, brings people to do what they are doing," Green's narrator comments on Alex's misunderstandings of Amabel (*PG* 466). In this moment he undermines with a radical uncertainty all his own fine notation of social motivation.

In short, Green wants to have it both ways in *Party Going*. He wants to demonstrate the complex artificiality of social selves with particular emphasis on the irony of questionable motivations for proper or supposedly charitable behavior, and yet he wants to suggest that inquiry into motivations is highly speculative. For the very reason that the characters misunderstand one another, the author cannot be relied on either. *Party Going* supports Green's realism of presentation through its content (revealing to what extent visible action can vary from true motivation), but it violates that realism stylistically (granting the author a privilege inconsistent with the limits Green's novel theory suggests).[31]

In several scenes Green describes a phenomenon the reverse of Evelyn's assertion that only appearances differ perceptively since motivations remain hidden: he suggests that social situations may generate identical behavior in different people for thoroughly different reasons. Standing alone as a paragraph unto itself is this bold authorial assertion: "People, in their relations with one another, are continually doing similar things but never for similar reasons" (*PG* 446). Again the statement is paradoxical since it both suggests the inaccessibility of the "reasons" and yet depends on knowing them to make its point. In context the comment refers to Angela and Julia's similar actions of "kiss[ing] their young men when these had been cross," but Green illustrates the same principle elsewhere. When Angela makes a vulgar joke in front of Robin and her new friends, Robin is heartened by the poor response it gets: "Of course she did not know them well enough to say things of that kind he thought, and he was wrong. In their day they had made too many jokes in that strain, they were no longer amused, so they took it just as

he had done for a different reason" (*PG* 405). This conclusion becomes a
sort of motto of cheerful misunderstanding in the novel. We see it illus-
trated again when the three women laugh at a remark of Max's: Amabel
laughs because "she had sufficiently established her claim over him";
Julia laughs "to save her face"; and Angela laughs "to keep in with them"
(*PG* 487).

Indistinguishable behavior and unknowable motivations characterize
the social world. Green uses narrative omniscience to point out the
limits of understanding, and he uses the party conversations to suggest
a frightening conclusion about our inability to encounter other people
except through a veil of misunderstanding and uncertainty. The performing nature of social interaction has grim consequences for Green
since it implies the fictitious and tenuous basis of all our personal relationships. If Green's novels are all about loneliness and the search for
love, as critics have suggested, then *Party Going* defines the nature of the
problem, the phenomenological source of our loneliness and isolation.[32]

Inescapable uncertainty suffuses the novel, even in dialogue uncomplicated by descriptions of motivation. Continually, the characters argue
about facts in a manner that converts certainty to confusion. When Alex
mistakenly identifies the mysterious man in the corridor as the hotel detective, it leads to several "how do you know" conversations in which
the question of who thinks he is the hotel detective and who thinks he
is not becomes even more muddled than the man's identity.

Claire breaks into tears from a confusion of feelings about her sick
aunt. She cannot decide whether to postpone her trip on account of Miss
Fellowes's illness, and she cannot determine if she is upset about the illness, the possibility of missing the party, or simply the confusion about
which action is socially proper. The narrator observes that, "Her tears
seemed to be quite separate from her, only a phenomenon," and her
words are also distanced from her emotions: " 'It's that I feel the whole
thing is so unfair. I do know Julia is rather counting on having me with
her this trip and now that Amabel has dropped out of the sky I do deeply
feel I can't let her down.' This was untrue. She went on and as people
will when they have just lied she began to speak out genuinely for once"
(*PG* 502). The characters in *Party Going* seem to be lying all the time.
Whether the topics of conversation are emotional or factual, people are
equally unreliable and the truth equally unapproachable. *Party Going* is

a comedy of insincerity in which radical doubt undermines characters' self-knowledge and self-presentation. As Lionel Trilling suggests in *Sincerity and Authenticity*, modernism begins with finding "To thine own self be true" problematic; Green's comedy plays on the connection between public dissembling and the private self-doubt and confusion it engenders, the relation between simple duplicity and genuine confusion about one's self.

The most inane and amusing manifestation of this confusion is the recurrent topic of conversation, Embassy Richard. This Richard Cumberland is the perfect item for party gossip because he is, it seems, a professional partygoer, particularly fond of attending embassy parties whether he is invited or not. A notice of regret appeared in all the London papers above Richard's signature in which he apologized for being "unavoidably prevented by indisposition from accepting His Excellency the Ambassador's invitation to meet his Prince Royal" (*PG* 392). Since Richard had not actually been invited, the ambassador angrily responded to the notice by denouncing him in the papers. It is widely assumed that someone else sent Embassy Richard's regret notice as a prank, but the possibility that he sent it himself provides the factual uncertainty that fuels several lengthy and absurd conversations in *Party Going*.

Embassy Richard is a celebrity, of course, in the sense of the word as I applied it to the characters of the gossip columns in *Vile Bodies*. His status is being debated "at length everywhere and in two solicitors' offices and in correspondence columns in the Press" (*PG* 392). Green adds an ironic twist to Waugh's mockery of celebrities, though: knowing the party crasher, Embassy Richard, grants one social status. Angela is labeled an outsider for not knowing this apparently vulgar uninvited guest, though typically, whether she actually knows him is uncertain: " 'D'you think Angela Crevy's ever met him?' 'No I don't,' Evelyn said to [Claire]. 'She's trying to be one of us' " (*PG* 470).

When the rich topic of Embassy Richard is exhausted, the guests find, in their fogbound stagnation, that they have little to say or do. A chorus of ennui grows overwhelmingly through the novel, intensifying as the evening progresses and paralleling the anxiety of the trapped crowd in the station below. Near the midpoint of the novel, Max, Amabel, and Angela sit together in heavy silence: "All three wondered and dreaded a little perhaps in their different ways but no one said anything, there was nothing to say" (*PG* 466). A few moments later, after a particularly tense conversation about the dilemmas of being trapped in the hotel, Evelyn concludes: " 'But surely that's just it . . . there's nothing to do' " (*PG* 471). When Robert Hignam, who has been cheerfully drinking in the hotel lobby, returns to the stagnated party, he remarks to the blank, bored faces: " 'Not of course that it isn't heaven our all being here together and all that, only there is so little to do, but have baths and gossip. Why, what's the matter, it's nothing I've said or done is it?' " (*PG* 490). Robert's understatement about little to do prepares for the double meaning of "it's nothing I've said or done." The choric "nothings" show the paralysis of the party transmuting healthy aspects of festivity into oppressive constraints; the festive purposelessness of the party turns to boredom.

Finally, the boredom reaches a crisis with Alex exclaiming, "Have you ever in your life known such a frightful afternoon?" and the party begins to panic about the best course of action (*PG* 514). A rumor spreads that the masses have broken into the hotel, and a frightened claustrophobia begins to strangle the partygoers as they debate whether a British crowd could possibly turn violent. Finally the end of this particular party releases them, as Max reports that the trains are leaving and preparations for departure create a new "fuss" which temporarily alleviates the pervasive boredom, a boredom that suggests a pointlessness to existence itself, a "nothing to do" transcending the particular moments of the fogbound party.

In a party characterized by fundamental insincerity and radical uncertainty about facts and motives, we may wonder what maintains any authenticity. The novel's beginning offers a clue: "Fog was so dense, bird that had been disturbed went flat into a balustrade and slowly fell, dead, at her feet." Miss Fellowes picks up the bird and "enter[s] a tunnel in front of her, and this had DEPARTURES lit up over it, carrying her dead pigeon" (*PG* 384). An eerie image, this entrance into a dark tunnel leading to departure, with Miss Fellowes bearing her pigeon, signals the beginning of the book's overt death symbolism. Behind the superficial party chatter, the performances, untruths, and frustrations of this anxious evening, lies a deeper ominous presence. The imagery of death provides a context for understanding the importance of the party and the nature of its failure.

Miss Fellowes is associated with death not simply because she picks up the dead bird, washes it in the ladies' room, wraps it in a parcel, and carries it about with her, but because she is taken ill mysteriously and rests in the room beside the party engulfed in feverish and morbid delusions. Any reading of *Party Going* must contend with the symbol of the dead pigeon and with the relation of Miss Fellowes to the party. Criticism of Henry Green invariably involves the elusiveness of his symbols, and the mysterious dead pigeon in *Party Going* is the prime example. What makes Green's symbolism difficult for exegesis is the disparity between the obviousness of the symbols and the lack of allegorical or analogical specificity. In *The Genesis of Secrecy* Frank Kermode uses *Party Going* (and particularly its symbolism) precisely to illustrate "a class of narratives which *have* to mean more, or other, than they manifestly say." [33] The symbolic nature of the narrative element resides in its absence of clear literal function, and the power of the symbolism arises from its lack of specificity, its openness to what Kermode calls "spiritual readings." In *The Literary Symbol* William York Tindall similarly lauds the controlled ambiguity of the dead pigeon as symbol in *Party Going*. He argues that its role is specific enough to suggest meanings connected to the book's themes but never definite enough to allow a conclusive interpretative connection. Thus he remarks that "the dead pigeon seems almost a sign of frustration," and concludes that "in enterprises of this kind we confront the penultimate at last." [34]

The dead pigeon certainly supports such metacritical readings since it poses interpretative problems for the characters as well as the reader: " 'I think what we are both afraid of,' said Evelyn, 'is that parcel she had and what was inside it' " (*PG* 503). But, ultimately, in reading Green we have to step from the metacritical to the text and venture readings of our own.[35] We can better appreciate the potency of Green's symbolic technique if we connect the icon of the dead bird to the patterns of death imagery in general and ask how this focus on death relates to the activity of party-going.

The death imagery is even more insistent and pervasive than the frequently echoed image of the dead bird suggests. We have already examined how the motif of waiting is connected to mortality through the image of the dead waiting at the heavenly gates and Miss Fellowes's deluded recollection of her argument with a waitress as an argument with death. The image of waiting for departure acquires an ominous double meaning that suggests how our common mortality combines certainty and uncertainty: death is inevitable, but the time of its approach is unknown. That the partygoers cannot rest comfortably, given the uncertainty of their train departure, suggests a similar lack of mature acceptance of mortality. Discussing the possibility of Miss Fellowes's imminent death, Alex says, " 'Well . . . we've all got to come to it some time, though why it should be here of all places I can't imagine' " (*PG* 490). Let her die, he seems to say, but not at our party. The servants below cynically recognize this attitude. Thomson remarks: " 'And if she did die why you'd never be the same, none of them would, not for three days at all events' " (*PG* 500). He admits that were he in their situation he would postpone his trip, but he senses that they will not do so because " 'they're different.' "

Death, whether the prospect of mortality, another's death, or merely hints of morbidity, spoils the fun, and it must be excluded from the world of the party. This is what Alex realizes when he angrily summarizes the nature of the party to himself:

> That is what it is to be rich, he thought, if you are held up, if you have to wait then you can do it after a bath in your dressing-gown and if you have to die then not as any bird tumbling dead from its branch down for the foxes, light and stiff, but here in bed, here inside, with doctors to tell you it is all right and with relations to ask if it hurts. Again no standing, no being pressed together, no worry since it did not matter if one went or stayed, no fellow feeling, true. . . . And in this room, as always, it seemed to him there was a sort of bond between the sexes and with these people no more than that, only dull antagonism otherwise. (*PG* 493)

This powerful passage puts the death imagery into perspective. Alex explicitly connects the "dull antagonism" of the party to an antiseptic attitude toward death, a need to isolate and forget it. And he associates the falling of a bird with natural death, an inescapable fact tumbling into the midst of life. The pigeon, then, represents death as natural and inevitable; washing it and wrapping it epitomize the desire to enclose death. In *Party Going* we see the festive triumph over mortality corrupted by a fear of death's uncleanness. The ritual incorporation of death into festivity turns into a desperate exclusion of all thoughts of mortality, which backfires, as it does in "The Dead," and manifests itself in inescapable signs of morbidity. Trying to exclude death only reveals its omnipresence; death's sacred force comes from its assertion of itself in spite of human attempts at control. The pigeon falling dead ironically reverses the image of Bede's swallow flying through the mead hall: life becomes the region outside, and the celebration inside becomes death.

Compartmentalizing death, one also sacrifices "fellow feeling," as is the case with Miss Fellowes, who is herself compartmentalized. Ushered off in secret to a separate room early in the evening, her presence becomes a scandal, a truth whose force grows from its inability to be concealed. Originally Claire and Evelyn wish to keep Miss Fellowes's condition secret, but eventually everyone learns of it, even the mysterious "hotel detective" who pronounces her "a goner." Miss Fellowes's name suggests her affinity with the masses, the grouped working-class fellowship in the station. And her meditations on the injustices of waiting for death echo the graveyard imagery Green uses to characterize the scene in the station. The piled luggage resembles "an exaggerated grave yard, with the owners of it and their porters like mourners with the undertakers' men" (*PG* 402). Green echoes this when he refers later to "gravestone luggage wait[ing] with mourners" (*PG* 497). When Alex looks down at the crowd he compares it to "a view from the gibbet," a simile that suggests a crowd of hungry spectators waiting for an execution (*PG* 430). Finally, when the morbid, unnamed man runs an errand for Robert Hignam, he makes his way "from one grieving mourner to another or, as they sat abandoned, cast away each by his headstone, they were like the dead resurrected in their clothes under this cold veiled light and in an antiseptic air. He dodged about asking any man he saw if he was Miss Julia Wray's, so much as to say, 'I be the grave-digger, would I bury you again?' " (*PG* 498). The image of assembled commuters as living dead suggests Eliot's application of Dante's words to a crowd flowing over London bridge: "I had not thought death had undone so many" (*The Waste Land*, l. 63). It implicates modern mass society in the destruction of a vital community and the creation of an anonymous deathlike assemblage.

The fog has forced these individual commuters into a mass gathering rather than allowing them to catch the train that takes them to their safe, individual, suburban homes. In the station we witness the creation of a reluctant community, and we see the impossibility of festivity in a group so large. In this remarkable vision, the failure of the group singing evinces the death of community-wide festivity: "Again, being in it, how was it possible for them to view themselves as part of that vast assembly for even when they had tried singing they had only heard those next them; it was impossible to tell if all had joined except when, perhaps at the end of a verse, one section made themselves heard as they were late and had not yet finished. Then everyone knew everyone was singing but this feeling did not last and soon they did not agree about songs, that section would be going on while another sang one of their own. Then no one sang at all" (PG 496). The movement toward stasis and inaction in this scene mirrors the ennui of the hotel party; Green offers two different but complementary visions of failed festivity. Upstairs the successful compartmentalizing of existence has sterilized the celebration into nothingness—safe, secure, and lifeless. Downstairs the horrors of mass society, of sheer numbers of people pressed together and rendered indistinguishable yet still not unified, makes community feeling impossible. Green presents the crowd's lack of fellow feeling in terms of decline and loss, though without nostalgia: "They were like ruins in the wet, places that is where life has been . . . with no immediate life and with what used to be in them lost rather than hidden now the roof has fallen in" (PG 497).

The worlds above and below suggest two extremes of failed festivity: the undifferentiated masses grown too large for a whole community to be viable; and the frightened rich cut off from so much of life. The masses waiting at death's gates and the dead pigeon neatly cleaned and wrapped are equal visions of desolation, two extremes of the horror of a mass, yet individualized, society. If human contact is possible, it must be in some other context.

After *Party Going* Green wrote his autobiography, *Pack My Bag*. It occupies an odd place in his oeuvre, written at age thirty-five, the midpoint in his life. He wrote it, he confesses, out of the feeling that he would not survive the coming war, out of a need "to put down what comes to mind before one is killed" (PB 5). Given this genesis, the book's preoccupation with passing time, marked transitions, and departures tinged with melancholy is understandable. Some of the memoir's finest observations concern departures, moments when "it is impossible . . . to be certain that where one is going will be any better than what is being left" (*PB* 199). Oddly appropriate to the uncertainties that shadow *Party Going*, these sentiments suggest some of the richness of experience that ties the party chatter to the grave images of departure and death. Recalling the bells at Oxford with their incessant tolling, Green compresses entering into adulthood in one potent paragraph: "Every day one died a little. The difference now was that one knew it" (*PB* 200). The emptiness that lies beneath the comedy in *Party Going* demonstrates Green's awareness of aging as diminution. And further it exemplifies the modernist ability to tie together great and small in experience, to understand how in dying we look to the minutiae of our lives: "It must be the greatest lump of all in dying if our condition is that we are conscious of it at the time. Regret, remorse, the broken bottles our lives are" (*PB* 199).

Such consciousness, simultaneously of mortality and of the tiny failures of connection weaving through our lives, perhaps eludes the characters in *Party Going*, but it does not elude author or reader. In *Pack My Bag* Green recalls the French saying that every farewell is to die a little and speaks of his memoir as a palliative: "Calling these to mind now may be in a way to die a little less" (*PB* 199). *Party Going* appears to be similarly motivated. It views its characters from above (more so than any other of Green's novels), but not with Waugh's satirical, rejecting eye. Rather the care in blending manners and mortality suggests a simple and loving touch that includes rather than excludes the characters. Green survived the war and wrote more novels. Like Embassy Richard when he suddenly joins the trip to France in *Party Going*, Green could turn to his wartime memoirs and say, " 'I can go where I was going afterwards' " (*PG* 528). In *Party Going*, however, he gives us a careful portrait of human uncertainty and loneliness moving darkly toward departures unknown.

Green's similarity with Waugh is significant: both expand the party into a larger symbol for failed community and both give the failure of human communion far greater emphasis than any hopeful alternative, past or future. Yet the difference between Waugh's satirical comedy verging toward apocalypse and Green's comedy of manners encountering individual mortality is equally significant. Waugh forces us to recognize the joy of a humor growing grimly from morbid roots. Green makes us temper our judgment of the characters' folly by linking us to the humanness of their shortcomings. In this sense Green is closer to the writers of classic modernism than Waugh, whose apocalyptic imagination presages, however obliquely, Thomas Pynchon.

PART 3

Beyond Decadence

The sense of "belatedness" that afflicted modernist writers hits contemporary novelists with a vengeance.[1] Their inheritance includes not only the encounter with the radical modernists as canonized masters but also the sense of coming after the dead-end decadence of the thirties and the apocalyptic savagery of the Second World War. The term "postmodernism" indeed captures the sense of coming after that characterizes these literary generations in much the same manner betweenness characterized writers of the thirties. John Barth, in his well-known essay, "The Literature of Exhaustion," describes the novelist's sense of the "used-upness of certain forms or the felt exhaustion of certain possibilities."[2] In the achievement of the best contemporary writers, however, this postdecadent sensibility is transformed from obstacle into creative catalyst and becomes a new raison d'être for the stoic comedians of our time.

The most daring works of contemporary fiction display a carnivalized consciousness, expressed both thematically and formally. In formal terms the modernist play with multiple narrative voices and self-conscious artifice is adopted wholeheartedly and often exaggerated beyond the bounds typical of early modernism. The incorporation of the languages of popular culture is expanded beyond the Joycean range, and the qualities of carnival blasphemy and the celebration of what Bakhtin calls the "lower bodily strata"—of the sort we noted in "Circe"—become central to contemporary fiction. The party gone wild or threatening to dissolve into chaos emerges as the paradigmatic form of celebration, and often the party scene becomes the site of the narrative transgressions of fictional decorum. Brian McHale goes as far as to assert: "[The] characteristic *topoi* of carnivalized literature are also characteristic *topoi* of postmodernist fiction."[3]

The festive visions of Pynchon and Coover are at once postmodern and postdecadent. Contemporary fiction includes, of course, a good deal of traditional narrative—novels composed, as John Barth has noted disparagingly, as essentially "turn-of-the-century-type novels, only in more or less mid-twentieth-century language and about contemporary people and topics."[4] But the work of recent generations that does not hearken back to nineteenth-century realism seems to possess qualities that relate it directly to modernist experimentation and yet distinguish it in fundamental ways. Discussions of postmodernism generally debate the extent to which those distinguishing qualities are fundamental (i.e., how radically the postmodern differs from the modern). Ihab Hassan, for instance, delineates postmodernist qualities as expansions of seven modernist parameters—urbanism, technologism, "dehumanization," primitivism, eroticism, antinomianism, and experimentalism. Yet Hassan has also posited a fundamental difference (rather than just differences in degree) by arguing that whereas modernism created artistic authority to replace absent spiritual and social authority, "postmodernism has tended toward artistic Anarchy in deeper complicity with things falling apart."[5] McHale argues similarly for a difference in kind: "Postmodernist fiction differs from modernist fiction just as a poetics dominated by ontological issues differs from one dominated by epistemological issues."[6] Other critics have questioned the claims made for the radical difference of contemporary fiction, as Robert Alter does in arguing that "the continuity of much of contemporary fiction with its literary antecedents is too substantial to be dismissed as mere vestigial reflex."[7] What is clear is that intelligent readers sense important and definitive similarities between contemporary and modernist literature and yet encounter, to varying degrees, substantial and equally definitive differences.

This complex relation to the past characterizes the contemporary vision of festivity and carnivalized form. In modernism failed festivity was typically a party stifled by too much control; thus the encounter with mortality (thematically) and the multiplying of narrative perspective (formally) served as transgressions to invigorate the festive potential. In the decadent model common to the between-the-wars writers, transgression became suspected of inauthenticity as it became the norm. As we look to fiction that moves "beyond decadence," we still encounter images of decadent stasis (in such memorable scenes as the party aboard the *Anubis* in *Gravity's Rainbow*), but an equally potent threat appears to be the party gone wild, an extreme transgression culminating in chaos and often violence. As Hassan argues, postmodernist fiction tends to be complicit with the breaking of order—particularly in terms of narrative authority and the consistencies of verisimilitude. And yet the new avatar of death at the party—whether it is the murder of Ros in *Gerald's Party* or the omnipresence of the rocket in *Gravity's Rainbow*—reminds us that tragic consequences can attend the societal discharge of violence. Coover and Pynchon insistently celebrate the festive spirit but not to the extent that they idealize the conflicts and potential catastrophes of the nuclear age. The party-gone-wild becomes the central literary festivity of the age precisely because it is a double-edged sword: the festive energy celebrates and encourages postmodernist decentering but can also work negatively as a cautionary force illustrating the dangers of contemporary chaos.

The significance of the party in contemporary fiction is also a legacy of the countercultural consciousness of beat literature, particularly the work of William Burroughs, but also the chronicles of counterculture of the fifties found in Kerouac and Ginsberg. Under beat influence the novel form further incorporated forms of popular culture (especially music), the subjective distortions of drug experiences, and the outcast's view of social, political, and military authority. Beat literature serves contemporary fiction as an influential example for vitalizing the postdecadent sensibility.

In *Gravity's Rainbow* and *Gerald's Party* the party becomes the location in which creative possibilities for literature and life are dramatized. Both texts are thoroughly carnivalized and manifest festive visions with important genre-shaping consequences. *Gravity's Rainbow* and *Gerald's Party* are, in different ways, sprawling texts that exhibit narrative multiplicity, the incorporating of genres (from comic books, fairy tales, and monster movies in Pynchon to detective fiction and slapstick in Coover), the celebration of the lower body, and the ridicule of authority (extending to the work's own narrative authority in ways likely to startle and disturb readers). These works do not necessarily "represent" the diversities of postmodernist literary style, but they do demonstrate once again the significance of festive vision in the development of the novel.

In their fascination with the festive element conceived of in popular terms, these novels are very much of our age—the age in which "party" has gained currency as a verb. We hear of "partying" as a popular activity and can often see individuals sporting T-shirts that announce, "I like to party," or bumper stickers that urge, "Party Naked." Disc jockeys exhort listeners to "party hearty," and there are nightclubs called "Party Party" and "Party Down" as well as a record collection labeled simply "Let's Party." Whether this usage signals an increasingly hedonistic age is difficult to say, but surely the popular slang valorizes the pursuit of leisure and festive release, while connecting the idea of the formal social gathering with the activities of dancing, drinking, and merrymaking, whatever the setting. It is likely that this verbal use of "party," as well as the ascension of "a social gathering" as the most common meaning of "party," testifies to the continuing importance of parties in our culture. Surely when the rock star Prince sings, "I want to party like it's nineteen ninety-nine" we sense the frightening self-consciousness that places our festive forms within the new fin de siècle.

5. Celebrating the Counterforce

PARTIES IN PYNCHON

You can't expect the fatted calf
to share the enthusiasm of the angels
over the prodigal's return.
—Saki, "Reginald in the Academy"

he party scene is a particularly congenial stage for Pynchon's narrative performances because it allows for the creation of a social microcosm in which the many-voiced struggle between the privileged and the dispossessed can be acted out. From the party inherited by the surrogate host in Pynchon's early story, "Mortality and Mercy in Vienna," to the surprisingly affirmative Traverse-Becker family reunion that concludes *Vineland*, Pynchon's fiction is fueled by festivity. The moments of countercultural potentiality often burst forth in the fertile chaos of celebrations, but the technologies of death also assert themselves in decadent parties-gone-bad such as Foppl's Siege Party in *V.*, the ship of fools debauch aboard the *Anubis* in *Gravity's Rainbow*, and the Thanatoid Roast '84 in *Vineland*.

Gravity's Rainbow (1973) is Pynchon's most clearly carnivalized work, both in terms of its significant party scenes and the explosively encyclopedic mixing of discourses that makes up its dense texture. Even its chronology appears to be based on the dates of a festive calendar.[1] I think, though, that we can best approach the complex and ambivalent role of festivity in *Gravity's Rainbow* by examining Pynchon's symbolic use of parties in the early story

"Entropy" (1960). In "Entropy" parties emerge both as important examples of the death-driven violence of the social order and as possibilities for subverting or transcending that deadly order.

Entropy provides the first of several crucial scientific metaphors Pynchon uses in his fiction.[2] Entropy becomes a potent cosmological metaphor applicable to societies and to life itself; the concept of entropy offers an alternative to teleological or cyclical models of historical progress. Pockets of antientropy do, of course, occur—all areas of human life exhibit the arrangement of matter into states of increased organization. But the laws of thermodynamics remind us that such human (as well as natural) efforts require energy, so that reversals of entropy are either temporary (destined eventually to tend toward greater entropy) or spatially limited (drawing energy from outside the limited system in question). Beyond the obvious nihilistic implications about the ultimate transience of all human endeavor, the concept of entropy poses a paradox concerning humankind's relation to the universe. As the antientropic unit of creation, humankind can be seen either as a futile antagonist of the universal process or as its complement. Most interpreters emphasize the former perspective, pointing out that entropy triumphs in the end. But the alternative interpretation, advanced by both Norbert Weiner and R. Buckminster Fuller, is worth considering.[3] Their interpretation describes entropy as the necessary condition for the human order-making propensity, which extends those antientropic tendencies evident in nature. Just as in *Gravity's Rainbow* when Slothrop's Calvinist ancestor advances the heresy that the elect *need* the preterite (those who are not saved) to secure their salvation, so too might one argue that entropy allows mind to create order, even if that creation is ultimately limited by time and space.

In "Entropy" Pynchon uses a party to make this scientific and philosophic concept palpable. "Entropy" narrates the events of one day in two separate Washington, D.C., apartments. Downstairs, Meatball Mulligan is hosting a wild "lease-breaking" party, presumably a party intended to continue until eviction. Upstairs a couple, Callisto and Aubade, live in a hothouse atmosphere among plants and birds, trying to create a wholly independent world—"a tiny enclave of regularity in the city's chaos" (E 83). Callisto is obsessed with the consequences of entropy. He sees evidence of the encroaching "heat death" of the universe all around him, particularly in the ominous fact that the temperature has remained stable at thirty-seven degrees for three days. We see Callisto engaged in two activities—trying to nurse back to health a sickly baby bird, and dictating his memoirs, or more exactly, his disquisition on entropy. Callisto, describing himself in the third person, narrates his discovery of entropy's implications then summarizes the two possible views of the relationship of man to universe implied by entropy—antagonist and balance: "He was aware of the dangers of the reductive fallacy and, he hoped, strong enough not to drift into the graceful decadence of an enervated fatalism. His had always been a vigorous, Italian sort of pessimism: like Machiavelli, he allowed the forces of *virtù* and *fortunata* to be about 50/50; but the equations now introduced a random factor which pushed the odds to some unutterable and indeterminate ratio" (E 87–88).

Callisto tries to alter those odds that lead to fatalism by constructing his own "ecologically balanced" world. Pynchon focuses here, as in all his fiction, on the nature of the strategies humans invent to cope with the forces that circumscribe and threaten them. Callisto's strategy amounts to creating his own more perfect world in which the entropic process can be reversed. But it is doomed to failure for two reasons: the created system cannot be wholly isolated (indeed noise from the party downstairs keeps disturbing the seclusion of the upstairs couple); and, furthermore, the attempt to create an isolated system approaches a death-in-life, an entombment in a "hermetically-sealed" world that foreshadows the grave. By the end of the story, the little bird dies, and Aubade shatters the window of their apartment with her hands and "turn[s] to face the man on the bed and wait with him until the moment of equilibrium was reached, when 37 degrees Fahrenheit should prevail both outside and inside, and forever, and the hovering, curious dominant of their separate lives should resolve into a tonic of darkness and the final absence of all motion" (E 98).

The musical metaphor returns our attention to the party below, scenes of which have been interspersed contrapuntally with the scenes of Callisto and Aubade.[4] There's plenty of music at Meatball's party, both on the stereo and from an avant-garde jazz band in attendance. Meatball Mulligan's lease-breaking party displays Pynchon's skill for briskly and economically communicating mood and milieu, especially in the case of one of his favorite subjects—a wild party veering out of control. A cymbal crash wakes the host who has drifted off to sleep in the party's fortieth hour while clutching an empty champagne magnum to his chest. His first spoken word is *Aarrgghh,* and he wanders blearily through a landscape that looks more like a party's aftermath than a party. This celebration of indefinite length is winding down, threatening, like Callisto's bird upstairs, to cease altogether. Amidst empty bottles and various semiconscious bodies, Meatball tries to wake up, and the party tries to gather its second wind.

The party that refuses to end signals decadence, as we have seen, in that it attempts to prolong the world of festive release out of despair with the normal world awaiting the participants at the party's conclusion. In that sense, Meatball's party might represent the decadent response of "enervated fatalism" that Callisto has so carefully avoided, and the participants, described as mainly hypocritical government employees longing to become expatriates, are likely candidates for the shallow desperation that precedes decadence. But the party also forms a community, a subworld like Callisto's apartment above, and thus exhibits its own entropic processes as well as human responses to society's entropy. This is a crucial characteristic of festivity: it is both a response to the everyday world and a world in itself. The party exhibits entropy's two characteristics, tending toward both undifferentiation and randomness—threatening to end prematurely in a hazy torpor, while new arrivals and awakenings threaten violence and increasing chaos. A depressed communication theorist crawls in from the fire escape, three female college students appear bearing bottles of Chianti, rowdy sailors arrive mistaking the party for a whorehouse, and in the background the Duke di Angelis quartet cheerfully plays music without instruments. The party turns violent as a "government girl" starts a fight with the drunken sailors and a woman screams for help as she begins to drown in the shower (she's sitting on the drain). Pynchon emphasizes the intensifying chaos: "The noise in Meatball's apartment had reached a sustained, ungodly crescendo" (E 96).

Meatball decides to salvage the party from utter disintegration and the possible violence that might accompany it. His jaded mind manages to sort out two alternatives: "(a) lock himself in the closet and maybe eventually they would all go away, or (b) try to calm everybody down, one by one" (E 96). The reader recognizes the first alternative as a version of

Callisto's hermetically sealed hothouse, and the reasons Meatball gives for rejecting it reveal the pitfalls of Callisto's approach: "But then he started thinking about that closet. It was dark and stuffy and he would be alone. He did not feature being alone. And then this crew off the good ship Lollipop or whatever it was might take it upon themselves to kick down the closet door, for a lark" (E 96–97). The retreat involves an unacceptable, deathlike withdrawal from humanity and, in any case, it is still subject to intrusions from the outside world: true isolation is possible only in death. Accordingly, Meatball opts for the latter alternative: "So he decided to try and keep his lease-breaking party from deteriorating into total chaos: he gave wine to the sailors and separated the *morra* players; he introduced the fat government girl to Sandor Rojas, who would keep her out of trouble; he helped the girl in the shower to dry off and get into bed; he had another talk with Saul; he called a repairman for the refrigerator, which someone had discovered was on the blink" (E 97).

Meatball's efforts, of course, do nothing to subvert the inevitable entropy: eventually the party will end. The reversal of entropy remains limited by time and space: not only are new guests ("young blood") needed to keep the party going, Meatball must also call out for a repairman to fix the decaying closed system of the refrigerator. But this alternative receives Pynchon's qualified endorsement, for it affirms life without attempting to ignore or escape universal forces. It opposes entropy without fatally denying it. Decadent though it might be, the party exhibits a contagious energy that is only equalled upstairs in the moment of Aubade's liberating gesture of breaking the window—a desperate saying yes to the outside world, even if it means death.

"Entropy" presents no simple solution, not even in its preference for a stoic, futile delaying of entropy over a stubborn, escapist denial of it. Meatball Mulligan's party remains the stew both his names imply, a mixed pot of vitality and degeneration. The party exemplifies decay and disintegration and yet offers the only hope for dealing with decay. Pynchon's perspective exemplifies the ambivalent relation of festivity to authority: festivity both subverts and supports the larger system. This crucial ambivalence and its stylistic correlative in Pynchon's writing emerge symbolically in the allusions to art in the story. The ecological balance of Callisto's apartment is compared to a "perfectly-executed mobile" in which each part contributes to the whole that exists complete in itself.

Pynchon contrasts this image with the erratic sounds from Meatball's party composed not only of the actual music but also of the many different voices, moans, and screams. As Aubade listens in her apartment to the "music" of a mimosa growing, her perfect world is disturbed by the noise from below: "That music rose in a tangled tracery: arabesques of order competing fugally with improvised discords of the party downstairs, which peaked sometimes in cusps and ogees of noise" (E 92). The perfect mobile of Callisto's apartment stands for the unity of Roland Barthes's "classic text," which embodies an artificial, created order resolving all tensions in a balanced conclusion. The classic text does not admit uncertainty or discord (though it may perceive that the world is less ordered than the text), and it offers a closed, rather than an open, ending. Pynchon endorses a carnivalesque vision of art that combines the two worlds; thus the highly ordered music forms but one voice in the story's complex fugue that also embraces "the cusps and ogees of noise."

Another side to the music at Meatball's party suggests the dangers entropy poses for art. The performing Duke di Angelis quartet tries to take its jazz further into the avant-garde. One player cites the example of Gerry Mulligan playing the saxophone part without a rhythm section so that the soloist had to think (rather than hear) the root chords and thus create new possibilities for melodic improvisation. The logical extension becomes merely thinking, not playing, all the parts—silent music. The quartet performs a silent version of "Love for Sale," commenting afterwards that at least they ended together. Pynchon, here, is satirizing those who see silence as the only authentic expression of art in an entropic world. Pynchon cleverly manipulates the musical imagery in the story to show how the end product of this extremism is indistinguishable from lockstep adherence to convention, the tonic-dominant-tonic pattern that, through Aubade, he identifies with death. The silences of redundant convention and nihilistic experimentation are identical, both involving a surrender of the artistic voice, which Pynchon is unwilling to countenance. The triumph of entropy may destroy illusions of art's immortality and perhaps even illusions of its ability to change consciousness, but it fails to negate the validity of the artistic process. Indeed, the entropic view of the universe renders art all the more necessary, not so much as a deciphering of the world's chaotic multiplicity of voices, but, rather, in Pynchon's words, as a "progressive *knotting into*" that chaos, a way of experiencing diversity (*GR* 3). As Mulligan's name and the nature of his party suggest, Pynchon is carnivalistic in Bakhtin's sense of all-embracing, transcending hierarchies and categories. Like Meatball Mulligan, Pynchon invites us to join a wild, inclusive carnival, to participate in the lease-breaking party until eviction, whether it be the end of the novel, or, ultimately, the end of our lives.

"Entropy" presents us with several unresolved tensions that continue through Pynchon's fiction. It uses the party as a social microcosm, mirroring in its movement toward chaos and disintegration the entropic tendencies of our entire world. But the party has possibilities as counter-culture as well as subculture; that is, it can counter or reverse the dominant tendencies of the official culture. Festivity continues to exhibit both of these contradictory characteristics in *Gravity's Rainbow:* the novel explores the possibilities and limitations of human celebration in the world following the Second World War, just as it outlines the possibilities and limitations of all human action in the age of the rocket. But festivity receives special prominence, as in the opening scene, a breakfast party that combines the two worlds of "Entropy" into a single celebration.

The first few pages of *Gravity's Rainbow* describe a dream of Captain Pirate Prentice, British special operations officer. Prentice wakes from his Kafkaesque nightmare of an unsuccessful bomb evacuation to a scene not unlike that which the awakening Meatball Mulligan actually encounters. Prentice, a tenant at a bachelor's officers' quarters in London during the Second World War, climbs over various of his colleagues and drinking companions strewn about the "maisonette" asleep on cots and chairs. He shakes himself from his dream to prepare another of his famed banana breakfasts. The action that follows resonates clearly with the spirit of Meatball Mulligan's party: people staging mock battles with bananas, searching bleary-eyed for "hair of the dog" drinks, singing popular songs and obscene parodies. But the scene has affinities with Callisto's hot-house as well. Before anyone else is awake, Pirate Prentice climbs to the rooftop where tropical bananas thrive in a glass greenhouse in the midst of war-torn winter London. The tropical foliage and heat of the greenhouse recall Callisto's Rousseau fantasy apartment and initiate the series of tropical images in *Gravity's Rainbow* that repeatedly oppose the overwhelming imagery of the arctic whiteness associated with the north and with death.[5]

The bananas grow in soil with a revealing history. The pre-Raphaelite builder of the house had "cultivated pharmaceutical plants" on the roof, a later tenant had kept pigs (which will also function through the novel as affirmative icons), and the remnants of these past tenants have combined with dead leaves and other forms of waste to create a fertile mulch: "all got scumbled together, eventually, by the knives of the seasons, to an impasto, feet thick, of unbelievable black topsoil in which anything could grow, not the least being bananas" (*GR* 5). Fertile waste is a crucial, recurrent symbol for Pynchon, who is fascinated with the creative powers of whatever the official culture designates as waste (as in the W.A.S.T.E. conspiracy in *The Crying of Lot 49* and the junkyard subculture in "Low Lands"). As in Joyce's image of the litter and the letter, the text uncovered in the middenheap, Pynchon sees literature embodying the all-encompassing trash heap of culture. Compost creates "the soil's stringing of rings and chains in nets only God can tell the meshes of, [allowing] the fruit [to] thrive often to lengths of a foot and a half" (*GR* 6).

Pirate Prentice harvests these giant bananas to transmute them in the kitchen below into myriad culinary delicacies. But not before his rooftop perch allows him the frightening glimpse of the new, horrible weapon that dominates Pynchon's novel—the V-2 rocket. Prentice, who is involved in British rocket intelligence, spots the distant vapor trail in the sky—"a new star." Aware of the physics behind the new rocket, Pirate can calculate the five-minute interval before the rocket should hit London. Nervous, he can think of only one thing to do: "he steps into the wet heat of his bananery, sets about picking the ripest and the best . . . moving barelegged among the pendulous bunches, among these yellow chandeliers" (*GR* 7). Helpless beneath the incoming rocket, Prentice uses the tropical bananas as a kind of exotic charm against death. As it turns out, this rocket falls short: "Banana Breakfast is saved" (*GR* 8). But the omnipresent threat from the sky is established to remain throughout the novel, and, as Pynchon implies, throughout all our lives in the age of the rocket.

Pirate's banana breakfast mingles the steamy, sheltered warmth of Callisto's retreat with the open festive communion of Meatball's party: we see the various officers and guests come to life as the banana dishes take form. As Pirate slices, blends, purees, whisks, fries, bakes, and flambés bananas, the atmosphere of the maisonette becomes transformed:

> Now there grows among all the rooms, replacing the night's old
> smoke, alcohol and sweat, the fragile, musaceous odor of Breakfast:
> flowery, permeating, surprising, more than the color of winter sun-
> light, taking over not so much through any brute pungency or volume
> as by the high intricacy to the weaving of its molecules, showing the
> conjuror's secret by which—though it is not often Death is told so
> clearly to fuck off—the living genetic chains prove even labyrinthine
> enough to preserve some human face down ten or twenty genera-
> tions . . . so the same assertion-through-structure allows this war
> morning's banana fragrance to meander, repossess, prevail. Is there
> any reason not to open every window, and let the kind scent blanket
> all Chelsea? As a spell, against falling objects. (GR 10)

This beautiful passage shows Pynchon's talent for mixing lyricism with
scientific metaphors. Again we see the banana invoked as a charm
against the loosely clustered forces of death—the war, the winter, the
rockets that threaten extinction from the sky. But the threat here is different from the disintegration of "Entropy." It is the malevolent *order* of
war, the grouping of death forces, which emerges in Pynchon's fascination with paranoia, a term as crucial to his fiction as "entropy." We will
return to this in greater depth later, but suffice it to say here that the war
threatens festivity; the two are diametrically opposed.

For a moment, under the spell of the banana fragrance, the festive
spirit of the party triumphs over the threat of falling objects. The richness
of the feast expands to epic and comic proportions:

> With a clattering of chairs, upended shell cases, benches, and otto-
> mans, Pirate's mob gather at the shores of the great refectory table . . .
> crowded now over the swirling dark grain of its walnut uplands with
> banana omelets, banana sandwiches, banana casseroles, mashed
> bananas molded in the shape of a British lion rampant, blended with
> eggs into batter for French toast, squeezed out a pastry nozzle across
> the quivering creamy reaches of a banana blancmange to spell out the
> words *C'est magnifique, mais ce n'est pas la guerre* (attributed to a French
> observer during the Charge of the Light Brigade) which Pirate has ap-
> propriated as his motto . . . tall cruets of pale banana syrup to pour
> oozing over banana waffles, a giant glazed crock where diced bananas
> have been fermenting since the summer with wild honey and muscat

> raisins, up out of which, this winter morning, one now dips foam
> mugsfull of banana mead . . . banana croissants and banana kreplach,
> and banana oatmeal and banana jam and banana bread, and bananas
> flamed in ancient brandy Pirate brought back last year from a cellar in
> the Pyrenees. (*GR* 10)

Behind the comically omnipresent banana, Pynchon captures the richness of the feast, which here provides a moment of magnificence that,
indeed, is *not* the war. It is something other, some life force opposed
to those invisible forces that fill the air with death and destruction. The
comic and festive worlds are not everlasting though, and the war asserts itself presently in the form of an official phone call for Prentice
concerning the misfired rocket he had spotted earlier.

Summoned to work Pirate must leave the breakfast party behind. Returning from the phone call he feels suddenly alone, separated from the
festive community he has brought into being: "He gazes through sunlight's buttresses, back down the refectory at the others, wallowing in
their plenitude of bananas, thick palatals of their hunger lost somewhere
in the stretch of morning between them and himself. A hundred miles
of it, so suddenly. Solitude, even among the meshes of this war, can
when it wishes so take him by the blind gut and touch, as now, posses-
sively. Pirate's again some other side of a window, watching strangers
eat breakfast" (*GR* 11). Pynchon uses the familiar dramatic technique of
the participant's withdrawal, again to a window, to put the party into
perspective. The war has the power to separate, to destroy community,
to devalue festivity. War expresses the official culture, the powers that
be, in paroxysms of greed, insisting on taking over more and more of
its citizens' lives. Throughout *Gravity's Rainbow* we see the war corrupt-
ing festivity, poisoning parties, and driving the carnival world further
into hiding. In this rich opening scene we first see the liberating power
of parties; then we see that power dwarfed by something greater and
bleaker.

Gravity's Rainbow is a war novel, but its unconventionality pushes the
scenes of literal combat far into the background. "But where *is* the war?"
the narrator asks after Roger Mexico and Jessica Swanlake fall asleep
together in their romantic hideaway in the evacuated sector of London.
Pynchon writes about the Second World War by writing around it. He

describes the conditions that make the Holocaust possible rather than describe the Holocaust itself, maps the forces that engineer war and peace and define the distinction, and describes the effects of the war on individuals powerful and weak.[6] Above all he describes the dynamics of the new world the rocket and the war bring into being—the world of push-button death, divided up by superpowers, in which individuals feel increasingly impotent. Pynchon poses a contemporary version of the age-old question of evil. What forces and what people are responsible for the malevolent order of reality, for the suffering and oppression of the masses, for the haunting prospect, in the age of the rocket, of instant pointless death? Who builds the rockets and fires them? Who destroys and devalues our lives?

To understand how Pynchon addresses these questions, it is necessary to understand the role of festivity and the carnival notion of two worlds: an "official" world of everyday routine, laws, values, and hierarchies sustained by the technology of the inanimate; and a carnival world of inverted or destroyed hierarchies, festive excess, and celebrations of the human and natural. We see this contrast of worlds throughout the novel but particularly clearly in one scene in which Roger Mexico identifies the war itself with his rival, Jessica's "official" fiancé: "Damned Beaver/Jeremy *is* the War, he is every assertion the fucking War has ever made—that we are meant for work and government, for austerity: and these shall take priority over love, dreams, the spirit, the senses and the other second-class trivia that are found among the idle and mindless hours of the day" (*GR* 177). There is no doubt about which side of this dichotomy Pynchon values, and yet *Gravity's Rainbow* depicts neither a static struggle nor a coexistence between official and carnival worlds but a conquest of the festive, comic world by the official world. The war will wreak a permanent change that peacetime cannot undo. Pynchon shows how the war mentality corrupts the spirit of play, how it corrupts children, sexuality, and festivity.

Just as the war threatens the fraternity and feasting of the banana breakfast, so too does the end of hostilities conversely manifest itself in the renewal of festive potential. "Now there's time again for holidays," thinks Ned Pointsman of "the White Visitation" (the bizarre Allied intelligence compound), as he spends his first postwar Whitsun by the sea (*GR* 269). Similarly, Pynchon opens "In the Zone" with a carnivalistic invocation to the Eis-Heiligen, ice saints of the North to whom winegrowers pray for early spring in a kind of Groundhog's Day ritual: "In certain years, especially War years, [the Eis-Heiligen] are short on charity, peevish, smug in their power" (*GR* 281). But this year (1945) peace has come and "the saints have refrained," winter sparing spring its wrath. "In the Zone" opens with the fertile hopes of spring: "Already vines are beginning to grow back over dragon's teeth, fallen Stukas, burned tanks. The sun warms the hillsides, the rivers fall bright as wine" (*GR* 281). Everything promises a festive blossoming into peacetime.

But the corruption continues to poison festivity even after the war. Pynchon applies the carnival metaphor to a telling parable of the war's indestructibility. At the White Visitation, which houses mental patients as a cover for its intelligence operations, lives a schizophrenic who believes he is the Second World War. When the Allies invade Normandy, his body temperature rises to 104 degrees; as the Axis troops retreat "he speaks of darkness invading his mind"; a late offensive in the war temporarily rejuvenates him, as does each rocket blast. "He's to die on V-E Day. If he's not in fact the War then he's its child surrogate" (*GR* 131). But the parable has a grim twist, for the reversal of the carnival world becomes reversed itself: "Come the ceremonial day, look out. The true king only dies a mock death. Remember. Any number of young men may be selected to die in his place while the real king, foxy old bastard, goes on" (*GR* 131). The true king is the war, and V-E day nothing but an illusion. Somehow, Pynchon tells us, the death-dealing spirit of the war survives, merely disguised in the rhetoric of peace. This parable augurs a complete corruption of festivity; it is as if winter were to survive its conquest by spring and slyly rule under May's guise. Festival celebrates a cyclical view of the world in which death feeds into regeneration, and winter into spring. War insists on progress, a linear movement toward one great goal, in which all steps, affirmative or horrible, are irreversible. War challenges the reversibility from which the festive spirit gains its power: "Nothing can really stop the Abreaction of the Lord of the Night unless the Blitz stops, rockets dismantle, the entire film runs backward: faired skin back to sheet steel back to pigs to white incandescence to ore, to Earth. But the reality is not reversible" (*GR* 139). The Blitz may stop, but the rockets will not be dismantled; in fact, the infant technology of the war will grow into ever more rockets with which modern society must live.

We see this in the post-hostilities festivals and parties, which are interrupted by "the authorities" and generally end in Slothrop's desperate flight. As the book progresses, Slothrop becomes increasingly identified as the carnival king, at once monarch and fool, honored guest and sacrificial victim. At the Casino Hermann Goering before V-E day, but after the liberation of that part of France, Slothrop begins a bright holiday with a trek down the beach and amorous flirtations with French girls. The episode accelerates into a wild farce that contains many comic, carnival elements; for example, Slothrop's varied costumes include a garish Hawaiian shirt, his naked body covered with seltzer water and feathers from a pillow fight, a purple bedsheet he wears after his clothes are stolen the next morning, and finally Major Bloat's British uniform. At one point the rain even provides him a clown's motley as he appears, "speckled, pied with rain" (*GR* 204). The amusing farce of Slothrop's disappearing clothes, however, grows increasingly ominous until his comic machinations appear no longer as liberating but as his preordained part in a game played with the forces in his pursuit: "Slothrop has been playing against the invisible House, perhaps after all for his soul, all day" (*GR* 205). Through this kind of play Slothrop not only becomes more clearly aware of the plots against him but also literally loses his identity—his uniform, his papers, and his identification. Bloat offers him a new uniform, with a stare having "nothing to it of holiday," and Slothrop accepts the ill-fitting garment, thinking "live wi' the way it feels mate, you'll be in it for a while" (*GR* 201). Slothrop accepts his future of changing uniforms and identities in the chaotic openness of the Zone; he becomes the Fool in a world hell-bent on destroying festivity.

The openness of the Zone into which Slothrop "escapes" holds possibilities as falsely promising as the cessation of hostilities itself. Geli Tripping tells Slothrop to "forget frontiers now. Forget subdivisions. . . . It's all been suspended. Vaslav calls it an 'interregnum'" (*GR* 294). Like Victor Turner's liminality, the Zone promises a creative state between systems of authority and enforcement. But as Slothrop discovers, that condition can simply multiply the figures of authority and mystify their interconnections. In the Zone authority repeatedly attacks festivity.

The greatest of these encounters is the Schweinheldfest, a "pigherofestival" in a small German village Slothrop passes through en route to Cuxhaven. As Slothrop drifts off to sleep in a small park, local children approach him and describe the upcoming festival. *Gravity's Rainbow* has several scenes in which children emerge at dusk to encounter Slothrop; as the outcast, victim, and fool he attracts these helpless orphans of the war. This night they tell him of Plechazunga, the Pig-Hero, sent by Thor to defend the town from a Viking invasion. Ever since the tenth century the epic tale has been reenacted on a Thursday (Thor's day) in late summer to commemorate the town's deliverance. "This year, though, it's in jeopardy" (*GR* 568). The festival's regular Plechazunga of thirty years' standing left for the war the preceding year and never returned. The children appeal to the portly Slothrop to play the pig, and, of course, as traveling fool of many guises, Slothrop accepts. In an earlier sequence he traveled in a Rocketman outfit with a Valkyries helmet and cape; now he dons a plush, padded, pig costume—bright pink, blue, and yellow.

Pigs have special significance in Pynchon. Their excrement fertilizes the soil where Pirate's bananas grow, and such positive, earthy associations continue throughout Pynchon's fiction. Pigs appear as the lowly charges of William Slothrop, Tyrone's heretical Puritan ancestor; in the form of a pig uterus nailed above the threshold of a party; and as Pig Bodine, a character in *V.* and *Gravity's Rainbow*. Pig Bodine is probably our best clue to Pynchon's view of pigs: a lusty, belching, obscene sailor, he is always good-hearted, loyal as a friend, and possessed of tremendous creative energy. Appropriately, he provides a choric voice urging "Party, party!" throughout *V.* We will meet him again in the climactic banquet scene of *Gravity's Rainbow*. Allon White claims that "Pigs in Pynchon all betoken a kind of frenzied, degenerate rejection of bourgeois order in the name of orgiastic revelry and crude appetite."[7] White calls the pig "the carnival animal par excellence" and follows Bakhtin in viewing the pig as carnival victim and king, representing human appetite and, when eaten, satisfying it. In the Schweinheldfest the pig seems to stand for the outcast and downtrodden as well as for bodily indulgence and general license; that is, for both the festive population and their behavior, the lower social strata and the lower bodily strata. The arrival of Plechazunga, defender of the meek, becomes the occasion for celebrative carnal indulgence.

The initial ritual proceeds without a hitch, Slothrop delivering his one line and driving out the children who are dressed as tiny Vikings. The simple drama is surrounded by the accoutrements of festival excess—fireworks, drink (a horrible liquor distilled from oatmeal and flavored with dill), and sensuously described food (beer and sausages and hot, dripping Kartoffelpuffer). But when the feasting gives way to a black market exchange, the police step in, viciously beating women and children. Pynchon, through Slothrop, speculates that the civil police, overshadowed during the war, have burst upon the postwar scene with renewed savagery, transmuting the war's militarism into peacetime ferocity. Protected by his padded suit, Slothrop withstands the billy-club blows longer than most of the villagers and wonders for a moment if he is expected "to repel *real* foreign invaders now" (*GR* 570). Once the police open fire, such heroic thoughts vanish and Slothrop, aided by a nameless girl, joins the flight. Still in his pig suit, Slothrop spends a romantic afternoon hidden in bed with his protector. Throughout *Gravity's Rainbow* Slothrop's last-minute escapes from parties and festivals stress the fleeting and abortive nature of all human contact in the Zone.

Slothrop leaves his protector nothing "but a last snapshot of a trudging pig in motley, merging with the stars and woodpiles" (*GR* 573). He has taken the identity of his carnival role and made love to her as Plechazunga. To survive he has gone one step closer to the complete dispersion of his identity. The everyday world is so corrupted that it offers no stability to return to from the communal loss of identity associated with festivity's upside-down world. The process of transformation and return is interrupted because of radical doubts about identity within the normal world. Indeed, Slothrop's next journey takes him further from the familiar. He encounters a real pig who travels with him as "a jolly companion" and leads him to Franz Pökler, who is living in the ghostly abandoned carnival town, Zwolfkinder, which is "perishing from an absence of children" (*GR* 575). The image of the empty amusement park with its enormous rusted Ferris wheel culminates the novel's treatment of the war's destruction of childhood, a theme that parallels the corruption of festivity and is reinforced by this particular image.

The pig festival, ripped apart by vicious cops, is but one of many parties and festivals from which Slothrop must flee. None offer him protection from those hunting him; the festival world seems to offer neither true liberation nor a temporary respite that would enliven the everyday world and render it livable. Perhaps the grimmest, most succinct example of the war poisoning festivity occurs when Slothrop attends a Schwarzkommando party held in honor of rocket scavenging. This affair usurps its form from older folk festivals in an ominous way: "It's a Rocket-Raising: a festival new to this country. Soon it will come to the folk-attention how close Wernher von Braun's birthday is to the Spring Equinox, and the same German impulse that once rolled flower-boats through the towns and staged mock battles between young Spring and deathwhite old Winter will be erecting strange floral towers out in the clearings and meadows, and the young scientist-surrogate will be going round and round with old Gravity or some such buffoon, and the children will be tickled, and laugh" (*GR* 361).

No longer commemorating the natural cycle of spring over winter, the new festival commemorates humankind's defeat of nature, a triumph over gravity, a festival illustrating "Plasticity's central canon: that chemists were no longer to be at the mercy of Nature" (*GR* 249). Pynchon specifically ties the failure of festivity to modern technological and social changes and suggests an inversion of the traditional festive relation with nature. Pynchon's vision of corrupted festivity does share a good deal with the anthropological devaluation of contemporary festivity I criticized in the Introduction. But it differs in that the importance of the rites depicted is never questioned, and the causes of failure are identified with antifestive social forces not with a simplistic vision of the superficiality of modern life. Several scenes of actual contemporary parties in *Gravity's Rainbow* do, however, illustrate corruption from within, a corruption beyond interference from authority. But the surfacing of repressed violence, or the transmuting of festive impulses into decadent desperation, remains linked to the stultifying powers of Them, which Pynchon is at pains to describe.

The best illustration of festivity corrupted by internal violence occurs at the party at Chez Raoul de la Perlimpinpin, in Cap d'Antibes. The party, near Slothrop's temporary home at the Casino Hermann Goering, is hosted by Raoul, the heir of a fireworks magnate (fireworks represent the festive incarnation of the rocket, somewhere between the transcendent dream of space travel and the brutal domination of weaponry). The party celebrates the end of hostilities, "if 'party' is the word for something that's been going on nonstop ever since this piece of France was liberated" (*GR* 243–44). The guests come from all over Europe, "linked by some network of family, venery and a history of other such parties whose complexity [Slothrop's] head's never quite been able to fit around"

(GR 244). Like so many systems in Pynchon, this party is presented as a code to be deciphered, a part of a possibly sinister pattern.

Slothrop dresses for the party in comically festive garb: he wears a green suit with a purple check, a flowered tie, brown and white golf shoes with white socks, and a "midnight-blue" fedora. In the paranoid world of *Gravity's Rainbow* Slothrop's odd costume marks him as a victim, an individual allowed neither to fade into the crowd nor to shape his own destiny. Slothrop's various costumes signal not only his developing role as the Fool, but also his qualified individuality, which renders him both prominent and helpless. His individuality emerges through the selectivity of his paranoia. Like Joseph Heller's Yossarian, Slothrop reads the life-destroying forces of the war as a conspiracy aimed specifically at him. And like Yossarian, the scandalous truth of his analysis generates a self-fulfilling prophecy: they *are* out to get him.

The party description opens by cleverly combining the motifs of feasting and intoxication through the announcement that some guest has spiked the hollandaise sauce with hashish. The guests have devoured the broccoli with enthusiasm while the rest of an elaborate dinner stands neglected. By the time Slothrop arrives, "a third of the company are already asleep, mostly on the floor" (GR 244). The ongoing party with guests falling asleep suggests chaotic festivity. At this point in the description, Pynchon switches to what I term panoramic description, his technique for communicating the crowded and varied activity of the party economically:

> There are the usual tight little groups out in the gardens, dealing. Not much spectacle tonight. A homosexual triangle has fizzed over into pinches and recriminations, so as to block the door to the bathroom. Young officers are outside vomiting among the zinnias. Couples are wandering. Girls abound, velvet-bowed, voile-sleeved, underfed, broad-shouldered and permed, talking in half a dozen languages. . . . Eager young chaps with patent-leather hair rush about trying to vamp the ladies, while older heads with no hair at all prefer to wait, putting out only minimal effort, eyes and mouths across the rooms, talking business in the meantime. . . . Dopers and drinkers struggle together without shame at the buffet and in the kitchens, ransacking the closets, licking out the bottoms of casseroles. A nude bathing party passes

through on the way down the sea-steps to the beach. Our host, that
Raoul, is roaming around in a ten-gallon hat, Tom Mix shirt and brace
of sixguns with a Percheron horse by the bridle. The horse is leaving
turds on the Bokhara rug, also on the odd supine guest. (*GR* 244–46)

This brief description maps the party room by room, cataloging the
guests by sex, dress, age, and preferred intoxicant. Pynchon uses the
ambiguous generalizing plurals to suggest a crowd. And the application
of specific adjectives to groups of people—"velvet-bowed" girls, chaps
with "patent-leather hair"—furthers the namelessness and generality of
the description. Pynchon's technique focuses on the mood of the party
and the nature of the crowd at the expense of describing individuals.
The occasional switch from the progressive tense ("officers are outside
vomiting") to the simple present ("a nude bathing party passes through")
suggests time passing. And direct narrative comment reinforces the chaotic mood: "What's happening is not clear"; and "[The party] is all out of
shape, no focus to it" (*GR* 244, 246). Pynchon uses these techniques to
communicate the chaotic richness and complexity of a party in this brief
passage.

In spite of the wartime setting, the party description clearly draws
on the American subcultures of the fifties and sixties and the beat fiction that celebrated it. We can see this in the emphasis on intoxication,
particularly through drugs, and the suggestion of an atmosphere where
anything is permitted, a festive oasis defiantly opposed to the decorum
of traditional society. The outside world, however, will reassert itself in
the form of the war. We begin to sense this in the scenario racketeer
Blodgett Waxwing tells to Slothrop: "a typical WW II romantic intrigue,"
involving many of the guests in a black market network of drugs, usury,
weapons, and prostitution and proceeding in the cheerful, capitalist wartime spirit of *Catch-22*'s Milo Minderbinder (*GR* 247). The true business
of the war is business.

As if on cue, one of the items in dispute in the black market loan controversy, a fully equipped Sherman tank, appears grinding through the
garden shrubbery, its driver, Tamara, intent on settling her debt with
Raoul without further ado. Guests flee shrieking, falling over each other
and into tubs of black market Jell-O. Tamara manages to load and fire

a three-inch shell (which sets a drape afire but fails to explode) before Slothrop pulls her from the tank and halts the destruction.

This chaotic, violent finale combines several qualities typical of Pynchon's parties and sketches both the affirmative and negative possibilities for festivity. The tank demonstrates, of course, the continuing power of the war: the postwar party, inevitably configured by the war it responds to, cannot escape the carnage central to that war, just as our postwar society has inherited the military and industrial values that originally made the war possible. But at the height of the confusion, Slothrop has a glimpse of freedom. After struggling with the beautiful Tamara in a wrestling bout that was not "without its erotic moments," Slothrop notices that "loud noise and all . . . he doesn't seem to have an erection" (his pursuers are considering both noise and violent destruction as possible stimuli explaining Slothrop's conditioned response to the V-2). Slothrop thinks, "Hmmm. This is a datum London never got, because nobody was looking" (*GR* 248). The chaos of the party at its height has temporarily freed him from surveillance, granted him a moment he can believe is his own. This moment is a refreshing alternative to the moments in which the excessive behavior of festive occasions is used to gather intelligence— when Slothrop gets Dodson-Truck drunk at The-Prince-of-Wales-has-lost-his-tails party in order to pump him for information (*GR* 211–17), or when Tchitcherine spies on the marriage initiation rituals of Asian tribal peoples to learn the location of the Khirgiz light (*GR* 356–59). Slothrop's moment of freedom offers a rare instance of hope in the developing importance of festivity to the informal resistance called the Counterforce. If the structure of the world reflects malevolent conspiracy, then perhaps chaos and disruption can become life-giving, not merely entropic.

But Pynchon symbolically sketches, at the same time, the direction parties can take *away* from true possibilities for liberation into the reactionary realm of decadence: "Turns out the projectile, a dud, has only torn holes in several walls, and demolished a large allegorical painting of Virtue and Vice in an unnatural act. . . . The burning drape's been put out with champagne" (*GR* 248). At first the destruction of Virtue and Vice might suggest a movement beyond good and evil, a postwar amorality. But the shell has destroyed not simply a picture of Vice and Virtue but a picture of Vice and Virtue "in an unnatural act," thus moving beyond

decadence itself. Pynchon views "unnatural acts" as a response to decadent boredom, an exhaustion of sexual possibilities, which has little to
do with "sin." The destruction of the already decadent painting suggests
accelerating decline, the corruption of the corrupt. Raoul's party possesses the familiar never-ending quality that decadent rejection of the
everyday world requires: we identified it in the narrator's opening qualification concerning the applicability of "party," and we see it again in the
brief mention of a girl "with a face like Tenniel's Alice" (*GR* 247), which
suggests that Ur-version of the desperate never-ending festivity, the Mad
Tea Party. Pynchon shows us festivity threatened from without and corrupted from within. But if parties create another world, characterized by
opposition to the dominant, everyday world, then they offer the creative
possibility of liberating new modes of existence as well as the repressive
alternative of futile decadence in which self-destruction substitutes for
external domination. Both possibilities receive fuller treatment in crucial
scenes we will examine in detail: the decadent floating party aboard the
Anubis and the liberating celebrations of the Counterforce (the affirmative
unofficial underground of *Gravity's Rainbow*).

The prolonged scene aboard the *Anubis*, a ship floating down the
Spree-Oder Canal in the Zone, is Pynchon's fullest, most imaginative
treatment of decadence. Like many of the great party scenes in *Gravity's
Rainbow*, it has important antecedents in Pynchon's earlier fiction, particularly his first novel, *V.*, in which he explicitly examines the forms
of decadent behavior: "Decadence, decadence. What is it? Only a clear
movement towards death or, preferably, non-humanity" (*V* 301). The
parties of "The Whole Sick Crew" and Foppl's siege party in Sudwest
Afrika illustrate this definition of decadence. No siege threatens the ongoing party upon the decks of the *Anubis* in *Gravity's Rainbow*, but the
ship functions as clearly as the siege in *V.* to create a closed system. When
the orgy on board reaches its highest point the guests form a "daisy-
chain" of sexually interlocked bodies, creating a closed system in human
form. Slothrop is led to the *Anubis* because he is briefly traveling with
German film star Margherita Erdmann, who is seeking her husband,
Miklos Thanatz, and her friends from the German cinema—"a yachtful
of refugees from the Lublin regime" including her estranged daughter,
Bianca. Slothrop, not one to miss a party, goes along for the ride.

The ship appears on the Spree-Oder Canal as a "cheerful array of lights, red, green and white," bowsprit adorned with a "gilded winged jackal" (Anubis, courier of death, laughing hound of hell). On board, the continual party surges forward, music mingling with the noises of the "chattering affluent in evening dress" (*GR* 459). Pynchon sets this party in the *Naarenschiff* tradition, explicitly marking it as a microcosm of human folly likened to the morbid, pilotless death ships of folklore. Slothrop, as an American, rounds out this floating League of Nations: " 'We are the ship of all nations now,' " a party guest remarks (*GR* 462). The ship, Pynchon implies, embodies human desire: "There are ships we can dream across terrible rapids, against currents . . . our desire is wind and motor" (*GR* 462).[8]

The ship of fools motif, best known from Sebastian Brant's *Das Naarenschiff* (1494), was a conceit for criticizing folly through a microcosmic society. But the notion of a traveling gang of fools also suggests a party in a positive sense, akin to the paradigmatic societies of Boccaccio's or Chaucer's pilgrimages. Brant attacks festive excess, as one would expect, treating "gluttony and feasting" with the rest of the embodied sins. Brant's list of historic personages felled by their drunkenness moves toward the rather hedonistic moral that sensual indulgence undermines worldly success: "Are wine and sumptuous food your itch? / You'll not be happy, not get rich."[9] Pynchon follows the ship of fools tradition in exploiting the notion of a social paradigm, but his moral perspective reverses Brant's: drunkenness and lust do not lead to social collapse but are responses to it; the prolonged party reacts to a preexistent perception of social decadence. The ship of fools becomes the inescapable metaphor for society when the complementary possibility of a penitential St. Ursula's ship sailing to salvation is no longer taken seriously.[10]

This scene's mixture of frenetic sexuality in various incarnations, obsessive fascination with pain and death, and the glittering role-filled world of pornographic film stars suggests another, more recent, literary influence, William Burroughs. Pynchon derives themes from other Beat writers of the American fifties, as well: the counterculture quest tales of Kerouac and Ginsberg, and the vision of society as oppressive machine crystallized in Kesey's "combine." Burroughs, however, is the dominant presence. Pynchon echoes him in his invention of imaginary mind-altering drugs and in his comically absurd gangs and conspiracies. Above all, he follows Burroughs in his fascination with death-riddled

pornography. The scene aboard the *Anubis* recalls "A-J's Annual Party" in
Naked Lunch.[11] Burroughs's pornographer, Slashtubitch, whose films feature sodomites experiencing final orgasms as nooses break their necks,
presages Gerhardt von Goll's masterpiece in which Margherita is gang-
raped by men wearing black hoods or carnival masks (this is how, it turns
out, Margherita's daughter, Bianca, is conceived). The varied sexual configurations aboard the *Anubis* echo Burroughs, about whom John Updike
has written: "Not since the Marquis de Sade has so much mechanical
copulation been so gravely arranged. Ejaculation is an explosion of sorts,
and the young male body the ultimate weapon."[12] These associations
of sexuality with the mechanical and with the destructive technology of
weapons provide Pynchon with his most powerful metaphor for how
society shapes individual desire. The ferocity and grim relish of the pornographer that make Burroughs (and some parts of Pynchon) such painful reading point ultimately to a vision of sexuality corrupted in the age
of the machine. Burroughs and Pynchon capture not the pornographer's
ability to shock but rather his penchant for grim mechanical repetition
and exhaustion of possibilities.

The party aboard the *Anubis* provides the clearest exposition of Pynchon's insistent linking of sexuality, death, and the rocket. A writer dedicated to mapping interlocking conspiracies, Pynchon depicts decadence
as a social phenomenon encompassing political and industrial, as well as
individual, behavior. Pynchon's panoramic survey in this scene offers a
glimpse of a party superficially organized around drinking and dancing
while the real fascination lies with sex and drugs. Waiters, for example,
offer exotic drug paraphernalia and sexual aids in addition to drinks.
Some people are emptying "sinister white powder[s]" into drinks while
other couples "[moan] together in life boats" (*GR* 463). The spirit of the
party strikes Slothrop as "the same old shit that was going on back at
Raoul de la Perlimpinpin's place." Perhaps, he speculates, it is even the
same party (*GR* 463).

The symbolic presence of death at this party reappears insistently. Not
only does the ship's name and symbol suggest a ferry to hell, but the
guests' names, songs, and party accoutrements all point to a particularly forceful morbidity. When Slothrop and Margherita are awaiting the
ship's arrival, they encounter a pale woman, dressed entirely in black
and carrying in her eyes "all the malaise of a Europe dead and gone" (*GR*

458). The woman seems a frightening apparition to Margherita, and it is only aboard the *Anubis* that Slothrop will discover why—the woman's dress recalls Margherita's when in the past she hunted and murdered small children. This grisly story is related, in a morbid parenthesis, by an oriental ensign fittingly named Morituri.

When Slothrop boards the ship, he is greeted with the song, "Welcome Aboard!" which ominously suggests that though the guests cannot recall how the "fabulous orgy" started, "there's only one way it can end." The song concludes:

> Come a-
> board the *Titanic*, things'll really be manic,
> Folks'll panic the second that sunken ice*berg* is knocked,
> Naughty'n'noisy, and very Walpurgisnacht,
> That's how the party will end,
> So—welcome aboard, welcome aboard, my friend!
>
> (GR 462–63)

The decadent party ends only in death; it admits no world to return to, no other way for the party to conclude. Indeed, Slothrop, when he makes his typical exit, nearly loses his life: after several days of comfortable elegance, a storm turns the party into a vomit-drenched debauchery with "barfing aristocracy sag[ging] all down the life-lines," and in the midst of the tempest Slothrop falls overboard hearing "the Iron Guard on the radio screaming *Long Live Death*" (GR 490, 491).

The segment of the festivities Slothrop observes between his death-bracketed entrance and exit is equally darkened by memento mori. The closest thing to a host is Miklos Thanatz, whose name suggests not merely death, but in this post-Freudian age, the subconscious desire for death. Thanatos plays into Pynchon's primary theme and echoes Freud's questions: How does civilization work against life? How do the structures created by life-affirming cultural growth turn against humanity?[13] We meet Miklos Thanatz—admittedly a weak personification for all the human fears Thanatos encompasses—armed with appropriate props: "drinking absinthe out of a souvenir stein on which, in colors made ghastly by the carnival lights on deck, bony and giggling Death is about to surprise two lovers in bed" (GR 464). This remarkably condensed image strikes at the heart of decadence. The green absinthe, the most narcotic of liquors (it causes Stephen's hallucinations in the "Circe" episode of *Ulysses*), fills the cup emblazoned with a traditional memento mori that plays on the old pun associating death with sexual climax. But death is no surprise in the already stylized world of the "souvenir cup," which suggests both memory and tawdry commercialism. Perversely, death has been rendered ghastly by carnival: the image suggests the overturning of the carnival treatment of death, which usually renders death's inevitability more palatable. This is consistent with the spirit of Thanatos: when alienation renders a culture incapable of celebrating life it can only turn to death, or more specifically to death obsessions couched in living behavior. Decadence, as Pynchon suggests, moves toward death through inhumanity, extending the process of dying to relish in putrefaction.

In an astounding Burroughs-like image, Pynchon depicts the flowering of decadence in a union of sex and death: "A girl with an enormous glass dildo inside which baby piranhas are swimming in some kind of decadent lavender medium amuses herself between the buttocks of a stout transvestite in lace stockings and a dyed sable coat" (*GR* 468). Heightening the association of sex with death involves an increase in decadent imitation; the penis-as-weapon becomes a piranha-filled glass dildo. Sex can only approach death's consummation but through perversity offers a convincing imitation. For Pynchon the perversity that transforms sexuality from life-engendering to death-desiring expresses the decadent exhaustion of human possibilities. This explains Pynchon's pornographic fascination in this scene and elsewhere. Pornography's essence is titillation through the forbidden. Like decadence itself, it is doomed to be ever-accelerating, encompassing more and more of a diminishing field. As the pornographic imagination conquers realms of forbidden sexuality, the remaining territory becomes increasingly narrow and brutal, closer to violence and death. Thanatz speculates that sadomasochism is the most forbidden form of sexuality because "submission and dominance are resources [the state] needs for its very survival" (*GR* 737). Whether or not one accepts Thanatz's "sado-anarchism," the progression toward violence remains unmistakable.

Sexuality divorced from feeling offers finite and diminishing possibilities. In the party's central scene Margherita's vicious public whipping of her twelve-year-old daughter excites her guests into a sexual frenzy, a mass orgy (*GR* 466–68). Within this closed circle of daisy-chain sexuality,

Pynchon, as stoic comedian, exhausts the pornographer's possibilities: only so many configurations of genitals, breasts, orifices, and sexual paraphernalia are possible. This vision of diminishing sexual possibilities reduces the human aspect of sexual intercourse so that mechanical coupling and bestiality become parallel manifestations of dehumanization. The orgy becomes the paradigm of all entropying levels of human behavior.

Pynchon follows the group orgy with a private sex scene between twelve-year-old Bianca and Slothrop. His page-long description of their lovemaking could come from any explicitly erotic novel until, approaching the climax, he inserts a bizarre twist as Slothrop suddenly feels his entire being concentrated inside his own penis: "Yes, inside the metropolitan organ entirely, all other colonial tissue forgotten and left to fend for itself, his arms and legs it seems *woven* among vessels and ducts, his sperm roaring louder and louder, getting ready to erupt, somewhere below his feet. . . . He is enclosed. . . . She starts to come, and so does he, their own flood taking him up then out of his own expectancy, out the eye at the tower's summit and into her with a singular detonation of touch. Announcing the void, what could it be but the kingly voice of the Aggregat [the A-4 rocket] itself?" (*GR* 470). We do not need that last sentence to recognize the parallel between penis and rocket and between this scene and Gottfried's being launched in the Rocket 00000, enshrouded in Imipolex-G, the synthetic erectile tissue. Slothrop, the man whose penis is not his own (see the song at *GR* 216–17), becomes contained in that penis, grotesquely determined, the rocket controlling his entire being. Oddly, the extremity of this experience jolts Slothrop into a rare awareness that his sexual partner exists as a person: "She *exists*, love, invisibility" (*GR* 470). But the crucial learning experience is hideously too late: he will never see her again, learning later, only obliquely, that her mother has killed her.

This scene unites the theme of behavioral control with the repeated phallic associations of the rocket. Thanatz, who, we will learn later, observed the firing of Rocket 00000, describes the assembled A-4 as "fueled, alive, ready for firing . . . fifty feet high, trembling . . . and then the fantastic, virile roar. Your ears nearly burst. Cruel, hard, thrusting into the virgin-blue robes of the sky, my friend. Oh, so phallic" (*GR* 465). Later, when Slothrop comes across a newspaper photograph of the bombing of Hiroshima, he sees the mushroom cloud as "a giant white cock, dangling in the sky straight downward out of a white pubic bush" (*GR* 693). And when Blicero finally launches Gottfried, the sexual imagery includes "a candle in a dead man's hand, erect as all your tissue will grow at the first delicious tongue-flick of your mistress Death" (*GR* 750). The elaborate thematic connection between rocket and phallus must signify more than the obvious link of the rocket with the masculine technologies of warfare and industry. Pynchon goes further to suggest that our sexuality responds to the entire complex of social forces that valorize domination under the aegis of free enterprise and the omnipresence of the rocket under the aegis of security. Pynchon wants to show how our sexuality expresses the inexorably negative progress of society for which "decadence" is but one word.

The same technology that built the rocket engendered Pointsman, who dreams of reducing all human emotion and action to stimulus and response. The dream of no longer being at the mercy of nature connects the radically different branches of the scientific, industrial, and military worlds; it unites the different metaphors of the White Visitation. Procreation gives way to artificial synthesis; the organic yields to the inanimate in the closed-system vision of Kekulé's dream-serpent swallowing its tail.[14] Depersonalized sexuality struggles suspended between two potent incarnations of the Word—equations and obscenity. This opposition tells us a lot about Pynchon's world.[15] *Gravity's Rainbow* is populated with dozens of men who worship the equation, from the sympathetic Roger Mexico to the evil Ned Pointsman. In the serene beauty of numbers they perceive a potent alchemy capable of calling things into being, of synthesizing rubber or gasoline or LSD or building a rocket. Beyond the illusion of the equation as impartial or pure signs (i.e., completely referential), lies the myth of scientific creation. The creative power of the equations is reified in the Mittelwerke, the rocket factory built in the shape of a double-integral. Death-dealing source for the rocket, this factory has a shape, Pynchon indicates, which can be read in many ways: as the double-integral that allows rocket flight to be captured in equations, as the SS of Hitler's Germany, as "the shape of lovers curled asleep," or as "the ancient rune that stands for the yew tree, or Death" (*GR* 302). This multiplicity of meanings eludes the scientist, however, who is blinded by the beauty of the equation, the impartiality of the "variable," the power "of finding hidden centers, inertias unknown" (*GR* 302). Precisely this predictive and creative power of science has led to other methods of understanding the world losing their truth status in modern society. And throughout *Gravity's Rainbow* the equation lurks as a language for reducing sexuality to function, to stimulus and response. The equation subsumes sexuality's organic, creative power and allows it to be thoroughly mechanized.

Against the power of the equation, Pynchon offers the obscenity. Pornography may be eroticism catering to a decadent, mechanical world, but obscenity remains, like the equation, a spell. The obscene yell or remark constitutes rebellion, an attempt to deny oppressive structures through the utterance of a magic word. When Slothrop first begins to sense the depth of conspiracy surrounding him, he appeals to obscenity for help: " 'Fuck you,' whispers Slothrop. It's the only spell he knows, and a pretty good all-purpose one at that. His whisper is baffled by the thousands of tiny rococo surfaces. Maybe he'll sneak in tonight—no not at night—but sometime, with a bucket and brush, paint FUCK YOU in a balloon coming out of the mouth of one of those little pink shepherdesses there" (*GR* 203). The scene recalls Holden Caulfield's vision of obscene graffiti on the insides of the great pyramids and testifies to some feeble yet irrepressible human spirit.[16] "Fuck you" becomes a cry from the carnival world, one of the carnivalistic blasphemies Bakhtin celebrates. It remains the cry of the preterite, the outcast, the Counterforce. Not a creative spell, it can only attempt to negate or ward off what has become repressive in the official world.

The melange of science and pornography in Pynchon's sexual universe thus presents an opposition that excludes the simply human. Obscenity, tool of the Counterforce, represents the language of sexuality stripped of everything but its capacity to shock and disrupt, while equations represent the language of sexuality reduced, along with all human behavior, into physical law. And the supposed impartiality of the equation has long since been lost to the rule of the rocket, pure science conquered by the kingdom of death (as demonstrated by the stories of Franz Pökler and Kurt Mondaugen). Between the metaphors employed by scientist and pornographer, humans grope for love and feeling, perhaps gaining it in fleeting revelation as Slothrop does in the postcoital insight he experiences in Bianca's embrace. That his lover is a person offers some hope that he may be also, though what is happening to him increasingly undermines that hope.

The obscenity becomes the weapon of the counterforce, the liberating power of the carnivalistic blasphemy that seeks to shake the grip of a rejected official world. But the undeniable potency of obscenity pales beside the powers of Them, as the description of Slothrop's plummet from the *Anubis* suggests: "Flipped that easy over the side and it's adios to the *Anubis* and all its screaming Fascist cargo, already no more ship, not even black sky as the rain drives down his falling eyes now in quick needlestrokes, and he hits, without a call for help, just a meek tearful *oh fuck,* tears that will add nothing to the whipped white desolation that passes for the Oder Haff tonight" (*GR* 491).

Carnival and parties are so important to Pynchon because he interprets the world in terms of the preterite and the elect, and this opposition finds expression in the antithesis between the carnival spirit and the official, everyday world. As a result the ambivalence about whether festivity subverts or supports the official culture is crucial to Pynchon's work. The *Anubis* episode captures the decadence of society's elite: the festivity on board mirrors social decline and offers no alternative vision. Slothrop's last glimpse of the boat (a couple of weeks after his stay on board) makes this clear: "The white *Anubis,* gone on to salvation. Back here, in her wake, are the preterite, swimming and drowning, mired and afoot. . . . Men overboard and our common debris" (*GR* 667). But the world excluded from the *Anubis*'s self-indulgent dance towards death holds out affirmative possibilities: "There is a key, among the wastes of the World . . . and it won't be found on board the white *Anubis* because they throw everything of value over the side" (*GR* 667–68).

These valuable wastes of the world form what Pynchon dubs the Counterforce, the carnival complement to the official world of the Elect: " 'For every They there ought to be a We. In our case there is. Creative paranoia means developing at least as thorough a We-system as a They-system—' " (*GR* 638). The efficacy of the Counterforce is seriously questioned in *Gravity's Rainbow*'s concluding section, which bears its name, but the countersystem at least exists and unites Pirate, Katje, Roger Mexico, Carroll Eventyr, Osbie Feel, and other sympathetic characters of the novel's roaming preterite. Slothrop becomes, in a sense, their spiritual ally, but the Counterforce never succeeds in liberating him from his pursuers. For, in the final section of *Gravity's Rainbow*, Slothrop fragments and dissolves until he is no longer recognizable as an entity. This dispersion of the main character is the most daring of Pynchon's attempts to frustrate his readers. We see characters familiar with Slothrop failing to recognize him; we learn that he is "scattered all over the Zone" (*GR* 712); we see him merging into nature, lying naked for days with insects crawling over his body; we see him becoming one with the preterite waste scattered over the countryside and with the countryside itself; and then we lose track of him entirely.

The last vision of Slothrop comes when Pig Bodine offers him a piece of clothing stained with John Dillinger's blood as an emblem of the Counterforce, Dillinger having "socked Them right in the toilet privacy of Their banks" (*GR* 741). But Bodine is the last one who can even see Slothrop, and Slothrop fades away leaving behind only what might be a photograph of him: "There's supposed to be a last photograph of him on the only record album ever put out by The Fool, an English rock group. . . . There is no way to tell which of the faces is Slothrop's: the only printed credit that might apply to him is 'Harmonica, Kazoo—a friend.' But knowing his Tarot, we would expect to look among the Humility, among the gray and preterite souls, to look for him adrift in the hostile light of the sky, the darkness of the sea" (*GR* 742). Slothrop the victim-quester, both seeker and sought, has become the Fool, patron saint of the outcast, the carnival king.

The outcast world of the Counterforce finds festive expression most powerfully in the banquet Roger Mexico attends after his initiation into the ways of the Counterforce. At the end of the war, relocation orders separate him from his lover, Jessica, who decides to marry a respectable gentleman, Jeremy or "Beaver." In a moment of blinding revelation, Mexico discovers that the whole separation was probably engineered by Pointsman, and he storms the new corporate London headquarters of the mysterious "Firm" in a fury. In a wonderfully executed comic scene, he searches the offices until he discovers Pointsman at a board meeting. Roger Mexico stands in the center of the table and urinates on the assembled board members. His liberating gesture reminds us of the carnival world's reliance on obscenity, the celebration of the "lower bodily strata." Mexico's escape leads him into the welcoming arms of the Counterforce where its dynamics are explained to him by Pirate Pren-

tice and Osbie Feel. "'We piss on Their rational arrangements. Don't
we . . . Mexico?'" Osbie Feel proclaims to the cheers of the assembled
gang (*GR* 639).

Before Jeremy and Jessica leave Roger's part of the world for good,
Jeremy invites Roger to a dinner, "an intimate informal party at the home
of Stefan Utgarthaloki" (*GR* 709). Roger accepts, realizing it may be his
last chance to see Jessica, but also realizing that the party will be filled
with high-level executives including "at least one ear to the corporate
grapevine that's heard of the Urinating Incident" (*GR* 710). The party is
destined to be a stiff and lifeless affair of the corporate elite, and Roger's
presence there clearly courts the danger of arrest. But Roger goes, taking
along for moral support that crown prince of obscenity, Pig Bodine. At
this climactic banquet Pynchon engineers the collision between the two
worlds of festivity—one clearly endorsing the material order, the other
clearly opposing it.

Bodine and Mexico epitomize the subversive potential of festivity.
Bodine is dressed as a walking distraction, a carnival figure in the color-
ful Slothrop tradition. Bodine wears a parrot-colored zoot suit that makes
Slothrop's old white suit with keychain pale in comparison. The giant
lapels are supported with coat hanger stays rising above a purple-on-
purple satin shirt, and the "paint-blue" pants are quintuple-vented: "At
gatherings it haunts the peripheral vision, making decent small-talk impossible. . . . A subversive garment, all right" (*GR* 710).

At the party the music is equally subversive, performed by a string
quartet that includes as "inner voices" two dope-dealing partners sympathetic to the Counterforce. Their offering tonight is "the suppressed
quartet from the Haydn Op. 76, the so-called 'Kazoo' Quartet in G-Flat
Minor, which gets its name from the *Largo, cantabile e mesto* movement,
in which the Inner Voices are called to play kazoos instead of their usual
instruments, creating problems of dynamics for cello and first violin that
are unique in the literature" (*GR* 711). The kazoo, as we saw in Slothrop's
epitaph, symbolizes the music of the preterite, the wicked yet comic
carnival stab at the gravity of the conventional and the classical.

Everything else at the banquet is proper and formal. The guests include
not only Jessica and Jeremy but corporate lions from ICI and GE, Pynchon's epitome of the They of the military-industrial complex. Printed
music programs and menus complement the arranged seating in what
Pynchon deems "the bosom of the Opposition" (*GR* 713). Indeed it is

the printed menus that first excite the suspicions of Bodine and Mexico as Bodine notices the Überraschungbraten or "surprise roast." Turning from the menu to a huge stone barbecue with iron spits, Bodine and Mexico share a vision: simultaneously they see themselves, horribly maimed, turning over the roaring fire. They realize they are to be the main course.

Pynchon, here, presents the most potent of carnival ambivalences, the sacred ambivalence of the *pharmakos*. The sacrificial victim attains sacred status and thus must be killed but cannot be killed; high and low meet in the outcast *pharmakos* raised to royal status by his selection. In this parody of that carnival ambivalence, the invited guest becomes the sacrificial victim; the party of the official world becomes a malevolent "surprise" for the emissaries from the carnival world. It is worth recalling the Last Supper here, where betrayal transforms honored guest into sacrificial victim. Christ subverts the official plan by offering himself as food to unite his countercommunity of followers against his persecutors. Mexico and Bodine's strategy differs in its technique for reversing the persecution of the official world, yet the setting is still explicitly sacral: "Going in to dinner becomes a priestly procession, full of secret gestures and understandings" (*GR* 713).

After their mutual vision, Mexico and Bodine share a secret gesture of their own, shouting loudly at the table about the absence of ketchup. Significantly they choose indecorous behavior as the code that initiates their "repulsive stratagem," their disruption of the banquet through verbal obscenity. Mexico and Bodine calmly begin to announce dishes missing from the menu:

> "I can't seem to find any *snot soup* on the menu. . . ."
>
> "Yeah, I could've done with some of that *pus pudding*, myself. Think there'll be any of that?"
>
> "No, but there might be a scum soufflé!" cries Roger, "with a side of—*menstrual marmalade!*"
>
> "Well I've got eyes for some of that rich meaty smegma stew!" suggests Bodine. "Or howbout a *clot casserole*?"
>
> "I say," murmurs a voice, indeterminate as to sex, down the table.
> (*GR* 715)

The game continues, pairing body parts and excretion with culinary dishes in obscene, alliterative splendor. One cheerful guest joins in, banging her spoon with delight, and the "inner voices" of the quartet offer suggestions during rests in the kazoo passages. The rest of the company, however, grows angry and nauseated. Guests begin to vomit and flee, while others ominously threaten the heroic pair.

The strategem succeeds: "The flames in the pit have dwindled. No fat to feed them tonight" (GR 716). Roger and Pig escape before the oppressive forces at the banquet can reassemble themselves. As they flee, they receive an appropriate blessing from a servant: "The last black butler opens the last door to the outside, and escape. Escape tonight. 'Pimple pie with filth frosting, gentlemen,' he nods. And just at the other side of dawning, you can see a smile" (GR 717). It is the most ecstatic, joyful, and hopeful moment in the novel. And this entertaining comic scene, which exploits in its style the same tension between decorum and obscenity operating in its content, draws its power from traditional carnival roots. Not only the obscenity per se but the combination of human excretion and food lies deep in the festive tradition. In discussing the "Palaver of the Potulent" scene in Rabelais (1.5) in which the eating of tripe affects the devourer's own intestine, Bakhtin demonstrates the symbolic importance of "the dividing line between man's consuming body and the consumed animal's body [being] erased."[17] This same ambivalence resides in the pig as symbol of gluttony and as object for satisfying the appetite. And indeed the pig has functioned historically in carnival as both hero and main course. In this scene, incidentally, not only is Pig Bodine present, but one of the members of the subversive quartet sports a Porky Pig tattoo. The genital and excremental obsession of the Counterforce stratagem becomes a celebration of what the official culture insists on repressing, and the success of Roger and Pig's disruption is directly proportional to the degree of repression that grants obscenity its power to shock. Discussing the episode in Rabelais, Bakhtin concludes that "the merry, abundant and victorious bodily element opposes the serious medieval world of fear and oppression with all its intimidating and intimidated ideology."[18] Surely Pynchon celebrates the same spirit here, in a specifically modern context.

But a reader of *Gravity's Rainbow* cannot help notice how rare these moments are in contrast to the bleak horrors of the *Anubis*, the Firm, and the rocket. Whatever hopes are offered by the Counterforce are clearly outweighed by society's evils. The apocalyptic ending in which the reader is destroyed by an onrushing rocket heightens this imbalance. Pynchon even suggests that the Counterforce may ultimately be part of Their design: "They will use us. We will help legitimize Them" (*GR* 713). Roger Mexico sees death as the only alternative to serving the ominously capitalized Them: "Which is worse: living on as Their pet, or death? . . . He has to choose between his life and his death. Letting it sit for a while is no compromise, but a decision to live, on Their terms" (*GR* 713). The ambivalence concerning festivity's ultimate function cannot be overcome. Pynchon, however, does capture the liberating energy of parties and the affinity between festivity and the powerless: in the banquet scene; in Slothrop and Pig Bodine and their relentless party spirits; in the vitality of the Whole Sick Crew in *V.;* in the outdoor family reunion that joyfully concludes *Vineland*. But Pynchon does not view the networks of the counterculture as a panacea, nor does he lose sight of the ultimate implications of our powerlessness in the nuclear age. He shows no more than the potential of festive vision in his complex, encyclopedic interpretation of the workings of the world.

The panoramic, encyclopedic richness of Pynchon's carnival world creates a tension between form and content that complicates our final response to Pynchon's parties and to his novel. *Gravity's Rainbow*'s dark conclusion conflicts with the liberating, comic force of Pynchon's language. Finally, most writing strikes us as hopeful or life-affirming by virtue of its persistence; it represents that the author's faith in art and communication is enduring enough to create a complete work. Something of this inevitable realization tempers our reading of Waugh's bleak satire or Fitzgerald's dark tragedy, just as it informs our interpretation of Pynchon. Pynchon's enormous novel exhibits the affirmative all-inclusiveness and encyclopedic breadth that leads Bakhtin to call the novel a carnivalized genre. The thematic function of festivity in Pynchon complements the stylistic carnival he creates. Pynchon absorbs and recasts the multiple languages of our age—from Plasticman comics and King Kong to the Tarot deck, entropy, and the Poisson distribution. Tony Tanner identifies Pynchon's polyglossia with carnival, which he sees as "an enactment of life freeing itself from old rigidifying forms" and which he finds expressed in *Gravity's Rainbow*'s "carnival of discourses" that captures the "carnival of modern consciousness." [19]

In Pynchon, party scenes serve as microcosms of the social order, either artificially isolated or open to external influence. They demonstrate the tension between stultifying order (paranoia) and degenerating but potentially liberating chaos (entropy). Finally, Pynchon's party scenes adumbrate a complex festive vision that pits the unity of the festive world against the violent struggle between the powerful and the powerless, which is characteristic of the official world. The capacity to celebrate becomes the voice of community and personal love in a world bent on annihilating both.

The same tension between festivity's capacity to preserve the oppressive order and its capacity to subvert it animates Pynchon's view of language, as Tanner realizes. Indeed, *Gravity's Rainbow* can be read as a vast, encyclopedic, modern gloss on George Eliot's observation that "all of us, grave or light, get our thoughts entangled in metaphors, and act fatally on the strength of them."[20] *Gravity's Rainbow*'s famous opening presents not only the fatal threat of death from the sky but also a problem in metaphor: "A screaming comes across the sky. It has happened before, but there is nothing to compare it to now" (*GR* 3). The failure of metaphor—its fatal entanglements—runs throughout *Gravity's Rainbow:* in the different metaphors scientists and psychics use at the White Visitation; in the power of mandalas, equations, Tarot decks, and the rocket; in the Kirghiz Light and the Angel of Bleicherode; in obscenity and the languages of the black market and the drug world. All the metaphors are inadequate, kept by gravity from piercing the sky to a realm of higher meaning or truth. Yet within the all-embracing inclusiveness of the comic, carnival world that is the novel itself, these failed metaphors make up whatever truth the book contains. With appropriate carnival ambivalence we can recall *The Crying of Lot 49:* "The act of metaphor then was a thrust at truth and a lie, depending where you were."[21] So too our celebrations in their desperation and their hope.

6. From Nightsticks to Nightmares

PARTIES IN COOVER

"All the style's gone out of your parties, Ger . . .
there's too much shit and blood"

"Contagious hysteroid reactions of this sort are
typical wherever masses are assembled—it's an
imitative ritualization of the bizarre and hallucinatory
tendencies of the odd few, and always, I've noted,
with a tinge of the burlesque. Frankly, it's the sort of
thing I see too much of"
—*Gerald's Party*

Gerald's Party (1985) is a bruising book. Gerald, the host, ends up with an assortment of literal bruises as must most of the surviving guests, who collide, trip, and fall through the novel, and are beaten with nightsticks, croquet mallets, and fists. The reader, too, emerges somewhat battered, worn by the novel's assaults upon time, coherence, and verisimilitude. The bruising shocks of *Gerald's Party* are of a piece, though, with its raucous humor, sexuality, and parody. These elements exemplify a particular carnivalesque vision that combines traditional elements of the festive—license, excess, masquerade, travesty, and sacrifice—with the powerful modern symbol of the party gone wrong, celebration turned into nightmare. *Gerald's Party* dramatically illustrates Bakhtin's contention that the carnival influence on the novel is both thematic and genre-shaping; the novel combines festive setting with the carnivalized mingling of different fictional discourses. *Gerald's Party* partakes of several fictional codes or conventions—ritual sacrifice, detective story, slapstick, masquerade, dream, and drama—and the symbolic form of the party is the central point upon which the axes of the novel converge. These codes are particularly compatible with the rich symbolic associations of the party.

To appreciate the richness of *Gerald's Party*, to get beyond its immediate power to shock and amuse simultaneously, it helps to see how the party assimilates, through its multiple incarnations, the competing fictional codes that animate the novel. Much of the novel's excitement and tension arises from the collision of different fictional conventions or set pieces: the patterns of detective story narrative collide with the patterns of slapstick comedy or the logic of nightmares. To modify Tzvetan Todorov's terms, different verisimilitudes clash, and the result is a displacement of the reader's expectations.[1] At the party Gerald himself speaks of "all these violent displacements . . . it was as though we'd all been dislodged somehow, pushed out of the frame, dropped into some kind of empty dimensionless gap like that between film cuts, between acts" (*GP* 99). Gerald might be describing the reader's experience, except that the reader's sense of being "between acts" comes from an overabundance of narrative cues; narrative codes are not absent but invoked in such profusion as to subvert reader recognition. These displacements can have effects disorienting and frustrating, or comic and parodic. Whether frustrating or comic, the collisions of narrative conventions create surprise, and the novel moves through a series of such surprises. The many voices of the party converge, in rich polyphony or outrageous cacophony; so, too, do the multiple fictional conventions.

When I speak of a fictional code or convention, I mean a subgenre of the novel characterized by a particular set of images, plot patterns, motifs, and modes of discourse. Just as the novel is capable of including extraliterary discourses, it can also include and modify various fictional modes of discourse.[2] A code consists, to borrow M. H. Abrams's modification of Barthes, "mainly of artifices, arousing conventional expectations, which function entirely within the system of literary writing itself."[3] But when an author modifies a code and combines it with other fictional codes, those conventional expectations can be deliberately frustrated. *Gerald's Party* is not a detective novel, for example, but it invokes enough of the elements of the detective code to generate (and then frustrate) conventional reader expectations. Coover sees the novel as an arena in which various fictions interact. "Every effort to speak of the world, involves a kind of fiction-making process," he has commented in an interview. "There are always other plots, other settings, other interpretations. So if some stories start throwing their weight around, I like to undermine their authority a bit, work variations, call attention to their fictional natures."[4] This "undermining" aptly describes Coover's narrative technique in *Gerald's Party*, where a hearty and remorseless dialogism, and an accompanying play with conventions and expectations, structures the novel. In the same interview Coover revealingly indicates his interest in group behavior as a festive locus for the interactions of different fictions, "especially [Durkheim's] image of 'collective effervescence.'"[5]

The most powerful convention a modern novelist manipulates is the convention of realism. A good deal of the innovations of contemporary fiction are modes of play with the realist frame, which has conditioned the modern reader to expect the events of a fiction to mirror standards of social and psychological probability commonly associated with real life.[6] An author may dispense with the convention of formal realism at the outset, either through an invocation of an alternate and exclusive convention, such as the fairy tale, or through the rapid violation of certain realistic consistencies (or reader expectations). Coover does not choose either of these nonrealistic paths. Instead, certain conventions of realism obtain throughout the novel so that the violations of realism continue to have a disruptive or absurdist effect. The setting, first of all, recalls much realistic fiction: a suburban house party of intellectuals and professionals with middle-class food, drink, and furnishings. The narrative, though it frequently flies off into the improbable or bizarre, never broaches the impossible: the dead do not speak, people do not turn into butterflies or armadillos. Finally, Gerald's perspective is presented consistently, and his concern and unease, and eventually his sorrow and inarticulate anger, suggest a realistic human response to the increasingly odd events. Within these realistic parameters, however, Coover challenges the convention in several ways. He creates a sense of absurdity by presenting unusual or startling events without any reactions of shock or surprise from witnessing characters. The novel opens with the discovery of a corpse—someone has been stabbed to death at the party. People gather about the body; the police and an ambulance are summoned. When the murdered Ros's husband goes wild with grief, the situation is still contained within realistic probabilities, but when the police beat him to death with croquet mallets and Gerald's wife (unnamed in the text) continues making hors d'oeuvres while the guests continue to eat and drink, the realistic frame threatens to dissolve. As the party continues, three more guests will die violently; still, the wife cooks and serves and cleans, still the guests flirt, tell jokes, and drink. Eventually the juxtapositions become more violent: " 'Yum!' enthused Bunky, stepping over Ros's body and plucking a melon ball" (*GP* 277).

The novel has many such discordant absurdities: as Gerald's wife is being tortured by police (for no apparent reason), she begs Gerald to check the nachos in the oven. When Gerald reports his best friend, Vic, has bled to death, his wife asks him to carry coffee cups into the living room. He responds by frantically shouting, "I'll, I'll . . . *I'll bring the whipped cream!*" (*GP* 272). As the police intimidate and torture people, as the plumber is drafted to be a video cameraman, as the child's toy soldiers are beheaded and his stuffed bunny dismembered, we discover this is not a typical party of realistic fiction. The reader's sense of verisimilitude is strained and revised but never revised so thoroughly that the power of unusual events to disturb is sacrificed. The novel depends on supporting and subverting the familiar realistic parameters.

At the same time, the novel mirrors the cacophony of a wild party through its narrative interruptions. Scenes, paragraphs, and sentences are constantly interrupted. Parentheses abound, usually placed in mid-sentence to maximize the disruption. Gerald muses that, like multiple parentheses, "all conversations were encased in others, spoken and unspoken. . . . It was what gave them their true dimension, even as it made their referents recede" (*GP* 103). To achieve this effect Coover interweaves many dialogues without attribution. The reader can, like a guest at a party, concentrate on one conversation and ignore the others as "noise." Or the reader can read the conversations as commenting on one another in patchwork or montage fashion. Or the reader can analyze a passage to disentangle the different conversational threads. Much of the book's power arises from Coover's masterful involvement of the reader in ways such as these.

If the reader of a party novel is analogous to a guest, the narrator is analogous to the host. Gerald's first-person perspective unwaveringly dominates this book: we see what he sees and hear what he hears; we share his memories, thoughts, emotions, and the unease of his confusion. The opening sentence of the novel—"None of us noticed the body at first"—initiates the confusion. It calls our attention not only to Ros's corpse but also to the fact that no one has noticed it. Gerald then comments on the strangeness of his mood and thinks that "this may not turn out quite as I'd imagined after all" (*GP* 10). Soon Gerald articulates further unease: "I felt there was something I should be doing, something absolutely essential, but I couldn't think what it might be" (*GP* 15). Throughout the novel Gerald is haunted by similar discomforts: he notices things out of the corner of his eye, forgets where he is headed at times, misplaces guests he is searching for, half-remembers apparently significant details, feels his emotion for the deceased guests mixed with doubt and confusion. We see through his eyes with immediacy, but they are not always well focused.

The party is blurred, but still the general outlines of the action are ascertainable. Unity of time and place help fix those outlines: the entire novel takes place at the party. Green's *Party Going* has similar unity but deviates from it, occasionally, to follow guests heading to the station. *Gerald's Party* strays no further than Gerald's lawn. The novel is structured somewhat by the homicide investigation that follows the discovery of Ros's body. Certainly the police alter the closed system of the party when they enter, and they are directly responsible for the deaths of Roger and Vic. In between those deaths Tania, the painter, dies mysteriously in the bathtub, evidently a suicide. Amidst much eating and drinking, a panoply of sexual activity ensues, particularly in the outside garden and the downstairs recreation room. Gerald has sexual involvements of sorts with Alison, Sally Ann, and his wife. A long-standing couple, Cyril and Peg, break up when Peg leaves the party with Dickie, a notorious playboy. Zack Quagg's theater company enacts a funereal drama built around Ros's corpse. Yvonne breaks a leg and Charley "Choo-Choo" Trainer slips a disc. Sally Ann and young Anatole become engaged. The party seems to epitomize Dick Diver's decadent desire in *Tender Is the Night:* "I want to give a really *bad* party . . . where there's a brawl and seductions and people going home with their feelings hurt and women passed out in the cabinet de toilette" (*TN* 27).

This brief summary gives an idea of the party's bizarre quality, but it fails to show how the novel coheres into a compelling tour de force. Its energy comes, as I have suggested, from the collision of fictional codes and from the rich symbolic associations of the party, associations that embrace the other generic patterns of the novel. The fictional codes disrupt coherence, but the party paradigm restores it by showing the dialogic possibilities of festive and novel form. If we examine these different codes or groups of motifs individually, we arrive at a better understanding of this great variety and richness of comic detail that enlivens the powerful set piece of the party.

The novel opens with the discovery of Ros's dead body; her character must, then, be constructed retrospectively through the memories of other characters. The character that emerges is shaped by male sexual fantasies so that the figure of Ros becomes almost entirely a projection of male libido. She is a beautiful, outgoing woman and a minor actress. "Mostly she was in chorus lines or shows where they needed naked girls with good bodies," Gerald explains to Alison, a newcomer unacquainted with Ros (*GP* 33). "I just like to be looked at," Ros once confirmed to Gerald. She is married to the insanely jealous Roger, but marriage has been unable to contain her generous sexuality. Gerald has had a long-standing affair with her; the skeptical Vic confesses she was his only love. Alison remarks to Gerald that she heard, " 'a thousand stories about [Ros] tonight. . . . You're right. You certainly weren't the only one' " (*GP* 66). Ros recedes behind her image of omnivorous sexuality: "We'd all been drawn to her, her almost succulent innocence probably, and a kind of unassuming majesty that kept you in crazy awe of her, even in intimacy" (*GP* 11). Ros is seen almost exclusively as a sexual and physical being. Her acting career is famous for a gaffe in which she misread a stage direction in sexual terms and fondled the astonished male costar. Memories of this story have multiplied into apocryphal variations with Ros misreading "clock" as "cock," "bells" as "balls," and so forth. Ros combines two virulent male stereotypes: the sexual allure of the femme fatale crossed with the all-giving fertile warmth of the earth mother. No longer deadly, this seductive female figure is, instead, dead herself. In *Gerald's Party* the stereotypes Ros embodies are maintained through the vivid recollections of the characters. Yet through her death and the various dark comedies surrounding her body at the party, the stereotype of woman as ideally a sexually giving being is exploded and criticized, revealed as a life-denying projection of male need.

The apotheosis of male sexual fantasy lies dead at the heart of the novel, signifying a dead end to desire. Ros's mysterious murder transforms her into a sacrificial victim, albeit a perverted sacrifice. Many elements of the ritual pattern are clearly present: the death at the celebration, the near-sacred or legendary status of the victim, the lack of an individual clearly responsible for the murder, the use of the body in ritual performances, and the sale of articles of clothing as relics. Like the traditional *pharmakos*, Ros has a status both sacred and vilified, and is elevated and killed, in a sense, by the whole community. The insistence that one's feelings for Ros are never unique but always shared ("You loved her very much." "Yes. Along with a thousand other guys" [*GP* 35]) suggests the shared emotions the community invests in the sacrificial victim. Traditionally, the victim was killed by being stoned to death or driven off a cliff so that no individual alone bore the guilt (or honor) of the deed. Here Ros is murdered, but, with the perpetrator unidentified, the party seems to share a vague and guilty sense of responsibility. Ros also lacks relatives—she's an orphan—which further improves her candidacy for sacred status.

The pattern of ritual sacrifice is as much a literary code as an ethnological one. Ritual is a kind of formal drama, and the ritual pattern is reproduced in fiction of all kinds, from passion plays to modern novels. Northrop Frye has discussed most thoroughly the ritual patterns in literature, and he has noted the theme of ritual sacrifice in *The Scarlet Letter*, *Billy Budd*, and, as we have seen, *Mrs. Dalloway*. Frye characterizes one version of the ritual sacrifice, in terms appropriate to Ros's role in *Gerald's Party*, as a "demonic erotic relation [which] becomes a fierce destructive passion . . . generally symbolized by a . . . tantalizing female, a physical object of desire which is sought as a possession and therefore can never be possessed. . . . The social relation is that of the mob, which is essentially human society looking for a *pharmakos*."[7] But Ros's death is not a primitive ritual; it is a murder at a contemporary party. There is a great deal to suggest that if Ros is a sacrificial victim, she is a victim of a confused and perverted sacrifice that is life-destroying rather than preserving. Certainly there is little in the events following her death to suggest communal revitalization, except that the party continues.

Ros exemplifies the body as independent sensual entity. At the party she becomes, literally, all body, all corpse. The police desecrate the corpse in their investigation—taking film exposures, revealing the gaping stab wound along with her breasts, making an incision to take the liver temperature, cutting up and selling pieces of her panties, encasing her in plastic bags. The true horror of the ultimate reduction to the physical—the separation of body and spirit—is revealed. The body remains on the floor throughout the party and is even used in an impromptu play staged by Zack Quagg's troupe: "'We got Ros playing herself—we use the corpse, I mean—but the rest of the cast interacts with it like she's alive, you dig? The trick being to make the audience get the sense she really *is* alive!'" (*GP* 226). But that trick fails, and Ros reminds us of death's finality and omnipotence. Once, perhaps, she was "the flame at which all chilled men might well warm themselves" (*GP* 39). But no phoenix arises from the ashes of that flame. Ros now symbolizes a boundary between art and life and reminds Gerald, "No, we were not going around in circles, Ros wasn't anyway" (*GP* 248).

The death of the projection of male fantasy suggests the morbid and destructive consequences of the sexual imagination. The nature of Ros's wound implies murder is a kind of sexual violation as well. Ros is stabbed to death, cut in her famous chest by some fearsome blade. Pointing to the corpse, the policeman Bob says, "Only one instrument could make a perforation like that! If we find the weapon that did it, we'll have our . . . our perpetrator" (*GP* 129). In *Gravity's Rainbow* the insistent linking of the penis to the rocket emphasizes the masculine technology of warfare; in *Gerald's Party* an equally insistent parallel links the penis with a weapon—knife or ice pick. The mysterious ice pick pops up repeatedly throughout the book, and always in a phallic and guilt-related context.

When Inspector Pardew first arrives, Gerald tries to calculate how much time has passed since the discovery of the body by figuring out how long it would take ice to melt in the pitcher of old-fashioneds he is carrying. "You were speaking of an ice pick," the inspector queries, and Gerald becomes flustered and defensive and responds that they do not even own an ice pick. Consequently, Gerald is startled to discover one later in the bathroom cabinet (*GP* 58). From that point on the ice pick becomes a menace that haunts Gerald. He tries to hide it in various ways, then shifts tactics and tries to give it to the police. It is misplaced but keeps comically reappearing. Throughout, the ice pick's phallic connotations are stressed. As Gerald ponders initially how to "get that thing out of the house," he sees above the bathroom hamper a picture drawn by his son: "It was a picture of a castle with a war going on, blood and flags flying, bodies scattered like jacks. There was a big figure on top that was presumably Daddy. He had a long thing hanging down between his legs which Mark said was for killing the bad guys, and he was throwing somebody off the ramparts" (*GP* 71). Penis, sword, ice pick are all united as instruments of violence belonging to the father. Gerald's irrational guilt takes the form of a desire to hide the ice pick. But the act of hiding or concealing the awkward device also recalls the murder act and the sexual act. For Gerald keeps thinking of hiding the pick *in* something: "I could hide it inside one of my wife's hatboxes . . . or her boot maybe, a sewing basket" (*GP* 80).

At times the phallic implications are made explicit, as in this scene where Sally Ann, a young teenager with a crush on Gerald, accidentally discovers the ice pick Gerald has concealed under his shirt:

> "Gerry—! My gosh!" she squeaked, stepping back, still holding her pricked thumb up with its tiny bead of blood.
> "It's not mine," I said lamely. "It just . . . turned up. . . ."
> She squatted to pick it up. "It's so—so *sexy*!" she gasped, stroking it gently. . . . "I'll never tell, Gerry!" she whispered gravely and, standing on her tiptoes, threw her arms around my neck and kissed me. "Cross my heart!" I tried to twist away, but she held on to my nape with one small warm hand, pointing down at the hard bulge in my shorts with the other: "See, you *do* like me, Gerry! I felt it pushing on my tummy—you can't hide it!"
> "Don't be silly, it gets that way by its—"
> "Can I see it?"
> "What? No, of course not!" (*GP* 80)

Gerald's denial and concealment of the ice pick merges into his denial and concealment of his erection, and the scene as a whole prefigures Sally Ann's loss of virginity later that night. This scene and many others in which Gerald's embarrassed handling of the ice pick suggests sexual guilt are wonderfully comic in spite of their morbid source. Part of the humor lies in the visual and aural pun that unites pick and prick (as does one version of the apocryphal Ros story).[8] But the universality of sexual guilt is a larger source of the theme's comic power. Desire seems inevitably linked to domination and possession, and thus the sexual urge remains tied to physical aggression.

Gerald's first thought is to bury the ice pick in the garden, to return symbolically to a prelapsarian sexual innocence. But the cold undercurrent of the mysteriously returning ice pick is the horrible realization that sexual desire exceeds individual control. Slothrop in *Gravity's Rainbow* learns that his penis is not his own because his erections are linked to the V-2 rocket; Gerald's repeated unwelcome discoveries of the ice pick suggest similarly unwelcome encounters with his own destructive desires. Eventually, we learn that the ice pick was planted by the Inspector: " 'One of the Old Man's favorite tricks. . . . His probe, he calls it. Stick it in, see what surfaces' " (*GP* 288). One thing that surfaces is the shared guilt of the party in the murder of Ros. As the inspector hyperbolically asserts: " 'The motive here was not merely irrational, it was *pre*rational, atavistic, shared by all, you might say, and thus criminal in the deepest sense of the word' " (*GP* 285). The party focuses the corruption of desire in a decadent world; the myriad desperate or ridiculous sexual liaisons (Dickie's girls, Sally Ann's crushes, Janny Trainer's flirtations, Gerald's pursuit of Alison, Vic's brutal relationship with Eileen, Malcolm's unassisted orgasms) find ultimate expression in Ros's corpse, in which the dream of vitalizing sexuality lies slaughtered.

The penis is the murder weapon, at least metaphorically. This conclusion is suggested not only by the comic links between ice pick and phallus but also by aspects of the homicide investigation, such as the "penis prints." The interplay of sexuality and violence has special significance in the festive setting because both forces are potentially dangerous products of festive release. Eros and Thanatos become liberated in a setting that debunks the myth of individual self-control. At the festival individual emotions give way to group expression. And though this may, as René Girard suggests, allow for the comfortable reestablishment of everyday lawfulness through catharsis, here the risks of libidinal chaos are grimly manifested in Ros's brutal death. Her death signifies finality to Gerald: not all wounds heal. That which does not kill me makes me stronger—but it may kill me just the same. The ice pick makes one final appearance to underscore this idea that the destructive force of sexuality has been intensified rather than purged by the festive release. In the house emptied of guests, Gerald and his wife make love. But, at one point, Gerald confesses to himself: "I was thinking about the ice pick, that improbable object. When the officer carried it away, I was glad to see it go—I thought at the time: Free at last! But now I was not so sure. I seemed to feel its presence again, as though it had got back in the house somehow" (*GP* 315). Ice pick as phallic symbol generates a powerful reading here: the destructive and guilt-ridden core of sexual experience remains inescapable. Even the release of the party fails to purify the shared sexual guilt.

Coover's development of the theme of sexual guilt around the murder of Ros illustrates how the phantasmagoric themes of the novel gain intelligibility through the festive setting. We understand Ros's centrality better when we connect the party to ancient rituals and festivals. Then the image of the guests dancing around the corpse loses some of its initial strangeness. Death at the party becomes no longer an aberration but part of the festive pattern. This ritual association does not diminish the horror or argue that, since Gerald's party follows a ritual pattern, it represents a revitalizing communal encounter with mortality. Rather it is the very superimposition of the modern celebration on the ritual pattern that reveals the alienation and despair in the world of Gerald and his friends. Ros's death does not discharge communal violence; it incites more violence in its wake (the murders of Roger and Vic and the various police beatings). Ros's communal being exists at the expense of her individual integrity, and her death reveals the life-negating aspects of the party's supposed sexual freedom. Ultimately we do not see in the partygoers' reactions to Ros a triumphant encounter with mortality; rather we witness frantic avoidance as the guests satiate their desires around the blood-soaked body. The sense in *Finnegans Wake* of celebration intensified by the encounter with death is transformed by Coover into a celebration rendered ghastly by its desperate need to ignore the accumulating corpses.

The death of Ros not only signals the ritual pattern of sacrifice and celebration but also introduces a modern means of controlling the violence of a community—the police investigation and criminal justice. The fictional code of the detective novel runs throughout *Gerald's Party* and provides the most marked example of how different fictional codes undermine one another. Detective fiction has a distinctive relationship to fictionality per se and to the party in particular. Coover exploits both of these fertile relationships in parodying and representing the detective story.

In general detective fiction shows an investigator creating a chronological and causal narrative retrospectively from its conclusion, the murder scene. To do so he must assemble narrative elements that have become disorganized like pieces of a puzzle (a common metaphor in detective fiction). Reader and detective share this perspective and the desire to render the scene intelligible through assembling the narrative pieces. The beauty and appeal of the game of detective fiction is often enhanced by limiting or closing the world of possible narratives, particularly by limiting the number of suspects. Thus the closed house party or country weekend becomes a frequent setting for murder drama, because the boundaries of the house double as boundaries for the "game." In detective fiction where a party is not the setting for the murder, it is often the setting for the resolution: the gathering of all suspects at a dinner or party where the detective reveals the murderer. *Gerald's Party* uses both of these intersections between the closed system of the party and the finite world of the detective novel. The murder clearly occurs at the party, and Inspector Pardew predictably warns: "*Nobody* moves! . . . Nobody leaves this house without permission!" (*GP* 37). Two hundred and fifty pages later, the Inspector initiates the classic detective denouement (the revelation of the supposed killer): "I have called you all here, here to the scene of the crime" (*GP* 281). In between Coover intensifies the dramatic unity by having the police conduct their investigation wholly at the party: there they set up a lab, interrogate witnesses, examine the body, develop and test theories, catalog evidence, and so forth. As in traditional detective fiction, the party becomes a social microcosm allowing the plot of narrative reconstruction to be dramatized more readily.

Todorov uses detective fiction as an example of how genres possess individual internal standards of verisimilitude, and he notes how the detective plot must be believable and logical but must conform to an apparent antiverisimilitude such as the rejection of the most likely suspect.[9] Thus the detective genre exists in a narrow margin between the need for surprise and the need for believability. Coover parodies the subgenre by skewing the investigation far from both poles: it is full of crazy illogic and implausibility, yet the denouement is absurdly anticlimactic. The humor emerges from the incongruity between the familiar detective form and its absurd content. A few examples will clarify this. Pardew initially (and predictably) tries to determine the time of Ros's death. He does this, however, by collecting all the guests' watches. Everyone cooperates as if this approach were reasonable; perhaps it exaggerates our tendency to look at a watch when asked how long ago something happened. The watch collection also comments on the temporal inversion of the detective act, working backwards from the conclusion. Pardew is fascinated with such metaphysical implications of his own investigations: "It's a little like sorting out the grammar of a sentence. . . . You have the object there before you and evidence of at least the verb. . . . But you have to reach back in time to locate the subject" (*GP* 130–31). Fascinated with such paradoxes, he sees no contradiction in concluding from the watches that the murder took place half an hour after he arrived and examined the body (*GP* 230). All this absurdity is presented without the characters commenting on its strangeness. The effect is to lampoon the surprise element of the classic detective resolution. Pardew's conclusion is so ingenious it is ridiculous.

Other absurdities enrich the investigation motif. The investigation also includes such things as penis exams, the dismemberment of Gerald's son's stuffed bunny, Peedie, and the videotaping and viewing of various moments of the party. Police laboratory procedures are comically exaggerated in the description of the temporary crime lab set up at the party. But the most elaborate mockeries are reserved for the narrative theories of detection themselves. The inspector speaks at times like a hard-boiled cop, at others like an obsessed literary critic analyzing crime detection. He is a self-parodying figure:

> "Holistic criminalistics *rejects* these narrow localized cause-and-effect fictions popularized by the media! Do you think that poor child in there died because of some arbitrary indeterminate and random act? Oh no, *nothing* in the *world* happens that way! It is just by such simple atavistic thinking that we fill our morgues and prisons, missing the point, solving nothing!" Pardew stormed about the room, waving his arms. . . . "Murder, like laughter, is a muscular solution of conflict,

biologically substantial and inevitable, a psychologically imperative
and, in the case of murder, death-dealing act that *must* be related to
the *total ontological reality!*" (GP 135)

The detective as interpreter or reader is similarly parodied in Pardew's
dramatic revelation to Gerald that he has found a blueprint of the murder:

> "Look at this! It's a drawing of the murder scene! Only it was drawn
> *before the murder!* We can *prove* this! Somebody was planning this homi-
> cide all along! You see? Somebody here, *in this house!* Down to the
> *last vile detail*—except that they apparently meant to strike her in the
> womb instead of the breast—at least that must be the true *meaning* of
> the crime—you can see here the blood, the hideous weapon between
> her legs. There's the killer standing over her. *Gloating!* One interesting
> thing: he's bearded. That might be a clue or it might not, of course. It
> might be a disguise, for example, or some fantasy image of the self, a
> displacement of some kind. . . ."
>
> "I'm afraid that's the, uh, Holy Family."
>
> "The what?" He looked pained, his eyes widening as he stared at
> me, as though I might have just grown horns myself and struck him.
>
> "It's the Christmas scene. You know, the manger and all that. My
> son drew it for nursery school."
>
> He slumped back into his chair, staring at the drawing in disbelief.
> "But—all this—*blood*—!"
>
> "There was a childbirth documentary on television the week be-
> fore that we all watched. Not surprisingly, my son put the two things
> together. The 'weapon' is the baby and the 'killer's' the father, and
> that, eh, 'diabolical accomplice' is a cow." (GP 128)

Pardew's language along with the italics and exclamation marks renders
his deduction speeches ridiculous. But this parody of morbid interpretations warns the reader as well against the potential solipsism of interpretative zeal. The inspector also interprets the party as a text and provides
a comic extreme against which we can measure and perhaps qualify our
own interpretations.

Since the police represent the maintenance of order, they are naturally opposed to the transgressive license of the party. Their reading of
the party thus provides an official and authoritarian perspective on the

celebration. When Pardew claims he can read "Lust, doubt, fear, greed" painted on people's faces, Gerald protests that "It—it's only a party" (*GP* 127). Pardew responds: " '*Only!* Do you think I'm *blind?* You've got drug addicts here! You've got perverts, anarchists, pimps, and peeping toms! Adulterers! You've got dipsomaniacs! You've got whores, thugs, thieves, atheists, sodomists, and out-and-out lunatics! There isn't *anything* they wouldn't do!' He seemed almost to have grown. He was rigid, power-ful—yet his hand was trembling as he picked up a piece of paper. 'In this world, nothing—*nothing*, I tell you—is ever wholly concealed! I *know* what's in their sick stinking hearts!' " (*GP* 127–28). Pardew's marvelous exercise in hyperbolic rhetoric should warn us against painting too dark a picture of a society from its transgressive behavior. And yet, Ros is still dead, and calmer voices than Pardew's (those of Gerald, Alison, and Vic) also question the value of these celebrations. The very comic expansion of Pardew's language of detection and revelation ("nothing is ever wholly concealed") undermines the force of his conclusions, how-ever. Caught between the fictional codes of detective story, parody, and realistic novel, Pardew is rendered absurd.

Detective fiction is a kind of metafiction because it always contains a narrative within the narrative; the detective functions as reader as he interprets and follows clues, and as writer as he presents them at the de-nouement. As part of the play with realism in *Gerald's Party*, the invented narratives or scenarios of the inspector upset the balance between plau-sibility and novelty typical of the detective genre.[10] We see this, not only in the anticlimactic "resolution" to this case, but in Inspector Pardew's stories of two earlier remarkable cases. In one, the murderer of a married couple is the woman's unborn fetus whose contractions cause an auto accident. In another the perpetrator of a series of murders is the first victim, whose careful planning incites a domino sequence of deaths after his own demise. In both cases the basic dividing line between the living murderer and the dead victim is erased, as are traditional notions of will and action. Both cases are rendered comically, the inspector unaware of his own absurdities. Pardew's authoritarian certitude is subverted by the growing ridiculousness of his interpretations. The novel does not pro-vide him the authority generally granted the inspector within detective fiction.

So when Pardew makes his triumphant announcement that he has solved Ros's murder, the climax is deflated by his own absurdities. The conclusion that the murderer is Vachel, a dwarf who arrives well after the murder, is neither logical nor stunning in its surprise: it simply does not make sense. And Pardew violates the detective frame by not explaining his detective process; he offers no coherent narrative in which Vachel is the villain. His climactic moment is further weakened by interruptions and slapstick physical comedy. He has to begin his speech three times because of different interruptions, and others follow—from slightly suppressed yawns to ribald jokes. In an elaborately detailed description, Pardew gets his fedora stuck first on one shoe, then the other, then both, until he finally shoots it off with his revolver. When the hat tricks give way long enough for the perpetrator to be revealed, the inspector's scene dissolves into a Keystone Kops melee as the vaseline-greased dwarf struggles with the police. The comical anticlimax reduces the power of the detective code so that it becomes but one of many voices in the text. The clumsiness and brutality of the police counterbalance the pretentious intellectualism of Pardew. And the physical comedy of the Inspector's hat, the police assistant's rough stuff, and the capture of Vachel introduce another essential fictional code—slapstick humor.

Coover is well known for using literary equivalents of film techniques in his fiction. His collection of fictions, *A Night at the Movies* (1987), brings together pieces (most written during the composition of *Gerald's Party*) that invoke cinematic themes or techniques. Certainly Coover exploits, in his earlier fiction, the montage and cut techniques of film, and he shows a concern for the force of the photographic image. But film's power to show motion as story—and the possibilities for imitating that power in language—seems the most significant cinematic legacy in *Gerald's Party*. In particular Coover seems interested in the pantomime comedy of slapstick. The pratfall belongs to precinematic forms such as circus and vaudeville, but it attained its greatest power in film, particularly silent film where gesture and body movement substituted for language. Coover's short story "Charlie in the House of Rue" brilliantly uses verbal equivalents of Chaplinesque physical comedy. Many of the extended passages of physical humor in *Gerald's Party* (such as the inspector's hat and shoe routine) echo specific passages of the "Charlie" story.[11] Physical comedy is even more appropriate in the festive setting because traditional decorum is suspended, intoxication encouraged, and the boundary lines between body and building blurred. The combination of celebration, drinking, and a crowd redefines physical space: touching becomes more permissible (indeed inevitable), and spilling, slipping, and falling become more common.[12]

Gerald's Party is filled with instances of physical comedy, and the humor of the slips and falls intensifies as they accumulate and become increasingly violent or theatrical. In the first (rather tame) instance, Gerald pours drinks to overflowing as his attention strays to the alluring Alison across the room (*GP* 8). Later, in the chaos of Roger's frenzy after Ros's death, there is much slipping and sliding on blood, and eyeglasses are shattered, drapes torn, and lamps smashed. Big Louise falls and, as Patrick comments later, "When she hit the floor I *skidded three feet in her direction*" (*GP* 44). Guacamole dip dribbles off dentures onto chins, ashtrays tumble, and beer froths and overflows. Naomi defecates in her pants in fright; Yvonne tumbles down a flight of stairs and breaks a leg; Charley Trainer falls down the same flight and slips a disc. Efforts to help all three contribute to more confusion and accidents. Throughout the evening Noble entertains with magic tricks some working, others failing; some involving his glass eye dropped in drinks or inserted backwards into his head. The party becomes an arena in which ordinary movement becomes difficult or impossible, relentlessly transformed into slapstick.

But there is a difference. The slapstick performer uses grace and skill to pretend to be clumsy and awkward. The pratfall is a planned, intentional replication of something by nature spontaneous—falling down. With the exception of Noble and his magic tricks, the physical comedy in *Gerald's Party* is largely unintentional. In substance, the falls and spills are not theatrical slapstick, but real. However, they take on, in the theatrical context of the party and the literary context of the book, the patterned artificiality of slapstick. Detective fiction plays with the tension between surprise and believability, and slapstick plays with the tension between the planned and the spontaneous. But both the detective code and the slapstick code are transformed in the context of the novel. We have seen how Coover manipulates the usual verisimilitude of the detective code. Slapstick is similarly transformed, almost inverted. The good slapstick artist falls hard enough so that the planned physical comedy appears spontaneous. The party guests' hard falls are patterned enough (by the author) that they appear theatrical and comic: life imitates art. Or, more appropriately, the literary representation of life imitates a cinematic representation called slapstick. One example should suffice for demonstrating Coover's descriptive technique:

> *"Hole on, Yvonne! God* DAMN *it! Ole Chooch is comin'!"* But his knees started to cave about halfway down to the landing and there was no negotiating the right angle turn there—Woody and Cynthia ducked, clinging to each other, as he went hurtling past behind them, smacking the banister with his soft belly and somersaulting on over the railing to the floor below: *"Pp-*FOOOFF*!"* he wheezed mightily as he landed on his back (I'd managed to jerk Mark out of the way just in time), bathrobe gaping and big soft genitals bouncing between his fat legs as though hurling them to the floor had been his whole intent. "Ohh, shit!" he gasped (Mark was laughing and clapping, my wife's mother shushing him peevishly), lying there pale and, except for the aftershock vibrations still rippling through his flaccid abdomen, utterly prostrate: *"Now* wha've I done . . . ?!" (*GP* 147)

The slapstick feeling here is created not only by the attention to gesture and physical detail (which creates an almost slow-motion effect as the prose unfolds more slowly than the action described) but also by Charley's drunken bravado turned into sheepishness, the comic book style sound effects, and little Mark's laughter and applause.

The point of the slapstick descriptions is, first of all, comical. The carnival spirit celebrates the body at play and the ability to laugh at the body's limitations. Pratfalls remind our minds of our bodies and make us laugh, perhaps because intellect has momentarily forgotten its corporeal shell. The fall also offers a pure illustration of loss of control. There exists a wild freedom in the moment between slip and impact—a moment of flight. But loss of control, as parties often remind us, can be frightening. The intensifying physical comedy of this party manifests its increasing chaos.

Like the codes of ritual sacrifice and detective fiction, slapstick complements the carnivalized spirit of the party. But its role in the novel stresses the book's basic ambivalence about the value of the party. On one hand slapstick fits perfectly and comically into the festive setting; on the other it hints at a darker loss of control and outlines the boundary between pleasure and pain. In "Charlie in the House of Rue" the hero's comical physical feats develop an increasingly morbid context as the members of the house of Rue die or decompose. In the final scene the slapstick tramp hero clings desperately to the corpse of a hanged woman wondering (as the story ends and the metaphorical film concludes), "What kind of place is this? Who took the light away? And why is everybody laughing?" [13] The final question is relevant to the many levels of humor in *Gerald's Party*. They inspire laughter, but also, through their grotesquerie, an insistent questioning.

Loss of bodily control also manifests itself in the attention to vomiting and excretion at Gerald's party. The novel is a sort of "vomedy" (*GP* 236), a dark comedy of festive excess. Parties accentuate what Bakhtin terms the "lower bodily strata," most obviously in their attention to physical appetite, eating, and drinking. Traditional carnivals also celebrated an earthy regard for the consequences of that physical excess, as Bakhtin examines in Rabelais. In contemporary Anglo-American parties, the taboos surrounding bodily waste are the least likely to give way. Intoxication may be acceptable and encouraged in the festive setting, but vomiting and passing out remain serious breaches of decorum. Fitzgerald pays considerable attention to the hangover as a consequence of intoxication, and Waugh grants greater prominence to the antidecorum of bodily waste. But of the works we have considered only in Pynchon's fiction is excrement celebrated for its transgressive power. Even in Coover's novel, which has obvious affinities with Pynchon's work, the excremental presence is largely negative, though admittedly comic in its excess. Excremental taboos remain strong, as Dickie's comment that Gerald's parties have "too much shit and blood" reminds us. Blood inspires fear and horror when it crosses the boundary of the flesh, when it is "spilled." Excrement is similarly taboo when it passes the bodily boundary. Taboos stem, as Mary Douglas has argued, from societal classifications or compartmentalizations,[14] the very classifications that festivity traditionally suspends. By assaulting and exposing those taboos least willingly suspended at the party, Coover dramatizes the transgressive force of the celebration and the increasingly futile attempts to control that transgressive force.

Ros's murder initiates the flow of blood and shit. Her blood (and later Roger's) darkens drapes, carpets, and clothing; her murder causes Naomi to defecate in her pants. Throughout the evening Gerald and his wife battle this rising tide with attempts to clean up. Gerald actually cleans Naomi and finds her new clothes to wear. His wife does several loads of laundry and lends out clothes of her own. Guests make various attempts (usually feeble) to clean up spilled ashtrays or to change their stained clothing, but their efforts never seem to catch up with the flood of waste and blood. The upstairs toilet clogs so badly that even the plumber cannot fix it, and guests begin to relieve themselves in the garden to the extent that it is transformed into a morass of urine and feces. The attempts of Gerald and his wife to clean up and get the toilet repaired recall Meatball Mulligan's efforts to sustain the party in "Entropy." The energy system of the party renews itself not only by taking in new guests but by successfully expelling waste products. The damming up of that process signals inescapable entropy. The breakdown of taboos becomes oppressive, not liberating in its reminder of the body's physical essence. Roger's blood-spattered suit, the begrimed bedsheets of the master bedroom, Naomi's shit-drenched clothes, the clogged toilet—all these images refer back to Ros's body.

"The grotesque body of carnival" is, however, essential to the festive spirit. As we see in Rabelais or in Pynchon, the destruction of bodily illusions and taboos *can* be liberating. Some such festive celebration of the body emerges in Gerald's party's relentless libidinal energy, which also glorifies the lower body. But that aspect, too, is frustrated or dammed up. Gerald's intense desire for the seductive Alison epitomizes frustrated desire as his attempts to rendezvous with her are repeatedly blocked, by her husband's intervention or Sally Ann's pretending to be Alison. By the end of the evening Alison has been abandoned to unspecified humiliations, and her exit from the party is marked by her husband pulling a long string of scarves from her behind in a grotesque parody of "theater." The bodily elements of carnival tradition are surely present at this party, but the context renders them negative; they reinforce a bondage to physicality rather than a reveling in it. Such "bondage" is epitomized ludicrously in Gerald's sexual encounter with Sally Ann, in which his penis becomes partially caught in her and has to be extricated by Jim. "I thought this was supposed to be fun," Sally Ann complains and someone replies, "You been going to the wrong church, kiddo" (*GP* 216). The exchange nicely encapsulates the paradoxical inversion of festive release; Sally Ann's sexual act hardly seems transgressive, but the bloody mess that results harshly parodies the spirit of libidinal release. The expressions of the lower body are everywhere blocked, and the body is rendered grotesque by the breakdown of its usual categories. Like the slapstick code, the motif of the "lower body" fits the festive frame but does not necessarily celebrate it. As a comic source the theme of the lower body is richly exploited by Coover; but its darker implications suggest the image of the party-gone-wrong as well as the ancient pattern of festive release. A profound ambivalence about the value of the party remains.

The futile attempts to clean or change clothes initiate a comic masquerade that highlights the body's monstrosity and illustrates Girard's contention that monstrosity and masquerade efface individual differences.[15] Gerald's party is not officially a masquerade, but it becomes one as blood transforms dress clothes into costumes and as the theater troupe joins in the act with liberal applications of stage makeup. In their desire to shed their stained clothing, many of the guests borrow clothes from the hosts. The result is an informal masquerade in which few of the guests are wearing what they wore at the beginning of the party. Much of the individual distinctiveness of characters magically disappears in the confusion of costume. This primitive phenomenon in which costume erases individuality emerges in the identity confusions caused by the clothes swaps. Gerald mistakes Kitty for his wife because she is wearing borrowed clothing (*GP* 179); Sally Ann pretends to be Alison with the aid of a dark room and Alison's knitted "peckersweater" (*GP* 209). Regina, arriving late, mistakes Yvonne for Ros. And the injured Yvonne is confused herself: "Honest to God, Jim, I think you guys pulled a fast one on me! This isn't my *body*" (*GP* 100). Talbot appears wearing a pair of Gerald's pants, as does Daffie later (*GP* 115, 219). In an extended comical scene, Ginger manages to don more and more articles of Inspector Pardew's clothing (overcoat, scarf, pipe); later, Fats appears wearing the inspector's fedora "like a party hat" (*GP* 274). Modern equivalents of motley emerge in a variety of "patched" guests: Steve, the plumber, wears a name patch; a nameless guest is identified only by his patched elbows; Sally Ann adds various sexually suggestive patches to her clothing during the party; by the end of the evening Alison sports a lewd patch as well. Earlier Sally Ann had imitated Alison in order to seduce Gerald; now Alison unconsciously imitates Sally Ann.

The metamorphosis of Alison's appearance illustrates the party's downward motion, its leveling of the guests and assault upon their individuality. She begins the evening in a beautiful silk dress with leotards; later she is "huddled up in a heavy checkered overcoat . . . her hair . . . snarled, her makeup gone, her eye shadow smudged" (*GP* 272). When she leaves, she wears Brenda's red pantsuit, flopping large on her and stained with blood. When her husband rips the pantsuit off and draws knotted handkerchiefs from her rectum, he concludes triumphantly with the inspector's white scarf (*GP* 293). Alison's changes chronicle her degradation from an angel in Gerald's eyes to a helpless victim in the mysterious rec room orgy.

The comical costume changes reflect a profound festive metamorphosis: the blurring of individual distinctions in the ritual setting. Identity depends upon certain categories, and in the chaos of the celebration those distinctions can disappear. The primitive qualities of festive chaos remind individuals of their primal and bodily nature. All clothing becomes a masking then of the bodily and "even bare skin is a kind of mask" (*GP* 152). Such confusions of identity are temporary, even momentary, but they reflect the frightening side of the exhilarating potential of the party. The party reveals, for better or for worse, a monstrous side to the human.

The monster is a figure that appears distorted because it blurs or perverts typically separate categories—human and animal, human and divine, animal and divine, and so forth. When monstrosity is recognized in a distorted or altered (costumed) human form, evil is externalized into a force that can "possess" the individual.[16] When the child, Mark, stumbles into the party from the (temporarily) protected realm of his bedroom, he is struck by the changed face of his father:

> "You look scary, Daddy!" he exclaimed, backing away.
> "We've been playing monsters," I laughed, and made a face.
> "Can I play?"
> "Not yet. When you grow up." (*GP* 68)

The party is adult play at monstrosity in that it allows a sort of free play to the repressed elements of the body. The party vision allows Gerald to see monstrosity in others as well, as when some younger guests appear to him "like bloated parodies of horny teenagers, papier-mâché caricatures from some carnival parade . . . wearing their mortality on their noses like blobs of red paint" (*GP* 88).

Coover's language of sartorial transformation reinforces the connection between modern and primitive celebration: the costume allows for and signals a release of that which is repressed by the mask of the everyday. As Terry Castle says of eighteenth-century masquerade, the transformation of public self represents "an almost erotic commingling with the alien."[17] The complement to loss of individuality is the discovery of the self's mutability, the possibilities for transformation of self-image. The dialogic natures of party and novel are especially receptive to the collective chaos of masking. The fictional code of masquerade fits naturally into the festive setting, but its context is deepened by the other codes of transformation: slapstick, injury, and waste, as we have seen, and also the codes of dream and theater.

Distortions of the human image, visions of monsters, and the metamorphosis of the body all suggest the logic of dream or nightmare, as well as the primitive festival. Gerald's party is not framed as a dream as are the *Alice* books or, in a sense, *Finnegans Wake,* but the party does contain specific retold dreams, and it does operate throughout with a certain visually associative dream logic. As we will see, the party itself is much closer to theater than to dream. Both theater and dream, however, present narratives in visual as well as auditory form, and it is worth considering how the fictional code of nightmare animates *Gerald's Party.*

Dreams violate the realistic conventions of fiction freely; in particular, time, causality, and probability are commonly altered or distorted. Dreams seem organized by vivid images and dramatic moments: "Parties are clocked by such moments: we all knew where we were in the night's passing when Roger's anguish was announced" (*GP* 12). Most important, the shape of dreams appears to be directed by repressed wishes and fears; dreams are weighted with a significance that we sense but do not understand. Dreams are always in the past, recalled through memory's double remove. The vagueness of retold dreams is always at least partly attributable to the limitations of memory. Narratives, then, remind us of dreams when they suspend normal notions of time and causality, move from one vivid image to another, and are vaguely suggestive of deeper significance. When the images are colored with horror or grotesqueness, narratives remind us of nightmares.

Literary works are not dreams, however. Even "Kubla Khan" reflects the deliberateness of authorship. But dreams do become narratives when we tell them, and thus they have a particular affinity to fiction. Jackson Cope sees the dreamlike quality of *Gerald's Party* (he calls it a "detective novel woven with dreams") in its obsessive searching for obscured origins. Dreamwork and fiction both struggle with memory, "the primal crime."[18] Thus Gerald's frequent reveries of vaguely remembered sexual encounters and Pardew's struggle to triumph over the force of time (which pushes the murder act into an unrecoverable past) are akin to dreamwork in their probing through confused memories to originating acts. Because the dream quality of narrative is defined by its blurring of spatial and temporal boundaries, the dream code is linked to other fictional codes operating in the novel. Most obvious is the link with masquerade, visual metamorphosis in which the familiar becomes disguised and symbolically coded. The group anonymity of disguise, which the masquerade motif suggests, hints at the collective unconscious theory of dream origins. The other fictional codes exhibit dreamlike qualities as well. The murder of Ros is nightmarish, to be sure, but its sacrificial quality reflects something of the psychologically purgative effect of dreams in which repressed violence is given free symbolic reign. The physical comedy of the novel, though primarily cinematic, pushes at the boundaries of body and gravity, which dream activity can erase. All these affinities suggest the connection between dreams and festivity, a connection developed fully in *Finnegans Wake*. Dreams and festivities are profound examples of human play occurring (typically) against the black background of the nighttime; they represent the strivings of consciousness against the unconsciousness of deep sleep and the night. Breaking boundaries and voicing repressed feelings articulate the transgressive common ground of dream and festivity. Dreams, however, are individual, and festivals are communal. The difference is crucial, and it reminds us that Gerald's party is not a dream, but dreamlike.

Dreams, however, do become communal when they are told, and several dreams are retold at Gerald's party. The novel contains five dream narratives and at least two dreamlike stories or visions. The most elaborately retold dreams belong to the inspector and to Michelle; they present opposite views of revelation, which comment on one another and on the novel itself. Pardew's tale presents his dream as access to a privileged realm where higher truth is revealed; Michelle's dreams cast doubts on the very concepts of higher truth and revelation.

Pardew tells of a dream of Truth as a seductive woman who gives him the clue to the bizarre serial murders he is trying to solve: " 'The victim is the killer' " (*GP* 204). This dream represents a metaphysical wish fulfillment for the inspector, since it reverses the causal time sequence that always limits detection; the murder is always in the past and the detective must interpret murderers from victims, move from corpse to living perpetrator. The identity of victim and killer, literal in this case, bears a figurative truth in ordinary cases for it is in the victim that the killer is inscribed. The inspector's retelling of the dream grows, however, into a riotous self-parody, as do all of the inspector's dramatic moments. The setting—Pardew confessing with his head in the lap of the stern mother-in-law—is ludicrous. And the developing dream story grows increasingly cliché-ridden so that the inspector's tale of his love for the dream vision of Truth becomes a mockery of dream as revelation. Pardew claims to have " 'loved her more than life itself' "; he was " 'given to violent extremes of passion and desire' "; and he was " 'fearing for [his] sanity.' " As he tells the story, "racking" sighs break from his lamenting body and his eyes are "feverish" (*GP* 206). His dream revelation is contaminated by the language of tawdry romance. The imaginative poverty of Pardew's dream narrative is further symptomatic of his self-aggrandizement as investigator, seeker for truth: " 'Facts in the end are little more than surface scramblings of a hidden truth whose vaporous configuration escapes us even as it draws us on . . . compelling revelation' " (*GP* 283). Pardew's self-characterization as truth-quester, while he is actually an overzealous and reductive interpreter, establishes him as the antithesis of the party's openness or dialogism. Seeking to resolve "clues" into the single voice of truth, Pardew sees the party as a forbidden domain as well as a "hysteroid reaction." Through Pardew's dream Coover parodies the idea of embodied truth made accessible through revelation. If there is an embodied truth, it is Ros, and she is, appropriately and significantly, dead. Pardew himself identifies the dream figure with Ros: " 'It was *her*! I *know* it was!' he wept. '*I've missed her so! Boo hoo!*' " (*GP* 207). Coover's satirical intent seems clear; it is certainly consistent with his admitted tendency to debunk privileged stories. Perhaps the great danger of dreams is that they invite grandiose interpretations because of their mysterious origin.

Michelle's two dream narratives counter Pardew's, however: Truth is not a seductive woman offering revelation but an infinite regress. Michelle's dreams are close to the party's spirit, not antithetical to it. Indeed she makes that connection explicit: " 'I once had a dream about something like this' " (*GP* 96). Michelle's second dream retelling clearly resists the inspector's reaching to a transcendent truth. In the dream Michelle encounters a scarred old woman on a mountaintop who tells her the worst thing about aging is that your navel gets deeper and deeper. Michelle looks at the woman's navel and it appears like a nail-hole, " 'like a kind of tunnel, going nowhere' " (*GP* 277). Then she notices creatures crawling out of the navel and a faint television-screen light at the back of the passage. One of these creatures (little people who turn into waterbugs) tells her " 'that's where heaven is' " (*GP* 278). Eventually, the woman disappears and Michelle is left standing there, the hole now in her navel. The dream is an eerie tale suggestive of human decrepitude, an endless search for origins and a never attainable heaven (as in the dreamlike bedtime story Gerald's grandmother tells of the infinite stairway to heaven).

While Michelle is narrating her dreams, Zack Quagg is organizing his play, particularly a "dream sequence" in which the stiff old mother-in-law will be accommodated into the play about Ros: "This is not a singalong, baby! We're not watching the bouncing ball! This is a dance of *death!*" (*GP* 250). The party, the play, the dream—all death-centered imaginative acts—are linked by their struggle with the irresolvable, the ever-receding. Dream uncertainty remains faithful to life's uncertainty. Michelle's dream and the bedtime story of Gerald's grandmother look at a receding heaven, not the ludicrous Truth of white-scarved Pardew.

The dream language in *Gerald's Party* participates in the festive blurring of boundaries and contributes to the sense that truth is the product of multiple viewpoints and experiences. The inspector's dream as revelation is subverted by its context, and Michelle's more ambiguous dreams are granted narrative support through their echoes of other themes and embedded narratives. Michelle equates her dreams with the surrounding party milieu, and the ambivalence of the dream images echoes Gerald's unease about his parties. One scene, however, playfully frames the whole party as a dream. At the end of the party Knud emerges from the television room having "slept through the whole goldarn party" (*GP*

308). He has had a remarkably vivid dream which he begins to recount: " 'I was like in some kind of war zone, see, only everyone was all mixed up and you didn't know who was on your side. . . . Since you couldn't be sure who anybody was, see, just to be safe you naturally had to kill everyone—right? Ha ha! You wouldn't *believe* the blood and gore! And all in 3-D and full color, too, I kid you not! I kept running into people and asking them: "Where *am* I?" They'd say: "What a *loony*," or something like that—and then I'd chop their heads off, right?' " (*GP* 308).

Metaphorically, Knud's dream is equivalent to the party; certainly the blood and gore suggest such a connection. The images of a confused war zone in an unknown location are darker. But they do evoke the neutral zone of festivity (recalling the liminal images of Pynchon's "In the Zone"), but here a festivity in which the only response to the breakdown of categories (no clear "us" and "them") is murderous violence. Perhaps the dream's most profound resemblance to the party is its hazy vagueness, a vagueness that is especially acute in the novel's concluding pages: "You know . . . sometimes, Gerald," his wife comments, "it's almost as if . . . you were at a different party" (*GP* 312). Certainly Knud was, and though he missed out on the communal festivity, he carries away some trace of it in his foggy dream memories.

" 'This widespread confusion of art and dreams is a romantic fallacy . . . derived from their common exercise of the brain's associative powers— but where dreams protect one's sleep, art disturbs it' " (*GP* 76). So pontificates Howard, the art critic, with, as Gerald admits, some validity. But such distinctions can break down; art can adopt dreamlike qualities and memory can transmute private dreams into public stories. The novel's ability to bring together different discourses allows for the juxtaposition or interweaving of discrete realms such as art and dream. Differences and distinctions still obtain, but the collision of discourses creates some fertile confusions. The description of Gerald's costumed afternoon of sexual performance with Ros offers a good example of how Coover brings various fictional codes to bear upon a single scene. When, at a photograph session, Gerald makes love to Ros at the photographer's request, he wears a variety of costumes from the theater trunk in order to preserve his anonymity in the photos. The scene wonderfully mingles imagery of dreams, masquerade, theater, play, photography, memory, and sexuality:

> [I] enjoyed an enchanted hour of what I came to think of as an erotic
> exploration of my own childhood. I was severally a clown, a devil, a
> scarecrow, skeleton, the back half of a horse, Napoleon, a mummy,
> blackamoor, and a Martian. I played Comedy to Ros's Tragedy, Inquisi-
> tor to her Witch, Sleeping Beauty to her Prince Charming, Jesus Christ
> to her Pope. Sometimes the mirrored images actually scared or ex-
> cited me, altered my behavior and my perception of what it was I was
> doing, but Ros was just the same, whether as a nymph, a dragon, an
> old man or the Virgin Mary: in short, endlessly delicious. . . . I prob-
> ably learned more about theater in that hour or so—theater as *play*,
> and the power of play to provoke unexpected insights, unearth buried
> memories, dissolve paradox, excite the heart—than in all the years
> before or since. After the third orgasm, it all became very dreamlike,
> and if I didn't have a set of prints locked away down in my study to
> prove that it actually happened, I probably wouldn't believe it myself.
> (*GP* 78)

This scene may recall Gerald's wife's protest that "Love is *not* an art . . .
It is a desperate compulsion! Like death throes!" (*GP* 27). But here Gerald
celebrates theatricality as participatory and joyful play. There is nothing
horrible or frightening in these manifestations of the monstrous. Instead
the spirit is clearly carnivalesque in its mixture of masquerade and sexual
transgression and its travesty (through the costumes) of religion, political
authority, high art, and mortality. Perhaps the only nonfestive element is
the photographer, whose prints come back to haunt Gerald at the party.

Gerald's Party brings extraliterary art forms and narratives into the
framework of the novel and the party. Art talk represents another discourse or fictional code, which radiates naturally from the festive setting.
Painting, photography, film, video, and, above all, theater, are recurrent
topics of party conversation. Since two of the characters who die in the
novel are artists (Tania, a painter, and Ros, an actress), Gerald's memories of them include memories of their works: Tania's paintings still hang
on his walls and are described; Ros's most memorable theatrical roles are
recalled in brief plot summaries. The presence of a professional art critic
and Zack Quagg's theatrical troupe keeps criticism and performance in
the air. Alison, too, is fascinated with theater, and, through the evening,
Gerald recalls theoretical discussions with her about the nature of drama.

One of the plays Gerald recalls is especially apposite to his party:

> I remembered a play I'd seen, Ros wasn't in it, in which the actors,
> once on stage—it was ostensibly some sort of conventional drawing-
> room comedy—couldn't seem to get off again. The old pros in the cast
> had tried to carry on, but the stage had soon got jammed up with bit
> actors—messengers, butlers, maids and the like—who, trapped and
> without lines, had become increasingly panic-stricken. In the com-
> motion, the principal actors had got pushed upstage and out of sight,
> only a few scattered lines coming through as testimony to their pro-
> fessionalism. Some had tried to save the show, some each other, most
> just themselves. It was intended to produce a kind of gathering terror,
> but though I hadn't felt it then (a stage is finally just a stage), I was
> suddenly feeling it now. (*GP* 221)

The stage delineates a play, because it is bounded—one can step off it.
Play activities differ from the whole of life precisely in their clearly drawn
boundaries. This drama incites anxiety by breaking the safe boundary of
the stage, creating a literal "no exit." When the roles cannot be shaken
off by the actors, the difference between art and life is eclipsed. Thus
this play with a marooned cast suggests the party, particularly as it is
closed off by the inspector's order that no one leave. Role-playing with
no escape, the party without end: these are the decadent variations on
the drawing-room comedy of the conventional "bounded" party.

Art figures in actual performance as well as discussion: e.g., Zack's
impromptu play in honor of Ros, and the video vignettes recorded at the
party (some acted for the camera intentionally, some merely "recorded").
Artistic themes and embedded works of art (the play within the novel)
generally function self-referentially in literature; that is, arts other than
literature inevitably comment on the literary art that frames them in
the novel. But in a work with an explicitly festive setting, the participatory nature of carnivalized art is emphasized over the self-referential
proclivity of the novel. Theater has traditionally been connected more
immediately to festivity, since it is by nature more open to active participation by the audience. In traditional carnival the dividing line between
performer and audience was broken down by popular participation in
games, feasts, sports, ritual dances, and even costumed dramas. In a
modern party the connection between theater and festivity is less obvious but still valid. Coover's use of theater consistently stresses the breakdown between audience and performer, and he highlights this aspect

of festival theatricality in several ways. First of all, the theatricality of human social behavior offers the continuing metaphor of role-playing, a metaphor invoked by all the writers we have considered. Coover intensifies this familiar metaphor by bringing an actual theater troupe into the party and having them recruit guests as performers. The party presents actors as party guests and party guests as actors; as more and more guests are swept into the drama (including resistant figures such as Alison's husband and Gerald's mother-in-law), the dividing line between performer and spectator is blurred. As the video cameramen film episodes of the party (taping over all Gerald's video collection), other guests become unwitting actors. Even Ros's death suggests this blurring of distinctions. Her death does, in a sense, become her final role, when she is incorporated into Zack's "dance of death." When Gerald first sees her dead body, the blood, ironically, looks "brilliant and alive, yet stagy, cosmetic" (*GP* 12). " 'Is this one of Ros's theatrical performances?' " Gerald wonders. Inspector Pardew's "white scarf fall[s] over Ros's breasts like theater curtains" (*GP* 23). Yet she will not stand and take a bow; she is really dead.

Malcolm Mee's mock stabbing of Benedetto (which ironically inspires Gerald's true rage) thrives, like Noble's magic tricks, on illusion and distraction. Like Gerald's reaction to the discovery of Ros's body, the ice pick murder suggests a confusion between mimesis and life, between performance and living. The theatrical discourse in *Gerald's Party* insistently returns to the creative power of the dissolution of traditional artistic boundaries. The theater motif enhances the carnival setting: creative energy erupts when everyday categories are suspended or broken down. And yet Ros's death seems to give the lie to this creative transgression. Her corpse seems to insist, at least for Gerald, that the cyclical uncertainties about what is theater and what is real are ultimately resolved. The distinctions of art and life (or death) reassert themselves. Benedetto, with his blood capsules and stage death, gets up to applause; Ros, with her stagy yet real blood, remains dead. Theater and festivity induce temporary destructions of barriers, but it remains to be decided if the creative force of those temporary destructions is worth the tragic losses sustained.

This artistic debate bears obvious similarities to the overarching issue of the party's worth and in turn reflects the anthropological debate over whether festivity is conserving or subversive. To frame the issue another way: to what extent does actual death challenge or undermine the symbolic life affirmations of art and festivity? Following the theoretical discussions of art that occur in the novel, we can see these questions explored, particularly through the characters of Tania, Howard, Gerald, and Vic.

Tania's description of her artistic aim in an unsuccessful painting, "Bluebeard's Chambers," mirrors Coover's technique in presenting Gerald's party: " 'I meant to have a lot of doors in my painting, doors of all sizes, some closed, some partly open, some just empty doorframes, no walls, but the various angles of the doors implying a complicated cross-hatching of different planes, and opening onto a great profusion of inconsistent scenes, inconsistent not only in content but also in perspective, dimension, style—in some cases even opening onto other doors, mazes of doors like funhouse mirrors—and the one consistent image was to be Ros. . . . Only from all angles, including above and below, sometimes in proportion with the scene around her, sometimes not' " (*GP* 56). Tania defends the multiplicity of viewpoints; she has a dynamic sense of art as struggle and she does not, like her husband Howard, glorify artistic expression in the abstract: "sometimes . . . art's so cowardly, Gerry. Shielding us from the truth" (*GP* 57). Here she is diametrically opposed to Howard and closer to Gerald's best friend, Vic, the other powerful voice of art criticism at the party.

" 'Watch out for art,' " Vic was known to exclaim, " 'it's a parlor trick for making the world disappear' " (*GP* 260). Vic is a forceful, outspoken, heavy-drinking cynic, who sees himself as an antidote to the sloppy thinking of the intellectual critics surrounding him. Gerald calls him "a hardnosed guy with a spare intellect, but . . . a weakness for grand pronouncements, especially with a few shots under his belt" (*GP* 40). Vic is a sort of anticritic counterbalancing the discourse of the novel-of-ideas code; he is a compelling force that warns against grandiose claims for art and fiction. Vic speaks with a vital intensity in rejecting critical formulations that turn existence into abstractions: " '*Fuck* your shadows! Man is . . . something *hard!*' " (*GP* 259). His extended death scene is a tour de force of rhetoric, description, and symbolic juxtaposition, possibly the most powerful passage in the book. The death of Vic (he is shot irrationally by a policeman) represents a loss of cynical sanity, as if one of the party's intellectual anchors is removed. Gerald responds to his death in such terms: "I felt a sudden pang of loss, of disconnection from something valuable. Something like the truth. . . . Not the truth so much, but commitment, engagement, the force of life itself: this is what Vic had meant to me" (GP 259–60).

Most of Vic's philosophical opinions that we hear occur during his slow death: shot in the chest he lies bleeding on the kitchen floor demanding drinks and lecturing about the excesses of critical abstraction. Coover extends the piece over forty pages, masterfully interweaving other conversations and concurrent scenes. Most of Vic's rage is directed at Howard, the art critic. At the end of the party Howard asserts: " 'Art, Gerald . . . is all we have. It is not a joke. . . . It is not a decoration' " (GP 299). Vic's dying speech, punctuated by groans, death rattles, and gurgling blood, can be read as a challenge to Howard's claims for art: " 'Ah well, what the fuck, it's all just a—fuff! foo!—fiction anyway,' " Vic rages, referring, presumably, to his life. Overhearing Howard evaluating an artist's skills, the dying Vic challenges: " 'So what's . . . next, Howard? . . . the old—hah! harff!—"language of the fucking wound"—? . . . The artist-as-visionary shuh-whooff!-shit?" (GP 261). Even Gerald is angered by Vic's bombast here, but the context renders his hyperbolic attack on critical clichés forceful.

At one point in the death scene Coover extends over two pages Vic's statement that: "What I hate is contrivance, triviality, obfuscation. I want lucidity, authenticity, a knowing moral center" (GP 262–63). The statement is interrupted not only by Vic's dying gasps but by the conversations and comments of at least twelve other people: Woody is looking for Noble; Gudrun is looking for food; Earl Elstob, returned from a sexual encounter, is telling lewd jokes; Mavis is recounting a dream of an ice sculpture with a wart on its behind; Gottfried is tape recording and interpreting Vic's remarks; Howard is disputing them. The dense scene is filled with comic and ironic juxtapositions. At the height of the conversational intermingling we have this passage:

> Howard was carrying on grandly about art as "man's transcendence
> of the specious present, his romance with eternity, with timelessness"
> ("But then what about Malcolm's tattooed prick?" Kitty interrupted)—
> and his eyelids fluttered again. "Doesn't exist!" he [Vic] bellowed. "I

beg your pardon?" said Gottfried. "Yes, it does," Kitty insisted. "I've seen it." "I think some strawberry shortcake passed me, going into the living room." "*Eternity!*" "Doesn't sound like the right thing to go with bourbon." "What're they up to in there now?" the man in the chalk-striped suit asked Scarborough. "Another . . . fucking *illusion!*" Vic yelled. (*GP* 263–64)

From this marvelous cacophony Vic's bass voice emerges, calling in dying accents that eternity does not exist. Eternity is not the right thing to mix with bourbon, according to, presumably, Gudrun. Yet the phrase comments savagely on the demise of Vic, the party's greatest bourbon drinker. Though Vic is judgmental and, in Howard's terms, monomania-cal, his credo is ironically a call to experiential openness. He resists the resolution of experience into interpretative abstraction and thus warns us against reductiveness. Throughout his long death scene he calls out vainly for, " 'More!' " and asserts " 'I'M NOT FINISHED YET!' " and " 'I *don't* . . . want it . . . *to end*' " (*GP* 266, 264, 269). Gerald shares this dread of eternal absence, the absence of the hard life Vic represents.

If Tania and Vic dramatize Coover's vision of the fragile balance of art, their deaths at the party are ominous. Combined with the death of Ros, the trio's demise seems to represent the lost or threatened values of sexu-ality, artistry, friendship, and love of life. Their loss in the festive context, which normally celebrates those very values, presents a powerful chal-lenge to Gerald. As the evening draws to an end, Gerald increasingly wonders about the value of his parties. He also displays anxiety about the value of sexual desire and art. The novel invites us to join Gerald in questioning the significance of his party; and in questioning Gerald's party, we interrogate the value of the eponymous novel as well.

A crucial characteristic of a party is the self-conscious awareness of the participants that they are indeed present at a festive occasion. The party depends on the awareness of the partygoers that they have entered a time and space consecrated to celebration, that different behavioral rules obtain. The self-consciousness of the partygoer includes a tendency to evaluate the party, in progress and at its conclusion. Charley Trainer's exit line, " 'Great goddamn party, Big G! Bess I ever wen' to!' " is typical (*GP* 302). In *Gerald's Party* Coover presents the party in terms that stress both its carnival sources and festive vitality, on the one hand, and the topos of the decadent failed party, on the other. Naturally the mingling of these two images of the party creates a recurrent tension in guests and host alike. The explicit references to the party throughout the novel develop a potent dialectic that reveals a great deal about the nature of parties.

Many of the explicit references to the party are negative. We have noted that Inspector Pardew views the entire affair as perverted, lawless hysteria. His voice is largely discredited, but the authoritarian dismissal of festivity continues to hold force when more sympathetic, involved characters echo aspects of Pardew's view of the party as aberrant, decadent, or failed. Charley Trainer (in an earlier, less genial mood) compares the party to "a goddamn funeral" (*GP* 157); Jim, the doctor, complains about having to spend the evening caring for the injured—" 'Some damn party *I'm* having' " (*GP* 248). Gerald wonders if "maybe these parties were a mistake" (*GP* 163); his wife muses, " 'You know, I think I'm beginning to like other people's parties better than my own' " (*GP* 107). The wonder is that the negative reactions are not all the more vehement: after all, four people die at the party. It is amazing that it continues at all. But the compelling force of the party is so great that it never threatens to end as a result of the tragic events. As we have noted, this quality creates a tension within the realistic frame but makes perfect sense in terms of other fictional codes: detective story, masquerade, nightmare, and sacrificial ritual. All these codes require the party to continue to reach their respective climaxes. Many of the negative comments thus assume an ironic force by virtue of their tameness. Except for the discredited Pardew, even the critical guests seem to accept that the festivities continue in the face of the deaths.

"If this is a party, Daddy, why aren't there any balloons?" wonders Mark (*GP* 145). The party does not fit Mark's innocent and childlike view of celebration, and yet Gerald twice defends the innocence of the occasion by saying: "It's only a party" (*GP* 127, 159). Though Gerald mourns the deaths, he never looks upon the party itself with horror. To him it somehow remains innocent, even if the activities within it are not. Though Vic assails him with his dying words—" 'Why . . . are they letting you even . . . *have* parties like this' "—Gerald responds with odd distance: " 'I don't know, Vic. Maybe they don't know any better' " (*GP* 266–67). The ambiguous "they" disguises the urges that "compel" the

parties, that compel celebration in general. And these mysterious motivations receive, from both Gerald and his wife, a tentative endorsement:
" 'Somehow,' [Gerald's wife] said . . . 'parties don't seem as much fun as
they used to. . . . It's almost as though the parties have started giving us
instead of us giving the parties . . . Still, I guess it's worth it' " (*GP* 305).
We need to understand the source of this vague affirmation.

The party is Gerald's party and his role as host is as central as his
viewpoint is to the novel. " 'I was serving drinks. I-I'm the host and
I—' " Gerald stutters to Inspector Pardew at the book's opening (*GP* 19).
"What *is* this 'we' when the I's are gone," he wonders as he makes love to
his wife at the evening's close (*GP* 313). This pair of quotations reminds
us of Dick Diver, his identity defined by his ability to be host (what,
here, Pardew defines as Gerald's " 'solicitude and hedonism' " [*GP* 133]).
But these quotations also bracket Gerald's haziness and uncertainty, his
doubts about memory and action, doubts that suggest a loss of identity
in the festive process. Paradoxically, the host also represents a convergence of identities; Gerald thinks of his mother-in-law and his son and
remarks: "I'd become in her eyes, as I was naturally in his, a kind of generalized cause" (*GP* 177). "Host" becomes another relation, like father or
son-in-law. Yet the position is, as Vic grudgingly realizes, one of generosity: " 'You're more considerate than I am. You give parties, I don't' "
(*GP* 85). The host as a role which is both fatherly and generous is further
echoed in Gerald's remarkable identification with his own penis, "that
most prodigious member, the host, as it were" (*GP* 313).

Many aspects of Gerald's character (from his desire to his vague sense
of responsibility and guilt) are interwoven with his sense of himself as
host. Like Clarissa Dalloway and Dick Diver, Gerald stands as party host
at the center of a community for which he reluctantly takes responsibility.
Out of that reluctant acknowledgment emerges this crucial conclusion
on the book's final page: "I lay there on my back, alone and frightened,
remembering all too well why it was we held these parties. And would,
as though compelled, hold another" (*GP* 316). The "why" is located outside the text for us to decipher. When Vic deems parties a " 'ritualized
form of release . . . just another power gimmick in the end,' " Dickie
lewdly responds, " 'For me, they're like solving a puzzle—I keep thinking each time I'll find just the little piece I'm looking for' " (*GP* 168–69).
The novel's final page invites a straight reading of Dickie's earlier sexist

comment: it presents the motivating force for the party as a kind of missing piece, its nature defined indirectly by the novel's developing context and conclusion.

In the final scene Gerald and his wife make love on the sofa amidst the abandoned wreckage of the house. Gerald has popped one of the newly made videotapes into the VCR, and a scene from the party plays an odd retrospective coda in the background. Knud, who has slept through the party, makes a late and sleepy departure, and Gerald and his wife seem finally alone, experiencing the familiar intimacy that follows a party. But they are not quite alone. As Gerald's wife gets up from their lovemaking, she suggests Gerald sleep on the sofa since the Elstobs are in their bed. The silence is punctuated by vague voices that Gerald's wife identifies as stragglers in the backyard. The novel concludes:

> "The backyard? But what are they doing out there?"
> "Nothing. Just telling stories, as far as I could tell. You know, the usual stragglers. But don't worry, I've locked up. Tomorrow . . ." Her voice seemed to be receding. "No, wait—!" I called, but she was already gone. Only the faintest fragrance remained and that, too, was fading. I lay there on my back, alone and frightened, remembering all too well why it was we held these parties. And would, as though compelled, hold another. At least she had turned the TV back on. Perhaps I had asked her to do this. Prince Mark was now riding through the Enchanted Forest. Or maybe this was the Walled Garden, maybe the Tattooed Dragon was dead already, quite likely. " 'Ass usin' yer ole gourd, Mark," Peedie was saying, with a loose drunken chortle. "I think we're awmoss there, ole son—juss keep it up'n—yuff! huff!— *don' look back!"* "Look! There she is! I can see her now! She's *beauti-ful!"* Yes, this *was* the Garden, I could see her, too: she was running bouncily toward me through the lotus blossoms, radiant with joy and anticipation, her blond hair flowing behind her, eyes sparkling, arms outstretched, her soft white dress wrapping her limbs like the frailest of gauze. I felt myself awash in glowing sunshine. "Gerry!" she cried, leaping across some impossible abyss, and threw her arms around me. Oh, what a hug! Oh! It felt great! I could hardly get my breath! Tears came to my eyes and I hugged her back with all my strength. But then suddenly she grabbed my testicles and seemed to want to rip them

out by their roots! I screamed with pain and terror, fell writhing to the ground. "No, no, Ros!" I heard someone shout. I couldn't see who it was. I couldn't even open my eyes. "That's 'Grab up the *bells* and ring them,' goddamn it—!" Oh my god! Get up! I told myself. (But I couldn't even move.) Turn it off. "Gee, I'm sorry . . ." (But I *had* to!) "Now c'mon, let's try that again! From the beginning!" No! *Now*—!
(GP 316)

The party reasserts itself through the guests who will not leave and their stories, through the dream vision captured on video cassette, through the operation of memory filling in the emptiness, through the vivid resurrection of Ros and her hugs, through a desperate compulsion to begin again, to live and celebrate. The "why" behind the parties is explicitly connected with the operation of memory as it is recalled only as Gerald's wife's fragrance fades. The television, which had earlier played a tape of the mother-in-law telling Mark a story, has now become a vision of that story—an impossible vision in which the stuffed rabbit talks and we return to the garden of childhood innocence and play. In that garden Ros has never perished and she emerges like a slow-motion vision from a shampoo commercial and bridges the "impossible abyss" between television screen and sofa, and, symbolically, between dream/memory and experience, impossible garden and living present. With painful and comic inevitability, the standard Ros joke recurs with a hard yank of Gerald's testicles, a sharp reminder of his frustrated sexual desires. So Gerald tries to break the vision, the vision that connects party, dream, memory, desire, and innocence. But he can't get up; he can't turn it off. Outside the text a director urges another take on the scene. Who is that director? Coover as novelist, or an embodiment of the urges that compel us from the outside, an embodiment of desire itself? In any case, that voice wins out through a tiny morphological change shuffling Gerald's "No" into the director's "Now—!" with all the powerful potentiality of repeated parties concentrated in dash and exclamation point.

Jackson Cope remarks that the novel's last line is Coover's nod to Beckett, and he is surely right.[19] Its spirit echoes the crucial Beckett line that Coover quotes elsewhere, "I can't go on, I'll go on."[20] As in Beckett, the strangely compelling force seems linked to the voice of narrative itself, to stories. The party ends with the guests telling stories and with a bedtime story turned into a dream vision, play video, and drama rehearsal. The fertile intersection of fictional codes at the axis of the party epitomizes the carnivalized spirit of the many-voiced novel. Many stories—ritual performance, detective fiction, nightmare, slapstick, theater, drawing-room comedy—are contained within the party and the novel. Teresa, a party guest, juxtaposes the two paradigms of carnival inclusivity: "Oh, I *like* stories . . . And I like *parties!*" (*GP* 162).

CONCLUSION

The Life of the Party

The vital connection between parties and stories is the central motivating argument of this study: the link between festivity and literature, originally manifested in ancient drama and carnivalized medieval texts, continues into the modern era and is evident in the importance of parties to the novel. Both the party and the novel create a space in which the many voices of our culture can be brought together. Both forms carry the possibility of celebration, which is to say, the shared affirmation of what is worthwhile and good in life. The insistently social character of the novel genre exists, however, oddly suspended between the essentially private acts of writing and reading. As I have suggested, the development of the novel parallels the increased individualization of culture (and the isolation of the individual within culture) and works to assuage or counteract that isolation; so too the modern party, which seeks to create festive communities in a mass culture.

I have also outlined, through the concept of controlled transgression, a typology of parties as a revealing approach to the development of the novel in the twentieth century. The life of the party works then as a life of the novel. Parties exist in a tension between control and release remarkably similar to the tension at work in novel form between narrative control and polyphonic discourse. Festivity gains its character from the struggle between authority and license; the successful novel grows out of a similar struggle. Though there are risks attending any generalization of literary history, we can see, in these terms, a suggestive parallel between festive form and novel form. In modernist fiction the typical failed party is characterized by an excess of control, that is, by the absence of any authentic sense of transgression or festive release. In response, the experiments with narrative form characteristic of the novel tend to celebrate multiplicity of narrative voice and the incorporation of popular cultural forms and other genres. In short, the modernist novel values and celebrates festive transgression, both thematically and in terms of the development of increasingly carnivalized aspects of the novel genre. In the period between the wars, we identified a social sensibility and aesthetic stance resistant to modernist experimentation. The typical failed party becomes one of false transgression, the decadent pose of excessive behavior not seriously experienced as release. Against this perceived sense of decadent artifice and stasis, the novel both records and resists festive multiplicity. The narrative distance of satire and the objective narrative stance of social realism thus work in conflict with the festive forms that occupy much of the attention of these writers. In more recent fiction in the postmodern vein, the typical party becomes festivity turned chaotic, the festive transgression veering out of control. Reinvigorating and often expanding modernist experiments with narrative, contemporary novelists tend to celebrate the spirit of carnival excess. Increased incorporation of popular culture and the celebration of the lower body (and all that is traditionally excluded from the realm of art) demonstrate the novel's complicity with festive license. But such complicity is not devoid of an awareness of the violence implicit in loss of control and its dangers. Though the overall development of the modern novel is too various and complex to be reduced to a linear pattern, these variations of festive experience implicit in the model of controlled transgression do capture the dominant trends and developments of each novelistic era in the twentieth century.

The bulk of this study, however, is composed of analyses of individual texts, with the faith that an understanding of an author's festive vision contributes to our understanding of the techniques and themes characteristic of that author's achievement. The arguments made here about the development of the novel and the centrality of the party scene are intended to enhance close readings of the literature. My belief is that it is still useful to offer readings of texts, still useful for the critical argument to be structured as a journey through the text, taken by critic and reader, in which a particular perspective offers illumination. Nevertheless, certain perspectives that emerge in this study can be summarized. In reading Joyce, we notice the centrality of the wake scene, the encounter with death at the celebration, and, viewing Joyce's work as a whole, we detect a pattern in which increasingly affirmative and successful encounters with mortality parallel increased stylistic openness and carnivalization. Woolf's use of parties provides a focus for her exploration of "the true self" and its social or communal character. Woolf's perception that traditional notions of self are inadequate then leads to a rejection of traditional narrative and to experiments rendering narrative voice as multiple. Fitzgerald also evidences a career-long struggle with point of view, and probably a less successful one. The search for a vital and nourishing community is paralleled by the author's search for a narrative perspective capable of being both "within and without." In reading Waugh we encounter modernist techniques turned against themselves, or at least against the perceived values of modern society. Waugh's conservatism generates a satirical approach to parties, but his fiction also evidences the use of popular forms and discourses, the development of a radically subversive black humor, and a strong attraction to the potential vitality of the social rituals he criticizes. Green's encounter with the nuances of insincerity and artifice reveals his central struggle with the epistemological stance of the novelist. The party scene provides the biggest challenge for Green's nonintrusive narrator, a challenge profound enough to alter his typical narrative technique. In Pynchon, writing after and about the Second World War, festivity is identified as the life affirmation of the oppressed and discarded, and Pynchon's carnival of discourses asserts the value of the carnivalized genre for the interpretation of contemporary life. Coover's party novel also celebrates the liberation engendered when differing discourses are set against one another. It is a liberation that opens creative and comic possibilities for the contemporary novelist.

Certainly all these works testify to the enduring quality of the impulse to celebrate; and they show us how closely that impulse is bound up with literature, with the desires that stimulate artistic creation and consumption. Finally, it is appropriate to point out, as we imagine ourselves reading about elaborate parties from the sheltered isolation of our separate homes, that the act of reading a text is ultimately a communal activity. The artist writes from within a society, and we read him or her within one. Inevitably, however, we cannot contain our readings. We continually re-create texts among a community of readers, applying, discussing, and restructuring our readings through literary criticism, in classrooms, or even, occasionally, at parties. Neither the party nor the novel is a panacea to cure our doubts and fears or deliver us from loneliness, but both begin from that shared isolation and work toward community and affirmation. The novel and the party both thrive as forces of life in our world.

NOTES

Introduction: Festive Vision

1. Burke, *Popular Culture in Early Modern Europe*, 178.

2. Plato, *The Symposium*, 71–72.

3. Petronius, *The Satyricon*, trans. William Arrowsmith, 84.

4. Kermode, *Shakespeare, Spenser, Donne: Renaissance Essays*, 84–115.

5. For a discussion of Jonson's complex attitudes toward festivity, see Marcus, *The Politics of Mirth: Jonson, Herrick, Milton, Marvell and the Defense of Old Holiday Pastimes.*

6. The coexistence of pagan rites and Christianity in the Middle Ages became the target of reformers in the sixteenth century who objected to the non-Christian elements and licentious nature of carnivals and feasts. For an excellent discussion of the reform movement see chap. 8, "The Triumph of Lent: The Reform of Popular Culture" in Burke, *Popular Culture in Early Modern Europe*, 207–43.

7. Stallybrass and White, *The Politics and Poetics of Transgression*, 103–4.

8. For a discussion of the shift in literary focus from heroic and historical themes to an examination of contemporary life, see Auerbach, *Mimesis: The Representation of Reality in Western Literature*, especially chapter 18 on French realism. See also Watt, *The Rise of the Novel: Studies in Defoe, Richardson and Fielding*. Watt treats the relationship between privacy and the novel form: the novel presents "a picture of life in which the individual is immersed in private and personal relationships because a larger communion with nature or society is no longer available" (185).

9. Castle, *Masquerade and Civilization: The Carnivalesque in Eighteenth-Century English Culture and Fiction*, 115.

10. Trilling, *Sincerity and Authenticity*, 98.

11. For the purposes of forming a general theory of festival, I have followed

writers like Roger Caillois and Emile Durkheim in grouping the celebrations of traditional cultures with the carnivals and festivities of antiquity and medieval Europe. In terms of overall structure and symbolism, the connection is strong among periods of festive license in primitive cultures, Greek Dionysian celebrations, Roman saturnalia, and medieval carnivals. Frazer's *The Golden Bough* is the most famous work connecting ancient rituals with surviving forms of festivity. Durkheim, *The Elementary Forms of the Religious Life*. Caillois, *Man and the Sacred*.

12. Durkheim, *Elementary Forms*, 250.

13. Ibid., 432.

14. Caillois, *Man and the Sacred*, 98.

15. Nietzsche, *The Birth of Tragedy* and *The Case of Wagner*, 46.

16. Caillois, *Man and the Sacred*, 101.

17. Bakhtin, *Problems of Dostoevsky's Poetics*, 124.

18. See the discussion of this remark in Pieper, *In Tune With the World: A Theory of Festivity*, 20.

19. Caillois, *Man and the Sacred*, 185 n. 22.

20. Unlike most writers on festival, Girard sees the joyousness of celebration not in the liberation of transgression but in the anticipation of the return to a rejuvenated normal state: "If the crisis brought on by the loss of distinctions and the subsequent advent of reciprocal violence can be celebrated in such a jubilant fashion, it is because these holocausts are seen in retrospect as the initial stages of a cathartic process . . . which will eventually manifest itself as a festive display." See Girard, *Violence and the Sacred*, 120. I find such a dismissal of the liberating quality of festive excess problematic, but Girard's theory is important for addressing the genuine dangers inherent in festive transgressions, threats all too often minimized or romanticized.

21. Bakhtin, *Dostoevsky's Poetics*, 125.

22. Bernstein discusses the relationship of Girard and Bakhtin, arguing that Girard's "vision of the 'mimetic violence' underlying the carnival rite . . . contains a salutary counterbalance to Bakhtin's optimistic affirmations." Bernstein, "When the Carnival Turns Bitter: Preliminary Reflections Upon the Abject Hero" in *Bakhtin: Essays and Dialogues on His Work*, 118.

23. Writers on modern literature, comedy, and festivity exhibit different approaches to the historical trend of secularization. In connecting comic fiction with the religious impulse, Polhemus defines "the main purposes and uses of religion" as follows: "To honor creation, to provide hope; to reconcile people to their harsh fates; to smooth over social enmity and to defend culture by authoritative moral sanction against selfish and destructive behavior; to organize and discipline the energies and emotions of a people; to make people feel

that they are important and part of a 'chosen' group; to institutionalize ways of getting rid of guilt; to allow people to identify with righteousness and let loose wrathful indignation and hostility in good conscience; to assure them of the possibility of future well-being; to lift them out of themselves and free the spirit." Polhemus sees these same functions served by nineteenth-century comic fiction, but it is instructive to consider how festival (and festivity in fiction) achieves these communal, religious ends. See Polhemus, *Comic Faith: The Great Tradition from Austen to Joyce*, 5.

24. See Cox, *The Feast of Fools: A Theological Essay on Festivity and Fantasy*. Cox sums up the connection: "Celebration requires a set of common memories and collective hopes. It requires, in short, what is usually thought of as a religion" (15).

25. Caillois comments that "there is no festival, even on a sad occasion, that does not imply at least a tendency toward excesses and good cheer." Caillois, *Man and the Sacred*, 97. See also Huntington and Metcalf, *Celebrations of Death: The Anthropology of Mortuary Ritual*, 1–2; and chap. 2, "The Emotional Reaction to Death" (23–34), which discusses the importance of funeral studies to Durkheim's overall interpretation of festivity.

26. Durkheim, *Elementary Forms*, 445.

27. Girard, *Violence and the Sacred*, 31.

28. In addition to Frazer and Burke, the following sources on carnival and other medieval festivities have been helpful in allowing me to generalize about festivity: Bakhtin, *Rabelais and His World*, 1–58, 196–277; Caputi, *Buffo: The Genius of Vulgar Comedy*, 21–94; Ladurie, *Carnival in Romans*, 305–25. Ladurie also provides a thorough bibliography on festival.

29. Perhaps Wallace Stevens articulates this paradox best in "Sunday Morning": "Death is the mother of beauty." In Stevens's "The Emperor of Ice Cream" the occasion of a death forms the context for celebration and affirmation of being.

30. Stallybrass and White, *Politics and Poetics of Transgression*, 189.

31. Caillois, *Man and the Sacred*, 163–80. The only other possibility he considers explicitly is the vacation, and he rightly dismisses it for being rooted in relaxation, not effervescence, and in isolation, not community. Other possibilities, including, one assumes, parties, are dismissed en masse: "Any other phenomenon [than war] seems indeed to be ridiculously out of proportion before the immense mobilization of energy represented by the festival" (165). War is indeed "a total phenomenon" and involves entire societies in a way little else does; this perhaps is its most potent analogical appeal. And Caillois does admit the basic difference: "Without a doubt, war is horror and catastrophe, the inundation of death, and the festival is consecrated to outbursts of joy and super-abundance of life" (165). Surprisingly, Caillois dismisses this difference as not bearing on "their function in collective life" (165).

32. Caillois, *Man and the Sacred*, 97.

33. Adherence to strict distinctions between sacred and secular also explains Gluckman's earlier and very influential dismissal of modern celebrative ritual. See his Introduction to *Essays on the Ritual of Social Relations*, 36–37.

34. The discussion of play in culture seems oddly polarized between those who view play very literally as competitive games and those who react to the play/work dichotomization by expanding the definition of play to include work and aspects of virtually all cultural activities. As a result, treatment of modern parties as adult play is virtually nonexistent. The seminal work on play theory is Huizinga's *Homo Ludens: A Study of the Play-Element in Culture*. Caillois's *Man, Play and Games* develops and criticizes Huizinga. Ehrmann and Hans are the most influential contemporary theorists of play; see Ehrmann, ed., *Game, Play and Literature*; and Hans, *The Play of the World*.

35. Turner, ed., *Celebration: Studies in Festivity and Ritual*, 11.

36. Manning, ed., *The Celebration of Society: Perspectives on Contemporary Cultural Performance*, 8.

37. Castle discusses this tension in terms of "innoculation and infection," *Masquerade and Civilization*, 89.

38. See Turner, *The Forest of Symbols*, chap. 4.

39. White, "Pigs and Pierrots: The Politics of Transgression in Modern Fiction," 60, 53.

40. Ladurie, *Carnival in Romans*, 316.

41. See also Burke, *Popular Culture in Early Modern Europe*, 199–204. Burke discusses whether carnival connotes "social control or social protest" and includes a list of famous carnivals that turned violent.

42. I have followed Wimsatt's balanced summary of theories of the origin of comedy and tragedy in his introduction to *The Idea of Comedy: Essays in Prose and Verse—Ben Jonson to George Meredith*. For the earliest persuasive arguments about dramatic origins see Murray, "Excursus on the Ritual Forms Preserved in Greek Tragedy," in Harrison, *Themis: A Study of the Social Origins of the Greek Religion*, 341–63; and Cornford, *The Origin of Attic Comedy*.

43. Frye, "The Argument of Comedy," 452.

44. Ibid., 456.

45. Ibid., 454–55.

46. Barber, *Shakespeare's Festive Comedy: A Study of Dramatic Form and Its Relation to Social Custom*, 6.

47. Ibid., 8.

48. Ibid., 10.

49. Frye, "The Argument of Comedy," 457, 452.

50. Bakhtin, *Dostoevsky's Poetics*, 124.

51. Bakhtin, *Rabelais and His World*, 246–57.

52. Ibid., 96.

53. Bakhtin, *Dostoevsky's Poetics*, 122, 123.

54. This emphasis on the existence of an ideally united community resonates with Nietzsche's panegyric to the Dionysian in *The Birth of Tragedy*, where he defines the Dionysian state as radically separate from ordinary existence: a "chasm of oblivion separates the worlds of everyday reality and of Dionysian reality" (59). And Nietzsche clearly opposes the Dionysian community to a society built of individuals.

55. Bakhtin, "From the Prehistory of Novelistic Discourse," in *The Dialogic Imagination*. Barbara Babcock has noted that "those scholars who have focused on the relationship of festival or carnival to 'high' literature—notably F. M. Cornford and C. L. Barber—have been concerned with drama . . . [which] is much more obviously comparable to ritual," "The Novel and the Carnival World: An Essay in Memory of Joe Doherty," 921.

56. Bakhtin, *The Dialogic Imagination: Four Essays*, 23.

57. Bakhtin, *Dostoevsky's Poetics*, 133.

58. Ibid., 134, 134–35.

59. See especially Bernstein, "When the Carnival Turns Bitter," 99–121.

60. Morson, "Who Speaks for Bakhtin?" 15.

61. Bakhtin, *Dostoevsky's Poetics*, 134.

62. Ibid., 130, 131.

63. Bakhtin, *Rabelais and His World*, 276, 120; see also *Dostoevsky's Poetics*, 164–66.

64. Bakhtin, *Rabelais and his World*, 276.

65. Frye, "The Argument of Comedy," 452.

66. Castle, *Masquerade and Civilization*, 27, 29.

67. Ibid., 105, 107.

68. Watt, *The Rise of the Novel*, 295.

69. Morson also mentions Bakhtin's exclusions: "[he] notably does not discuss the works of Jane Austen, George Eliot, and Henry James. Bakhtin should have called his book *The Great Anti-Tradition*." In Morson, "Who Speaks for Bakhtin?" 15.

70. Watt, *The Rise of the Novel*, 297.

71. Austen, *Emma*, 220, 262.

72. Polhemus, *Comic Faith*, 182.

73. Virginia Woolf, "On Re-Reading Meredith," in *Collected Essays*, 1:235.

74. In passing we might note such memorable scenes in Victorian fiction as Lewis Carroll's Mad Tea Party or Thomas Hardy's marvelous drunken party scene in *The Mayor of Casterbridge*.

75. James, *The Art of the Novel*, 110.

Part 1. Death at the Party

1. I am aware that many readers consider *The Waves* to be Woolf's most radical experiment with narrative. Still, I think the development of a plural narrative consciousness as revealed in *Between the Acts* and the work-in-progress, *Anon*, represents a further development in Woolf's career of daring experimentation.

2. Bakhtin, *The Dialogic Imagination*, 11.

1. "The Dead" and the Wake

D   *Dubliners*
U   *Ulysses*
FW   *Finnegans Wake*

1. Hayman, "Forms of Folly in Joyce: A Study of Clowning in *Ulysses*," 260. For a discussion of the recent critical tendency to stress the continuities and similarities throughout the Joyce canon see Donoghue, "Bakhtin and *Finnegans Wake*," in *We Irish*, 120–23.

2. Abbreviations of major works discussed are keyed to the lists of abbreviations, which precede each chapter's notes.

3. In his study of Joyce's narrative technique, Riquelme notes how "In 'The Sisters' the repetition of related phrases lends an iterative coloration to the past perfect." Riquelme, *Teller and Tale in Joyce's Fiction*, 101.

4. Walzl, "Joyce's 'The Sisters': A Development," 389.

5. Ibid., 379–80.

6. Ibid., 415.

7. Duffy, " 'The Sisters' as the Introduction to *Dubliners*," 424.

8. See Torchiana, *Backgrounds for Joyce's "Dubliners*," 151.

9. Hodgart, "Ivy Day in the Committee Room," 120.

10. See Blotner, " 'Ivy Day in the Committee Room': Death Without Resurrection," 210–12.

11. The most articulate proponent of an opposing view is Pecora who challenges affirmative and open-ended readings of "The Dead" in " 'The Dead' and

the Generosity of the Word," 233–45. Pecora argues that the reader longs for escape as much as Gabriel and thus reads the passage blind to Joyce's criticism of the Christian paradigm of self-abnegation. Gabriel's affirmation is conditioned, Pecora asserts, by the very society Joyce criticizes throughout *Dubliners*. Pecora's argument is compelling, and his tracing of Joyce's use of *generosity* is particularly brilliant. Nevertheless, his claim that the reader is caught in the same ideological web as Gabriel and thus unable to attain sufficient distance from him betrays precisely what Pecora wishes to deny: that "The Dead" is fundamentally different from the other *Dubliners* stories. Because we can identify with Gabriel's complexities, a more ambivalent judgment seems warranted. Gabriel shares with other creations of the mature Joyce (Stephen, Bloom, Molly, HCE) a complex nature not subject to either a thorough dismissal or acceptance.

12. Caillois, *Man and the Sacred*, 113.

13. Brown examines the opening paragraph of "The Dead" to argue that the narrative voice "represents the kind of group mind of the occasion," a sort of communal narrator, consistent with "the awareness of mutual dependency of all the living and the dead that Gabriel Conroy comes to at the end of the story." Brown, *James Joyce's Early Fiction*, 90.

14. Girard, *Violence and the Sacred*, 125. For the reading that follows of Gabriel's encounter with the Other I am indebted to Girard's analysis of mimetic desire in *Deceit, Desire and the Novel*. Girard does not discuss Joyce, but his concept of triangular desire is suggestive for "The Dead."

15. Rabate discusses this scene in terms of images of sound and silence. See Rabate, "Silence in *Dubliners*," 65–67.

16. Riquelme, *Teller and Tale in Joyce's Fiction*, 127.

17. The symbolism, from the funeral and Easter association of "Lily" to the ice and water combination of snow, supports such a reading. See the discussions of ambivalent symbolism in Tindall, *A Reader's Guide to James Joyce*, 42–49; and Walzl, "Gabriel and Michael: The Conclusion of 'The Dead.'"

18. Riquelme, *Teller and Tale in Joyce's Fiction*, 122.

19. See Hayman's contention, "In a book that approximates the integral texture of experience, clowning is a convenient shorthand capable of linking norm to universal, consciousness to the unconscious, rational to irrational perception. In other words it provides a magic substance that moves the everyday beyond itself," "Forms of Folly in Joyce," 265.

20. Tucker, *Stephen and Bloom at Life's Feast*, 98.

21. Janusko, *The Sources and Structures of James Joyce's "Oxen,"* 18.

22. See Blamires, *The Bloomsday Book*, 163–64.

23. Tucker, *Stephen and Bloom at Life's Feast*, 107.

24. Kenner, *Ulysses*, 123. See also Kenner's essay on "Circe" in *James Joyce's "Ulysses": Critical Essays*, 341–61.

25. See especially Shechner, *Joyce in Nighttown*.

26. Vickery discusses the importance of carnival tradition in "Circe" in his study of Frazer's influence on modern literature, *The Literary Impact of "The Golden Bough*," 358–407.

27. Hayman, "Forms of Folly in Joyce," 283.

28. Bakhtin, *Dostoevsky's Poetics*, 122.

29. Ibid., 129–30.

30. Ibid., 133.

31. Vickery, *The Literary Impact of "The Golden Bough*," 381.

32. Bakhtin, *Dostoevsky's Poetics*, 133.

33. Riquelme's *Teller and Tale in Joyce's Fiction* discusses the correspondences to Christian history in "Circe" (146–47) and the importance of drunkenness to the Homeric parallels (142–44).

34. Bakhtin, *Rabelais and His World*, 78–79.

35. See Vickery for a discussion of Joyce's debt to Frazer with regard to the *danse macabre*, *The Literary Impact of "The Golden Bough*," 377–78.

36. Donoghue qualifies this connection by noting that "it may be better to think of Joyce's technique in the *Wake* not as setting the language of travesty in a derisive relation to an official discourse but as relativizing two or more forms of perception by confounding the privilege any of them might be expected to have," *We Irish*, 135.

37. Ibid., 127.

38. Bakhtin, *Dostoevsky's Poetics*, 131.

39. See Glasheen, "Notes Toward a Supreme Understanding of the Use of 'Finnegan's Wake' in *Finnegans Wake*." See also M. J. C. Hodgart and Mabel Worthington, *Song in the Works of James Joyce*, 28–29. See also Bishop, *Joyce's Book of the Dark*, 71ff.

40. Bishop, *Joyce's Book of the Dark*, 137, 419n.

41. Tindall, *A Reader's Guide to "Finnegans Wake*," 34. *Bockalips* is one of those especially potent *Wake* words: it contains "apocalypse" and "Bacchus," bock beer and the lips that drink it.

    2. *The True Self*

    BTA   *Between the Acts*
    CE   *Collected Essays*
    DVW *The Diary of Virginia Woolf*

MD   *Mrs. Dalloway*
MDP   *Mrs. Dalloway's Party*
W   *The Waves*

1. The figure of Percival in *The Waves* concentrates the imagery of violence, blood sacrifice, and the victim-as-beloved throughout the novel. Behind the social gatherings of the friends at Hampton Court and at restaurants lies the language of ritual:

> "Like the dance of savages," said Louis. . . .
> "The flames of the festival rise high," said Rhoda. "The great procession passes, flinging green boughs and flowering branches. . . . They throw violets. They deck the beloved with garlands and with laurel leaves. . . .
> "Death is woven in with the violets," said Louis. (W 140)

I'm grateful to Patricia Joplin, who is working on a study of ritual and Virginia Woolf, for calling these scenes to my attention.

2. Forster, *Virginia Woolf*, 21–23.

3. Guiget calls *Mrs. Dalloway* "the urban novel *par excellence*," *Virginia Woolf and Her Works*, 413. Zwerdling treats the novel as an examination of the social mechanics of a declining "governing class," *Virginia Woolf and the Real World*, 120–43.

4. For a sociological analysis of interaction as role-playing, see Goffmann, *The Presentation of Self in Everyday Life*, 240.

5. Woolf's fiction is full of scenes describing the seductive dangers of solitude and how nature is no secret sharer but the inhuman force that "in the end will conquer." Scenes of solitude in Woolf's fiction are discussed in Naremore, *The World Without a Self*.

6. Miller, "Virginia Woolf's All Soul's Day: The Omniscient Narrator in *Mrs. Dalloway*," 103.

7. Naremore, *The World Without a Self*, 91.

8. Naremore provides the most detailed account of this aspect of Woolf's technique; he focuses on how, in *Mrs. Dalloway*, it allows for the adept movement between points of view without breaks in the narrative, and his central thesis argues that Woolf creates a "qualitative unity" of different selves through the ego-subsuming voice of the narrator.

9. This quality of Woolf's writing is what leads Auerbach to make her the subject of the concluding chapter of *Mimesis*. Auerbach chronicles the increasing attention in Western literature to "minor happenings" in characters of unexceptional social standing.

10. Miller, "The Omniscient Narrator in *Mrs. Dalloway*," 104.

11. Hawthorn, *Virginia Woolf's "Mrs. Dalloway,"* 79.

12. Miller, "The Omniscient Narrator in *Mrs. Dalloway,"* 104.

13. Naremore, *The World Without a Self,* 91.

14. Fleishman, *Virginia Woolf: A Critical Reading,* 73. See also the map contributed by Morris Beja to the *Virginia Woolf Miscellany* 7 (Spring 1977): 4.

15. Ruotolo, *"Mrs. Dalloway:* The Unguarded Moment," 158–59.

16. See Hawthorn's discussion of this passage, *Virginia Woolf's "Mrs. Dalloway": A Study in Alienation,* 82–84.

17. Woolf herself uses the term in her introduction to the Modern Library edition of *Mrs. Dalloway* (New York: Random House, 1928), vi. Since then it has been adopted or alluded to by almost all critics discussing the novel.

18. For suggestive typologies of the double, see: Albert Guerard, Introduction to *Stories of the Double* (Philadelphia: Lippincott, 1967); C. F. Keppler, *The Literature of the Second Self* (Tucson: University of Arizona Press, 1972); Robert Rogers, *A Psychoanalytic Study of the Double in Literature* (Detroit: Wayne State University Press, 1970).

19. Frye, *Anatomy of Criticism,* 179.

20. Fleishman, *Virginia Woolf,* 88.

21. Miller argues that the parallel between the characters suggests their communal participation in a unified humanity: "All individual minds are joined to one another far below the surface separateness," Miller, "The Omniscient Narrator in *Mrs. Dalloway,"* 105.

22. Fleishman, on the other hand, argues that "the two main actions of the plot—suicide and party—are parallel in intention and effect" and he suggests that this "blunt[s] the distinction between life affirmation and death wish," *Virginia Woolf,* 87. I would argue that Woolf offers Clarissa another alternative, embodied by the old neighbor woman.

23. See, for example, Apter: "The old woman Clarissa sees through the window . . . represents the purely personal, private life which Clarissa pilfered in her desire for social success." *Virginia Woolf: A Study of Her Novels,* 72.

24. In the Modern Library introduction, Woolf writes, "Mrs. Dalloway was originally to kill herself" (vi).

25. See especially the writings of R. D. Laing. To some extent, this sentiment emerges in the conclusion of Michel Foucault, *Madness and Civilization,* trans. Richard Howard (New York: Vintage, 1973).

26. The conclusion of Lionel Trilling's *Sincerity and Authenticity* provides a good antidote to the romanticization of madness: "Who that has spoken, or tried to speak, with a psychotic friend will consent to betray the masked pain of his

bewilderment and solitude by making it the paradigm of liberation from the imprisoning falsehoods of an alientated social reality?" (171).

27. Miller, "The Omniscient Narrator in *Mrs. Dalloway*," 122–25.

28. The criticisms Peter and Richard make of Clarissa's parties are echoed by a variety of critics who attack the novel on the grounds that Clarissa and parties are essentially superficial. Woolf spoke of bringing "innumerable characters to [Clarissa's] support" in anticipation of such criticisms. The most notable (and predictable) attacks come from the Leavis school, in works by Leavis and William Troy that attack the "almost continuous state of moral and intellectual relaxation" of Woolf's characters. See Troy, "Virginia Woolf: The Novel of Sensibility," 343. Hawthorn, approaching the book from a Marxist perspective, also finds parties per se superficial: "Isn't it . . . work rather than parties which brings people together in a real sense?" *A Study in Alienation*, 92. For appreciative considerations of Clarissa's party see Baldanza, "Clarissa Dalloway's 'Party Consciousness' "; and Philipson, "Mrs. Dalloway, 'What's the Sense of Your Parties?' "

29. Wilson, "A Comparison of Parties, With a Discussion of Their Function in Woolf's Fiction," 216–17.

30. Ruotolo, *The Interrupted Moment: A View of Virginia Woolf's Novels*, 115.

31. DiBattista, *Virginia Woolf's Major Novels: The Fables of Anon*, 62.

32. Some critics reach this conclusion. See, for example, Rachman, "Clarissa's Attic: Virginia Woolf's *Mrs. Dalloway* Reconsidered," 15.

33. See Miller, *Fiction and Repetition*, 211.

34. Ibid., 222.

35. Ruotolo, *The Interrupted Moment*, 2.

36. Bazin discusses the affinities between "The Waste Land" and *Between the Acts*, *Virginia Woolf and the Androgynous Vision*, 215–18.

37. Ruotolo comments: "In a novel so steeped in literary allusion, it is notable that newspapers . . . serve to guide almost every inhabitant of Pointz Hall. Like the pageant, literature remains at best a marginal enterprise, something to pursue literally between the acts." *The Interrupted Moment*, 209.

38. For interesting discussions of music and literature see Robert Wallace, *Jane Austen and Mozart: Classical Equilibrium in Fiction and Music* (Athens, Ga.: University of Georgia Press, 1983); and his *Emily Bronte and Beethoven: Romantic Equilibrium in Fiction and Music* (Athens, Ga.: University of Georgia Press, 1986).

39. Leaska's edition of the early drafts of *Between the Acts* reveals this fascinating meditation on the narrative limitations attending the presentation of emptiness or nothingness. See Leaska, *Pointz Hall: The Earlier and Later Typescripts of "Between the Acts,"* 61–62.

40. See Bazin, *Virginia Woolf and the Androgynous Vision* (216–17) and Leaska, *Pointz Hall* (220–21) for discussions of the Swinburne allusion.

41. Zwerdling, *Virginia Woolf and the Real World*, 311.

42. Ibid., 307.

43. Bakhtin, *Dostoevsky's Poetics*, 126.

44. Ibid., 130–31.

45. Ibid., 134–35.

46. Barth, "The Literature of Exhaustion," 71.

47. Bakhtin, *Dostoevsky's Poetics*, 108.

48. Ibid., 127.

Part 2. The Party Between the Wars

1. Cunningham, *British Writers of the Thirties*, 77.

2. The word *decadence* is indispensable in discussing parties and their literary treatment. Because it is so rich and suggestive a word, it has meant many different, even contradictory, things in its varied history. The classic study of *decadence* as a word of many meanings is Gilman's *Decadence: The Strange Life of an Epithet*, a curious book. It effectively discusses the periods to which the term has most often been applied—Rome around the beginning of the fifth century, France in the 1860s and '70s, England in the 1890s. Gilman is best when demonstrating that *decadence*'s pejorative, accusatory application is always part of a moralistic strategy for posing a golden-age, classical mean from which to judge human behavior. He is clear in deploring this moralistic use of *decadence* almost as much as he is in deploring the chic contemporary usage.

Gilman's discussions of the casual contemporary meaning as roughly, "self-indulgence" reveal the true passion of his study. "One result of this tropism of 'decadence' toward the sensual," writes Gilman, "is that the word loses any status it might have had as a moral, spiritual, or cultural term" (16). He argues that the word has lost its moral seriousness: " 'Decadence' was once a word that lived in the depths, under the pressure of extreme consciousness. Now it exists in the thin air of the pretense of extremity, a device for the imitation of spiritual or moral concern, or for mocking them" (7).

Gilman is aptly describing an alteration in usage, and he is correct that the twentieth-century uses of *decadence* do not approach the moral force of Baudelaire's poetry. But Gilman's valid observation loosely conceals an attitude even more fascinating: his discussion of the "cheapening" of the usages of *decadence* echoes remarkably the language of decay and decline itself. The very process he describes is, in one sense, decadent. Gilman uses the words *debasement, degradation,* and *trivialization* to chronicle the word's decline (see 169). In discussing the word, Gilman catapults himself into the very role of positing a golden age from which our usage has fallen, and he heartily adopts the judgmental tones he associates with the moralistic uses of *decadence* as an epithet.

The closest Gilman comes to making this parallel explicit is in his discussion of recent meanings of *decadence*: "To crave decadence would rightly be regarded as a pose, would be thought of in fact *as a sign of decadence itself*, the posturing quality of which has come to be one of its prominently regarded features. When Kenneth Tynan chats about decadence as though it were a charming native dance or jet-setters hold parties with a theme of 'decadence,' the testimony is only to falseness, pose, the inauthentic" (166; emphasis mine). This is a crucial observation, but one in need of more examination than Gilman grants it. I would argue that the desperation underlying the pose of decadence is inextricably related to the aspects of decadence Gilman endorses as "retain[ing] a core of thoughtfulness." To celebrate evil, pure sensuality, and decay because the contemporary manifestations of the good, reason, and progress are hollow and lifeless is a desperate action inevitably destined to harden into a pose. To make deviations and extraordinary behavior the norm is to accept damnation at the hands of social authority, to accept the tyranny of mediocrity by opposing it so. Thus the *pose* of decadence, the self-conscious desperation of adopting an adversary position to what one views as the norms of a dying culture, is inextricably related to the earlier "purer" decadence. Occasionally certain figures, such as Baudelaire, may appear to transcend the decadence they are associated with by virtue of their position in history. At other times, writers may use their art to distance themselves from the decadent aspects of their own subculture— this is what I believe writers like Fitzgerald, Waugh, and Green accomplish.

If we see decadence as a desperate response to loss of faith in traditional forms of behavior beginning with a moral rigor but necessarily abandoning it, we can see that the phenomenon embraces both the "core of thoughtfulness" Gilman endorses *and* the chic pose he rejects. They are two sides of the same coin; they represent the initial rebellious exuberance of the party and the eventual weightlessness of the late stages of the party without end.

3. Relevant Waugh articles are collected in *The Essays, Articles and Reviews of Evelyn Waugh*, edited by Donat Gallagher. They include such pieces as "The Youngest Generation," "Too Young at Forty," "The War and the Younger Generation," and "Such Appalling Manners." Fitzgerald's articles include material reprinted in *F. Scott Fitzgerald in His Own Time: A Miscellany*, edited by Matthew J. Bruccoli. These articles include "Our Young Rich Boys" and "What I Think and Feel at Twenty-Five." Other articles include pieces cowritten with Zelda. See the excellent bibliography in Bruccoli, *Some Sort of Epic Grandeur: The Life of F. Scott Fitzgerald*, 545–69.

4. Duffy, Introduction to *Etiquette*, xvii.

5. For a good discussion of the political distrust of aestheticism in thirties literature, see Stevenson, *The British Novel Since the Thirties*, 30–67.

6. Bakhtin, *Rabelais and his World*, 38; see also chap. 1, "Rabelais in the History of Laughter," 59–144.

3. Charioted by Bacchus

BD   *The Beautiful and the Damned*
CU   *The Crack-Up*
GG   *The Great Gatsby*
TN   *Tender Is the Night*

1. See Fitzgerald's story "The Baby Party" for a dramatic example of adults taking over a party from the younger generation.

2. Wilson, "F. Scott Fitzgerald," 34–35.

3. See Lehan, *F. Scott Fitzgerald and the Craft of Fiction*, 84–86. Lehan draws an interesting, if disapproving, comparison between "May Day" and *The Beautiful and Damned*.

4. Mizener, *The Far Side of Paradise*, 153; Lehan, *F. Scott Fitzgerald and the Craft of Fiction*, 90.

5. Wharton to Fitzgerald, June 8, 1925 (*CU* 309).

6. See Long, *The Achieving of "The Great Gatsby."* See also Tuttleton, *The Novel of Manners in America*, 180. He cites Gilbert Seldes's comparison of Fitzgerald's scenic method to the narrative techniques of Wharton and James. The dramatic approach to fiction is also discussed in terms of Fitzgerald and literary modernism in Perosa, *The Art of F. Scott Fitzgerald*, 76–79.

7. The quest for the elusive host suggests a significant parallel between Conrad and Fitzgerald. Conrad's influence on Fitzgerald has been discussed primarily in terms of the use of a participant narrator (see Long, *The Achieving of "The Great Gatsby*," 79–118 and Stallman, "Conrad and *The Great Gatsby*"). But Nick's perspective on Gatsby's first party suggests another technical parallel with Conrad's impressionism: the mystery of Gatsby is developed in a manner similar to the mystery of Kurtz. Gatsby attains mythical stature through the awestruck reports of others; his actual appearance rarely matches that stature. Nick's search for the host parallels, perhaps comically, Marlow's search for the ambiguous Kurtz. In both cases the narrative strategy arises from the conception of the "great" character as an embodiment of an emptiness or horror that actually belongs to the society he represents.

8. Compare Jane Austen writing in *Emma*: " 'This is the luxury of a large party,' said [Mrs. Weston]:—'one can get near every body, and say every thing.' " Earlier the narrator comments on the intimacy possible at a large gathering:

"They were too numerous for any subject of conversation to be general; and while politics and Mr. Elton were talked over, Emma could fairly surrender all her attention to the pleasantness of her neighbor" (231, 224).

9. Fitzgerald had considered titling the novel *Trimalchio*. The standard study is MacKendrick, "*The Great Gatsby* and Trimalchio." He argues that the most profound link with Petronius is Fitzgerald's use of the excessive individual to criticize society as a whole. Fitzgerald, he argues, sees in Trimalchio, "the symbol of a sick society." One might also note that the comparison suggests Fitzgerald's awareness of a tradition of festivity (and corrupted festivity) stemming from classical literature.

10. From Fitzgerald's "General Plan" for *Tender Is the Night*, published in Bruccoli, *The Composition of "Tender Is the Night*, 76.

11. Obviously, I am arguing for the superiority of the original 1934 edition of the novel over the rearranged version published by Cowley. The 1934 text is essentially the standard text in contemporary criticism and has been the more commonly available text from 1934 to the present. The importance of the Villa Diana scene throughout the novel is one of many arguments for the aesthetic superiority of the original version. See Cowley, Introduction to *Tender Is the Night—A Romance*, xiv–xv. Bruccoli argues against the superiority of Cowley's version in *The Composition of "Tender Is the Night*," 10–11.

12. Lehan cites this passage as "vague and badly written," *F. Scott Fitzgerald and the Craft of Fiction*, 147. Leslie Fielder cites it as evidence supporting his assertion that "all his life, point of view baffled [Fitzgerald]." "Some Notes on F. Scott Fitzgerald," 180.

13. Fitzgerald to H. L. Mencken, April 23, 1934, quoted in Bruccoli, *The Composition of "Tender Is the Night*," 129–30. Fitzgerald writes: "This is what most of the critics fail to understand . . . that the motif of the 'dying fall' was absolutely deliberate and did not come from any diminution of vitality, but from a definite plan."

14. For a discussion of the relevance of "Au clair de la lune" to *Tender Is the Night* see Grube, "*Tender Is the Night:* Keats and Scott Fitzgerald." The verse quoted in *Tender Is the Night* is:

> Au clair de la lune
> Mon ami Pierrot,
> Prête-moi ta plume,
> Pour écrire un mot.
> Ma chandelle est morte.
> Je n'ai plus de feu
> Ouvre moi tu porte,
> Pour l'amour de Dieu.

15. Green and Swan discuss the significance of commedia dell'arte tropes in modern literature, music, and the arts in their joint study, *The Triumph of Pierrot—The Commedia dell'Arte and the Modern Imagination.* Green devotes considerable attention to Fitzgerald's "commedic" imagination, but, oddly, does not cite this scene in *Tender Is the Night.* Green also discusses the use of commedia dell'arte figures in Waugh's early fiction.

16. For a perceptive discussion of Fitzgerald's use of dialogue in this scene and throughout the novel, see Hall, "Dialogue and Theme in *Tender Is the Night.*"

17. Fitzgerald's revisions of the novel heightened the delaying or suspension of Dick's eventual decline. See Bruccoli, *The Composition of "Tender Is the Night,"* 109.

18. The phrase "plagued by the nightingale" comes from Marianne Moore's poem "Marriage." Fitzgerald's use of the phrase probably follows Kay Boyle's use of it as the title (and, with following lines, the epigraph) of her 1931 novel.

19. Doherty, *"Tender Is the Night* and the 'Ode to a Nightingale,'" 198.

20. Lowry and Lowry, *Notes on a Screenplay for F. Scott Fitzgerald's "Tender Is the Night,"* 68.

21. For a discussion of the Murphys, the American expatriates in the twenties, and the importance of parties to their milieu, see Tomkins, *Living Well is the Best Revenge* and Donnelly and Billings, *Sara and Gerald: Villa America and After.*

22. Bruccoli makes this point in *The Composition of "Tender Is the Night,"* 6–16.

23. Bloom, *The Visionary Company,* 437.

24. Trilling, "F. Scott Fitzgerald," 246.

25. Fitzgerald, quoted in Perosa, *The Art of F. Scott Fitzgerald,* 109.

26. See DiBattista, "The Aesthetic of Forbearance: Fitzgerald's *Tender Is the Night.*"

27. See Allen, *Candles and Carnival Lights: The Catholic Sensibility of F. Scott Fitzgerald.* Allen provides a thorough compendium of carnival imagery in Fitzgerald's work, including a discussion of this scene. In arguing for Fitzgerald's "catholic sensibility," though, she simplifies his approach to social entertainment and pleasure into an opposition between the City of Man (epitomized by the carnival or a "world's fair") and the City of God (represented by a salvation Fitzgerald and his characters somehow fail to attain). In her view, all the appeals of carnival are illusory, and *Tender Is the Night* becomes the story of "the man who allowed himself to be emasculated by masked female destroyers, irretrievably damned by his choice of a life of folly in the carnival of the City of Man" (131). While Allen's book perceives the sacral issues involved in celebration, it continues, remarkably, in the tradition of Church hostility toward secular festival.

28. James Joyce to Stanislaus Joyce, September 25, 1906, *Letters of James Joyce,* 2:165.

29. Fitzgerald saw melodrama as a threatening debasement of both emotion and art; tragic illusions temper and transform the predictable pattern of the melodramatic. In his notebooks Fitzgerald recorded: "Fifty years ago we Americans substituted melodrama for tragedy" (*CU* 208).

30. Fitzgerald, *The Letters of F. Scott Fitzgerald,* 3.

31. Ibid., *Letters,* 16.

32. DiBattista, "The Aesthetic of Forbearance," 31, 30.

33. Ibid., 31.

34. Trilling, "The Fate of Pleasure," 58.

35. Ibid., 74.

36. Fussell, "Fitzgerald's Brave New World," 258.

4. Dark Visions of the Bright Young Things

VB   *Vile Bodies* (Waugh)
PG   *Party Going* (Green)
PB   *Pack My Bag: A Self Portrait* (Green)

1. *Crome Yellow* is the best example of Huxley's party fiction, and *Afternoon Men* is the most thoroughly party-centered of Anthony Powell's work. Parties remain important through all of Powell's fiction though most notably in his twelve-volume series, *A Dance to the Music of Time.* The best discussion of Powell's use of parties as "a means of better understanding oneself and the world at large" is found in Butterfield, "Party Politics: Novelistic Uses of the Party in Waugh, Green and Powell." Butterfield also discusses the relation of all these writers' fictional parties to accounts of parties in their memoirs.

2. Waugh, *Decline and Fall,* 1.

3. Quoted in Green, *Children of the Sun: A Narrative of "Decadence" in England After 1918,* 201.

4. Ibid., 209–10.

5. Stannard, *Evelyn Waugh: The Early Years, 1903–1939,* 180.

6. Heller, *Catch-22,* 450.

7. The best discussion of Waugh's relation to modernism is McCartney, *Confused Roaring: Evelyn Waugh and the Modernist Tradition.* Farr provides a concise summary of one approach to Waugh: "One must account for the dichotomy between Waugh's theme, which is basically a conservative attack on modernism, and his form, which is essentially modern." "Evelyn Waugh: Tradition and a Modern Talent," 507.

8. Waugh, "Fanfare," in Gallagher, *The Essays, Articles and Reviews of Evelyn Waugh*, 304.

9. Stannard discusses how Waugh's satire of youth slang actually served to popularize it. This is one manifestation of *Vile Bodies*'s ambivalent caricature and its popularity with the set it depicts: "In attempting to undermine the glamorous image of his young characters [Waugh] had inadvertently enhanced their image as an object of fashionable imitation," *Evelyn Waugh*, 204.

10. Stopp, *Evelyn Waugh: Portrait of An Artist*, 75.

11. Boorstin, *The Image: A Guide to Pseudo-Events in America*.

12. I find this image of the stationary engine a more effective encapsulation of the machine age than the more strained metaphor that follows of the automobile illustrating the "metaphysical distinction between 'being' and 'becoming.'" Waugh suggests that the racing car exploiting technology in a ridiculous quest for high speed represents eternal "becoming" while the family auto valued for transportation represents a stabler "being." The racing cars "are in perpetual flux; a vortex of combining and disintegrating units; like the confluence of traffic at some spot where many roads meet, streams of mechanism come together, mingle and separate again" (*VB* 228). The divorce of technology from genuine improvement of life seems to be the target of both passages, though this latter one reads as more deliberately didactic.

13. See Susan Sontag's discussion of camp: "[Camp] is the love of the exaggerated, the 'off,' of things-being-what-they-are-not. . . . Art Nouveau objects, typically, convert one thing into something else: the lighting fixtures in the form of flowering plants, the living room which is really a grotto." "Notes on 'Camp,'" in *Against Interpretation and Other Essays* (New York: Dell, 1966), 276.

14. Kenner, *The Stoic Comedians*, xix. Kenner's definition is useful for considering Waugh, though I doubt Kenner would extend the definition to someone so explicitly anti-modern in attitude as Waugh.

15. Cunningham discusses this theme in connection with several other scenes from thirties' novels that depict aerial views of civilization inspiring revulsion. *British Writers of the Thirties*, 203–5.

16. The English country house is an important element in Waugh's fiction; it stands for lost tradition and community and often serves to ridicule the desire to live in the past. For a full discussion of this symbol in Waugh's work, see Gill, *Happy Rural Seat: The English Country House and the Literary Imagination*.

17. Stannard discusses the effect of the breakup of Waugh's marriage on the structure and tone of *Vile Bodies*. The sudden split occurred during the time Waugh was working on the novel and may well have exacerbated the bitterness of the latter parts of the work. Stannard, *Evelyn Waugh*, 186–214.

18. Ryf, *Henry Green*, 3.

19. Gill, *Happy Rural Seat,* 12.

20. North argues that Green is, in many significant respects, characteristic of the "Auden generation." He also discusses the tendency of other writers on the period to neglect Green or to view him as an aberration. North, *Henry Green and the Writing of His Generation.* I do not dispute North's assertions but think that approaches to Green other than considering him in terms of the zeitgeist may well be useful.

21. Ibid., 12.

22. North discusses the setting of *Party Going,* with the fog stopping the trains: "It is as if the thirties symbol of progress were being purposely inverted to be used as a symbol of the helplessness of technology against the simple elements, and by extension, of the wreck of the political hopes associated with technological symbolism," ibid., 82. The other obvious literary antecedent for the use of fog as an image of paralysis is Dickens's *Bleak House.*

23. Kermode, *The Genesis of Secrecy,* 8.

24. Hynes discusses the importance in thirties literature of the image of waiting passively for disaster. Hynes, *The Auden Generation: Literature and Politics in England in the 1930s,* 335–37. See also North, *Henry Green and the Writing of his Generation,* 82–83.

25. Goffmann, *The Presentation of Self in Everyday Life,* 208–37.

26. Goffman discusses this sort of behavior in a section on "Protective Practices" and "tactful inattention," ibid., 229–34.

27. See Cunningham's discussion of this scene as an image of the thirties' writer in problematic retreat to a "still center." Cunningham also uses the scene as a paradigmatic discussion of the importance of social and literary context for interpretation, *British Writers of the Thirties,* 6–9.

28. Stokes, *The Novels of Henry Green,* 192–93.

29. Green, "A Novelist to His Readers—II," 425.

30. Green quoted in Taylor, "Catalytic Rhetoric: Henry Green's Theory of the Modern Novel," 82.

31. In "The Structure and Technique of *Party Going,*" Clive Hart argues that various inconsistencies in the novel subvert the reliability of the authorial statements: "*Party Going* is informed throughout by the idea of the abnegation of authorial control. . . . the novel itself warns us against accepting at face value its apparently omniscient statements" (187). Hart is right on target in defining the problem raised by Green's uncharacteristic use of authorial access to the characters' thoughts, but I am not convinced that inconsistencies in facts or time scheme clearly "reveal the privileged information offered on other occasions to be a sham," as Hart contends (188).

32. See Stokes, *The Novels of Henry Green:* "It would not be a gross over-simplification to say that the basic theme of Green's work is that of love versus loneliness" (133).

33. Kermode, *The Genesis of Secrecy*, 7.

34. Tindall, *The Literary Symbol*, 94–95.

35. The best discussion of the pigeon, and Green's symbolism in general, is in Stokes, *The Novels of Henry Green*, 139–48. Stokes offers a useful alternative to critics who argue like Giorgio Melchiori that "preoccupation with style is so strong that the content is overpowered," (*The Tightrope Walkers*, 197) and Rod Mengham, who calls Green's preoccupation with motif "perverse" and claims "the dead bird is robbed of its interpretational value and returns the narrative to an impasse" (*The Idiom of the Time*, 31, 33).

Part 3. Beyond Decadence

1. For a good discussion of modernist "belatedness," see Meisel, *The Myth of the Modern: A Study in British Literature and Criticism After 1850.*

2. Barth, "The Literature of Exhaustion," 64.

3. McHale, *Postmodernist Fiction*, 173.

4. Barth, "The Literature of Exhaustion," 66.

5. Hassan, *Paracriticisms: Seven Speculations of the Times*, 53–59.

6. McHale, *Postmodernist Fiction*, xii.

7. Alter, *Partial Magic: The Novel as Self-Conscious Genre*, 230.

5. Celebrating the Counterforce

E   "Entropy"
V   *V.*
GR   *Gravity's Rainbow*

1. Weisenburger, *A "Gravity's Rainbow" Companion: Sources and Contexts for Pynchon's Novel*, 10.

2. For discussions of scientific and technological metaphors in Pynchon see Friedman, "Science and Technology." See also Freidman's earlier article with Manfred Puetz, "Science as Metaphor: Thomas Pynchon and *Gravity's Rainbow*."

3. See for example Fuller, *Utopia or Oblivion: The Prospects for Humanity*, 311.

4. See Redfield and Hays, "Fugue as a Structure in Pynchon's 'Entropy.' "

5. See Fowler's discussion of the contrast between the tropics and the North in *A Reader's Guide to "Gravity's Rainbow,"* 19–21.

6. For an excellent article on Pynchon's use of historical sources see Khachig Tololyan, "War as Background in *Gravity's Rainbow*," in Clerc, *Approaches to "Gravity's Rainbow*," 31–68.

7. White, "Pigs and Pierrots: The Politics of Transgression in Modern Fiction," 57.

8. Note how desire in this image appears as the propelling force both internally and externally.

9. Brant, *The Ship of Fools*, 98.

10. Another interesting source for Pynchon's depiction of the decadent orgy may be Aubrey Beardsley's unfinished novel *Under the Hill*. See Beardsley and Glassco, *Under the Hill*.

11. Burroughs, *Naked Lunch*, 88–103.

12. Updike, "Dark Smile, Devilish Saints," 86.

13. This theme is discussed in detail in Wolfey, "Repression's Rainbow: The Presence of Norman O. Brown in Pynchon's Big Novel." Wolfey quotes Brown to articulate Pynchon's theme: "Mankind unconscious of its real desires and therefore unable to obtain satisfaction, is hostile to life and ready to destroy itself" (875). Wolfey compares the action of repression in shaping the psyche to the role of gravity in shaping physical matter. Wolfey's article is one of the most original and useful approaches to *Gravity's Rainbow* I have encountered, though I think his emphasis on repression gives short shrift to Pynchon's recurrent theme of external oppression and conditioning.

14. See the remarkable treatment of Kekulé's famous dream in *Gravity's Rainbow* in which Laszlo Jamf asks, " 'Who sent this new serpent to our ruinous garden, already too fouled, too crowded to qualify as any locus of innocence—unless innocence be our age's neutral, our silent passing into the machineries of indifference—something that Kekulé's Serpent had come to—not to destroy, but to define to us the loss of" (*GR* 413).

15. I discuss this opposition of discourses in greater depth in "Power and the Obscene Word: Discourses of Extremity in *Gravity's Rainbow*."

16. Salinger, *Catcher in the Rye*, 204.

17. Bakhtin, *Rabelais and His World*, 225.

18. Ibid., 226.

19. Tanner, "Games American Writers Play: Ceremony, Complicity, Contestation and Carnival," 115, 130, 136.

20. Eliot, *Middlemarch*, 111.

21. Pynchon, *The Crying of Lot 49*, 95.

6. From Nightsticks to Nightmares

GP *Gerald's Party*

1. See Todorov, "An Introduction to Verisimilitude" in *The Poetics of Prose*, 80–89. Todorov argues that verisimilitude is the relation of a work to its genre, not the relation of a work to an external "referent": "There are as many verisimilitudes as there are genres" (83).

2. See Todorov, "The Typology of Detective Fiction" in *The Poetics of Prose*, 42–52. Todorov uses the term "genre" for the kinds of codes or conventions I term subgenres. I prefer to reserve "genre" for the larger classifications of novel, epic, lyric, and so forth.

3. Abrams, *A Glossary of Literary Terms*, 190; Barthes, *S/Z*. Barthes defines codes more generally (as in hermeneutic or cultural codes). Nevertheless, his notion of the text as a polyphonic interplay of codes applies well to Abrams's modification and to my use here: "Each code is one of the forces that can take over the text (of which the text is the network)" (21).

4. McCaffery, "Robert Coover on His Own and Other Fictions: An Interview," 50.

5. Ibid., 57.

6. My argument here presupposes a workable definition of the much-vilified term "realism." A full discussion of the nature of realism would fill another book, but I find it useful to employ the term as a nonevaluative description of a particularly powerful novelistic convention. Watt's definition is particularly illuminating: "[Formal realism refers] to a set of narrative procedures which are so commonly found together in the novel, and so rarely in other genres, that they may be regarded as typical of the form itself. . . . The premise, or primary convention, [is] that the novel is a full and authentic report of human experience, and is therefore under an obligation to satisfy its reader with such details of the story as the individuality of the actors concerned, the particulars of the times and places of their actions, details which are presented through a more largely referential use of language than is common in other literary forms" (*The Rise of the Novel*, 32).

7. Frye, *Anatomy of Criticism*, 41, 149.

8. Coover comments: "I like the pun for its intense condensation, but for me it's only a second-rate version of the more exciting idea of the juxtaposition of two unexpected elements—structural puns you might call them." Quoted in McCaffery, "Robert Coover on His Own and Other Fictions," 55.

9. Todorov, *The Poetics of Prose*, 43, 49.

10. In fairness I should note that Todorov objects to the representations of degrees of external verisimilitude: a work is only more or less true to its genre. While I agree that subgenres possess particular internal requirements, I think

it is also true that readers judge entire subgenres as more or less believable or "realistic." Thus readers are aware of the different internal codes of a romance novel or a detective novel, but they may also perceive such codes to be "unrealistic" to varying degrees. Detective fiction thrives in the margin between the requirements of external verisimilitude and the genre-based antiverisimilitude of surprise and novelty.

11. Examples from Coover's "Charlie in the House of Rue" echo the Keystone Kops' comedy and drink-spilling escapades of *Gerald's Party*: "Suddenly [the policeman's] arm flashes out of the gray bathwater, his fist clutching a billyclub: he brings it down with all his might—*pow!*—on one of the rubber ducks" (107). "This time, however, the old man does not stop pouring. . . . Charlies stumbles to his feet, grabs up another glass and holds it under the flow, drinks down the full one just in time to thrust it back under as the new glass brims over. The old man, as though transfixed, continues to pour. Charlie thrusts more glasses under the gurgling bottle" (93). *A Night at the Movies: Or, You Must Remember This*, 87–114.

12. Goffmann discusses this phenomenon as "region behavior" in *The Presentation of the Self in Everyday Life* (106–40), and as "The Territories of the Self" in *Relations in Public: Microstudies of the Public Order*.

13. Coover, *A Night at the Movies*, 111.

14. Douglas, *Purity and Danger: An Analysis of Concepts of Pollution and Taboo*, 29–40. Also discussed in Goffman, *Relations in Public*, 53–54.

15. Girard, *Violence and the Sacred*, 143–47.

16. Ibid., 165.

17. Castle, *Masquerade and Civilization*, 62.

18. Cope, *Robert Coover's Fictions*, 122–23.

19. Ibid., 135.

20. Coover, "The Last Quixote: Marginal Notes on the Gospel According to Samuel Beckett," 132.

WORKS CITED

Abrams, M. H. *A Glossary of Literary Terms*. 4th ed. New York: Holt, 1981.

Allen, Joan M. *Candles and Carnival Lights: The Catholic Sensibility of F. Scott Fitzgerald*. New York: New York University Press, 1978.

Alter, Robert. *Partial Magic: The Novel as Self-Conscious Genre*. Berkeley: University of California Press, 1975.

Ames, Christopher. "Power and the Obscene Word: Discourses of Extremity in *Gravity's Rainbow*." *Contemporary Literature* 31 (1990): 191–207.

Apter, T. E. *Virginia Woolf: A Study of Her Novels*. London: MacMillan, 1979.

Auerbach, Erich. *Mimesis: The Representation of Reality in Western Literature*. Trans. Willard Trask. Princeton: Princeton University Press, 1953.

Austen, Jane. *Emma*. Ed. Ronald Blythe. New York: Penguin, 1966.

Babcock, Barbara. "The Novel and the Carnival World: An Essay in Memory of Joe Doherty." *Modern Language Notes* 89 (1974): 911–37.

Bakhtin, Mikhail. *The Dialogic Imagination: Four Essays*. Trans. Caryl Emerson and ed. Michael Holquist. Austin: University of Texas Press, 1981.

——— . *Problems of Dostoevsky's Poetics*. Trans. and ed. Caryl Emerson. Theory and History of Literature Series: Vol. 8. Minneapolis: University of Minnesota Press, 1984.

——— . *Rabelais and His World*. Trans. Helene Iswolsky. Cambridge, Mass.: MIT Press, 1968.

Baldanza, Frank. "Clarissa Dalloway's 'Party Consciousness.'" *Modern Fiction Studies* 2, no. 1 (1956): 22–30.

Barber, C. L. *Shakespeare's Festive Comedy: A Study of Dramatic Form and Its Relation to Social Custom*. Princeton: Princeton University Press, 1972.

Barth, John. "The Literature of Exhaustion." In *The Friday Book: Essays and Other Non-Fiction*, 62–76. New York: Putnam, 1984.

Barthes, Roland. *S/Z: An Essay*. Trans. Richard Miller. New York: Hill and Wang, 1974.

Bazin, Nancy Topping. *Virginia Woolf and the Androgynous Vision*. New Brunswick: Rutgers University Press, 1973.

Beardsley, Aubrey, and John Glassco. *Under the Hill*. New York: Grove Press, 1959.

Beda Venerabilis. *A History of the English Church and People*. Trans. Leo Sherley-Price. Harmondsworth, Middlesex: Penguin, 1955.

Bernstein, Michael André. "When the Carnival Turns Bitter: Preliminary Reflections Upon the Abject Hero." In *Bakhtin: Essays and Dialogues on His Work*, ed. Gary Saul Morson, 99–122. Chicago: University of Chicago Press, 1986.

Bishop, John. *Joyce's Book of the Dark*. Madison: University of Wisconsin Press, 1986.

Blamires, Harry. *The Bloomsday Book: A Guide Through Joyce's "Ulysses."* New York: Methuen, 1966.

Bloom, Harold. *The Visionary Company*. Garden City, N.Y.: Anchor-Doubleday, 1963.

Blotner, Joseph L. " 'Ivy Day in the Committee Room': Death Without Resurrection." *Perspective* 9 (1957): 210–17.

Boorstin, Daniel. *The Image: A Guide to Pseudo-Events in America*. New York: Atheneum, 1971.

Boyle, Kay. *Plagued by the Nightingale*. 1931. Reprint. Carbondale, Ill.: Southern Illinois University Press, 1966.

Brant, Sebastian. *The Ship of Fools*. Trans. Edwin H. Zeydel. New York: Columbia University Press, 1944.

Brown, Homer Obed. *James Joyce's Early Fiction: The Biography of a Form*. Cleveland: Case Western Reserve University Press, 1972.

Brown, Norman O. *Life Against Death*. Middleton, Conn.: Wesleyan University Press, 1954.

Bruccoli, Matthew J. *The Composition of "Tender Is the Night": A Study of the Manuscripts*. Pittsburgh: University of Pittsburgh Press, 1963.

———. *Some Sort of Epic Grandeur: The Life of F. Scott Fitzgerald*. New York: Harcourt Brace, 1981.

Burke, Peter. *Popular Culture in Early Modern Europe*. New York: New York University Press, 1978.

Burroughs, William. *Naked Lunch*. New York: Grove Press, 1966.

Butterfield, Bruce. "Party Politics: Novelistic Uses of the Party in Waugh, Green and Powell." Paper presented at the annual meeting of the Modern Language Association, New York, December 1981.

Caillois, Roger. *Man, Play and Games.* Trans. Meyer Barash. New York: Free Press of Glencoe, 1961.

———. *Man and the Sacred.* Trans. Meyer Barash. Glencoe, Ill.: The Free Press, 1959.

Carroll, Lewis. *The Annotated Alice: Alice's Adventures in Wonderland and Through the Looking Glass.* Ed. Martin Gardner. New York: New American Library, 1974.

Caputi, Anthony. *Buffo: The Genius of Vulgar Comedy.* Detroit: Wayne State University Press, 1978.

Castle, Terry. *Masquerade and Civilization: The Carnivalesque in Eighteenth-Century English Culture and Fiction.* Stanford: Stanford University Press, 1986.

Clerc, Charles, ed. *Approaches to "Gravity's Rainbow."* Columbus: Ohio State University Press, 1983.

Coover, Robert. *Gerald's Party.* New York: New American Library, 1985.

———. *A Night at the Movies: Or, You Must Remember This.* New York: Linden Press, 1987.

———. "The Last Quixote: Marginal Notes on the Gospel According to Samuel Beckett." *New American Review* 11 (1971): 132–43.

Cope, Jackson. *Robert Coover's Fictions.* Baltimore: Johns Hopkins University Press, 1986.

Cornford, Francis MacDonald. *The Origins of Attic Comedy.* 1934. Reprint. Garden City, N.Y.: Anchor-Doubleday, 1961.

Cowley, Malcolm. Introduction to *Tender Is the Night—A Romance: With the Author's Final Revisions,* by F. Scott Fitzgerald. New York: Scribner's, 1951.

Cox, Harvey. *The Feast of Fools: A Theological Essay on Festivity and Fantasy.* New York: Harper and Row, 1972.

Cunningham, Valentine. *British Writers of the Thirties.* New York: Oxford University Press, 1988.

DiBattista, Maria. "The Aesthetic of Forbearance: Fitzgerald's *Tender Is the Night.*" *Novel* 11 (1977): 26–39.

———. *Virginia Woolf's Major Novels: The Fables of Anon.* New Haven: Yale University Press, 1980.

Doherty, William E. "*Tender Is the Night* and the 'Ode to a Nightingale.'" In *"Tender Is the Night": Essays in Criticism,* ed. Marvin J. La Hood, 190–206. Bloomington: Indiana University Press, 1969.

Donnelly, Honoria Murphy, and Richard N. Billings. *Sara and Gerald: Villa America and After.* New York: Holt, 1984.

Donoghue, Denis. *We Irish.* New York: Knopf, 1986.

Douglas, Mary. *Purity and Danger: An Analysis of Concepts of Pollution and Taboo.* New York: Frederick Praeger, 1966.

Duffy, Edward. " 'The Sisters' as the Introduction to *Dubliners.*" *Papers on Language and Literature* 22 (1986): 417–28.

Duffy, Richard. Introduction to *Etiquette: The Blue Book of Social Usage,* by Emily Post. New York: Funk and Wagnall's, 1934.

Durkheim, Emile. *The Elementary Forms of the Religious Life.* Trans. Joseph Ward Swain. 1915. Reprint. New York: The Free Press, 1965.

Ehrmann, Jacques, ed. *Game, Play and Literature.* Boston: Beacon Press, 1971.

Eliot, George. *Middlemarch.* New York: Penguin, 1965.

Farr, D. Paul. "Evelyn Waugh: Tradition and a Modern Talent." *South Atlantic Quarterly* 68 (1969): 506–19.

Fiedler, Leslie. "Some Notes on F. Scott Fitzgerald." In *An End to Innocence.* Boston: Beacon Press, 1955. 174–82.

Fitzgerald, F. Scott. *The Beautiful and Damned.* New York: Scribner's, 1922.

———. *The Crack-Up.* New York: New Directions, 1956.

———. *F. Scott Fitzgerald in His Own Time: A Miscellany.* Ed. Matthew J. Bruccoli. Kent, Ohio: Kent State University Press, 1971.

———. *The Great Gatsby.* New York: Scribner's, 1925.

———. *The Letters of F. Scott Fitzgerald.* Ed. Andrew Turnbull. New York: Bantam, 1971.

———. *Tender Is the Night.* New York: Scribner's, 1934.

Fleishman, Avrom. *Virginia Woolf: A Critical Reading.* Baltimore: Johns Hopkins University Press, 1975.

Forster, E. M. *Virginia Woolf.* New York: Harcourt Brace, 1942.

Fowler, Douglas. *A Reader's Guide to "Gravity's Rainbow."* Ann Arbor, Mich.: Ardis, 1980.

Frazer, James George. *The New Golden Bough.* Ed. Theodor H. Gaster. New Jersey: S. G. Philips, 1959.

Friedman, Alan J. "Science and Technology." In *Approaches to "Gravity's Rainbow,"* ed. Charles Clerc, 69–102. Columbus: Ohio State University Press, 1983.

Friedman, Alan J., and Manfred Puetz. "Science and Metaphor: Thomas Pynchon and *Gravity's Rainbow.*" In *Critical Essays on Thomas Pynchon,* ed. Richard Pearce, 69–81. Boston: G. K. Hall, 1981.

Frye, Northrop. *Anatomy of Criticism: Four Essays.* New York: Atheneum, 1969.

———. "The Argument of Comedy." In *Theories of Comedy,* ed. Paul Lauter. Garden City, N.Y.: Anchor-Doubleday, 1964.

Fuller, R. Buckminster. *Utopia or Oblivion: The Prospects for Humanity.* New York: Bantam, 1969.

Fussell, Edwin. "Fitzgerald's Brave New World." In *"The Great Gatsby": A Study,* ed. Frederick J. Hoffmann, 244–62. New York: Scribner's, 1962.

Gill, Richard. *Happy Rural Seat: The English Country House and the Literary Imagination.* New Haven: Yale University Press, 1972.

Gilman, Richard. *Decadence: The Strange Life of an Epithet.* New York: Farrar, Strauss and Giroux, 1979.

Girard, René. *Deceit, Desire and the Novel: Self and Other in Literary Structure.* Trans. Yvonne Freccero. Baltimore: Johns Hopkins University Press, 1965.

―――. *Violence and the Sacred.* Trans. Patrick Gregory. Baltimore: Johns Hopkins University Press, 1979.

Glasheen, Adaline. "Notes Toward a Supreme Understanding of the Use of 'Finnegan's Wake' in *Finnegans Wake.*" *A Wake Newslitter* 5, no. 1 (1968): 4–15.

Gluckman, Max. Introduction to *Essays on The Ritual of Social Relations.* Manchester, Eng.: Manchester University Press, 1962.

Goethe, Johann Wolfgang von. *Italian Journey.* Trans. W. H. Auden and Elizabeth Mayer. New York: Pantheon, 1962.

Goffman, Erving. *The Presentation of Self in Everyday Life.* Garden City, N.Y.: Anchor-Doubleday, 1959.

―――. *Relations in Public: Microstudies of the Public Order.* New York: Harper, 1972.

Green, Henry. *Living, Loving and Party Going.* New York: Penguin, 1978.

―――. "A Novelist to His Readers—II." *The Listener* 45 (1951): 425.

―――. *Pack My Bag: A Self Portrait.* London: Hogarth Press, 1940.

Green, Martin. *Children of the Sun: A Narrative of "Decadence" in England After 1918.* New York: Basic Books, 1976.

Green, Martin, and John Swan. *The Triumph of Pierrot—The Commedia dell'Arte and the Modern Imagination.* New York: MacMillan, 1986.

Grube, John. "*Tender Is the Night:* Keats and Scott Fitzgerald." In *"Tender Is the Night": Essays in Criticism,* ed. Marvin J. La Hood, 179–89. Bloomington: Indiana University Press, 1969.

Guiget, Jean. *Virginia Woolf and Her Works.* Trans. Jean Stewart. New York: Harcourt Brace, 1965.

Hall, William F. "Dialogue and Theme in *Tender is the Night.*" In *"Tender Is the Night": Essays in Criticism,* ed. Marvin J. La Hood, 144–50. Bloomington: Indiana University Press, 1969.

Hans, James S. *The Play of the World.* Amherst: University of Massachusetts Press, 1981.

Harrison, Jane Ellen. *Themis: A Study of the Social Origins of the Greek Religion.* Cambridge: Cambridge University Press, 1912.

Hart, Clive. "The Structure and Technique of *Party Going.*" *The Yearbook of English Studies I* (1971): 185–99.

Hart, Clive, and David Hayman, eds. *James Joyce's "Ulysses": Critical Essays.* Berkeley: University of California Press, 1974.

Hassan, Ihab. *Paracriticisms: Seven Speculations of the Times.* Urbana, Ill.: University of Illinois Press, 1975.

Hawthorn, Jeremy. *Virginia Woolf's "Mrs. Dalloway": A Study in Alienation.* London: Sussex University Press, 1975.

Hayman, David. "Forms of Folly in Joyce: A Study of Clowning in *Ulysses.*" *ELH* 34 (1967): 260–83.

Heller, Joseph. *Catch-22.* New York: Dell, 1961.

Hodgart, M. J. C., and Mabel Worthington. *Song in the Works of James Joyce.* Philadelphia: Temple University Press, 1959.

Hodgart, M. J. C. "Ivy Day in the Committee Room." In *James Joyce's "Dubliners": Critical Essays,* ed. Clive Hart, 115–21. New York: Viking, 1969.

Huizinga, J. *Homo Ludens: A Study of the Play-Element in Culture.* Trans. R. F. C. Hull. London: Routledge and Kegan Paul, 1949.

Huntington, Richard, and Peter Metcalf. *Celebrations of Death: The Anthropology of Mortuary Ritual.* New York: Cambridge University Press, 1979.

Hynes, Samuel. *The Auden Generation: Literature and Politics in England in the 1930s.* New York: Viking, 1977.

James, Henry. *The Art of the Novel.* Ed. R. P. Blackmur. New York: Scribner's, 1934.

Janusko, Robert. *The Sources and Structures of James Joyce's "Oxen."* Ann Arbor, Mich.: UMI Research Press, 1983.

Joyce, James. *Dubliners.* Viking Critical Edition. Eds. Robert Scholes and A. Walton Litz. New York: Viking, 1969.

———. *Finnegans Wake.* New York: Viking, 1958.

———. *Letters of James Joyce.* Vol. 2. Ed. Richard Ellmann. New York: Viking, 1966.

———. *Ulysses: The Corrected Text.* Ed. Hans Walter Gabler. New York: Vintage, 1986.

Kenner, Hugh. "Circe." In James Joyce's "Ulysses": Critical Essays, ed. Clive Hart and David Hayman, 341–61. Berkeley: University of California Press, 1974.

———. *Ulysses.* London: Allen and Unwin, 1980.

———. *The Stoic Comedians: Flaubert, Joyce and Beckett.* Berkeley: University of California Press, 1974.

Kermode, Frank. "The Banquet of Sense." In *Shakespeare, Spenser, Donne: Renaissance Essays,* 84–115. New York: Viking, 1971.

———. *The Genesis of Secrecy.* Cambridge: Harvard University Press, 1979.

Ladurie, Le Roy. *Carnival in Romans.* Trans. Mary Feeney. New York: George Braziller, 1980.

La Hood, Marvin J., ed. *"Tender Is the Night": Essays in Criticism.* Bloomington: Indiana University Press, 1969.

Leaska, Mitchell. *Pointz Hall: The Earlier and Later Typescripts of "Between the Acts."* New York: University Publishers, 1983.

Lehan, Richard. *F. Scott Fitzgerald and the Craft of Fiction.* Carbondale, Ill.: Southern Illinois University Press, 1966.

Long, Robert Emmet. *The Achieving of "The Great Gatsby."* Lewisburg, Pa.: Bucknell University Press, 1979.

Lowry, Malcolm, and Margerie Bonner Lowry. *Notes on a Screenplay for F. Scott Fitzgerald's "Tender Is the Night."* Bloomfield Hills, Mich.: Bruccoli Clark, 1976.

McCaffery, Larry. "Robert Coover on His Own and Other Fictions: An Interview." In *Novel vs. Fiction: The Contemporary Reformation,* ed. Jackson I. Cope and Geoffrey Green, 45–63. Norman, Okla.: Pilgrim Books, 1981.

McCartney, George. *Confused Roaring: Evelyn Waugh and the Modernist Tradition.* Bloomington: Indiana University Press, 1987.

McHale, Brian. *Postmodernist Fiction.* New York: Methuen, 1987.

MacKendrick, Paul L. "*The Great Gatsby* and Trimalchio." *The Classical Journal* 45 (1950): 307–14.

Manning, Frank E., ed. *The Celebration of Society: Perspectives on Contemporary Cultural Performance.* Bowling Green, Ohio: Bowling Green University Popular Press, 1983.

Marcus, Leah S. *The Politics of Mirth: Jonson, Herrick, Milton, Marvell and the Defense of Old Holiday Pastimes.* Chicago: University of Chicago Press, 1986.

Meisel, Perry. *The Myth of the Modern: A Study in British Literature and Criticism After 1850.* New Haven: Yale University Press, 1987.

Melchiori, Giorgio. *The Tightrope Walkers: Studies of Mannerism in Modern English Literature.* London: Routledge and Kegan Paul, 1956.

Mengham, Rod. *The Idiom of the Time: The Writings of Henry Green.* Cambridge: Cambridge University Press, 1982.

Miller, J. Hillis. *Fiction and Repetition: Seven English Novels.* Cambridge: Harvard University Press, 1982.

———. "Virginia Woolf's All Soul's Day: The Omniscient Narrator in *Mrs. Dalloway.*" In *The Shaken Realist: Essays in Modern Literature,* ed. Melvin J. Friedman and John B. Vickery, 100–127. Baton Rouge: Louisiana State University Press, 1970.

Mizener, Arthur. *The Far Side of Paradise: A Biography of F. Scott Fitzgerald.* New York: Vintage, 1959.

Moore, Marianne. *The Complete Poems of Marianne Moore*. New York: Viking, 1967.

Morson, Gary Saul, ed. *Bakhtin: Essays and Dialogues on His Work*. Chicago: University of Chicago Press, 1986.

———. "Who Speaks For Bakhtin?" In *Bakhtin: Essays and Dialogues on His Work*, 1–20. Chicago: University of Chicago Press, 1986.

Naremore, James. *The World Without a Self: Virginia Woolf and the Novel*. New Haven: Yale University Press, 1973.

Nietzsche, Friedrich. *The Birth of Tragedy* and *The Case of Wagner*. Trans. Walter Kaufmann. New York: Random House, 1967.

North, Michael. *Henry Green and the Writing of His Generation*. Charlottesville: University Press of Virginia, 1984.

Pecora, Vincent P. " 'The Dead' and the Generosity of the Word." *PMLA* 101 (1986): 233–45.

Perosa, Sergio. *The Art of F. Scott Fitzgerald*. Trans. Charles Matz and Sergio Perosa. Ann Arbor: University of Michigan Press, 1968.

Philipson, Morris. "Mrs. Dalloway, 'What's the Sense of Your Parties?' " *Critical Inquiry* 1 (1974): 123–48.

Pieper, Josef. *In Tune with the World: A Theory of Festivity*. Trans. Richard Winston and Clara Winston. New York: Harcourt Brace, 1965.

Plato. *The Symposium*. Trans. Walter Hamilton. New York: Penguin, 1951.

Polhemus, Robert M. *Comic Faith: The Great Tradition from Austen to Joyce*. Chicago: University of Chicago Press, 1980.

Powell, Anthony. *Afternoon Men*. Boston: Little Brown, [1963].

———. *A Dance to the Music of Time*. 4 vols. New York: Popular Library, 1955–75.

Pynchon, Thomas. *The Crying of Lot 49*. New York: Bantam, 1967.

———. "Entropy." In *Slow Learner*, 77–98. Boston: Little Brown, 1984.

———. *Gravity's Rainbow*. New York: Viking, 1973.

———. *V*. New York: Bantam, 1963.

Rabate, Jean-Michel. "Silence in *Dubliners*." In *James Joyce: New Perspectives*, ed. Colin MacCabe, 45–72. Bloomington: Indiana University Press, 1982.

Rachman, Shalom. "Clarissa's Attic: Virginia Woolf's *Mrs. Dalloway* Reconsidered." *Twentieth Century Literature* 18 (1972): 3–18.

Redfield, Robert, and Peter L. Hays. "Fugue as Structure in Pynchon's 'Entropy.' " *Pacific Coast Philology* 12 (1977): 50–55.

Riquelme, John Paul. *Teller and Tale in Joyce's Fiction: Oscillating Perspectives*. Baltimore: Johns Hopkins University Press, 1983.

Ruotolo, Lucio. *The Interrupted Moment: A View of Virginia Woolf's Novels.* Stanford: Stanford University Press, 1986.

———. "*Mrs. Dalloway:* The Unguarded Moment." In *Virginia Woolf: Revaluation and Continuity,* ed. Ralph Freedman, 141–60. Berkeley: University of California Press, 1980.

Ryf, Robert. *Henry Green.* New York: Columbia University Press, 1967.

Salinger, J. D. *Catcher in the Rye.* New York: Bantam, 1981.

Shechner, Mark. *Joyce in Nighttown: A Psychoanalytic Inquiry into "Ulysses."* Berkeley: University of California Press, 1974.

Stallman, Robert Wooster. "Conrad and *The Great Gatsby.*" *Twentieth Century Fiction* 1 (1955): 5–12.

Stallybrass, Peter, and Allon White. *The Politics and Poetics of Transgression.* Ithaca, N.Y.: Cornell University Press, 1986.

Stannard, Martin. *Evelyn Waugh: The Early Years, 1903–1939.* London: J. M. Dent, 1986.

Stevenson, Randall. *The British Novel Since the Thirties: An Introduction.* Athens: University of Georgia Press, 1986.

Stokes, Edward. *The Novels of Henry Green.* London: Hogarth Press, 1959.

Stopp, Frederick J. *Evelyn Waugh: Portrait of An Artist.* Boston: Little Brown, 1958.

Tanner, Tony. "Games American Writers Play: Ceremony, Complicity, Contestation and Carnival." *Salamagundi* 35 (1976): 110–40.

Taylor, Donald S. "Catalytic Rhetoric: Henry Green's Theory of the Modern Novel." *Criticism* 7 (1965): 81–99.

Tindall, William York. *The Literary Symbol.* Bloomington: Indiana University Press, 1955.

———. *A Reader's Guide to "Finnegans Wake."* New York: Noonday Press, 1969.

———. *A Reader's Guide to James Joyce.* New York: Noonday Press, 1959.

Todorov, Tzvetan. *The Poetics of Prose.* Trans. Richard Howard. Ithaca, N.Y.: Cornell University Press, 1977.

Tomkins, Calvin. *Living Well is the Best Revenge.* New York: Signet, 1972.

Torchiana, Donald T. *Backgrounds for Joyce's "Dubliners."* Boston: Allen and Unwin, 1986.

Trilling, Lionel. "F. Scott Fitzgerald." In *The Liberal Imagination: Essays on Literature and Society,* 243–54. New York: Scribner's, 1976.

———. "The Fate of Pleasure." In *Beyond Culture: Essays on Literature and Learning,* 50–76. New York: Harcourt Brace, 1965.

———. *Sincerity and Authenticity.* Cambridge: Harvard University Press, 1982.

Troy, William. "Virginia Woolf: The Novel of Sensibility." In *Literary Opinion in America*, ed. Morton D. Zabel, 324–37. New York: Harper and Row, 1951.

Tucker, Lindsey. *Stephen and Bloom at Life's Feast: Alimentary Symbolism and the Creative Process in James Joyce's "Ulysses."* Columbus: Ohio State University Press, 1984.

Tuttleton, James W. *The Novel of Manners in America.* Chapel Hill: University of North Carolina Press, 1972.

Turner, Victor, ed. *Celebration: Studies in Festivity and Ritual.* Washington, D.C.: Smithsonian Institution Press, 1982.

Turner, Victor. *The Forest of Symbols: Aspects of Ndembu Ritual.* Ithaca, N.Y.: Cornell University Press, 1967.

Updike, John. "Dark Smile, Devilish Saints." *New Yorker* (11 August 1980): 82–89.

Vickery, John B. *The Literary Impact of "The Golden Bough."* Princeton, N.J.: Princeton University Press, 1973.

Walzl, Florence L. "Gabriel and Michael: The Conclusion of 'The Dead.'" In *Dubliners*, eds. Robert Scholes and A. Walton Litz, 423–43. New York: Viking, 1969.

———. "Joyce's 'The Sisters': A Development." *James Joyce Quarterly* 10 (1973): 375–421.

Watt, Ian. *The Rise of the Novel: Studies in Defoe, Richardson and Fielding.* Berkeley: University of California Press, 1957.

Waugh, Evelyn. *Decline and Fall.* Boston: Little, Brown, 1928.

———. The Essays, Articles and Reviews of Evelyn Waugh. Ed. Donat Gallagher. London: Methuen, 1983.

———. *Vile Bodies.* Boston: Little Brown, 1930.

Weisenburger, Steven. *A "Gravity's Rainbow" Companion: Sources and Contexts for Pynchon's Novel.* Athens: University of Georgia Press, 1988.

White, Allon. "Pigs and Pierrots: The Politics of Transgression in Modern Fiction." *Raritan* 2 (1982): 51–70.

Wilson, Edmund. "F. Scott Fitzgerald." In *A Literary Chronicle: 1920–1950*, 30–37. Garden City, N.Y.: Doubleday, 1956.

Wilson, J. J. "A Comparison of Parties, with a Discussion of Their Function in Woolf's Fiction." *Women's Studies* 4 (1977): 201–17.

Wimsatt, W. K. Introduction to *The Idea of Comedy: Essays in Prose and Verse—Ben Jonson to George Meredith.* Englewood Cliffs, N.J.: Prentice Hall, 1969.

Wolfey, Lawrence C. "Repression's Rainbow: The Presence of Norman O. Brown in Pynchon's Big Novel." *PMLA* 92 (1977): 873–89.

Woolf, Virginia. *Between the Acts.* New York: Harcourt Brace, 1969.

————. *Collected Essays.* 4 vols. London: Hogarth Press, 1967.

————. *The Diary of Virginia Woolf.* 5 vols. Ed. Anne Olivier Bell. New York: Harcourt Brace, 1977–1984.

————. *Mrs. Dalloway.* New York: Harcourt Brace, 1925.

————. *Mrs. Dalloway's Party.* Ed. Stella McNichol. New York: Harcourt Brace, 1973.

————. *The Waves.* New York: Harcourt Brace, 1931.

Zwerdling, Alex. *Virginia Woolf and the Real World.* Berkeley: University of California Press, 1986.

INDEX